THE LEAN
TREASURE CHEST

Using Lean to Locate, Recover, and Maximize Your Hidden Capacity and Potential

Jay R. Hodge

ISBN 978-0-692-18476-9

Printed in the United States of America.

DEDICATION

To you, the countless Executives, Directors, Managers, Supervisors, and Team Members who tirelessly give of yourselves each and every day. Your dedication, determination, discipline, and perseverance does not go unnoticed and is the catalyst for a legacy of Cultural and Operational Transformation.

and,

To my dear friend Jay Rice. A Marine who served his country with honor, integrity, discipline, and Esprit De Corps. Through his battle with brain cancer, he has continually inspired, motivated, and encouraged me to persevere. His example of strength and selfless commitment to others will always be humbling. Semper Fi Brother!

TESTIMONIALS

"I had the pleasure to work with Jay Hodge for nearly 3 years. He helped us immensely in an urgent operational turnaround situation that resulted in multi-million-dollar increases in EBITDA at three different production facilities. Jay has incredible skills in analyzing and determining deficiencies and inefficiencies in an operation and then working with the teams at every level to determine and implement significant improvements in all areas of the operation. He is extremely perceptive and experienced in his approach to Lean. His efforts resulted in a positive culture change, staff engagement, process efficiencies, and increased profits!"

Dan L. Williams
General Manager (Retired), KIK Custom Products, Inc.

"Jay Hodge has a unique combination of excellence in Lean methodology as well as a deep understanding of the realities of health care operations, communication, and people skills. He brings common sense and a practical way of problem solving, involving everyone in the organization. From the bedside to the board room, Jay breaks down the walls and silos, engaging everyone to problem solve together. Jay demonstrated his ability to transform an organization's culture from reactive to proactive, demonstrating the value and critical importance of Gemba. Jay challenges leaders to engage and support teams rather than just critiquing and leaving them to struggle."

Kerri Jenkins, RN, MBA, FABC, CENP
Executive Vice President, SSM Health St. Mary's Hospital

"My experience with Jay Hodge to implement 'Lean Daily Management' into our 400-bed acute care hospital was nothing less than spectacular. Jay is so methodical, knowledgeable, and patient that it not only made this large undertaking a great learning experience for our team, but we were able to execute quickly and start to see the benefits of our work in just a few short weeks. We are now celebrating one year into our Lean Daily Management program, and we have 40 Gemba Boards representing 54 departments, all of them realizing significant improvements and engagement by the staff. Thank you for helping to change our hospital forever."

Edward F. Littlejohn
Chief Operating Officer, Fountain Valley Regional Hospital and Medical Center

CONTENTS

Introduction   13
    Lean isn't a Program or Initiative   13
    Common 20%   14
    What This Book Offers   18
Foreword: a Tale of Two Ships   21
    Inside The Lean Treasure Chest   25
    A Look in the Operational Mirror   27
    Lean is for Everybody   28
    My Personal Commitment   30
Chapter 1: What is Waste, Really?   31
    The 8 Wastes   31
    Zero Value   33
    The Hidden Potential   34
    What's in It for Me?   37
Chapter 2: A Little Red Lawnmower   39
    Efficiency Isn't Robotic   42
    Understanding Their Perspective   44
    What's in It for Me?   44
Chapter 3: The Gorilla on Your Back   47
    Your Operational Gorilla   50
    The Slow Decay   53
    A Cultural Shift   55
    What's in It for Me?   56
Chapter 4: Waste Immunity?   59
    It's in the Air   59
    Pigs Smell   60
    The Ever-Increasing Dosage   62
    What's in It for Me?   64
Chapter 5: Sustainability = Process, Not People Dependent 67
    Standards Require Standardization   67
    Design, Consistency, and Reliability   69
    Simple Math   69
    Standards Impact Lives   71
    Effective Standard Work   73
    Cycle Time vs. Takt Time   75
    Leader Standard Work   78

The Sad Little Penny   79

Driving in the Slow Lane   81

What's in It for Me?   82

Chapter 6: Waste and Value – Choices, Not Results   85

Understanding Waste and Value   85

The Teeter-Totter Relationship   87

Who Defines Value?   88

Using Resources to Produce Value   90

Danger, High Tide!   92

Limited Means Valuable   94

Value Has Shifted   96

A Hospital's Customer   98

The Tow Truck Mentality   100

What's in It for Me?   101

Chapter 7: Leadership for the Future   105

Teflon Coated Leadership   105

We've Always Done It That Way   107

The Permanent Band-Aids   109

Super Heroes Are for Comic Books   110

You Can't Fake True Leadership, for Long   112

Demonstrated Leadership   115

What's in It for Me?   117

Chapter 8: The Iceberg and the Oak Tree   121

The Old Melting Iceberg   122

The Mighty Oak Tree   124

Have You Lost Your Marbles?   126

What's in It for Me?   127

Chapter 9: Negative Value   131

Patients and Patience   131

The Value Thermometer   132

A Strategic Failure   134

Credibility Through Behavior   137

Mowing Air   137

What's in It for Me?   138

Chapter 10: Waste – The Capacity Parasite   141

Hope   141

Waste Consumes Capacity   142

An "Aha" Moment   143

You Need Capacity Now, Not Tomorrow   144

Maximizing Value   147

Protecting Your Processes   150

What's in It for Me?   151

Chapter 11: The 8 Wastes Explosion   153

     An Exponential Impact   153

     The Waste Correlation Explosion   159

     What's in It for Me?   160

Chapter 12: Waste #1 – Defects   161

     A Defect Can Be Anything   161

     Wasted Joy   164

     Devastating Consequences   166

     Getting Real   168

     Defects Don't Just "Happen"   169

     What's in It for Me?   170

Chapter 13: Waste #2 – Overproduction   173

     Chicken Not-So-Little   174

     Pulling, Not Pushing   176

     A Paradigm Shift   179

     What's in It for Me?   181

Chapter 14: Waste #3 – Too Much Inventory   183

     The Deal of the Century   184

     A Steel Steal   186

     Inventory Is a Tool   190

     What's in It for Me?   191

Chapter 15: Waste #4 – Excess Motion   193

     It's Everywhere   193

     A Not-So-Sharp Process   194

     Motion Takes Time   194

     Value Based Decisions   197

     Making Motion Productive   198

     What's in It for Me?   200

Chapter 16: Waste #5 – Waiting   203

     Fast is a Relative Term   205

     A Prescription for Waiting   206

     Patients Dressing for Success   209

     Value Under Pressure   210

     Stamping Out Waiting Waste   211

     Everybody Wins   213

     What's in It for Me?   215

Chapter 17: Waste #6 – Transportation   217

     Unanticipated Consequences   218

     Free Home Delivery   220

     Moving Without Value   222

What's in It for Me?   224

Chapter 18: Waste #7 – Over-Processing   227

    Above and Beyond?   227

    Slow Boiling Water   228

    Delivering Expected Value   230

    Taxing My Patience   231

    A Rainbow with No Gold   233

    What's in It for Me?   235

Chapter 19: Waste #8 – Underutilization of People   237

    The Market Downturn Opportunity   237

    The "We Know More" Opportunity   241

    What's in It for Me?   242

Chapter 20: The Corporate Crutch   247

    The Value of Consultants   248

    Transferring the Torch, not the Crutch   250

    Consultants as Partners   251

    The Parable of the Onion   252

Chapter 21: The Taking Action Toolbox   255

    Kaizen & Kaizen Events   257

    The 5S Way of Life   262

    Value & Non-Value Analysis   278

    The "New Shoes" Matrix Tool   283

    Value Stream Mapping (VSM)   285

    The Pareto (Reality) Chart   288

    5-Why Problem Solving   294

    The Fishbone Diagram   298

    SMED (Single Minute Exchange of Dies)   301

    Cardboard Cities   306

    The Spaghetti Mapping Tool   309

    Standard Work   311

    Time Studies   314

Chapter 22: A Lean Management System   325

Summary: A New Horizon   351

What Now?   355

Acknowledgments: An Impossible Task   357

About the Author   359

Recommended Readings   361

Index   367

INTRODUCTION

Lean Isn't a Program or Initiative

There are several things in life I would consider myself passionate about: my family, my God, my country, my friends, helping others, and Lean. In reality, the last two go hand in hand. When I refer to helping others, I am mostly referring to my passion for working with those with disabilities and those who are struggling in life, but I am also referring to those who are struggling at an organizational or professional level. The last item I mention in my list is Lean. I have been a disciple of Lean for many years and am still only scratching the surface of its potential for transforming operations at every level. There is indescribable satisfaction in watching others benefit from the application of the Lean principles and tools, witnessing their "aha" moments as the reality of what they are accomplishing finally sinks in. I would like you to experience this same level of accomplishment as you read and apply the Lean concepts outlined in this book.

> **"Lean is the most efficient and effective utilization of our limited resources to minimize waste and provide the maximum value to our patients, customers, and stakeholders."**

Unlocking The Lean Treasure Chest is important to you. If it wasn't, you wouldn't have picked up this book. You understand the value of Lean and where it can take you and your teams. You are not alone, but you may feel under-qualified to start the Lean journey. In today's world of Lean and Lean Six Sigma certifications, we often make the mistake of thinking that understanding and utilizing Lean is beyond our competency and ability without a piece of paper that documents our belt level. You may not realize that the experience you already possess is what makes Lean so valuable. Lean by itself holds little benefit without the understanding of the processes it can influence.

Regardless of the size of your company or the industry in which you operate, you can use Lean to change your world. Certifications add value through the accompanying training, but they are not the impenetrable gate through which you must pass in order to utilize and benefit from Lean. Lean is based on common sense and rational thought – it's not rocket science. It requires a foundational understanding of your processes and a willingness to take an honest look in the operational and leadership mirrors. You must be willing to:

- Make tough decisions

- Admit when you are wrong

- Accept that you don't know everything

- Lead by example

- Set clearly defined expectations

- Drive true accountability

You can no longer accept the endless excuses and the "we've always done it that way" rhetoric that will be thrown in your face repeatedly.

Lean works, and it will impact every single fiber of your organization's operational fabric. It will be woven into your quality, service, customer satisfaction, safety, growth, and financial processes. Lean depends on the process, not people, but it requires committed people to understand and utilize it. It works because it isn't a "program" or new initiative; it is a mindset that is reflected in your behaviors, your habits and, ultimately, your culture.

Whether you are a Lean Six Sigma Master Black Belt, a Shift Supervisor in a small machine shop, a rising star on the hospital Administration Team, or the VP of a multinational company, this book will provide you with insight, understanding, and confidence to utilize Lean to transform your operational reality.

The Common 20%

Remember this number: 20%.

On a cloudy and rainy Saturday afternoon, you take your entire family to the local theater to watch the newest superhero thriller. Everyone is excited – you've all been talking about this movie for months, since the first trailer came out. You pay a mind blowing $15 per ticket for the IMAX experience, and then spend twice that amount on popcorn, drinks, and small boxes of stale candy. You and the family jump into the best seats and then sit through what feels like an endless number of previews. As the previews finally conclude, the theater lights fade, and the long anticipated main feature begins. It starts with a visually explosive action sequence that instantly pulls you into the captivating plot. Eighteen minutes into the movie, the screen suddenly goes blank, the theater lights come on, and the cinema attendants start sweeping the floors, picking up trash, and directing you to leave. You walk out confused and frustrated.

Later that evening, you and your spouse go out to a nice expensive dinner at an up-scale restaurant downtown. The lighting is perfect, the atmosphere is quiet and cozy, and you find yourselves in a secluded back corner. Perfect! You order a nice glass of red wine and a delicious looking appetizer and entree. You were hungry even before you arrived, and your appetite intensifies while you wait. Fifteen minutes later, the waiter brings out your food, but the appetizer and dinner plates contain only 20% of the amount of food shown in the menu picture. The waiter politely drops off the bill once you finish your meals. To your surprise, the charges on the ticket are for the full amount of each meal.

Hungry and frustrated, you pull into a gas station after dinner to fill up your car, which is running on fumes. As a cost-conscious shopper, you have scoped out the station with the best fuel price, $2 per gallon. Since the station is pre-pay only, you walk inside, patiently wait behind three people redeeming lottery tickets, and then hand the cashier $20 to be applied to pump 6. You walk out to the car, remove the gas cap, grab the pump handle, and select the 87-octane button. You start pumping gas. As the pump display reaches $4 and 2 gallons, it stops dispensing gas, but the cost display continues climbing all the way up to $20. Something isn't right.

The next week, you head to the airport for a flight from Jacksonville, Florida, to San Diego, California. The $800 Business Class ticket was not cheap, but since it was such a long flight, you thought the cost would be worth it. You arrive to the airport early, get through the TSA checkpoint, and even have enough time to grab an overpriced cup of coffee. A short time later, you board the plane with Group 1 and sit back and watch as the remainder of the passengers board with their oversized luggage, car seats, pillows, dog carriers, and backpacks the size of small vehicles. The plane takes off, but at 24,000 feet and 50 minutes into the 5-hour flight, the pilot comes over the intercom and instructs the flight attendants to prepare for landing. Ten minutes later, you are being welcomed to beautiful New Orleans, Louisiana. How did that happen?

Since you are now stranded in New Orleans for 6 hours until the next flight to San Diego, you start looking through the airport for something to occupy your time. Down one of the small concourses, you see a booth that advertises thrilling skydiving adventures. You strike up a conversation with the man at the counter, and he convinces you to experience a tandem parachute jump. He escorts you out of the airport and gives you a ride to the jump school just a couple short miles away.

Over the next hour and a half, you go through the jump instructions and get suited up. As you step onto the small plane, the realization of what you are about to do hits home. As the plane rolls down the short runway and lifts off, you ask yourself, "What was I thinking?" What seems like hours later, your jump instructor turns around to inform you that the plane has almost reached the target altitude. The instructor reviews the plan with you one more time, secures your goggles, attaches the tandem connections, positions you at the door, and then…"aaaaahhhhhhhhh!"

You are terrified and trying to catch your breath for the first 10 seconds, but your fear is quickly transformed into wonder and amazement as you soar through the cloudless blue sky. Over the years, you have enjoyed watching eagles and hawks effortlessly float over the earth and wondered what the world looked like from up there, and now you know. A few moments later your instructor tells you to prepare for the chute deployment. He pulls the cord, but nothing happens. "Not to worry," he yells in your ear. "We always carry a backup chute." Pulling the cord to the backup, the parachute deploys. To your dismay, the chute lines gets tangled and only deploys to 20% capacity. The remainder of the story is painfully obvious, so no further details are necessary.

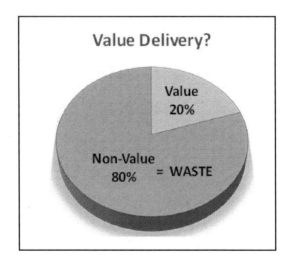

Why would I use these examples for the introduction of a book, and why did I tell you to keep the number 20% in mind? Well, in each of these five examples, you received only 20% of the value you expected and paid for. I can't imagine that you would accept the outcome of any of these situations. On the contrary, I would expect that you would take every action necessary to ensure that the movie theater, restaurant, gas station, and airline did, in fact, provide you with the value you paid for. The jump school example will unfortunately have to be handled by someone else. Here is the main point, or the "hook," as my editor calls it. Nobody in their right mind would be content receiving only 20% of the expected value, right? Well, in the real world, it happens every day, and it's taking place right under your nose. It's called *waste.*

It happens in hospitals, manufacturing facilities, government offices, telecom companies, retailers, airlines, and every other organization that could possibly come to mind. It's a reality, regardless of whether you are for-profit or non-profit. It happens when your processes are filled with inefficiency and problems. It's the reason you short or miss customer orders, fail to meet patients' medical care expectations, keep customers on hold for 30 minutes, lose inventory and supplies, struggle with quality, never seem to meet financial performance targets, and dread the company's End-of-Month Performance Review Meetings.

> **"Data by itself has never solved a single problem. Finding solutions requires taking actions that result from a deep understanding of what the data is telling you."**

There are a host of tools and methodologies available to dig into your process and identify waste and inefficiency. You can use TPS and Lean, Six Sigma and DMAIC, PDEA (Plan Do Check Act), SPC (Statistical Process Control), TPM (Total Productive Maintenance), SMED (Single Minute Exchange of Dies), and any of a hundred other systems. You could get so lost in the data that you cover the walls of your offices with control charts, pie graphs, histograms, scatter plots, bar charts, and spider graphs. All of it means nothing and is a "waste" of your time and effort if you and your teams are not using the data to take action and address your problems and inefficiencies.

To be perfectly clear, data without action is a jet without engines, a turbine without wind, and a rocket without fuel. Action is what gives data its value. It takes people to analyze the data and make decisions that lead to actions that result in improvements.

Do you know how much value you and your customers are missing out on? I use the 20% figure simply to get you thinking about what your reality is. Understanding is the catalyst for taking that first step in addressing the opportunities – it enables you to make informed and productive decisions that drive value and reduce waste. You can recapture and take advantage of the capacity and potential that exists within your organizations; you just need to have a proven, effective, and sustainable plan. This book will enable you to develop such a plan.

What This Book Offers

This book contains 22 chapters. The first 11 chapters are dedicated to developing a deeper understanding of what I believe are the greatest barriers for success to your organization – process waste and inefficiency. I also believe that addressing process waste holds the greatest opportunity for your organization to achieve greatness by solving problems, addressing process design flaws, and eliminating waste that permeates every aspect of your operations. If you want to locate The Lean Treasure Chest and take advantage of the enormous capacity, productivity, and potential that already exist within your organization, then it is certainly worth spending a substantial amount of time to first gain a new and deeper understanding of waste and inefficiency.

Chapters 12 through 19 provide in-depth discussion and detailed examples for eight types of process wastes to enable you and your teams to understand and identify them within your processes. Chapter 20 provides a word of warning as you progress in your journey. Chapter 21 is the "toolbox" to help you do something about process waste and inefficiency. This chapter translates understanding into action, allowing you to systematically and effectively address the waste opportunities in a way that leads to positive and sustainable results. Chapter 22 highlights the need for a Lean Management System that enables you to sustain the improvements and build upon them for the long-term.

At the end of every chapter, I have included a short section titled "What's in It for

Me?" This small section drills down to the heart of the matter – it provides examples, removes excuses, and offers direction and insight. This section is designed to take you beyond the knowledge and understanding phase and drop you right in the middle of the "process mud puddle" – the action phase. As you move into chapters 12-19, the "What's in It for Me?" section provides detailed directions for applying specific tools for uncovering The Lean Treasure Chest by identifying and addressing each unique type of waste and inefficiency. The Applicable Tools section lists what I believe are effective tools for addressing the opportunities unique to that chapter's subject matter. The use of these identified tools is detailed at length in Chapter 21.

The tools are most effectively utilized as part of a higher level system approach to Continuous Improvement or Operational Excellence. I personally call this approach a Lean Management System, but I have implemented it under a multitude of different names. What is important to understand is that a Lean Management System is based on a strategic, long-term, organizational level perspective that translates these individual tools into tactical activities that deliver measurable, meaningful, and sustainable results.

I can make the bold statement in the previous paragraph based upon my own experience. I have used these tools and seen firsthand how they can transform an organization, as well as its employees, customers, community, and future. In my 25 years of experience working at Toyota, GM, Ford, Caterpillar, Tenet Healthcare, and other industry leaders, I have utilized these tools. I have worked with multiple teams to uncover problems, implement solutions, recover capacity, create effective flow, drive true employee and leadership engagement, and ensure sustainable performance. Don't get me wrong – I have slipped, tripped, and fallen flat on my face numerous times, but such is the nature of learning. Some of my most valuable lessons have resulted from an "operational black eye and bloody lip."

Understanding process waste at a deeper level will enable you to truly understand the critical nature of both value and efficiency. You will look at your operations from a different perspective, without blinders and unfiltered. You can set a new standard for performance and develop a reputation for excellence many aspire to, but few ever demonstrate. The hidden capacity will become painfully obvious as you see the waste, inefficiency, obstacles, barriers, and problems that clog your operations. You will be able to utilize the tools to change your reality, your velocity, and your future. There are potentially millions of dollars, thousands of hours of capacity, countless flow improvements, and untold operational, quality, and safety improvements just waiting for you to find them. They are the Treasure Chest. Don't expect to become an expert just by reading this book though – it will require repeated and continuous application of the tools. Be realistic in your expectations for buy-in from your teams. Your current reality did not happen overnight, so be patient, yet diligent in driving toward your new operational horizon.

As Great Britain's former Prime Minister Winston Churchill once said in a 1941 speech, "Never give in, never give in, never, never, never..."

FOREWORD:
A TALE OF TWO SHIPS

It is a beautiful ship. Sleek and steady with the enormous main mast reaching high above the deck. Its first voyage is a 6-month route through the Atlantic to deliver supplies and trade other goods. You have been chosen to join the crew out of a large group of applicants – your credentials and experience stood out to the Captain. Great things are expected of you, and your reward will be substantial. It is indeed a privilege to be part of this maiden voyage on such an advanced and nautically sound vessel.

The seas are calm, and the weather remarkably beautiful. Almost daily, dolphins or porpoises seem to swim alongside the ship, escorting her through the deep blue seas. A continual breeze cools your brow and fills the sails with purpose. Life is good, and, though hard at times, the days are not a dread. As the normalcy of your duties slowly settles in, you find a routine taking shape. Each day is filled with the same tasks, accomplished in roughly the same order, and completed in nearly the same amount of time. After the first month, the routine requires very little conscious effort.

As you are working in the bilge of the ship one day, you notice a small trickle of water flowing across the floor and puddling in the corner. You aren't worried – just a small leak and to be expected. Several weeks later, while manning the wheel, you notice that the rudder seems to lack a crisp responsiveness, but no worries – it still works, and someone else will fix it.

Weeks go by. One day while working to store supplies in the stern compartments, you see a small crack in the wooden keel, but it doesn't appear to be getting bigger, and it's nothing that a little tar won't fix. You just need to remember to come back to fix it, or at least let someone know.

Then, on a windy afternoon as you walk through one of the middle decks, you see water spraying in from the sea. You find that the porthole cover seal is missing. It's only a little ocean spray, so nothing to get concerned about.

Late one evening, you are abruptly awoken from your sleep by the Captain. Everyone is running around, yelling, and grabbing buckets. It's hard to maintain balance, as the ship seems to be dropping out from under your feet. The dim lanterns reveal a look of terror in your shipmates' eyes. You ask others what has happened, and they explain that a storm has come upon the ship, and she is taking on water and listing heavily. You are thousands of miles out at sea, with no land in sight. Enormous waves crash over the deck, and the sea tosses the vessel around like a small piece of drift wood. The ship that for the last three months has been your unwavering fortress of strength and confidence now feels like a small floating wooden coffin. You try to make sense of the situation, asking yourself, "How could this have happened?" The answer comes instantaneously as you reflect back on the small leaks, problems, cracks, and concerns that were previously of no concern to you or the crew. Now, in the middle of a hurricane and with no safe harbor in sight, you understand the devastating consequences of your lack of action and complacency. If only you could go back in time and fix those issues, you wouldn't be in this situation.

Suddenly you are aware of an annoying buzzing noise. What is it, and where is it coming from? Slowly you drift out of your slumber. Your eyelids feel like they are glued together as you slowly gain enough consciousness to realize that the alarm is going off on the nightstand next to the bed. That was a weird dream, considering the closest body of water is your neighbor's koi pond, and the nearest ocean is 1,200 miles away. Maybe the dream was a result of watching Disney's *Pirates of the Caribbean* a couple of weeks ago.

Anyway, time to get ready for work. It's another early Monday morning. As you drive toward the office, you run through the endless list of things you need to accomplish. Arriving at work, you park and walk up to the building to discover a large group of employees standing outside the front door. The doors are locked – all of them. A single white piece of paper hanging inside the glass reads, "Temporarily Closed – Will Re-Open Next Week – Possibly."

On the drive home, you frantically make several calls to try to find out what's going on, but no luck. Everybody you call is asking the same question. Why would the company shut down for a week, and what are you going to do if the sign is still there next week? Why was there no advance warning? Is this a precursor to a permanent closure?

Over the next week, while sitting at home, you attempt to piece together what could have caused this to happen. You know things have been tight recently, but nobody expected this. Two questions seem to remain at the front of your mind, constantly surfacing: "Am I out of a job?" and, "How many of my friends and co-workers are asking the same question?"

How could this be happening? Thinking about a typical day at work and so many different process issues come to mind. Could this be a result of the mountains of finished goods inventory that just continues to grow, or maybe the enormous amount of raw material purchased far in advance of production needs? Might it relate to the ever-growing pile of quality defects or the recent loss of valuable and longtime customers? Those process flows filled with waste and inefficiency – could they have played a part in this? Maybe it was the escalating transportation costs resulting from partial shipment and expedited deliveries to customers. Was it the constant knee jerk decisions and direction changes from management that resulted in out-of-control overtime costs? Could I have done something to change this? The answer to every one of these questions is a resounding "YES."

Both scenarios are real. Both the ship and the company will either falter or persevere based on the decisions made and actions taken by you, your teams, and your leadership on a daily basis. This scenario isn't intended to scare you – I use it to ask a simple, yet purposeful question. If this situation did actually play out in your organization, what would you, your leadership, and your teams be willing to do to open those doors back up? Would you be willing to change the way you operate daily – to start seeing every single action as either a value producer or value consumer? Would you be willing to question the old ways of doing business? Would you stop to fix problems as they arise instead of looking the other way? Would you look for every imaginable way possible to improve quality, promote efficiency, increase productivity, satisfy customers, and eliminate waste? Would you stop settling? How hard would you work, and how much effort would you be willing to put forth in order to right the ship and save the company?

So, why wait for "rough operational seas" or the "market hurricane" to toss you around and put you at risk? Why not use this insight while the sea is calm to prepare the ship for a long and successful voyage? Take time right now to fix the leaks, seal the holes, and solve problems. You can build the ship that will stand the test of time, endure through the roughest of seas, and stand out as the flagship of your industry. You can build this.

The Lean Treasure Chest

You may be part of an organization that is extremely successful, or your company may be struggling. It doesn't matter. Every organization possesses a hidden operational treasure. It exists everywhere and is embedded in each and every process. Unlike a shiny gold coin, this raw gold is dull and dirty, providing no reason to be noticed, but it's there. There are "process jewels" buried deep inside your day to day activities – rough and uncut, just below the surface, but they are there. The potential they possess can only be realized when you find them, but their combined value is beyond estimation. These jewels make up the contents of The Lean Treasure Chest.

A treasure chest is probably not an analogy you would associate with your organization. After all, when you think of a treasure chest, you most likely envision a crusty and dirty old wooden box, filled by some pirate with gold and jewels, sealed tightly with an old skeleton key lock. As children, we all dreamed of finding buried treasure out in the back yard, in the woods across the street, or at the beach while on summer vacation. This dream was real, especially if you had ever watched the classic Warner Bros. 1985 movie *The Goonies,* in which a small group of kids search for the lost treasure of a fabled pirate named "One-Eyed-Willy." What they find is beyond imagination and changes the lives of their families and the entire community. For kids watching the movie, it was impossible to see the treasure and not start dreaming.

What's interesting about this movie story line and many like it is the fact that One-Eyed-Willy's treasure had been there, located in the same spot within the cliffs, for hundreds of years, just waiting for someone to search for and locate it. In the same way, a Lean Treasure Chest waits for you. It's there under your feet, embedded deep within your operations, just waiting for you, your team, and your organization to discover it.

Like One-Eyed-Willy's treasure, it's worth is more than you can imagine, and its value is beyond estimation. Inside your Lean Treasure Chest are gold, silver, and jewels in the form of improved quality, increased productivity, employee engagement, satisfied customers, efficiency, innovation, growth, financial strength, accountability, ownership, servant leadership, and so many others. Like a buried pirate's treasure, The Lean Treasure Chest will remain where it is, undiscovered and of no value. It will hide there, silent and undisturbed, buried under layers and layers of waste and inefficiency, until you make a conscious decision to search for and discover it.

You won't find it on your own – you will need a team of so-called "Goonies" to join you on the adventure. Situations will arise where you need someone to reach down and pull you up from the edge of the cliff. In those moments when you trip and fall, the steady and reassuring hand of a team member will provide the balance you need. There will be danger, risks, and tough decisions to make, but upon finding it, you will open The Lean Treasure Chest to reveal unimaginable value, worth, and potential that few organizations would dream of possessing.

Inside The Lean Treasure Chest

So, if you've picked up this book and immediately flipped to the Foreword or Introduction to see if it relates to your need or situation, you probably understand that The Lean Treasure Chest actually exists. Chances are you're searching for it in order to impact at least one, but most likely several of the operational areas listed in Figure F:1. This book will function as a metal detector that will enable you to locate the treasure.

FIGURE F:1

Problem Solving Expertise	Benchmark Productivity
High Quality	Increased Capacity
Effective Communication	Fast Service
Operational Agility	Cross Functional Collaboration
High Employee Retention	Low Overtime Cost
Employee Engagement	True Organizational Alignment
Reduced Defects and Errors	Pride and Respect
Team Loyalty and Trust	Increasing Demand
Exceptional Safety	Innovative Growth
Defined Expectations	Accountability and Ownership
Standardized Processes	Regulatory Compliance
A Culture of Success	A Legacy of Excellence
Satisfied Customers and Patients	Industry Leadership

You may have looked at the list in Figure F:1 and subconsciously muttered to yourself, "Yeah, I wish," "Wouldn't that be nice," or maybe even, "That could never happen where I work." Each one of us has worked in organizations where we felt that way. The question is, did we accept defeat, or did we rise to the challenge? Don't make the mistake of thinking that simply reading this book will result in The Lean Treasure Chest popping open and treasure pouring out. It doesn't work that way. No, this book will provide you with the knowledge you need to find the jewels, as well as the skills you need to realize their value.

What could your organization accomplish if you were able to drive improvement in just half of these areas? Unfortunately, simply wishing won't make it happen. If it could, every board room, hospital, factory, and office would be equipped with a wishing well. You are right in thinking, "Wouldn't that be nice," and if you truly believe, "That could never happen where I work," then you are also right. As Confucius once said,

"He who says he can and he who says he can't are both usually right."

Your company doesn't need more followers; it needs people who believe in a vision for the future, who are not intimidated by a challenge, and who are willing to venture off the commonly traveled path of contentment and complacency. Your company doesn't need people who are there just for a paycheck; it needs people who are there to make a difference. It needs leaders who are willing to remove the standard-issue "operational rose-colored glasses" and come to grips with their reality. It needs people who understand waste at a whole new level and refuse to accept it as an unfortunate, but acceptable part of doing business. Your company, its leaders, its managers, and its team members all need to understand the basic equation for success.

$$CAPACITY = VALUE + WASTE$$

$$OR$$

$$CAPACITY - WASTE = VALUE$$

Burn this equation into your mind. Your customers expect value. Your capacity is designed to produce the value that is in demand by your customers, clients, and patients. But, it is limited, so maximizing value creation is critically important. As shown in the two equations, the independent variable is waste. By reducing or eliminating process waste, you increase your available capacity to use for value creation.

A Look in the Operational Mirror

If you understand and believe this analysis of capacity, waste, and value, and if you are willing to step out and away from the crowd content with "average," then read on.

The survey contained in Figure F:2 contains seven questions. Answering any one of them in a manner that is less than 100% honest will make the whole survey invalid and is a confession that you are either not willing or not ready to utilize Lean to its full potential. Don't complete it quickly. Read the questions, and then take a few days to observe your operations. Come back after spending time knee-deep in the processes, and then complete the survey.

FIGURE F:2

A QUICK LOOK IN THE OPERATIONAL MIRROR	YES	NO
1) Do you have adequate equipment, machinery, and tools, but always seem to be behind schedule and looking for ways to increase capacity?		
2) Is your team fully staffed, but you continually struggle with low productivity numbers, excessive overtime, and poor quality?		
3) Do you have the infrastructure to succeed, but continually fall short of your goals and customer expectations, never truly understanding why?		
4) Does getting the simple things done, or completing even the most basic tasks, sometimes feel like trying to move a mountain or solve world hunger?		
5) Does getting different groups within your organization to communicate effectively and work together collaboratively seem to require an act of Congress?		
6) Do you doubt that the five previous answers will change over the next year?		
7) Are you willing to think differently, see from a new vantage point, take decisive action, teach others, challenge the norm, and be a transformational leader?		

I know, it probably isn't standard practice to start a book with a survey, but chances are you're looking in the very front of this book to gather a quick perspective of if and how it can help you, your team, and your organization. If it shows potential, reaching beyond simple theoretical discussion and into the world of activity-based application, then you may decide it's worth the cost. If not, then you may decide that it's probably better to place it back on the shelf and keep looking.

Let's get to the point. As you took the survey, some of these questions may have already been floating around in the back of your mind. These questions may have been recent topics of discussion between you and your team, or maybe even you and your leadership. These questions may be the same ones asked over and over for years at your company, but never truly addressed. They are the same questions that 99.9% of all organizations ask on an almost daily basis, so join the club.

Actually, don't join that club! Use the contents of this book to start your own club – a new club with members who are out-of-the-box thinkers, ready to pave new roads and set higher standards for their industry.

So, how did you answer the questions? If you answered "Yes" to any of the first six questions, and *if and only if* you also answered "Yes" to question 7, you will find this book to be an invaluable tool. If you answered "No" to question 7, then put the book back on the shelf. An answer of "No" to question 7 means you are probably better served by any one of the ten-thousand feel-good, warm and fuzzy, "I'm a winner," "Let's all stand in a circle and sing campfire songs" books that fill the bookstore shelves.

If you did answer "Yes" to question 7, then keep reading, but get ready to see, think, smell, and hear differently – very differently!

Lean Is for Everyone

This book is for everyone in your organization. It is not intended to simply fill shelf space, as its value is realized in the office of the CEO as well as at the process level of every department. Its value is realized as the pages get dirty, the cover gets torn, and the binding gets bent and cracked. Few things give me more satisfaction than seeing one of my books worn out, held together only by duct tape or some industrial adhesive. Your executives, directors, managers, supervisor, and team members should each have a copy of their own, so they can write notes on the pages, underline paragraphs, and highlight specific points that relate directly to them and their departments. A rainbow of different colored sticky notes should protrude from between the pages like a bad haircut. This book is a tool to be utilized by every employee to change the face of their processes.

These pages serve both as a wake-up alarm and a call to action for every board member, CEO, executive, director, manager, supervisor, and team member. Basically, if you are breathing, have a job to do, and value to add, this book applies to you. The discussions and examples are not simply "word candy," intended to temporarily excite your professional taste buds and then gradually melt away. They are examples that are meant to open your eyes to the ugly truth about the waste and inefficiency that exist within your organization and processes now, right under your nose.

The contents of this book are applicable to you and are meant to drive you to the leadership level, where decisions are made and strategies are developed. It is designed to drive you to the process level, where the organization actually creates and delivers value, down to the production floor, over to the Emergency Room, to shipping, engineering, quality, customer service, HR, and, ultimately, to a state where you and your teams see the waste, inefficiency, and problems for what they really are – both risks and opportunities.

As a firm believer in the importance of clear expectations and accountability, I think it only appropriate that we hold ourselves to the same level of commitment that we expect of everyone else. That said, it only makes sense that your first action prior to diving into this resource would be to formalize this commitment on the next page. As you progress through this book, utilizing the ideas, concepts, and tools to change your reality, this formal statement will provide you with a constant reminder of why you are fighting through the barriers, digging in the trenches, and climbing over the walls.

Reflect on it often.

My Personal Commitment to Success

I, _____ , am formally committing to myself, my team, and my organization (_____), to use the concepts and tools contained in this book to change our reality, transform our culture, and establish a new level of performance in the following areas of operation:

		Performance		Actual Performance		
	Process	Current	Goal	3 Month	6 Month	1 Year
1)	_____	_____	_____	_____	_____	_____
2)	_____	_____	_____	_____	_____	_____
3)	_____	_____	_____	_____	_____	_____
4)	_____	_____	_____	_____	_____	_____
5)	_____	_____	_____	_____	_____	_____
6)	_____	_____	_____	_____	_____	_____
7)	_____	_____	_____	_____	_____	_____
8)	_____	_____	_____	_____	_____	_____
9)	_____	_____	_____	_____	_____	_____
10)	_____	_____	_____	_____	_____	_____

I understand that this process will not be easy, but I will remain focused and disciplined. I will not provide or accept excuses that would compromise our journey toward excellence. I will set an example for my team, peers, and leadership, refusing to accept good or adequate in place of exceptional.

_____   _____
Your Signature   Today's Date

CHAPTER 1:
WHAT IS WASTE, REALLY?

As an organization, you have access to and utilize a pool of limited resources to produce value for your customers. Resources can refer to time, money, manpower, intrinsic knowledge, supplies, equipment, facilities, space, capital, reputation, and even confidence. Every resource is both limited and valuable. When those resources are being utilized in processes that are sub-optimal, only delivering, for example, 20% of the value they are capable of producing, what's happening to the other 80% of the potential value? Put simply, it is wasted – thrown in the trash, washed down the drain, gone for eternity, never to be recaptured and realized.

The 8 Wastes

Waste can be categorized for the most part into one of the following eight categories:

1. **Defects:** An outcome that does not meet an expectation as defined by a standard

2. **Overproduction:** Producing more than your current customer demand supports

3. **Too Much Inventory:** Holding more inventory than required to support current production

4. **Excess Motion:** Movement of people that doesn't add value

5. **Waiting:** Time spent between value creation processes

6. **Transportation:** Movement of material, assets, supplies, and inventory that adds no value

7. **Over-Processing:** Adding more value than the customer is willing to or has agreed to compensate you for

8. **Underutilization of People:** failure to utilize the talent, experience, knowledge, and skills of employees

Each waste is unique in its definition, but all are connected and can be generated by any other waste. Confused? In Chapters 12-19, we will break each one down individually to make it clearer.

If we learn to see waste in a new way, our eyes will open to what it truly is. The word "waste" can mean a multitude of things to any number of people. A formal definition of waste, according to Dictionary.com, is "to consume, spend, or employ uselessly without adequate return; use to no avail or profit; squander; and anything unused, unproductive, or not properly utilized." From a personal and professional perspective, waste may refer to the items you place in the trash can that you drag out to the end of the driveway each week, the time spent at the airport waiting 4 hours for a delayed flight, or the three tomatoes that went bad in the back of your refrigerator's produce drawer. As a manufacturer, it could refer to the 6% of machined aluminum parts produced that don't meet quality standards and must be dispositioned. Waste could be the five days a paving contractor spends ripping up a 2-mile section of asphalt that was not formulated correctly prior to application.

THE SPARK PLUG CATASTROPHE

I recently changed the spark plugs in my 2003 Suburban. I purchased the plugs at the local auto parts store and then drove the 30 miles home, pulled into the garage, and began the installation process. As I attempted to remove the first spark plug wire, the wire end pulled out of the boot, rendering the spark plug wire useless. Even more aggravating, I had considered also purchasing a wire set while at the auto parts store but had decided against the $60 purchase. I got in my other car and drove 30 miles back to the store, purchased the wires, and then drove 30 miles home. As I started replacing the plugs and wires, I noticed that the wires were too short. The store attendant had given me the wrong wire set. I jumped in my other car and once again drove 30 miles to the store. After verifying the new wires were, in fact, correct, I drove 30 miles back home.

The entire process should have taken me 45 minutes at most, but as a result of the multiple issues and the fact that is was snowing heavily, it took me a total of 5 hours. In addition to the wasted time, I spent about $18 on fuel, experienced elevated levels of frustration and anger, and missed out on time with my family on a Saturday. What a waste! This example may play out daily in your operations a result of poor planning and execution. Projects and operations both require you to plan ahead and focus on the details, giving special attention to the "what if" contingency planning and avoiding process chaos.

In a hospital, it may be the extra linens and towels in every in-patient room that must be laundered between patients, or the time spent taking a patient to X-ray just to be turned away because of a scheduling error. At a contract manufacturer, it may be the 3,000 gallons of body wash formula sitting in the batch tank that was contaminated during transfer and must be treated and then disposed of. At a retailer, it might be the entire shelf of cereal boxes an employee must relabel because they were mistakenly marked with the wrong price. It could be as simple as sending an email but forgetting the attachment, leading to a follow-up email and wasted time for both the sender and recipients.

In the winter, it could be the 10% of your heat that is lost through inadequate insulation or drafty doors and windows, or the 10% of air conditioning lost in the summer from the same issues. It may be as basic as the 2-inch vein of fat you trim off a steak that was hidden beneath four others in the package from the local grocery store. On another, often overlooked level, it could be the potential and talent that has been disregarded by a gifted athlete, brilliant student, or a promising employee.

My point is, this waste exists whether you want to admit it or not. You can choose to bury your head in the sand and continue to pretend it doesn't exist, fabricating excuses for poor performance, or you can acknowledge the tremendous impact waste has on you at a personal, professional, and organizational level. Once you do this, you can then do something about it.

Zero Value

The fundamental premise behind waste is universal – it is something that you place zero value upon. You don't want it, you don't need it, and you most certainly would not pay for it. It adds no value, consumes limited and valuable resources, and demoralizes your teams. Waste and inefficiency are often embarrassing, but doing something about them requires effort. Unless the pain and discomfort resulting from the waste becomes unbearable, often organizations chose to simply live with what they mistakenly perceive as inconsequential waste. This applies both in your personal and professional lives. The problem with waste, though, is that, whether or not you choose to acknowledge it, you do pay dearly for it – far more than you probably realize.

As we'll discuss later, all too often people make the mistake of missing the greatest opportunity to take advantage of hidden capacity, which leads to increased productivity, improved service and quality, satisfied customers, elevated profitability, and, ultimately, growth. They mistakenly assume that, to accomplish any of these things, they must either invest in new equipment or capital, hire more people, build new facilities, or upgrade IT systems. These investments may provide some positive results, but they are an expensive and often unnecessary undertaking, considering the enormous amount of potential and capacity that already exists within current operations, but remains hidden from sight under layers of operational waste.

> **"Processes consume limited resources and produce either value or waste."**

I use the term "hidden" because it is an accurate description of what happens when operations are buried underneath piles of waste and inefficiency that only continue to accumulate over time. As the piles grow, their negative impact becomes more burdensome, weighing down the operations to the point where any dream of industry excellence is replaced with a desperate desire to simply survive. When organizations ignore process symptoms, using "operational Band-Aids" as permanent solutions and continually working around the root cause of problems, they bury themselves, pulling the dirt pile of waste and inefficiency down on top of their own organizational coffin.

FIGURE 1:1

THE HIDDEN POTENTIAL QUESTIONNAIRE	YES	NO
1) Is your team proficient in the "Just get it done" methodology?		
2) Do you have a small group of "superheroes" who can always make it happen?		
3) Do you and your team spend a large percentage of the day fighting fires?		
4) Do your operations contain "process Band-Aids" instead of permanent solutions?		
5) Is your employee turnover rate higher that you think it should be?		
6) Is your employee productivity low, but your overtime cost high?		
7) Is your equipment utilization number high, but your operational efficiency low?		
8) Are your defects/errors climbing while your quality performance is falling?		
9) Have you ever wondered how your company is still in business?		
10) Is an employee RIF always your company's first line of defense in a market downturn?		

The Hidden Potential

Look at the questionnaire in Figure 1:1. Read the questions and then check the appropriate boxes to gain a quick, but deeper understanding of your current situation. Some of these questions aren't fun to answer, and some may make you downright uncomfortable. That is to be expected and is absolutely necessary if you are serious about "seeing the invisible to realize the potential." Keep in mind that the answers you provide may not match those of your team, peers, and managers. That is to be expected and is in itself a huge part of the opportunity.

Ask those around you to answer the same questions, but not to write down their names, unless they really want to. After you review the results on your own, meet as a team to discuss the group's answers. You will experience what I commonly refer to as "an honest look in the operational mirror" and gain a new perspective of the organization's *reality.*

> **"As you read this book, I would expect that many of you will be literally shaking your heads in both agreement and disbelief, as the examples I use are mirrored in perfect clarity within your own experience on an almost daily basis. You'll feel as if I had been standing on a wooden box outside your facility, secretly observing you through a very low window. I haven't."**

Of course, not every process in your organization yields only 20% value – some may yield 30, 40 or even 50 percent! Does a 50% yield make you jump up and down with excitement? Would you burst into the office of your Manager, Director, COO or President and exclaim, "We did it, we reached 50% value delivery this month!?" I kind of doubt it. Keep in mind that, even after an enormous amount of work and effort, a world-class process and organization may eventually see anywhere from 60-90% value delivery, depending on the industry and process itself.

But how do you get there?

Understanding the "how" is why you are reading this book. You may have spent years looking for a way to enable your company and teams to reach levels of performance that you've always known they were capable of but seemed just beyond grasp. The potential for world-class performance already exists within you, your teams, and organization – it's just not realized yet. It's similar to the potential you see in your children – you know it's there, and you see it every day, but, ultimately, it's up to them to do something with it. Unrealized potential is akin to the finest Japanese sword ever forged – meticulously crafted, hardened and strong, with a razor edge and an almost glass-like sheen. Despite the sword's breathtaking beauty, until it is wielded, its purpose fulfilled in the skillful hands of a Samurai master, it is useless – a simple wall decoration.

This is an opportunity for you to accomplish something that you and everyone else in your organization may have never imagined possible – something that may have been nice to think about but was just a pipe dream. You have the ability to develop a vision for the future that previously has seemed out of reach, and to create a legacy that will become the cornerstone of a truly world-class organization.

To be completely transparent, this book is not just for reading and storing on a shelf with hundreds of other improvement, transformation, and motivational books. It is a tool! It's no different than a lathe in the machine shop, the X-ray machine in an imaging department, a fork truck in a warehouse, a computer system at a software company, or a website for a retailer. Its sole purpose is to add value.

I will make a bold statement up front. You are without a doubt very busy, and most of the hours in your day are probably already spoken for several times over. You probably get to work too early and leave later than you anticipated the majority of the time. You may have moved into your current role expecting a better work-life balance, only to find that now the days are actually longer, and you rarely seem to be able to disconnect from work. You may often find yourself rescheduling dinner dates with your spouse and missing your children's piano recitals, football games, wrestling matches and school plays.

THE NON-VACATION

If you've ever sat on a sunny beech in Mexico or been hiking in the picturesque mountains of Colorado while on vacation and felt the uncontrollable need to check your work emails or messages, I am talking directly to you. I can say this from personal experience and expect that you can completely relate.

So, understanding that your time is extremely valuable, if reading this book is nothing more to you than a trendy eye exercise program, put it down. If this book does not lead you to a transformation in how you see and understand waste, donate it to Goodwill. If reading this book doesn't result in meaningful action that drives value through you and into your team and organization, then the act of reading this book is a waste.

If you are an executive who sits in your office or in the board room, running through report after report trying to understand why the financials are consistently floundering while volume and productivity are soaring, you should be the first one reading this book, and then personally infusing its principles into your entire organization. If you are a director wedged between the rocks known as "the team" and "the executives," desperately attempting to support, motivate, and placate each group, but always feeling like you are failing both, this book is for you. If you are a manager, supervisor, or team member who carries duct tape or zip-ties in your back pocket, constantly working around, though, over, under, and between your standard processes to "just get it done," this book is for you.

If you are looking for a feel-good, easy read that validates your list of excuses and reasons for remaining content with mediocrity and complacency, this is not the book for you. If you see yourself as a leader who possesses a vision for the future and wants to pass on a legacy of greatness – someone who can bring a dream to life within an organization and is disciplined, servant minded, and dedicated to more than just your own individual success, this book is for you.

WHAT'S IN IT FOR ME?

At the end of every chapter, I have included a short summary explaining how the content applies to you and what value it can deliver when applied in your own world. The ideas, examples, and concepts are intended to provide you with the tools and insight needed to go beyond your visible performance horizon. What you do with the tools will determine your future progress as well as the future of your team and organization. No pressure, right?

To be perfectly clear, there is not one standard answer or solution that applies to every situation or problem. Every hospital, manufacturing plant, and service organization is unique. Each uses different equipment, employs different people with different backgrounds, follows different standards, utilizes different IT systems, and possesses a history of its own. Even companies that reside under the same corporate umbrella operate differently. Walking through sister facilities located perhaps only a couple of miles from each other, looking around and watching the operations, you might swear there was no way they were affiliated.

If you are reading this book, hoping to find a nice pre-packaged can, tube, or bottle of industrial strength "Fix-All Problem Remover," sorry – it doesn't exist, and it never will. If you are looking for a special offer full of empty promises and lies, just watch late night TV and be ready to call within the next 10 minutes. There is no single book that will lead you to a state of corporate utopia, no one tool that will fix all of your problems, no one solution that answers all the questions, no one management skill that will engage every employee, and no single person who can make it all happen, regardless of degrees, certifications, awards, and licenses.

The journey described in this book is to be taken together as a team, so that when challenges and difficulties arise – and they certainly will – the combined strength and resolve of the team will lead you to victory.

Eliminating waste takes effort, determination, and resolve. You will get dirty and may even scrape your elbows and knees, so grab a pair of gloves, some first aid ointment, and a shovel. Such is the path to greatness!

CHAPTER 2:
A LITTLE RED LAWNMOWER

At this point, you have made the commitment to yourself, your team, and your organization. In the Foreword and Introduction, you asked yourself some hard questions that were probably not easy or pleasant to answer truthfully. You now find yourself standing in front of the operational mirror looking at a bad case of bed head, pillow wrinkles imprinted on your face, dried drool marks down your chin, crusty goobers in your eyes, and teeth in desperate need of a good brushing. This is where you want to be, face to face with reality – not pretty, but very real. I have stood in front of that same mirror many times.

So, to understand the context of this book and what would lead me to take the time to write it, you must first understand where I am coming from. This chapter will better explain how you and I both arrived together in this paragraph at this specific moment in time. So, bend down, step inside my cardboard refrigerator box time machine, and join me as we travel back in time to a small mid-western town in Indiana called Avon.

Forty years ago, we find a nervous 8-year-old boy moving into a brand-new neighborhood. At the time, Avon was not large enough to be classified as a town – it was simply considered a community. It was the epitome of a middle-class neighborhood and, as this young boy took notice of the yards that surrounded his own, he quickly realized the calling for his young life. So, with the permission of his mom and dad, and the use of their 19-inch red Murray side discharge push mower, he started mowing yards.

You probably guessed it already, but that 8-year-old boy was me. I was an undersized kid from the beginning, as most of my friends usually stood at least a head's height above me. My father was (and still is) short as well, and he counseled me that my lack of stature was simply a fact of life – it would not change miraculously overnight, and it was never to be used as an excuse for lack of effort or failure. I knew early on that my chances of being the star center on the varsity basketball team or receiving a college football scholarship were slim, but luckily my passion wasn't basketball or football – it was wrestling.

My preoccupation with efficiency and waste started in the front yards of this small neighborhood. A summer day was limited to 16 hours of sunlight, and I needed to get as much out of each as possible. As I carefully evaluated each new yard, I would mentally calculate the possible mowing routes. I would consider the number of turns, the direction of the grass discharge, and the number of bushes, trees, and other obstacles. I would take into account the area consumed by driveways, the location of parked cars, and any other obstacle that would interrupt my flow, like dog kennels and yard ornaments. I would test different routes and always arrived at a standard way of mowing each unique yard. This dedication to efficiency would ultimately be realized in the time required and fuel consumed to mow each yard. Or, when translated into the language of an 8-year-old, it meant extra time to play with our beagle named Posey and extra money for those important things in life like comic books, sling shots, and miniature army men.

Being small in stature, I had difficulty pushing the mower using the top handle, so my progress was slow and grueling at times, especially in taller grass. This problem was quickly addressed and overcome when I realized that I was actually small enough to stand inside the handles and push the mower using the middle cross bar of the handle assembly. Yes, it looked very strange to people driving and walking past, but I wasn't getting paid for looking cool; I was getting paid for mowing yards. The faster I finished mowing, the sooner I could jump on my bike, ride around with my friends, and go to the local Hooks Drug Store for a candy bar, root beer, and a quick game of PAC-MAN or Galaga. I imagine that many of you are smiling as you remember your own summer days filled with the same activities and the same games that are now considered archaic by our kids.

This passion for efficiency followed me through my teenage years, my time as a U.S.

Marine, and, ultimately, through multiple roles over the last 25 years as my career has progressed. It has impacted the way my wife and I manage our finances – how we paid for our children's college, maintain our home and vehicles, schedule our vacations, and plan for our future. All three of my children were exposed to this passion for efficiency as they grew up. As a result, they have become quite proficient in their own ability to evaluate and plan for any number of different situations in their lives. Honestly, it is extremely rewarding to find myself being coached by one of my kids as they stop me in my tracks and say, "Dad, that isn't the most efficient way to do that – let me show you why." BAM! Drop that microphone!

Efficiency has permeated every area of my life, but not in a way that you may be thinking. If you are envisioning a stark white, sterile, monotone, and almost robotic existence, we are not on the same page. To clarify, it is critical to understand that everything you do is ultimately a process, whether at home or at work – from brushing your teeth to paying the monthly electric bill, treating a patient, or assembling an automobile. The simple act of reading this book, whether on a tablet, via audio, or in printed form, is a process.

THE LEAN OIL CHANGE

My car needs an oil change every 5,000 miles. Committed to Lean, preventative maintenance, and the efficient use of resources, I do it myself for about $25, as compared to paying someone else to do it for $45. When I'm changing the oil in my vehicle, I make sure that I have all the supplies, equipment, and tools available when I lay down and crawl under the car for the first time. It is very aggravating, uncomfortable, and a complete waste of time and energy to squirm out from underneath the car to go get something I forgot or positioned out of reach. This means that I must plan ahead and, as a result, improve the overall efficiency of the process.

Our Normal Life

Consider Indiana – what comes to most peoples' minds are corn fields and hogs. That is not far from reality, and I am ok with that. Indiana actually has a lot of technology – biomedical, manufacturing, and other industries – but where I live out in the country, corn fields and hog farms act as a fairly accurate summary. Our lives are like most of yours, with the normalcy of daily existence consuming the lion's share of our days. Even with that said, my family tends to operate on the Lean side, and it does have its benefits. Here are some quick examples from our simple, yet rewarding life.

From October through February, we use our fireplace almost every day – not for heating the house, but because there is something warm and comforting about a glowing and crackling fire. When storing wood outside for use in the fireplace, my son Jordan and I look for a location that's close, easily accessible, safe in slippery and snowy conditions, and that would not promote an all-out termite infestation of our home.

Regarding our home entertainment, like many of you, we keep the remotes for the TV, satellite, and Blu-ray all in one place. By doing this, we avoid spending hours digging through couch cushions lined with potato chips, dog toys, dirty socks, and loose change just to find the remote. Some cable and dish companies have even engineered their systems to contain a button on the console that will set off a beeping alarm on your remote control so that you can easily locate it. Another national crisis averted!

As previously mentioned, since I am vertically challenged (short), in my shed I organize the tools so that the ones used most often are at chest level. Every tool also has its own "home" on the pegboard wall.

We have a pond on our property, and the air filter for the aerator system pump is changed at specific time intervals to avoid mechanical failure and costly repairs.

We keep a cabinet in the laundry room stocked with LED light bulbs ranging from 40 to 100 watts, available to use when a ceiling or lamp light decides to burn out.

My son always keeps an extra bag of chicken feed in the shed, so that once the feed container is emptied, he has another bag on hand, available to pacify our feathered egg-laying friends.

My wife Barbara uses a simple Kanban Trigger System (see Chapter 21) for different food items. When we empty the peanut butter jar in the kitchen cabinet, she retrieves the full one from the pantry and then adds peanut butter to her shopping list.

Efficiency Isn't Robotic

These actions should not seem sterile and robotic – they are part of a life lived efficiently. I would expect that you can completely relate with each of these examples within the context of your own day-to-day life. Efficiency, or waste reduction, is not confined to the manufacturing floor or operating room. It is almost instinctive, applicable to our personal and professional lives. Most of us demonstrate it every day without even realizing it. Need me to prove it? Take a look in your silverware drawer. I would wager your paycheck that the forks and spoons are side by side right next to each other and that the knives are on the outside of one or the other. Why? It's because you almost always use a fork and spoon together, but if you're like my family, you rarely use a knife. You may have organized it that way unconsciously, or perhaps purchased a drawer insert that was designed that way by the manufacturer because they already understood the concept of efficiency. I know you need to go to the kitchen to see if it's true, so go ahead.

To be perfectly transparent, though, the whole efficiency thing does have its limitations, and if these limitations are not clearly understood, you can find yourself in a "hurt locker." Case in point: after sponsoring, leading, and participating in many Lean and Continuous Improvement activities focused on waste reduction, efficiency improvements, and visual management system implementation, I made a sincere offer to help my wife organize her kitchen and improve flow. There were numerous examples of what I observed as inefficiencies, waste, and opportunities for improvement that stood out, literally screaming for resolution. I was all too eager and happy to help. My heart was in the right place, but I didn't realize that my life was in imminent danger.

As I proceeded to explain the proposed plan to my wife for rearranging, organizing, and right sizing her inventory levels, it became obvious from her lack of any recognizable facial expression that we were not on the same page. In fact, I would say that we were probably also not in the same book, the same library, the same country, or potentially even the same solar system. I felt like I was watching one of the nature channel specials documenting the feeding habits of the great white shark. I recalled in vivid detail how its big, black, lifeless eyes would roll back into its head right before its jaws opened and it took a massive bite out of an unsuspecting seal. I was the seal, preparing for the attack that would launch my lifeless body 20 feet out of the ocean.

Then, in a way that only a compassionate and loving wife can, Barbara, peering through my eyes and into the very depths of my soul, tenderly explained to me that since I didn't enjoy cooking, her kitchen was, indeed, her kitchen. She continued to expand on her thoughts, stressing that, from a life expectancy standpoint, I would probably find a mine field and the core of a nuclear reactor a safer place to drive Lean than in her perfectly organized kitchen. Wow, what a wonderful, sincere, remarkable woman! So, at that point I tucked my tail between my legs and scurried to the farthest corner of the house, where I contemplated the magnitude of my near-death experience.

Understanding Their Perspective

This example was, in reality, a very good learning experience for me. Even after many years in operational roles, it made me realize that, when we peer outside our own realm of control and start looking at others' processes to address opportunities, we often experience a similar reaction to my wife's. Waste and inefficiency are not always seen for what they are, especially if you are the person standing in the middle of the "process forest," neck deep in the underbrush day after day. If we don't approach each unique situation correctly, we can find ourselves alienating the very people we want to help – those who need to understand it the most. Instead of being viewed as a resource, we can be perceived as an outsider, troublemaker, and boat rocker. Once this happens, the walls go up, and the job of helping, no matter how sincere your intentions, becomes 10 times more difficult.

You must be patient and present opportunities in the right manner, in the right context, and in a way that demonstrates the real value and benefit to the process owners. As we will discuss in the Chapter 21 section on "New Shoes," you must observe the world from others' perspectives in order to understand the potential impact to their realities. Nobody likes being told to make a change without first understanding the reason for the change – the "why." Whether you are a CEO, Director, or Manager, when driving any type of improvement, you need to engage the people directly involved in the value creation so that they are part of every solution process, not just the recipients of a supposed improved outcome. This book is an attempt to enable you to do just that.

WHAT'S IN IT FOR ME?

This chapter was intended to explain why this book originated in the first place, and to show how waste and inefficiency are part of our everyday lives. If these apply to the personal examples I show above, how much more applicable are they in our complicated and chaotic professional lives as team members and leaders of organizations? You may think that these concepts don't apply to you. You may be telling yourself that your situation is unique, but it would be a big mistake to assume that.

For example, if you work in healthcare and automatically assume that the mere mention of the terms waste, efficiency, and Lean is somehow negatively prophetic, forcing you to sacrifice the quality of patient care to promote profitability, you have completely and absolutely missed the true meaning. We improve every aspect of patient care by reducing operational waste, increasing efficiency, and utilizing Lean concepts. Case in point – patients hate to wait, but what do they spend the vast majority of their time doing? Waiting!

When you reduce waste and improve efficiency, this increases the value that you are able to provide to customers, patients, and clients. These groups return because you provide what they want, what they expect, and what they value. They consciously chose you over any number of direct competitors who offer the exact same product or service as you. By seeing, understanding, and reducing process waste, you can increase the value offered to current customers, patients, and clients. This not only promotes their future loyalty, but also creates reasons for the competition's customers to jump ship and choose to do business with you instead.

You also provide your most valued asset – your employees – with the ability to win and to be successful every day, avoiding the frustration that drives them over the fence to what they perceive as greener pastures.

Improved performance then provides an opportunity to deliver greater value to your stakeholders and investors. When stakeholders are confident in how you operate, they are confident in your future, and they demonstrate it through additional investment.

CHAPTER 3:
THE GORILLA ON YOUR BACK

Efficiency and waste reduction are natural in both our professional and personal lives. We strive for both without even realizing it sometimes. Our subconscious is programmed to walk the shortest distance, to look for the dish soap bottle with the highest fill level, to avoid the longest line at the supermarket, and to multi-task at work. So, based on this almost instinctive predisposition for efficiency, how do we find ourselves in the situation that most managers, employees, and organizations are in – struggling to overcome the waste, inefficiencies, and repetitive problems that weigh us down operationally?

To understand that, you must understand the journey that led you to this point. It didn't happen overnight, no text message alert was sent, and there was no red light flashing to notify you of the impending struggles. One day you turned around and realized that the operational steering was no longer crisp and responsive, reacting to even the slightest adjustment. Have you ever felt like the dog being wagged by the tail? Has it ever seemed like you were a 14,000-pound elephant being chased around the plains of Africa by a .68-ounce mouse? If so, then simply follow along.

I know that once we leave grade school, our imagination skills start to diminish, and the world becomes more black and white. Leading a company or department seldom returns you to the carefree days of Winnie the Pooh and kindergarten playgrounds, but let's take an imaginary journey together to the jungles of Africa.

Keep in mind that this is a fictional story, so kindly allow me a little leeway in the realm of reality.

It's your 40th birthday, and you decide to finally do it. You've wanted to see and experience the African Congo Basin for as long as you can remember. You remember in vivid detail reading as a child the *National Geographic* articles detailing the danger and mystery of the Congo. Countless hours over the last 10 years have been spent researching, watching documentaries, reading books, and attending college classes, just dreaming about this moment. In fact, this was item #2 on your bucket list. So, you book the trip and a couple of months later find yourself smack dab in the middle of the Congolese rainforest. You work with a local team to get the guides lined up, purchase your supplies, get clearance from the local authorities, and then head out on a 1-year trek to navigate the Congo Basin.

Few people have done it, and there are some inherent risks involved, but your family is supportive, and all the preparation and hard work will be worth it. When it's all said and done, you will have accomplished something monumental.

So, early one morning you and your team set out. It is even more amazing than you had imagined. During your fist week, you find yourself walking along in the unbelievably dense brush, stepping over pythons, brushing off large tarantulas, and swatting at the persistent mosquitoes that appear to be the same size as small birds back home. You are taken back by the variety of plants and insects that are within fingers' reach, most of which you have only previously seen on nature documentaries. In real life, they are even more fascinating and colorful. Your trek brings you face to face with swamp monkeys, bats, anacondas, otters, macaws, and the somewhat unnerving paw prints of a jaguar.

The daily torrent of rain is unrelenting. The humidity seems so heavy and thick that you wonder if you might have made a mistake in coming here, but your guides inform you that you are simply acclimating to the conditions and that it will get easier as the days progress. Then one morning, as you reach the crest of a tall hill, you look out over an endless expanse of jungle, clouds of mist lying deep within the troughs and valleys. Your ears are filled with the sound of thousands of insects, birds, and monkeys. The sight is both breathtaking and inspiring. The realization that you are finally here motivates you

to forge on.

One day, about a month into the expedition, as you slowly push through the under-brush-covered path, from the corner of your eye you catch sight of something that seems out of place about 10 feet off the trail. You cautiously move toward the large black mass lying motionless on the jungle floor. It isn't making any noise, and you walk all the way up to it. You realize that it is a large gorilla that has fallen from the trees above and sadly has died from the impact. You are taken back a little, as this is the first time you have seen a gorilla up close in the wild, and this is not how you would have liked the first meeting to have gone.

Suddenly a faint noise grabs your attention. You lean over the deceased gorilla and realize that there was a small baby in her arms. When the gorilla fell, the baby must have been still clinging to its mother's chest. You look around, hoping to see or hear other gorillas that would take care of the baby, but no such luck. It is so small and helpless, and you can't just leave it there to perish, so you gently reach down and pick up the small, scared mammal. He has big brown eyes and little hands that look remarkably similar to your own. His fur is soft, and he appears to be smiling at you – at least you think he is. He isn't afraid of you – quite the opposite. He immediately attaches himself firmly to your chest. He is only a couple pounds, so he will be no big deal to take care of. Your guides warn you that what you are doing is not a wise decision and that nature has a way of maintaining a balance, but you disregard their advice. You decide to name him "Tiny."

Over the next couple of weeks, you modify and rig up your pack to accommodate the new passenger. It is an easy addition, and you hardly notice that the little guy is there ex-cept for the constant squirming and chatter. You do have to stop more often than before to feed him, and he has developed a liking for your food instead of the fruit you find on the jungle floor. Still, it is not a big deal, and the journey is going well. You are only slightly behind schedule. No worries.

As the days turn into weeks and the weeks turn into months, Tiny starts to put on some weight and demands increasingly more of your attention. The stops become even more frequent, and, in some cases, you find yourself abandoning the trail and objective to chase the not-so-little fella around the jungle whenever he decides to jump from your back and run off. It is becoming painfully obvious as he grows that this small gorilla is not so small anymore. In fact, at this point, you have had to empty your backpack completely to make room for his considerable size. Others are now having to carry your supplies.

There is also the unpleasant realization that gorillas do not use the bathroom in the same manner that humans do – they just "go" when the urge makes itself known. As a result, your backpack is starting to take on an odor and requires constant cleaning. Though fruit is available, Tiny makes it clear that he likes your food and starts to consume more of your team's resources and time, and certainly your energy. Your initial purpose and enjoyment of the journey have taken a back seat to accommodating Tiny.

You spend most of your time tending to Tiny and keeping him out of trouble. He does not sleep according to your schedule, so most of your sleep at night is at most a shallow slumber – you wake to every sound and make sure Tiny is still there and out of danger. His weight has taken a toll on your back – he is becoming heavy and has caused you to slip and trip while carrying him. His strength is incredible for such a small creature. Looking back to the beginning of the journey, you faintly recall the original objective of the trip, which has now been transformed into nothing more than an exercise in babysitting your gorilla.

Eleven months into the adventure, the reality of your situation has become painfully clear. Tiny is not tiny anymore, and in fact he is so big that you can't carry him any longer. He is too heavy, so you now hold onto his hand and walk together down the trails. Your progress is considerably slower now, and your team is discouraged, losing faith that you will ever complete the trek. You calculate your position using your GPS and realize you are about 3 weeks behind schedule. This is not good. There is no way you can complete your objective under these circumstances. Reluctantly, you contact your transport company and schedule an early pickup. You turn Tiny over to the local animal rehabilitation authority and take the long flight home, defeated, dejected, and demoralized.

So, what happened? How did you transition from an excited, energetic, and motivated adventurer into this battered, bruised, and defeated person traveling home with your tail between your legs? In essence, you allowed your objective to be compromised. Your original goal was to traverse the Congolese jungle, but along the way you became preoccupied with what was at first a very small deviation to your plan – something so small and insignificant that it was almost unnoticeable.

Unfortunately, you did not see this little gorilla for what it really was, what it would become, and how it would eventually control you and your destiny.

Your Organizational Gorilla

Companies make this exact same mistake every day. Organizations start out strong, with robust strategies, efficient processes, new layouts, well trained employees, and standardized processes. Everything is going well, and the teams are making great progress. Margins are high, quality is good, overtime is low, productivity is improving, and you are riding on top of a wave of positive results.

Then it happens. You experience a problem within the manufacturing, patient care, or service process. It may be a quality issue, an engineering weakness in the design, or a simple work flow or information gap. Instead of driving to the root cause and fixing the problem, you just assume it's a one-off issue – an operational anomaly. Then down the road a little way, it happens again, so instead of fixing the issue and interrupting the process, you implement a quick work-around that adds extra processing time or even product rework. You lie to yourselves, convinced that your team will only use this work-around until the demand surge or patient volume weakens, and then you will get in there and fix the root cause. Right?

Unfortunately, volume does not decrease. The temporary solution is forgotten about and now becomes a permanent part of the process, reducing overall efficiency and impacting productivity and contribution margin. Today's problems are not problems tomorrow, since tomorrow will have enough problems of its own, and you quickly forget what happened yesterday. This Band-Aid also tarnishes your previously stellar quality record by promoting a risky practice of reworking product that is known to be defective, potentially allowing a quality defect to slip through to the customers. Instead of setting the example by demonstrating an unyielding commitment to producing quality products and services, you subvert your reputation and produce a defective product or service that will now consume additional resources to fix.

"You can do it right, or you can do it again. Your choice."

You make the mistake of thinking that, since we don't have time now, there will be time to fix it later, not realizing that over the next year you will potentially consume 10 times more resources by living with the problem than it would have taken to just stop to fix it. You send a very clear statement to your employees that work-arounds and Band-Aids are an acceptable method of operations, potentially resulting in hundreds of these temporary solutions permeating your processes, most of which you may never be made aware of. This leads to a domino effect of more out-of-control processes and quality risks. It goes back to the old adage one of my mentors used to tell me – "Do it *right* or do it *again*."

THE PROCESS COCKROACH

A problem ignored is like ignoring a single insignificant cockroach. German cockroaches, for example, only live for roughly 20 weeks. Within that 20 weeks, that single ignored female cockroach can produce between 30,000 and 35,000 offspring. Do the math. Within a couple of months, you have cockroaches living in every wall, nook, crevice, cupboard, and cabinet of your house. Ignoring a single and seemingly insignificant problem leads to the same results, with issues, defects, barriers, and interruptions soon permeating every department, system, and process in your organization.

Even in a hospital, this can all too often be the case. I worked with a very modern hospital, complete with a state of the art Emergency Department, Cath Lab, Surgery Center, Women's Services, and many other service lines. It was the nicest hospital in the area. Leadership utilized a staffing matrix based on the daily census and real time ED volumes. Staff were excited, and patient satisfaction and physician satisfaction scores were the highest many had ever experienced. The operations were efficient, providing tremendous value to patients through excellent quality care.

After 6 months working with the facility, we started to notice a trend in the ED – blood draws were being contaminated at an increasing rate. The ED manager worked with the lab to understand the problem and realized that the ED RN's and techs were not following defined protocols when drawing blood, resulting in the substantial increase in contamination. Action had to be taken quickly, considering that every contaminated sample had to be redrawn, consuming additional time and resources, not to mention the discomfort and inconvenience to the patient. The ED was also seeing a corresponding impact on patient satisfaction scores, as patients didn't particularly like being "stuck" twice due to a hospital mistake. It diminished their confidence, creating a perception that the ED teams didn't know what they were doing.

In response, the ED and lab managers made the decision to allow only lab techs to draw blood samples in the Emergency Department. Since this was their main responsibility up on the in-patient floors, they would take this responsibility out of the ED RNs' and techs' hands and give it to the experts. Problem solved, right? Well, not really. What they discovered was that now, every time the ED needed to have blood drawn, they had to call the lab, which was on the other side of the hospital. There were also a limited number of lab techs in the hospital, so, quite frequently, the ED patient had to wait for the lab techs to finish what they were doing on the in-patient floors before they could come over to the ED.

This resulted in increased patient wait time for the entire ED. Considering the number of patients sitting in the ED waiting room at any given time, this also increased the time that those just arriving had to wait to be seen, as all the observation rooms were full. Waiting for the lab techs also impacted the effectiveness of the entire ED staff of physicians, nurse practitioners, physician assistant, and RN's, as they also had to wait longer for the lab test results. Provider satisfaction, employee satisfaction, and patient satisfaction scores continued to drop. People were getting tired of waiting and were leaving the ED waiting rooms and going to the urgent care center down the road. Lab techs were being overworked and starting to resign. Quality of care, productivity, and ED volumes were negatively impacted.

All this operational carnage resulted from a single decision to work around the problem – ED RN's and techs not following correct blood draw procedures. By working around the root cause of the problem, the team introduced waste into the process and ultimately impacted at least 10 other areas. They were not victims of this situation; they were the cause, and the responsibility rested squarely on the ED and lab managers' shoulders. If the decision would have been to retrain the ED RN and tech staff and to develop a robust process to reinforce clear expectations and drive accountability, they would have addressed the root cause of the problem and avoided most of the chaos resulting from the work-around.

The Slow Decay

The baby gorilla named Tiny in the story represents the waste in your organizations. It starts out small, requiring very little attention or effort to manage. As only a minor distraction from your daily goals and objectives, it is hardly worth mentioning. Over time, and almost unnoticeably, your process stability begins to decay, like a tree dying from the inside out. Gradually, the waste starts to become more cumbersome. You set a precedent in one area by using a work-around, so people in other departments now see this as an acceptable way to address issues. They start implementing their own process quick fixes in an effort to avoid any interruption in production or service that would put them in the cross-hairs of upper management. The waste is now firmly embedded into their processes, no longer seen for what it is. You will realize that more and more of your resources, formerly dedicated to adding value, are now dedicated to the management of processes encumbered by waste and inefficiency.

GETTING BURNED

My family and I were in Gulf Shores, Alabama. The weather was fantastic, and we had already toured the USS Alabama battleship, as well as the submarine and the aircraft museum. It was time for the beach, and we were prepared. It was a perfect temperature, with the clouds providing some respite from the glare of the sun. We brought sunscreen, and I sprayed myself down. I asked my oldest son if he wanted some, but despite my suggestion, he was confident that he wouldn't get burned. I smiled as I realized that a life lesson was in the making. Toward the end of the day, we packed up and headed back to the hotel.

It was shower time, and we each took turns. Sitting there on the couch, we heard my oldest son make a sound like that of a dog with its tail caught in a gate. When he emerged from the shower, he informed us that the hot water was very painful on his unanticipated sunburn. Surprise! He had gotten burned and never knew if until it was too late. Organizations get "operational sunburns" by not addressing risks, waste, and problems. Avoiding or ignoring problems won't make them go away – it only delays their imminent impact, leading to a condition far worse and more painful to rectify. Develop the habit of addressing the risks and fixing the problems before you get burned.

You may hire outside quality groups to come in with literal armies of people to unpack, inspect, and repack your product prior to shipping to customers. Additional fork trucks are purchased, and more fork truck drivers are hired to move product around that must now be inspected and re-inspected. You lease warehouses where finished product is taken to sit, waiting to be inspected. You pay trucking companies to transport the finished product to the warehouses, where it sits, waiting to be inspected. The company installs countless vision systems to verify the integrity of your production process. You hire so many additional quality staff that they resemble an army, outnumbering the actual production staff.

You do everything *except* address the root cause of the problem, because doing that would require you to stop the line, develop standards, and hold people accountable.

As an operation, you turn around one day to realize that the little gorilla in the story named Tiny, who started out so small and helpless, has transformed into something that now controls you. It consumes your resources, manages your time, tells you where and when to go, wears you down, and, ultimately, prevents you from reaching your goals. Like the Congo adventurer, you have become a servant to the very thing you saw only as a minor distraction, not knowing that before long it would call the shots and rule the day.

A Cultural Shift

I would be daring enough to say that the you can certainly relate to the relevance of this example from a previous or maybe even current role. How you address opportunities and problems dictates whether your organization is building a culture of value or a culture of waste, a culture that excels or a culture that exists, a culture that succeeds or a culture that secedes. You have the ability to stop this madness, and it starts with your desire to change how you see waste.

> **"Great performance doesn't result in a great culture. Quite the opposite – a great culture drives great performance."**

A culture is not something you change overnight, and transforming it requires you to come to grips with your current culture. Your culture isn't defined by your brochures, advertising, or even your Mission, Vision, and Values. It is what you and the team demonstrate on a daily basis. Your culture is defined by your continual habits and behaviors. It is defined when you overlook a near-miss, walk past a hospital room where the call light is going off, get short with a customer on the phone, ship a part that is questionable according to the specs, and talk behind patients', customers', and employees' backs. This is your culture – not what you say or advertise, but what you do.

On the other side of the spectrum, your culture could be one of operational excellence, a high-reliability organization dedicated to uncompromising safety and quality. You may demonstrate daily the values and priorities that reflect your organization's dedication to satisfy customer needs and expectations. No different than in the previous case, your culture is defined by the daily habits and behaviors of everyone on your team. Culture is a result of leadership. The culture in a five-star restaurant is different than that of a fast food restaurant because the expectations are different, driving the habits and behaviors of the teams. These expectations are established and driven by leadership.

THE HOLIDAY WORLD SURPRISE

All amusement parks are the same, or so I thought. Then one day my wife convinced me to take the kids to a small amusement park in southern Indiana called Holiday World. I expected the same old same old – not-so-attentive attendants, $10 sodas, litter-lined walkways, and long lines. What we found was quite the opposite. We were amazed at the cleanliness of the park, observing employees constantly picking up even the smallest piece of trash. The employees and attendants were so courteous that, more than a few times, I looked around to see if I was part of a video training program. The lines were not long, and the rider flow was very fluid. To top it off, every 200 feet or so, a covered booth provided access to free pop, lemonade, and water. My wife and I were amazed, never having experienced an amusement park like this. I stopped one of the supervisors and conveyed my amazement and delight. Her comments made me realize that what I was both witnessing and experiencing was not a show – it was their culture, demonstrated through behavior, attitude, and habits. The culture was built on clear expectations and an absolute commitment to safety, quality, and customer satisfaction. It was driven by leadership – not on a daily or even hourly basis, but minute-by-minute. Their culture wasn't just a shirt taken on and off for work – it was part of who they were as Holiday World employees. Imagine what this level of cultural cohesiveness would look like in your organization, and how it would impact your future.

WHAT'S IN IT FOR ME?

Please do not go the local zoo and borrow a baby gorilla to validate my story above. The "operational gorilla" you are carrying was probably picked up, fed, and raised by multiple people who previously held your position. As roles changed, the furry problem was just passed on from leader to leader, each assuming that carrying it was just part of the job description. Currently, you hold the gorilla. It's time to put the backpack down and let the gorilla go.

At this point, realizing the magnitude of your opportunity, you are going to either throw your hands up in the air in defeat, or, armed with a new resolve, charge into action with a new and clear understanding of your enemy – waste. You may feel overwhelmed by the amount of waste and inefficiency you now realize exists in your operations. Don't be discouraged! As said by many great leaders, "Nothing worth doing is ever easy." Instead of getting overwhelmed, start documenting your opportunities to reduce and eliminate the waste. Get your teams and leadership involved. Once you document the opportunities, prioritize them so that you can start effectively addressing them. Don't attack them all at once, but make a plan and then execute it. Use the tools in Chapter 21 to accomplish this.

Admittedly, some of you may now look at your processes and realize that the tail is, in fact, wagging the dog, in almost every area. You may be completely overwhelmed, clinging desperately to a lifeline as you hang perilously close to the edge of the bottomless pit of despair. Don't let go!

Seeing what has been invisible, or maybe even ignored, is where your journey begins. Waste and problems don't fix themselves. Solutions require work by you and your team – the experts who design the processes.

Start with one area, with a team that is engaged and ready to make a difference. Provide each of them a with a copy of this book, and give them a couple of weeks to read it. Afterwards, sit down with them and talk about what they learned and how it has changed the way they see their processes. From my personal experience, you will be overwhelmed by the hundreds of opportunities that will immediately surface as a result of your excited team's new perspective and understanding of process waste.

This newfound understanding of waste is the spark that ignites the fire of employee engagement. This fire will set your organization ablaze with the inferno of promise, hope, and belief in your vision for the future. Like fire to gold, this inferno serves to purify your purpose, melting away old cultural skepticism that categorizes every initiative as simply the "flavor of the month." This excitement within your team is a result of the potential they see in improving their own world. It enables them to envision their role as a team in building something greater. It opens doors that allow them to be both successful and valued. It changes the culture.

Kindle a fire in your organization, and then fan those flames!

CHAPTER 4:
WASTE IMMUNITY?

After spending considerable time trampling through the foliage in the Congolese rainforest and being bitten by a vast array of insects, it probably makes a lot more sense now as to how your organization reached this point. It took time and, unfortunately, that time was permeated with instances of temporary solutions, relaxed standards, overlooked mistakes, and misaligned priorities. You may be part of a culture that has made a habit of looking the other way. Now is the time to change that culture – to stop looking away and start getting face-to-face with your reality. You may have gotten so caught up in simply surviving that you lost sight of the ultimate goal. As T.F. Tenney explained so well in his book *The Main Thing*, you were distracted and forgot your "main thing."

Having now stated the obvious, why does it appear that so much waste surrounds us? When I say "surrounds," I mean at home, while driving, on vacation, when eating, at the doctor's office, while traveling, at school, in government offices, and most certainly at our place of business. Is "surrounds" too strong of a word? I don't think so, and as you continue to read this chapter, I believe you will understand why.

It's in the Air

Look at the air that surrounds you. It's in your car, your home, your office, the elevator, the racquetball court, the middle of the lake, the top of the mountain, and even the bottom of the coal mine. "Look" may not have been the most appropriate term to use, as air is most often invisible, but this verb does, in fact, make a point. In most instances, you don't see the air; you simply accept and take for granted that it is present. You breathe thousands of times every day without a second thought. You can't see it, but air is powerful. It can bend and break mighty trees and create massive waves that are capable of capsizing enormous ships and flooding cities. The invisible air is capable of fueling enormous forest fires and carrying mountains of dust and sand in the form of dust storms in Arizona called Haboobs. It can destroy any structure in its path in the terrifying form of an EF5 tornado that can pick up houses and livestock, take thousands of lives, and cause damage that reaches into the hundreds of millions of dollars. How can something we can't see be so powerful and devastating?

When it comes to waste, for the most part, you don't see it either. It's like cruising in a Boeing 747-8 airliner at 34,000 feet – the sky outside your window is perfectly clear, but the force of the air shakes and twists the fully-loaded 970,000-pound aircraft like a paper clip.

In the same manner, waste may have become invisible to you, surrounding you, baked into your processes like the ingredients in a chocolate chip cookie or a loaf of bread. Unfortunately, as outlined in the list above, not being able to see waste has no bearing on its ability to yield catastrophic results on our people, processes, and plans. Just like the sugar in a cookie, we don't see it, but we taste it and feel the impact of its presence when we step on the scale. It's then we realize that the half a bag of Oreo cookies we consume every night with a glass of milk while watching TV has transformed us into something quite different than the lean, mean, fighting machine we were in high school and college.

Pigs Smell

When I was growing up, I would spend time each summer working on my Uncle Larry and Aunt Sally's pig farm with my cousins, Mark, Mike, and Mary Ellen. I lived with my parents and sister in more of a suburban setting, so, for the most part, any manual labor was limited to mowing yards, pulling weeds, tilling in the garden, raking leaves, trimming trees, occasionally digging a hole, and other menial domesticated chores.

The only animal care that I was responsible for was feeding the dogs and cleaning up their piles of unmentionables scattered around the yard. I also tended to the needs of my hamsters in their spacious and luxurious resort, better known as a "Habitrail."

Time on the pig farm was one of my favorite experiences each year. Yes, it was hard work, but like anything else that requires effort, it was rewarding in its own way. Each summer, my parents and I would make the 1-hour drive across Indiana from Avon to my Uncle Larry's farm out in the country just north of Kokomo. We would pull into the farm on a hot, muggy, and humid summer day when the air seemed to just stagnate. Opening the car door, we would be immediately greeted by and immersed in an odor that was beyond adequate description. Going from the smells of fresh cut grass and hot asphalt to the smell of 2,000 hogs and what they did in their pens was overwhelming and would take our breath away, or at least make us want to temporarily stop breathing. Honestly though, today, years later, as I drive through the country and smell the hog farms, it brings back nothing but good memories of my younger days on the farm and the valuable lessons I learned.

Once on the farm, I couldn't wait to get my boots and overalls on and head out to the barns with my cousin Mark and Uncle Larry. After a couple of days feeding the hogs, driving tractors, drying grain, moving the pigs around from pen to pen, cleaning and shoveling up their "stuff," and assisting in the birthing and castration processes, the odor's offense to my nasal passage would slowly diminish. After a week of living literally knee-deep in it, I didn't even notice the smell anymore. My clothes would be covered with piggy material, and my boots would be caked in muck, but I no longer noticed the odor. Even when we had the pleasure of collecting the manure and dispersing it on the fields with the "honey wagon," the air seemed almost normal. In essence, I had become acclimated to its presence and was no longer offended by it. After my weeks on the farm, I would return to my suburban home, and my mother would rewash all my clothes, multiple times. I didn't think they smelled that bad, but from the perspective of my mom, who was not living on the farm, my clothes most certainly smelled.

In the same manner, you may see or smell waste in your processes for a short period of time, but after a while of living in the conditions permeated by it, you become acclimated to it, losing conscious awareness of its existence. Like the picture in Figure 4:1 illustrates, the smell of waste fades away, filtered out by complacency and a false sense of security. The waste becomes the norm and no longer "stinks." Like working on the hog farm, you spend day after day in it – shoveling it, cleaning up after it, spreading it around, and then, all a sudden, you find that it doesn't smell anymore. Make no mistake, though – the waste is still there, and you absolutely feel the impact of its presence in your operations.

FIGURE 4:1

Problems, delays and interruptions

Waste and Inneficiency

If you don't smell it anymore, ask others who don't live on your "operational hog farm" to step into your processes and make some honest and sincere observations about what they see and smell. We always say that fresh eyes are valuable, but when it comes to waste, I believe a fresh nose is of equal value. Chances are they will almost immediately start to smell the process waste and opportunities that you have become insensitive to, so don't be surprised, and don't take offense when they point these opportunities out.

The Ever-Increasing Dosage

I call this condition "Waste Immunity." It happens when the waste and its impact are no longer seen as a danger or threat. People who handle poisonous snakes for a living do something that most of us find very disturbing. They inject themselves with small amounts of venom, slowly increasing the amount over time until their body builds up an immunity to the venom and its effects. They live with the adverse reactions of small amounts, slowly increasing the dosage until the snake bite no longer causes a reaction and isn't seen as a threat to their lives. You do the same thing when you and your teams live with small amounts of waste that over time become larger and larger doses. One day you get to the point where even a massive amount of waste is not seen as a threat. You have achieved "Waste Immunity."

OUR SLOW INTERNET

My family and I live out in the country on 16 acres. We have a couple of ponds, a beautiful stream, and lots of woods. We even have a fenced horse pasture complete with no horses. The price for living in this picturesque environment is very slow internet. We do not have access to DSL or fiber-optic data delivery – only wireless coverage using the same tower signal as our phones. It is slooooooooooooooow! It is what it is though, so we just accept it and live with the waiting. We don't even think about it as slow anymore, as it is simply our new norm, our reality. That is, until we visit my parents. There they have internet speeds that boggle the mind. My son, Jordan, will even take his Xbox One with us to update his games because our service is so slow at home. You experience the same effect in your processes. You become numb to the inefficiency and waste. You forget what fast, efficient, and effective look like and how if feels to experience them. Visiting another company that is serious about Lean, you see what is possible. This realization of your potential should motivate you and your team.

Keep in mind that as you start to look at waste at the granular level, a problem, whether it involves waste, safety, quality, service, or engineering, is most often not actually the real issue, but a superficial indication or symptom of the real problem. What your teams all too often see as the problem is only a symptom of the root cause when a standardized process has failed or was never actually developed and implemented.

Rarely does the obvious and apparent condition, or symptom, turn out to be the true issue. It's usually a side effect of something that is normally buried two, three, or more layers deep somewhere upstream of the process. Everyone tends to make the mistake of attempting to remedy the first thing you can fix, not realizing that the condition you are observing is only a superficial indication of a deeper issue. This book is not directly about problem solving, but as you start to understand where your wastes exist, problem solving becomes a part of the method for eliminating them.

As outlined later in Chapter 11, problem solving is not a quick activity. It is rarely a one-and-done event and is seldom straight forward or linear. Problem solving is like wrestling a "waste octopus." Just as you get one tentacle under control, you realize that there are seven more that must also be dealt with. Regardless of your role or industry, the operational octopus exists, and wrestling it is a reality, so developing and utilizing an effective method for doing so is important. Otherwise, you run the risk of being dragged down to the dark and dreary depths of the "operational abyss" where many-a-ship-

wrecked manager, department, and organization silently reside.

WHAT'S IN IT FOR ME?

This chapter is intended to open your eyes, and your nose. Waste Immunity is a real condition – just look around. How many Band-Aids and temporary fixes exist within your processes right now as you read this? What was your defect rate yesterday? How many patients walked out of your ED or left a bad review on one of a hundred social media platforms? Are you struggling to meet customer deliver dates even though your warehouse is full of raw material or finished inventory?

I am just as guilty of becoming waste immune as anyone reading this book. It happens slowly and almost without you realizing it. It happens when you become complacent, relax your expectations, or bend the rules "just this once." Doing so ultimately destroys your credibility with the teams who expect you to set the example and demonstrate an unwavering dedication to the organization's quality and service standards. It happens when you experience an out-of-the-ordinary day that yields a high defect rate, low customer service score, high inventory shrinkage, and low customer fill rates. Instead of immediately diving in while the situation is fresh, we wait and lose the clarity of the moment that gets clouded by time. Without a dedication to immediately investigating and resolving the underlying reasons, those so-called out-of-the-ordinary days become the new norm.

Open your eyes. If necessary, just stand in the middle of a process and watch what takes place. Sit in the ED waiting area and just observe people coming in, their interactions with the hospital staff, and their attitude and disposition. Stand in the middle of the manufacturing floor and observe the assembly process, the fork truck traffic, the inventory levels, and the movement of material and people. Sit in the middle of a call center and listen to the conversations with customers, the tone of your employees' voices, and the variation in how they respond or ask questions.

Now, go find five people who don't work in your department or process. Go to people who don't interact with your processs daily and who have not become immune to their smell. Give each of them a pad of paper and a clipboard. As a group, just take a walk in the warehouse and look at the storage shelves, observing whether parts are in the right locations, if the bins are correctly labeled, and if items are damaged or past their expiration dates. If you manage a department in a hospital, take a walk through your ED, patient floors, lab, or waiting room. Just let them walk around and make observations. If you supervise a call center, let the group observe your teams, watching how they complete tasks and listening to the conversations they have with the customers who have called in. Sit down afterward and review what these "fresh eyes and noses" observed. You will be amazed.

Just go and see. Open your eyes and see what has become invisible to everyone else. Take off the mask and smell the process.

CHAPTER 5:
SUSTAINABILITY = PROCESS, NOT PEOPLE DEPENDENT

Waste and inefficiency may be invisible, but, as described in the last chapter, they are anything but harmless. They have the power to cripple a department and organization, erasing a previously impeccable record of performance and customer satisfaction. Many organizations fail to realize the power of that tiny "waste raindrop," seeing it only as a slight nuisance that temporarily blurs their vision. Eventually, that insignificant raindrop, combined with thousands of others, creates a perfect storm those organizations never believed could happen and that eventually sweeps them away.

Underestimating the impact of waste and inefficiency is very dangerous. So how can you move forward, accepting the responsibility for what opportunities already exist while also operating in a way that avoids the addition of any future risk? You start by defining your processes – by developing Standard Work.

> **"Standard Work is the documented form of how you define and measure success."**

Standards Require Standardization

A customer at a fabrication company at which I worked had become very particular about what are called "bb's" on the painted weld assemblies. A welding bb is simply a splash of hot metal that originates from the welding process, bouncing around for a short second until it cools and solidifies. These bb's normally fell to the floor or ended up underneath the jig on the welding platform, so for the most part, there had never been any big concern. Sure, some of the weld bb's ended up sticking to other surface areas of the weldment. Considering that the weldment was only a small part of a gigantic piece of heavy equipment that, when completely assembled and put into service, immediately gets covered with mud, dirt, and dust, nobody would see the bb's or care. Right?

Wrong! The end customer had tightened their specs, and the presence of bb's was no longer acceptable. On a raw weldment, the bb's were somewhat difficult to locate since they visually blended in with the metal, but once the weldment was painted, the bb's stood out like an ostrich in a birdbath. This became a real problem since, once the weldment was painted, any rework to grind off the bb's damaged the paint, resulting in a potential shipping delay as the part had to be completely repainted. So, we identified a robust and detailed process for both preventing bb's and then removing them. We trained everyone and made sure that all welders were comfortable with the expectations.

Things were good for about a week. Then we started noticing that a high percentage of the weldments produced by the night shift were coming to the paint department containing bb's. The manager met with the supervisors and teams to reiterate the importance of following the standard in order to meet customer expectations. Ok, a quick reset and things went well, for about two days. It was critical that we fix this issue immediately, as we were risking a production impact to the customer.

One day, we had a group meeting between shifts with all department welders and support staff. What we discovered was enlightening. The standard was very robust and explicit, detailing the process to remove the bb's, but what the leadership had not considered were the tools and equipment being used by the 12 welders to identify and remove the bb's. Some welders were using grinders; some were using scrapers. Some of the welders had their own high-intensity flashlights to see into the dark hidden areas, whereas others had company issued generic flashlights that provided only minimal visibility. Some welders were hoisting the parts up with a crane to manipulate the part orientation, providing better perspective for identifying the bb's, while others kept the weldment on the jig. Some of the welders were using a weld wire that produced fewer weld bb's, while others were using the standard weld wire.

What had happened is something that happens in almost every organization. You create a standard that defines a process that is intended to produce a specific outcome. What the team learned in the above example demonstrates that success is in the details. Each welder had followed the standard as they understood it. As always happens, the welders each started coming up with their own "personal standard" to fill in the gaps for the documented Standard Work. People used the tools they preferred, the flashlights they had at their disposal, and the welding wire they had available.

What's encouraging about this example is that some of the welders had actually already identified ways to improve the process. Unfortunately, the improvements were theirs alone since everyone else was following their own standards. Over the next couple of days, the manager, supervisors, and welders all worked together to integrate additional details into the Standard Work that covered tools, equipment, weld processes, and part orientation for inspection. All welders were provided with standard tools and equipment that would enable them to consistently produce high quality parts every time. It worked, and the team succeeded, even getting recognized by the customer for outstanding quality.

Design, Consistency, and Repeatability

Sometimes companies and leaders are quick to blame behavior as a driving factor in process failure. However, if a process' success or failure is overly reliant on an individual's behavior, then as the people within the process change, rotating in and out with each shift change, you find yourself at the mercy of their unique preferences and individual behavior patterns. When documented Standard Work does not exist or is not detailed enough, then the opportunity for variation is introduced. The process' outcome becomes completely dependent on how different people learned to accomplish the same task. The lack of an effective standard leads to ambiguity, which leads to variation, ultimately resulting in problems and inconsistent results.

> **"If you don't have a documented standard that defines the specific process steps between both input and output, then how can you expect a consistent and predictable outcome? If you can't predict a consistent outcome, then how can you claim to have a problem when the process produces something other than what you expected?"**

How can you expect anything other than chaos when the process is designed to produce inherent variation? A process standard, by definition, dictates the output, so without a process standard that defines both input and process parameters, it is impossible to ever expect a consistent outcome. By establishing the Standard Work, you design and engineer repeatability into the process, which drives consistency in outcomes and results in improved efficiency, productivity, safety, and quality.

Simple Math

The example is Figure 5:1 perfectly demonstrates this. In the first calculation, the resulting total will be 4 every time, but in the second calculation, the resulting total can never be predicted. The second calculation contains variables that are not defined, and, as a result, the total will always result in a different outcome.

FIGURE 5:1

$$(4 + 8 + 7 + 8 - 3) \div 6 = 4$$

$$(4 + \text{?} + 7 + 8 - \text{?}) \div 6 = \text{?}$$

Let's look at a couple more examples. I was working with a hospital that had contracted with an environmental service provider to clean patient rooms. Once a patient was discharged from the hospital, the floor nurse informed the environmental services department that the room was ready to be cleaned in preparation for a new patient. One EVS (Environmental Services) person went into the room, cleaned the bed, wiped down the furniture, cleaned the bathroom, cleaned the windows and mirrors, wiped off the phone, mopped the floor, and took out the trash.

"By documenting the process Standard Work, you design and engineer *repeatability* into the process, which drives consistency and reduces variation, resulting in improved quality, productivity, safety, and efficiency."

The next day, that same room had a patient discharged, but this time a different EVS person cleaned the room. This EVS person cleaned the baseboards, mopped the floor, cleaned the bathroom, wiped down the walls, cleaned out the drawer on the food tray, filled the paper towel dispenser, and wiped down the mattress, but he did not wipe down the furniture or clean the windows and mirror.

What we discovered was that, without a documented standard that detailed the process at a granular detail, each room was cleaned according to each EVS person's individual standard.

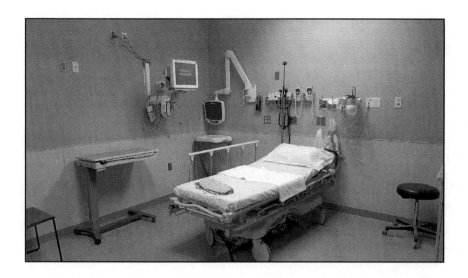

Both people had cleaned the room according to their own personal standard, but did their individual standards meet the expectation of the hospital or, more importantly, the patient? No, how could they when a standard had never been developed to instruct them?

As a result, there was an enormous amount of variation in the cleanliness from room to room, leading to inconsistency in patient satisfaction scores. Understanding this, the hospital worked with the EVS department to create a very detailed and all-inclusive standard for cleaning the rooms. The standard included not just what was to be cleaned, but how it was to be cleaned, the sequence of the process steps, the materials and chemicals to be used, and the time each step and overall process should take. Also, in a demonstration of effective 5S (Chapter 21), the team developed room visuals that mapped out the standard location of all furniture and equipment. The hospital went as far as to include the input of patients, not just clinical employees. The variation was eliminated, and patient satisfaction scores increased very quickly. Success was defined and documented, and the team was trained, enabling them to meet expectations and, ultimately, succeed.

Standards Impact Lives

Let's look at another example – one that will hit home, or, to be more specific, the garage in your home. Assume you buy a new car from the local dealership. It is a fine ride, and you just love that new car smell. It has all the amenities, and the family can't wait for the road trip to Florida next week. Wi-Fi, individual DVD players, heated and air-conditioned seats, and an outrageously large sunroof make this the perfect vehicle. A couple of days after you buy it, you notice a little vibration in the front end. Hmm, you should have the dealer check that out before you head out to Florida. So, you take it to the dealer, and they put it up on the stands.

The first thing they check is the front wheels. You watch them through the window in the waiting area, and they all seem to be talking and pointing to the front left wheel. A few minutes later, one of the service technicians comes in and lets you know what they found. He explains to you that the lug nuts on the left front wheel were all loose, and the wheel was starting to make its way off of the hub, so you are very fortunate that you brought it in. He then explains that the front right wheel lug nuts are so tight that their air-gun isn't powerful enough to loosen them, and they need to use a special tool.

You think to yourself, "How can one wheel be too tight and the other too loose when they were put on in the same factory?" The simple answer is a lack of standards. As a vehicle rolls down the assembly line, there is a person on the left side and a different person on the right side who put the wheels on and then attach the lug nuts. If they are not both following an established and documented standard that clearly defines the process, then what chance is there that they are both using the same standardized tool and tightening the lug nuts to the same torque level? None!

I use this example for two reasons. First, it is somewhat ridiculous, as automobile manufacturers utilize very clear standards and perform robust quality checks for the assembly and installation of wheels on vehicles. But what would the potential impact be if those standards didn't exist and were not followed? It would be catastrophic, as millions of lives depend on those standards being followed. Secondly, it drives home at a personal level the importance of documented standards. Your safety, your health, your job, your investments, and, ultimately, your overall existence are dependent upon established standards.

Standards impact how fast you drive, where you walk, how electricity is delivered to your house, how you pay for a meal, how restaurant food is prepared, how you board a plane, how you file your taxes, and how you receive medical treatment. They dictate how bright vehicle headlights are, when and where you can hunt for deer, the location and color of lights on boats and airplanes, the fill level in your bottle of Dr. Pepper, the force your car's seatbelt must absorb, and the size limitations of the semi-trailer driving next to you on the highway. Our world is filled with standards, and you live a comfortable and relatively safe life because these and other standards exist.

Eliminating waste requires you to understand a process so deeply that, as you dig deeper and deeper, the waste raises its hand and screams at you, "I add no value!" Like an old California prospector panning for gold, you must sift through the huge pile of "process dirt." As you shake the screen or sieve, the value-added activities fall through, leaving only the little chunks of process waste. Eureka! These tiny bits of waste you discover are pure gold, a fortune that's realized as you and your teams work together to eliminate them from your processes.

A MAP FOR SUCCESS

I love Google Maps and could probably not exist without it anymore. Look at the map below. It shows how to drive from San Diego, California, to Peru, Indiana. Do you know where Peru, Indiana, is, let alone how to get there? If you were in San Diego and I told you to drive to Peru, Indiana, but you could not use a map, GPS, compass, or stop to ask for directions, would you ever get there? I think not, and, in fact, I would expect you to probably end up in North Carolina or Maryland. The journey looks easy on the map, but, in reality, there are roughly 70 different actions you must take to arrive there. The Google map and the accompanying written and audio instructions are the Standard Work for a trip from San Diego, California, to Peru, Indiana. I follow the instructions, and I end up at my destination. The same applies to any process. The Standard Work is literally a *map* for success!

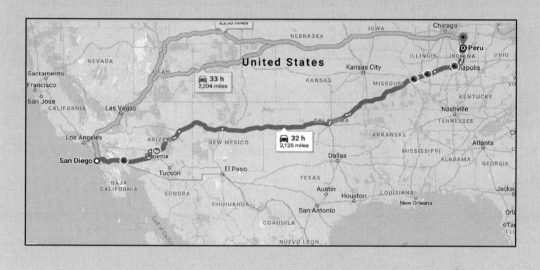

Effective Standard Work

To eliminate waste, you must first identify and document your current process. You must document your current standard in a consistent and well-defined manner that maximizes value, efficiently utilizes your limited resources, and delivers consistent results. Now, if you don't already have a standard, work with your team and write one out. Understand that up front that it will not be perfect, and almost immediately people will start saying, "Well that's not how I do it," or, "That isn't how I was trained," or, "I know of a better way." The fact that your teams are saying these things only validates your need for a standard to begin with.

Standard Work is intended to proactively answer the questions regarding the consistent, effective, and timely completion of a process, before your team finds itself in a confusing situation that could result in process variation. Figure 5:2 as an example of a basic Standard Work document.

Now, keep in mind that there are many versions of Standard Work that can be used, but, regardless of the format, several non-negotiable items must be included to ensure its effectiveness.

FIGURE 5:2

STANDARD WORK DOCUMENT					
Standard Work Description:					
Written by:					
Revision Date:					
Department Ownership:					
Purpose/Objective:					
Step #	Process Description		Step Owner/s	Cycle TIme	Progressive Time

At a minimum, and to be effective, all Standard Work should contain the following:

1. Standard Work Description: What process are you creating Standard Work for?

2. Written By: If there are questions about the process or the need for future revisions, you need to know who the author is and who has the authority to make changes.

3. Revision Date: Standard Work is not stagnant – it changes and improves over time as new processes are developed. Including the revision date is critical because over time there may have been multiple revisions, and your team needs to know which version is current.

4. Department Ownership: There cannot be multiple departments that own the process and have the ability to change or modify it. There needs to be one department that owns and has responsibility for maintaining the Standard Work.

5. Purpose & Objective: Briefly describe why this Standard Work is needed and what you expect it to accomplish.

6. Step #: Standard Work defines not just the steps within a process, but also the sequence and order in which they are performed.

7. Process Description: Provide a brief, but detailed description of what action is being performed in the step.

8. Step Owner(s): Identify who is responsible for performing the actions in the step.

9. Cycle Time: Document how long each step should take. Without an expectation of how long a specific step should take, every individual will take the amount of time he or she personally believes is appropriate to complete the step.

10. Progressive Time: This is the running total of time consumed as the individual steps progress. This provides a total time for the entire process and, thus, a way to measure your success in meeting the identified standard.

Cycle Time vs. Takt Time

What is the difference between cycle time and takt time? Cycle time is the time required to complete a single step or element within a process. You can also calculate what is called the process cycle time, which is simply the sum of all the step cycle times to complete the entire process. For example, completing an end-of-shift report may require you to run three reports. Running the reports takes 10 minutes, so the cycle time of that individual step is 10 minutes. If, with all of the other steps, completing the end-of-shift report takes 30 minutes, the process cycle time is 30 minutes. The process cycle time for filling up your car may be 2 minutes and 30 seconds, made up of individual step cycle times as follows:

- Open the door and step out   10 Seconds

- Process debit card   15 Seconds

- Fill the tank   1 Minute and 40 Seconds

- Replace the nozzle and cap   10 Seconds

- Get back in the car and close the door   15 Seconds

Takt time, on the other hand, is the customer rate of demand divided into the available time in the work day. Takt time can be listed in seconds or minutes, based on the product or service. See the Figure 5:3 chart below for a quick example. The columns list the number of shifts available, with each shift adding an additional 480 minutes. The left column shows the daily customer demand.

FIGURE 5:3

		Takt Time		
		1 Shift	2 Shifts	3 Shift
		480 Minutes	960 Minutes	1440 Minutes
	100	4.80	9.60	14.40
	200	2.40	4.80	7.20
	300	1.60	3.20	4.80
	400	1.20	2.40	3.60
Customer Daily	500	0.96	1.92	2.88
Demand (Pieces)	600	0.80	1.60	2.40
	700	0.69	1.37	2.06
	800	0.60	1.20	1.80
	900	0.53	1.07	1.60
	1000	0.48	0.96	1.44

Takt Time = Available Time / Customer Demand

If customer demand is 400 per day and the company is running only one shift, your takt time is 1.2 minutes (1 minute and 12 seconds). That means you must produce a part every minute and 12 seconds to support your customer's needs. Utilizing three shifts, the takt time is 3.6 minutes (3 minutes and 36 seconds). This means that you must be producing a part or product every 3 minutes and 36 seconds to be able to meet customer demand. If your cycle time is greater than your takt time, this means that you are taking longer to produce a part than it takes your customer to consume the part, and eventually you will fail to meet their needs. By decreasing process waste, you increase your capacity and reduce your cycle time.

CYCLE TIME> TAKT TIME = UNABLE TO SUPPORT CURRENT DEMAND

CYCLE TIME< TAKT TIME = ABLE TO SUPPORT CURRENT DEMAND

If you want to take the Standard Work to the next level, you can include pictures of the parts, tools, and equipment used. The pictures can also show details regarding part or material orientation, location, direction of movement, color coding, required personal protective equipment, safety risks, and so on. If you are familiar with the use of work instructions in manufacturing companies, you would see these levels of details included in many of them. Just remember that your Standard Work can be as detailed as you need it to be to deliver consistent and high-quality results.

Now, you may be thinking, "I don't see an enormous amount of waste in our processes." You may be correct, but you are only entitled to make that statement if your processes are supported by documented Standard Work and if a formal method is in place that continually ensures adherence to it.

In most cases, though, you as an individual do not comprise the entire company, so your statement may be premature. Most likely, you and your department are only a small part of a much bigger organization. You are a single spoke in a company wheel that may be made up of 50, 1,000, 10,000, 100,000, or even more employees. It is easy to make the mistake of assuming that the universe revolves around us, but a simple walk on a pitch black and cloudless night, looking up at the countless stars, makes us realize we are only a tiny part of something much greater.

Leader Standard Work

Standard Work does not just apply to processes. Leader Standard Work is the documentation of what a leader must accomplish to be successful in his or her role. For obvious reasons, as the role gets further away from the day-to-day and minute-by-minute management of a specific process, the less rigid the Standard Work becomes. For instance, a vice president's day is very fluid and unpredictable compared to the day of a first line supervisor. Therefore, the Leader Standard Work will dictate a smaller percentage of the VP's day than the supervisor's.

FIGURE 5:4

OR Charge Nurse - Leader Standard Work

Name: _____   Week Of: _____   Signature: _____

	Task #	Activity	S	M	T	W	TH	F	S
Pre-Shift	1	Check OR board for add-ons							
	2	Check/make team assignments							
	3	Take report from night shift							
	4	Check announcements for the day - update as needed							
	5	Check schedule for ICU cases and write on the board							
	6	Complete break assignment schedule							
Start of Shift	7	Staff huddle - announcements and follow-up							
	8	Call ICU about cases to make sure they are ready and consent forms are completed							
	9	Validate OR room 5S audits are assigned and completed							
During Shift	10	Hourly rounding of the OR rooms							
	11	Manage add-ons and keep pre-op up to date							
	12	Complete work orders as necessary							
	13	Hourly - touch base with pre-op clinical coordinator							
	14	Review status and updates with mid-shift staff as they arrive							
	15	Approve PTO and trade requests							
	16	Update staff schedules (PTO, trades, etc.)							
	17	Elevate critical staffing issues with the OR manager							
	18	Complete 5S audits for open rooms							
	19	Attend/delegate OR Gemba Board report-out at 9 a.m.							
	20	Calculate call sign-ups and verify that employees have completed							
End of Shift	21	Daily huddle at 1:30 p.m. in scheduling to review next day cases							
	22	Provide report to evening charge nurse							
	23	Complete assignment for afternoon/evening shifts							
Weekly	24	Co-facilitate staff meeting/In-service with the OR manager (Wednesday at 6:35 a.m.)							
	25	Complete narcotic counts in Onmicell (Monday and Thursday)							
Monthly	26	Put code cart, neuro cart, temp, and humidity logs into cabinet							
	27	Meet and greet new new hires							
			S	M	T	W	TH	F	S

Leader Standard Work applies to a specific role. For instance, one hospital with which I worked had three levels of leadership in one department: the director, manager, and charge nurse. There always seemed to be confusion as to who was covering and completing what. The leaders in those roles had changed so many times in recent years that the lines of responsibility had been blurred, as each role was required to cover for the others during the transitions. Leader Standard Work defines a role, regardless of who is filling it. As shown in Figure 5:4, we defined the OR charge nurse's role, detailing what the person in that role needed to accomplish on a daily, weekly, monthly, and quarterly basis.

By defining the role, as well as that of the manager and director, we were able to eliminate the cross-functional confusion, duplication of efforts, and dropped balls that occurred on a daily basis. Each leadership role knew what he or she needed to accomplish individually and what the other roles were responsible for. Everyone was now on the same page. We as a team had defined what success looked like, and as a result we experienced success.

The Sad Little Penny

Standard Work enables you to separate the trees from the forest. Take a look at the unfortunate penny. Every day, you probably walk through a parking lot on your way to work, the store, a restaurant, or your car. During that walk, you may see a shiny copper penny laying on the ground. A single penny is only worth one cent and is as close to meaningless as any monetary form we have in the United States. I doubt that you even give it a second thought, and, most likely, you just step right over it. If you have kids, they may have started to pick one up, leading you to immediately respond with something like, "Don't pick that up Jordan; you don't know where it's been."

When did the unfortunate penny become so meaningless? A mere 75 years ago, the penny meant something, and discovering one on the ground was quite a find. In your organization, you may find yourself doing the same thing, and the sad part is you know that you're doing it. In your processes, you walk right past the little "penny wastes" every day, fully aware that they are there, but not seeing the value in doing anything about them. You tell yourself, "It just isn't worth the effort," or, "It would be more expensive to fix it that it is worth." What would happen if you had the ability to add up all of the pennies that people walk over in all the parking lots, malls, fairgrounds, stores, and parks in our country on a single day? Suddenly, you realize that the total dollar amount is quite substantial – not one of us would turn down a cashier's check for that amount. They are still just pennies, though, so what changed?

What changed is you have realized that the tiny penny, though almost meaningless, when combined with others across the country, amounts to a substantial sum that is absolutely worthy of your attention. In most organizations, team members walk over pennies, nickels, dimes, and quarters every day, but tend to only see value in picking up and addressing the nickels, dimes, and quarters. This is a very big and quite costly mistake. When you change your individual perception and see each waste penny as valuable and meaningful, and when every department starts picking up the pennies in its own parking lot, you take an organizational perspective. An organizational perspective views the sum total impact of waste for what it truly is – an enormous opportunity.

Let's be honest – a major difference between your own company and the company considered as the benchmark for the industry may be how you and they "see" these pennies. Chances are, they are considered the benchmark, in part, because they understand the value of a penny and have made it a priority to pick up and address each one. They don't simply step over them, and they have developed a top-to-bottom culture that refuses to ignore the pennies' existence and impact.

A PIGGY BANK FULL OF INSIGHT

My family and I were enjoying a beautiful day walking through a park. The sun was out, the birds were singing, and a soft breeze quietly accompanied us on our stroll. We came upon a large fountain in the middle of a nice sitting area. Barb and I decided to sit down and enjoy the scenery, but Jordan, who was only 4 years old at the time, went to look at the fountain and watch the multiple streams of water squirting back and forth.

All of a sudden, he turned and ran up to me with a look of excitement and wonder. "Dad, there's treasure in the water – enough to fill my piggy bank!" Grabbing my hand, he dragged me to the edge of the fountain. At the bottom lay thousands of pennies, shiny and glistening. There were a few dimes, nickels, and quarters, but mostly pennies. I humored his excitement, but inside I knew that the value of the pennies was minimal.

Sitting back down, it hit me. Unlike my small son, I had lost that wide-eyed amazement with the shiny penny. Instead of seeing their total value, I saw individual insignificance. It's amazing what the innocent and unintentional insight of a 4-year-old can teach us.

If I was to condense this book's roughly 360 pages into a definitive single purpose, it would be this:

> "To enable you, your teams, and your organization to open your eyes, ears, nose, and minds, and understand waste for what it truly is – a gold mine of unrealized potential and opportunity."

It all starts with taking process waste seriously. I liken the purpose of this book to the Animal Planet show *The Monsters Inside*. The show goes into graphic detail regarding the germs, bacteria, parasites, bed bugs, and other creepy crawlers we are surrounded by daily. For the most part, they are not visible, so we don't normally give them a second thought; we just go about our day as if they don't even exist.

Well, if you have ever watched this show, you will become instantly aware of what could be right there at the end of your fingertip, crawling across your floor, snuggling up to you in bed at night, swimming in the stream behind the house, or hiding inside that big, juicy pork chop you had for dinner last night. The show goes into painfully explicit detail about how these nasty organisms can enter the body, make themselves at home, and wreak total havoc on our physical health. As if that wasn't bad enough, the show also illustrates these creatures with highly magnified images that send shivers up our spines, making us want to spend the remainder of our lives isolated from the environment, locked in a personal hermetically sealed bubble. The organisms are nothing short of gruesome and grotesque, resembling miniature horror movie monsters or dinosaurs.

The connection here is in the fact that, after I watched the show just one time, it had my attention. These organisms were no longer invisible; they were very real, and I wanted nothing to do with them. I saw things differently, and the reality of what was out there waiting for me was now part of my existence. I became consciously aware of the serious nature of their potential impact on my life and health. It was a shock factor that drove the point home for me. I hope that, as we dig further into this book, learning about the waste you live with every day has the same kind of shock value for you, and that ultimately you become both sensitive to and aware of its existence.

Driving in the Slow Lane

The reality of waste is self-evident in the United States. In the U.S., we have felt the impact of waste in our organizations over the last 60 years as we have watched millions of domestic manufacturing and service jobs move to other countries. We were not victims; we were just fooling ourselves into believing that nobody could do it better than we could. We were fat, happy, content, and comfortable with being good at what we did, unaware that someone out there wasn't satisfied with good and had this crazy idea to become great. We set our cruise control and motored along in the slow lane, never looking in the side or rear-view mirrors to see what was coming up behind us. We were passed before we realized it. Once passed, it was too late; we were too bloated and cumbersome to react fast enough to quickly regain our lead position.

This topic applies to any company in any country, but my perspective is based on what I have seen and experienced personally in the United States. Make no mistake – United States companies are capable of competing at any level with any other country in the world. But we must stop looking to quick fixes and new "programs" and start looking internally, within our own processes, to understand, identify, and eliminate the process waste that weighs us down.

Over the last 20 years, U.S. companies have proven repeatedly that they have the skills, technology, workforce, and drive to be the best of the best. The global competition for customers will only get fiercer, and the competitors will only become even more determined to take possession of your existing market share. It's time for you to put on your seatbelt, adjust your mirrors, get in the fast lane, and stomp on that "operational gas pedal."

WHAT'S IN IT FOR ME?

I can't answer this question for you. What I can tell you is that the people who work in your organization want to succeed, even those employees who you would prefer to see just walk out the door and never come back. As humans, we all want to believe that we provide value through our efforts. But if you don't have detailed and documented standards and Standard Work that outlines what you as an organization define as "success," then how can you expect anyone who works for you to succeed?

If people don't believe they can succeed, they will leave. The issue is not with the bottom 10% of your performers – they will stay for the paycheck for as long as you let them, leaving a trail of "operational slime" behind. The problem you face is with the other 90% who actually care. When this group leaves work day after day feeling like failures, they already have one foot out the door.

Start with a simple process, and write the Standard Work. People may roll their eyes and shake their heads, but that's okay. When the first quality or service failure occurs, you and the team can quickly walk through the Standard Work and identify where the process failed. It may have been a person who chose not to follow the standard. You can quickly address this through training and clarification of expectations. The interesting thing about Standard Work is that it makes the role of managing easier. Since following the Standard Work is not optional, employees who repeatedly choose not to follow it make the de-hiring decision for you.

A fallout could also take place simply because the Standard Work was not detailed enough or was confusing. Confusion creates ambiguity and process variation, resulting in fallouts and defects. Understanding this enables you to continually improve the Standard Work and drive consistency in outcomes.

To demonstrate the need for documented Standard Work, meet with your team and perform the following exercise. Write the following calculations on a white board:

$$1 + 2 + 4 + 10 - 6 + 5 - 8 = ?$$

$$3 + 9 + 3 - ? + 2 - 6 + ? = ?$$

Tell everyone to complete both calculations on their own, not as a group. Obviously, the first one should yield the same results for the entire team (8). The second calculation will require them to insert numbers of their choice (variation), ultimately leading to a final result – one that is probably unique to each individual. Ask the team for their answers, and discuss why there were so many different answers for the second calculation. This is the perfect lead-in to the value of Standard Work. When their processes are not clearly defined, containing ambiguity or confusion, people make choices that they believe are best, inserting their own "numbers," as shown in the example above. This leads to inconsistency in results or output, which equates to waste, inefficiency, and potential quality problems.

If you and your team are not versed in creating Standard Work, design one using the example on page 78 as a template. Document a simple process like using a copier to make copies. Next, ask someone who was not involved in the development of the Standard Work to complete the task following the steps exactly as documented. As you watch, you and the team will become immediately aware of the gaps in your Standard Work. These exist because you assumed that the task of making copies was simple and obvious, when in fact the process should take roughly 20 steps when documented in the appropriate amount of detail.

CHAPTER 6:
WASTE AND VALUE – CHOICES, NOT RESULTS

As outlined in Chapter 5, standards are critical to achieving sustained levels of performance. That said, the standard must be comprehensive and complete. By "comprehensive and complete," I mean that it must contain all the information needed to enable employees to perform a task consistently. The standard must also be detailed enough to prevent confusion and avoid ambiguity, which leads to individual interpretation. The sequence and steps must be efficient, with all waste and inefficiency removed or reduced to a minimum during the process design. Standard Work, when not designed correctly, can actually promote or even create waste and inefficiency, negating its benefit altogether. This is why we have to define what waste is and is not.

I suspect that your experience has probably provided you with many opportunities to both observe and address process waste. You may be confident that your understanding of waste is adequate. I personally believe that we all have infinitely more to learn about a great many things. In this chapter, we are going to venture into what some of you may initially perceive as some sort of 1960's induced abstract fantasy trip into an eighth dimension. No worries – just throw on some bell bottom pants, download some Beatles songs, stream a couple of episodes of *The Andy Griffith Show,* and follow along.

Understanding Waste and Value

Before you can truly understand waste, you must first define it. To define it, you must first understand both what it is, and what it is not. Remember what they say about the art of war: in order to be victorious, you must clearly understand your enemy – you must study them and put yourself in their shoes. You must learn how they think, how they operate, and how they react in different situations. One formal definition of an enemy is, "one that wants to harm or defeat something else." Process waste fits that definition perfectly – it is most certainly your enemy.

To understand what waste is and is not, you must dig deeper and first understand who defines it. To understand who defines waste, you must understand where it originates, and to understand where it originates, you must understand why it exists to begin with. Yes, I agree that this was a very convoluted way of saying that waste is far more complicated that the five letters of the alphabet that make up the word. But, if we don't clearly understand these things, we can very easily find ourselves focusing on the wrong targets and objectives as we try to eliminate it.

THE VALUE PIZZA

I like pizza – a lot! My favorite pizza is pepperoni, sausage, and onion. In addition, my perfect pizza would have no ring of crust. If I am going to pay $20 for a pizza, I want what I value – lots of cheese and toppings. If I want crust, I can order bread sticks. By understanding what I value and am willing to pay $20 for, you are now able to identify what I am not willing to pay for, what I consider waste – crust. By understanding what I value, you can now identify and eliminate anything that does not provide this; in other words, you can remove the "process crust."

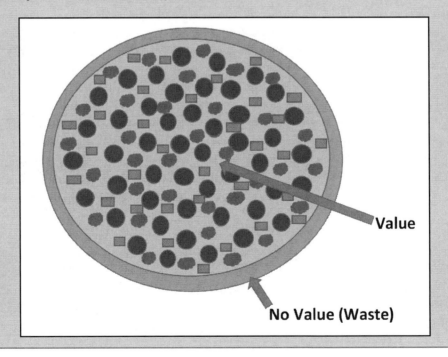

Value

No Value (Waste)

As noted before, waste is something of zero or even negative value. The key word is **value**. So, how do you define value? That question leads you down the same path as before, requiring you to ask, "Who defines value?" What at first appears to be an easy question – "What is waste?" – is, in reality, a very tricky one to answer meaningfully and effectively. The same difficulty applies when you try to put into words what value is. Organizations talk about both waste and value all the time, but do we really understand either? Try sitting in a room with a group of 20 people attempting to formulate a definition for each that everyone can agree on. You will be there for hours, if not days.

The Teeter-Totter Relationship

One thing is for certain – waste and value are direct opposites; they have a completely inverse relationship. There is no waste contained in value and most certainly no value contained in waste. Look at Figure 6:1. If you use the simple, yet oh-so-fun example from our childhood, a playground teeter-totter, you can see how the inverse relationship works.

FIGURE 6:1

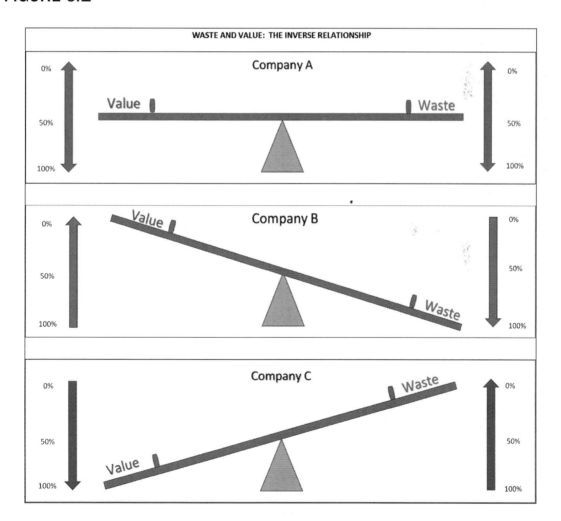

The scale used shows that as the burden of waste increases and decreases, value does the opposite. They reside on opposite ends of the platform.

In the "Company A" example, you see that there is an equal amount of waste and value, so the process is only producing 50% of its potential value, and the organization is only realizing 50% of its potential value.

In the "Company B" example, the process is heavy with waste, burdened with inefficiencies and sub-optimal activities. As the waste within its processes increases toward 100%, the value produced on the opposite side decreases toward 0. Company B will not be in business much longer, so, as an investor or stakeholder, you should sell, sell, sell!

In the "Company C" example, a company has realized the inverse relationship between waste and value and has taken actions to identify, eliminate, and reduce the burden of waste contained within the processes. Doing so has enabled the organization to provide a greater percentage of value. In all three examples, the resources available are equal and limited. The only difference between the three companies is how efficiently each consumes and utilizes those resources to produce value.

Having said that, maybe we modify our vantage point and attempt to understand waste by first understanding value. After all, everyone understands value, right? How much value to you place on the 45 minutes you sit waiting in a doctor's office even though you arrived on time for the appointment? When you go to a nice, expensive, five-star restaurant, how much value do you place on the 15 minutes it takes the waiter to simply take your drink order? Taking a flight to Dallas, how much value to you place on the 50 minutes you spend sitting at the gate while the pilots run tests on the engines and subsequently wait for signatures from the maintenance crew? Where do you find value while driving on Interstate 5 in California, waiting in traffic backed up for 6 miles as a result of construction crews painting lane lines during rush hour?

Who Defines Value?

Why does value exist? Well, it exists because of you and me. In essence, value is what you believe is important and has worth. Value permeates your personal and professional lives. For instance, I value my time with my family above any other activity. No movie, recreational activity, concert, race, or football game is of more value. My family is extremely important to me, and I find great worth in spending time with them.

Our economies are based upon value. For example, let's say you just bought a new smart 65" 4K flat screen TV. You paid $3,200 for it. You will watch the entire Star Wars series, all the Lord of the Rings movies, football, baseball, and soccer games, the Discovery Channel, the History Channel, as well as hours and hours of family videos. Your kids will play Xbox or PS4 games on it. You can hook your camera up to it and look at this year's vacation pictures. You can connect to the internet, Googling and watching You-Tube videos to your heart's content. You can stream movies from Amazon and Netflix. All this entertainment is brought to you in three times the standard 1080p picture quality with accompanying ear drum-shattering surround sound.

MR. BINKY

On the corner of my desk, leaning up against a couple of books, stands a rubber chicken. This rubber chicken is named Mr. Binky, and, when squeezed, he makes this amazingly annoying sound. Why would I have a rubber chicken in my office? Well, this rubber chicken has a long history with my son Jordan and me. When Jordan was little, we would play with Mr. Binky, and he would laugh and laugh. Years later, as I would drop him off at school, sometimes I would take Mr. Binky along, and, as Jordan got out of the car, Mr. Binky and I would wish him a great day. Now that I think about it, once Jordan turned 14, he didn't seem to laugh much and almost acted like he didn't know me.

You see, Mr. Binky is only a $5 rubber chicken to you, but to me he is priceless. He represents so many wonderful memories. Just looking at him or squeezing him makes me smile, and I would never sell him. Mr. Binky is valuable to me in a way that can't be expressed in monetary terms. Again, he is only a $5 rubber chicken, but that $5 is not his value. I determine his value, and his value is beyond measure. Understanding what your customers value is how you define your own path to success. You are in business to provide a product or service that is in demand. Identify what is important to your customer, and you define what should be important to you.

What you have stated by making that purchase is that you determined the value of what the 65" TV provides to you is greater than the value of the $3,200 you paid. In addition, your decision implies that the value of the TV was also greater than the numerous alternative options of how you could have spent that $3,200, like a new refrigerator, a new set of high-end tires for the SUV, or a new living room set. You personally just created implied value by defining the value of the experiences you will have by owning the new TV. That is the key – value is not necessarily always something that you can hold. It is based on your individual perception and, thus, is created when you define and quantify a need or desire. Filling that need or desire is where we create value. If this was not true, why would people pay $500 for a concert ticket that has a face value of $75?

Next time you're driving around, look at the vehicles on the road with you. Most of them have four wheels, doors, windows, engines, a radio, air conditioning and heat, and comfortable seats. Automobiles are the perfect example of how we as consumers define value. Please don't think less of me, but I make it a habit of keeping a car for around 8 to 10 years. All my cars are paid off, and having no car payment allows for additional investments or charitable giving. My wife and I have been Chevy Suburban fans for many years and are currently on our third. The Suburban is my personal point of reference, so please don't assume this is a quick advertising segment for the Chevrolet, as there are many very nice SUV's on the market.

Now, does my 10-year-old Chevrolet Suburban Z71 have all the creature features of the newer model? No. I don't have Wi-Fi, air-conditioned seats, a heated steering wheel, automatic folding seats, pop-up navigation, a two-tone leather interior, collision prevention sensors, a backup camera, digital dash display, or countless other amazing features new models possess. The interesting thing is, though, that my 10-year-old Suburban will get me anywhere that the new model Suburban will go – I just may not look as good. So why do people trade in a 5-year-old Suburban that is paid off for a new model that can cost upwards of $60,000? The simple answer is value.

A new Suburban is beautiful and sleek. It has an overwhelming number of features, gadgets, and gizmos. It is exceptionally comfortable, and the ride is quite dreamy. The interior is aesthetically pleasing, catering to both driver and passengers. Let's also be honest – pulling up to the office in a brand new Chevy Suburban carries with it a degree of personal pride and status. It feeds our egos! All that said, the things I just described are part of what you find important, of worth. You value them and have deemed them important enough to surrender hundreds of dollars per month on vehicle payments and insurance. If these items were not valuable, everyone would keep their paid-for 5-year-old vehicles.

Using Resources to Produce Value

Where you choose to expend your resources impacts your ability to satisfy customers and, ultimately, grow. For example, by properly maintaining an older piece of equipment that operates just as efficiently as a new shiny one, you conserve capital that can now be invested in other areas. In your organization, value and waste are in direct competition with each other for your limited resources. When you have a highly efficient process, you can deliver an exceptional amount of value, based on how resources are manipulated and consumed. When I say "resources," I am referring to every single item that went into the delivery of the value. A resource can mean almost anything. If I asked an accountant for an example of a resource, I would probably get a definition centered around finances. If I asked a manufacturing manager the same question, I would probably get an answer relating to machinery or equipment. If I asked a hospital's chief nursing officer, the answer would probably have to do with the talented clinical staff who care for patients.

A resource could be the money used to purchase raw materials, the time it took to produce a part or provide a service, the space consumed in the storage of materials, the energy and effort required to transport something or someone, the energy consumed by the equipment and lights, the tables and chairs used in the processes, the team members who make up our organizations, and the knowledge and experience needed to accomplish a task or perform a function. You could probably fill an entire book just by listing out the resources that you utilize and consume on a daily basis while producing a product or providing a service.

> **"Resources are the ingredients in the 'value stew,' and you make conscious decisions to *create* or *consume* value based on how effectively you utilize those resources."**

In any process, regardless of industry or company, resources are your limiting factor. Resource limitations have been the downfall of entire countries, powerful armies, organizations, and individuals. They are a reality regardless of how high your market share percentage or how enormous your market capitalization. All too often, employees, and even leaders, have the misguided perception that a company, regardless of its size, operates on a different playing field than we do as individuals. When it comes down to it, a company must follow the same rules that you and I follow on a personal level. It pays taxes, has expenses, incurs debt and interest payments, saves for the future, and follows a budget. I have not worked for or read about a company that had a bottomless checkbook or infinite supply of financial resources, but I have seen people in organizations who have made decisions that would have led you to think that.

Danger, High Tide!

Have you ever noticed that when the market is growing, times are good, and your bottom line is healthy, with profits reaching record levels, companies tend to worry less and less about how effectively they use their resources? You tend to shrug off the small uptick in material, scrap, and overtime costs, and don't really see any need to panic about the minor dip in productivity and equipment utilization. Times are great, and everyone is riding high, even with these insignificant details that indicate a problem. There is already talk of the end of year bonus payout percentages!

FIGURE 6:2

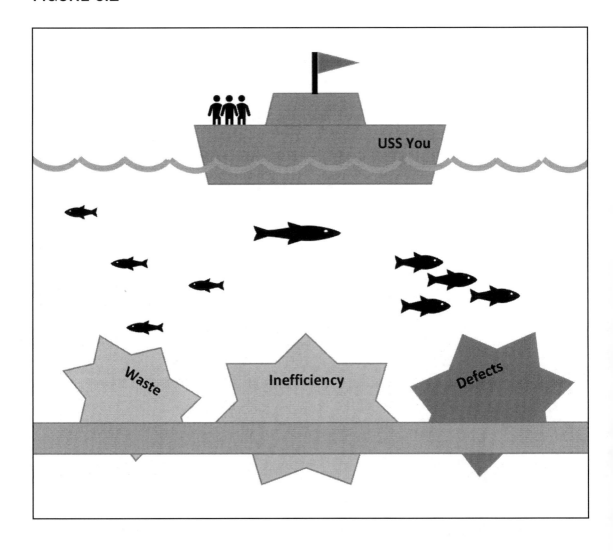

Truly exceptional companies do not let the high water level resulting from record sales and profits cloud their vision. They manage their resources as if the water level was dropping, refusing to compromise efficiency, productivity, service, quality, and performance standards. They understand that the market is, in some ways, like the ocean tide. Regardless of the enormity of the ship, if not understood and planned for, the "market tide" can leave you beached or trapped on a reef. While the water level is high, truly exceptional companies plan for the tide and do something about the hidden rocks and reefs that exist (see Figure 6:2). They map the risks, always checking the depth and wind direction, so that if and when the water level drops, they are still able to operate effectively and maneuver safely.

Not-so-exceptional companies take for granted the current high water level and make the mistake of assuming it will always be that way. These companies fail to proactively plan by identifying and addressing the opportunities that will later become risks if and when something happens to put their current operating model in jeopardy.

FIGURE 6:3

As shown in Figure 6:3, these are the companies that realize too late that the reality has changed, the market tide has retreated, and a devastating impact is imminent.

It reminds me of the difference between being 20 years old and 40 years old. At 20, I could eat anything, climb anything, pick up anything, and risk life and limb. My body seemed impervious to damage, almost as if I were destined to be a future member of the Marvel Avengers.

Then the 40's hit. In an instant, there seemed to be a direct connection between food consumption and weight gain, a correlation that I had never been made aware of until that point. There were also the numerous aches and pains that burst on the scene during activities like hiking, climbing a tree, chopping wood, playing basketball, and simply bending over to tie my shoe. All the articles I read over the years said this would happen and that it was very important to take care of my body in my 20's and 30's so that when I crested the hill at 40, my body would be capable of supporting life for at least another 40 years. I didn't listen, as I believed this obviously didn't apply to me! Now looking back, I can see that I wrongly assumed the water level of my health would always be high. Organizations do the exact same thing, failing to prepare. The question has never been if the water level will drop, but rather *when* the water level will drop.

Limited Means Valuable

I used to work with an old crusty maintenance supervisor names Ruffus. He wasn't the most social or friendly of people, but, for some reason, we connected. Sitting down, talking one day, he explained to me that, at one point, he had one really good flashlight for use around the plant while working on equipment and machines. The flashlight was so bright, according to him, that it would blind an astronaut looking down from the International Space Station. One day, while at a local hardware store, Ruffus came across an amazing find – the same expensive flashlights on sale for 75% off. He went ahead and bought three more, just because they were so useful and durable. Here is the interesting part of this story, which correlates to what takes place in your organizations. When he only had one of these flashlights, Ruffus was absolutely committed to keeping it in one place, making sure it was charged, and taking care of it. It was a valuable and limited resource, so he monitored and maintained it to ensure it performed correctly and provided the value that he needed.

Once he had four of them to use, it became less important to Ruffus that he manage the flashlight with the same level of discipline. He explained that if he couldn't find the one, he would just grab another. If one was not charged, he could always pull another out of the toolbox. If one got dropped and broken, or left outside in the rain, that was ok – he could use one of the other three. See how this works? When Ruffus only had one flashlight, he managed it like the limited and valuable resource that it was, but when he had four, he became complacent and lazy, giving less attention to how he managed, maintained, and utilized the resource. Ruffus had adopted the all too common "there's plenty more where that came from" attitude. Sound familiar?

You probably do the same thing in your organization sometimes and don't even realize it. When there are plenty of parts on the shelf, lots of orders coming in, and the "operational checkbook" is fat, you tend to pay less attention to how you utilize and manage those resources. By creating a culture of complacency and laziness, unaware of the importance in the small and seemingly insignificant details, you set yourself up for a dangerous and bumpy ride when the market tide turns and starts to head back out toward open ocean.

Getting your teams to understand this is of more value than I can convey through this book. Your effectiveness and efficiency in utilizing these resources determines how much value you can produce and provide.

Try this simple exercise. Get a group of 10 people together. The group could be made up of anyone: team members, directors, mechanics, groundskeepers, executives, and so on. Give them each a single sticky note. All the notes need to be the same color. Ask this group one seemingly simple question: "What percentage of your day is spent on non-value activities, or waste (fighting fires, looking for equipment and info you should already have, fixing your own or others' mistakes, asking questions that should have already been answered, preparing reports that nobody will read and that will not lead to meaningful action, and so on)?" Have them each write their individual answer on the sticky note, fold it up, and toss it to the middle of the table.

Historically, this question is met with both laughter and frustration. Laughter because the reality of their answer is so ridiculous, and frustration because they see the wasted potential, but feel helpless to do anything about it. Review the sticky notes with the team, reading each aloud. From my experience, the range is normally between 30% and 70%. Seriously?! This means that if I averaged this to 50% among the 10 people, and if each person works 8 hours a day (80 hours total), in a normal day we are only realizing 40 hours of value.

How many people work in your company, and how many hours of non-value activity does that equate to? How much is that costing you financially in productivity, overtime, utilization, and so on? How much is it costing your customers in lost derived value? How many high caliber employees have one foot out the door as a result of this reality? I would expect that the answer is somewhat mind boggling when you consider the extent of the impact. Good, now you understand the opportunity that lies before you.

Let's look at this idea from an organizational perspective. A hospital is in business to provide excellent patient care to the individuals who make up a community. A hospital is also in business to be profitable in order to reinvest financial resources and provide improved care through new service lines, innovative equipment and procedures, and employment of well-trained and talented staff and specialists. If, for example, a piece of new robotic surgery equipment becomes available in the market, the hospital must weigh several factors when deciding whether to invest the $1.3 million. These factors may include:

1. The additional cost of training staff

2. The financial and operational impact of deciding whether to keep or trade in the old equipment

3. The space required to utilize this new equipment. Will it fit in the current layout, or will we need to make structural modifications to the facility?

4. The current and anticipated patient and physician demand that would necessitate and validate the need for this new equipment

5. The difference in the effectiveness of the surgical service provided to patients with the current equipment vs. the new equipment (outcomes)

6. The opportunity cost of investing that $1.3 million in other departments or areas that could potentially return greater value

7. Oh yes, we must also ask if we have the $1.3 million in free cash flow or in the capital budget to invest in the first place?

8. The "cost of money" – if we do have to finance the purchase of the equipment, what is our interest rate expense?

These factors being considered are how the hospital defines value, creating the perception of potential value. If the value provided by purchasing the equipment is perceived (using both financial data and market studies) as greater than the other options available, then the hospital will most likely purchase the equipment. If not, the value must be created in another place. Either way, value will be created. Value is also something that changes with time and customer expectations. Value is anything but stagnant. It is a fast-moving and ever-changing target, as companies such as Kodak, Compaq computers, Blockbuster, RadioShack, Kmart, and others unfortunately realized far too late.

Value Has Shifted

Tell me if the following situation sounds familiar. In the 1990's, the VCR was the technological benchmark. My children were young and completely captivated by Disney movies, which is why I have two large tubs filled with nothing but VHS tapes sitting up the attic collecting dust. Why are these VHS tapes stored up in the attic, you ask? Well, there was this cool thing that came out in the 2000's called the DVD player. I remember spending big money on several DVD players, and thousands of dollars on the DVD movies themselves, even though I already had VHS copies of many of them. These DVD's now reside in the back of the cabinets in our living room. Why are they in the back of the cabinets, you ask?

VALUE DRIVES DEMAND

"I don't want to go on a cruise." These were the infamous words I shared with my wife back in 2001. I preferred camping or relaxing on a houseboat. Cruising was of no interest to me and made me think of the haughty people on the 1970's ABC show *The Love Boat*. She finally convinced me to go on one, and it was nothing short of amazing.

Since then, we have been on 10 cruises total and plan to venture out on many more. What changed? My definition of value changed. I realized how affordable a cruise was, considering that food, lodging, exotic destinations, and entertainment were all included. I am not promoting the cruise industry, but look at the number of people who cruise now vs. in the 1970's. The number of cruise ships has skyrocketed to over 300 worldwide, servicing over 25 million passengers annually. It is no longer only the elite and wealthy who enjoy cruising; it's the delivery driver, school teacher, firefighter, office worker, and millions of other middle class citizens. More people now value what a cruise has to offer, so demand increases. As demand has increased, the number of cruise lines and ships has increased to provide that value.

Value drives demand.

Well, several years ago, this really cool thing came out called a Blu-ray player. The picture quality and sound were light years beyond the old DVD, so of course I subsequently purchased several Blu-ray players, along with countless Blu-ray discs.

You think that this is where the story stops, don't you? Well, at this point, I don't even worry about the Blu-ray or the numerous Blu-ray discs I have sitting in the cabinet in front of the old DVD's. Currently, I just pay for several subscriptions to stream movies and shows. To top it off, if I do get the urge to watch an old DVD or Blu-ray, I don't even need to use the obsolete players; I just use my son's PS4 or Xbox One.

Value absolutely changes over time with the expectations of those who define value, namely you and me. Here is another example for you to ponder. Ten years ago, did you have any need for or expectation of Wi-Fi access when you took a flight? The answer is no, but if you look at how you currently define value when you fly, for the most part, Wi-Fi access is an expectation, not an option. How much value do passengers place on having access to Wi-Fi during their flight? Just watch people become unglued at 10,000 feet when the pilot gets on the intercom and informs the passengers that the Wi-Fi system is not working. It is reminiscent of the airplane scene in the 2013 Brad Pitt movie *World War Z,* when zombies take over the plane. Can you even imagine not being connected to social media for 3-4 hours? How would we survive?

So, we have established that value starts with us. But who are we? Well, we are customers, the consumers of products and services. Value is defined by the customer, but don't be fooled into thinking that this now makes everything crystal clear. To my point, every organization has far more than one customer that must be considered when working to define its specific value offerings.

A Hospital's Customer

Let's look again at your local community hospital, for example. For the most part, a hospital has one customer that probably stands out in everyone's mind first, the patient. If the patient is always happy and receives value in the form of quality care and timely treatment, the hospital will succeed. Correct?

But wait, is the patient really the only customer the hospital needs to consider as it works to understand value in its journey to becoming the #1 provider of care in the region? What about the patient's family? What do they value? Are patients' family members really customers even though they are not being medically treated? Well, if the waiting room is dirty and uncomfortable, the Emergency Room wait times are outrageous, the cafeteria food is less than appetizing, the staff is rude, and the doctors don't communicate well or basically ignore them, will these patient family members be happy? Will they find any value in their own experience? Probably not.

So, is it really that important to satisfy the expectations of family members? Based on the above factors, a dissatisfied family member can make the decision to not bring her family member back to you, and to instead drive 5 miles past you to be seen at another hospital. She could also choose to not come to you when she herself needs medical treatment. Even worse, she will most likely proceed to share her bad experience with her entire family, as well as her friends at work, church, bowling league, and at her son's soccer games. Even worse than worse, she will also most likely detail her entire experience on some social media platform for the entire world to review. Her social media review will be based 100% on her perception of the experience (her reality), whether it's completely accurate or not.

According to different studies regarding social media, it takes anywhere from 10 to 13 positive reviews to counteract the impact of a single negative review. Acquiring a new customer will always require substantially more effort and resources than keeping an existing customer, so keep your customers happy and ensure their repeat business. If you have ever been dissatisfied enough to tell someone about it, it is estimated that you will tell five to 10 times as many people about a negative experience vs. a positive experience.

If you doubt the impact of a negative experience shared on social media, and the potential fallout, Google a Canadian musician named Dave Carroll, and read about his experience with a global airline in 2008 over a $3,500 guitar. The financial impact to this specific airline, caused by one bad experience shared on social media, was measured in tens of millions, not thousands, of dollars.

So, are we done with hospital customers? What about the physicians and surgeons? What do they value? Aren't they customers as well? If, for example, the facilities are not clean and sterile, the staff is not friendly, knowledgeable, well trained, and experienced, the equipment is not up to date, inventory and supplies are always lacking or missing for procedures, and the procedure scheduling system is not effective, the physicians and surgeons will most likely decide to practice at any one of the other five hospitals within a 30-mile radius. Contrary to what most people think, the majority of physicians and surgeons do not work directly for the hospital – they work for contracted physician groups or have their own practices outside the hospital. If the physicians and surgeons do not perceive greater value working with your hospital, they will find their value somewhere else. In addition, in their private practices, the physicians and surgeons will also most likely not refer their patients to your hospital.

So, are we finished following the value map in this example?

What about the nurses, lab techs, administrators, and other employees? Wait a second – these are employees, not customers, right? In reality, they are customers in the same sense as the patients and physicians. People normally start a position wearing what we will call "cloud nine goggles." They are excited about the new role and paycheck. Whether they are new to the organization, new to the role because of a promotion, or simply new to the role because of a transfer from another department in search of greener pastures, most people are not aware of the challenges that already exist in that position. Slowly, reality sets in and they realize that the new role is just as stressful, unchallenging, political, or chaotic as their previous role, if not even more so.

The employee starts to evaluate his situation and seeks to understand the value he is receiving from working in that role. Value for employees means several things: are they capable of succeeding in this environment, are they appreciated, do they receive the support they need to be successful, are their home and work lives balanced, are they respected and treated with respect, do they have opportunities to grow professionally, and does the salary they receive adequately compensate them for the time and energy they provide in exchange?

The patients, family members, physicians and surgeons, and hospital employees are all customers or stakeholders, each with their own definition of value. Each group's value definition is unique, but, considering that the hospital cannot continue to operate without all four groups, as organizations, we had better understand clearly how to provide that value better than anyone else.

FIGURE 6:4

Value Delivery Audit	Yes	No
1) If customers have other options, are they making a conscious decision to choose you?		
Why?		
2) Are customers recommending your organization to people they care about and work with?		
Why?		
3) Do you have a line of customers waiting to exchange something with you for the value that you provide?		
Why?		
4) Can your customers articluate why you are or are not their first choice?		
Why?		
5) Are your competitors tryng to gain an understanding of how you operate in order to mirror the value you provide?		
Why?		
6) Given the choice, would you choose to do business with your organiation over the competition?		
Why?		

The real test of whether you are providing the value as defined by your different customers is fairly simple and often quite enlightening. Look at Figure 6:4. Complete this audit to gain a better understanding of the value or lack of value your organization offers. Some of the questions will require an attitude of honest humility and take time and some very deep consideration.

The Tow Truck Mentality

There are additional books out there about waste, what it is, where it exists, and what to do about it. However, after 25 years in manufacturing and healthcare, I believe that we need to take a different approach. Some companies have made the mistake of assuming that the way to effectively eliminate waste and fix problems is to hire consultants or outside groups to swoop in and carpet bomb their organization with one-size-fits-all solutions. Some companies create large departments comprised of Six Sigma Black Belts and Lean certified experts who are then tasked with eliminating waste and inefficiency within the organization. The problem with both strategies is that, for the most part, they shift the responsibility of Continuous Improvement and waste elimination away from the people who own the process and are actually responsible for creating value on a daily basis.

An organization that does this treats their value-add departments like a broken-down car on the side of the road. There they sit, stranded and unable to move or progress, until someone arrives to help them. This creates a culture of victimization and defeat. The Continuous Improvement team or consultants become no more than a team of tow truck drivers called out at all hours for emergencies when someone is in trouble. Instead of a team of tow truck drivers, the Continuous Improvement team should be an integral part

of the department's day-to-day maintenance team, working hand-in-hand and side-by-side with the value-add level process owners. They should not be perceived as outsiders pulling the department out of trouble, but as valuable and engaged partners in the every-day journey toward excellence.

Consultants and internal Continuous Improvement departments should be utilized as resources and coaches, embedded at the value creation level alongside the process experts. The consultants and Continuous Improvement departments should never own the improvement activities, but rather develop partnerships with the operational teams to create an environment of shared responsibility and accountability. I have worked in operations and operational excellence in roles from production supervisor to manager, director, and up to vice president. I have become convinced that the real potential for eliminating waste, which is, in essence, a profit-eating "black hole," is to utilize the expertise and knowledge of the actual "value-adding" team members who often get overlooked and underestimated.

WHAT'S IN IT FOR ME?

Let's get straight to the point. Waste is your enemy, your adversary, and it desperately desires to consume every ounce of your time, energy, and resources. It does not care if you succeed or fail. Waste can drive your best employees out the door, send your most loyal customers running to the competition, cripple your operations, stagnate any growth plans, and, ultimately, drive you out of business.

Waste likes hiding in the shadows, just around the corner and out of view. We live out in the country, and some evenings I have to walk out to my barn in the dark. The long, narrow driveway leading to the barn is surrounded by thick woods and, every once in a while, as I shine my flashlight into the trees, I see two, four, or six eyes looking back at me. The eyes are from possums, raccoons, or coyotes. Their reflective eyes are creepy and make me glad that I have a flashlight. The point is this: if I didn't shine the flashlight into the woods, I would never have known that these animals where there. Waste works the same way – hidden, sneaky and creepy, just waiting for you to walk on by.

In some cases, though, if the waste or problem is so large and intimidating that nobody wants to mess with it, waste is just as comfortable out in the open, staring at you as you walk by the process over and over throughout the day. It has no problem getting up in your face like a professional wrestler, as if to say, "You want some of this?" It isn't afraid of you or anybody else. Why should it be afraid? It has occupied the same spot for months or years, and nobody has ever addressed it.

Value, on the other hand, is your ally, your partner in success. Value validates your reason for existence. Value will attract the best and brightest employees, persuade your competitors' customers to do business with you, provide justification for stakeholder investment, and pave the path for future organizational growth and market leadership.

The interesting thing about this chapter is that both waste and value are choices, not results. You can choose to sacrifice your resources on the altar of waste, or you can choose to effectively utilize your limited resources to deliver value and emerge victorious on the battlefield of operations.

There are no victims here, only willing participants who have chosen to put on the uniform, lace up the cleats, pop in the mouthpiece, and step onto the "operational football field." The game you play depends on the calls you make, the speed of your actions, communication to the team, and the execution of the plan. Victory or defeat? It's your decision.

Waste will not surrender without a fight. It will not throw up a white flag and quietly walk out from behind your front-line processes. You will have to eradicate it from your operations by first acknowledging its existence, then identifying it, and finally taking the actions required to remove it.

As you know, one of the most successful marketing tools ever created was the Nike "Just Do It" campaign. It was so successful because it inspired people like you and me to grit our teeth, ignore the voices in our heads telling us to quit, work through the pain, and "Just Do It." It was simple, straightforward, motivating, and it ignored any potential excuses.

If your process is producing defects, then your process is broken, yielding waste. Just fix it!

If your teams are not following standards, failing to deliver consistent quality service to your customers, then your process is broken, yielding waste. Just fix it!

If your machine utilization and efficiency are lower than what they should be, given your volumes, then your process is broken, yielding waste. Just fix it!

If leadership is sending mixed signals, failing to engage and empower the experts on the front lines, then your process is broken, yielding waste. Just fix it!

It's time for an organizational workout. Pick up those weights, grab that jump rope, climb up on that pull-up bar, and lace up those running shoes. Break a sweat, grit your teeth, ignore that voice in your head telling you to quit, work through the pain, and "Just fix it!"

CHAPTER 7:
LEADERSHIP FOR THE FUTURE

So, we've now taken the excuses away and paved the road ahead. You have jumped into the front seat of the car, snapped your seat belt, and put the key in the ignition. The fuel tank is full, topped off with the excitement stemming from the realization that you can really make this happen. This journey is no longer just an idea; it's a reality that now stretches out ahead of you, far beyond the visible horizon. Now it's time to start the engine that will propel you forward and provide the momentum for a successful journey. That engine is called leadership, and the fuel is your engagement.

Teflon Coated Leadership

It's a Monday morning. You're sitting in a staff meeting with the leadership team, directors, and managers. You start talking about the plan for this week, including corporate visitors, regulatory deadlines, orders at risk, and any plant operations activities that everyone needs to be aware of. You then start to review last week's less-than-stellar performance. Everyone immediately starts looking around, checking their phones, hiding behind their laptops, or lapsing into "corporate walking dead zombie mode," complete with glazed-over facial expressions and a lack of any identifiable respiration or pulse. Some people go as far as to fake a text or urgent call to excuse themselves from the impending discussion.

Everyone knows how we did last week, and everyone knows what questions are coming, but the resulting discussion won't be any different than that of last week's meeting, or the one before that, or even the one before that. The finger pointing starts, and the masterful art of diversion is demonstrated with ninja-like skills that rival those of Bruce Lee. It gets so bad that you could swear the staff coated themselves with grease prior to joining the meeting. Nobody can tell you why you missed target, and nobody is taking responsibility. As the meeting ends, the teams stand to demonstrate the "Teflon Salute" (non-stick accountability coating) as the corporate flag of responsibility flaps majestically in the ever-changing winds of blame (see Figure 7:1). It's back to the old corporate version of lawn darts. Throw a problem up, and whichever unfortunate soul the dart lands on gets the blame.

FIGURE 7:1

Teflon
Salute

What is going on? You just completed your annual strategy (Hoshin) development sessions. Where is the engagement and excitement to make improvements and perform at levels defined through your Vision and Mission as "world-class"? As the CEO, COO, director, or manager, you may go back to your office afterwards and ponder the results and effectiveness of the meeting. Where did you get off track?

How have you arrived at this point? Why, with a room filled with such talent, do you seem to be stagnated? You may even be tempted to take the easy road by pulling out and spraying yourself with a can of industrial grade "corporate non-stick responsibility," thrusting blame for the situation on prior leadership. Don't do it! The apparent stagnation isn't the real problem – it is merely a highly visible symptom of a deeper issue embedded within the culture.

You are a determined and progressive leader, so you take the proactive approach and schedule some open forum meetings with different groups throughout the organization. You want to hear from every level in the organization to understand what is going on, based on their unique perspectives. You provide beverages and snacks to make the events more attractive and avoid the perception that the open forums are punitive. You go to your first forum and watch the people stream in and almost instinctively fill the back rows first, as if they had received assigned seating prior to the meeting. You start on time, and people continue to filter in for the next 5 minutes, making it obvious to you that most were not excited about attending in the first place.

You start the meeting with a brief explanation of why you invited everyone, your appreciation for their attendance, and your hope for an open and honest discussion. Your humble demeanor and tone are not an act, and you have no hidden agenda, as you sincerely care about every single person in the room. You also clarify that the discussion is not a "moan and groan" exercise, but is intended to surface legitimate opportunities and issues that impact the entire organization. You spend time explaining to everyone how valuable they are to the organization and the positive impact their engagement in the open forum process will have.

People are slow to respond at first, and the initial discussion is somewhat superficial. After about 15 minutes, though, people become more comfortable and trusting, opening up about their reality, which is also your reality – you just don't realize it yet. They start explaining how they work in processes that are filled with problems, confusion, duplication, and ambiguity. Some examples take you by surprise, making you literally scratch your head. You try to maintain your composure as a leader, but some of the things people are telling you cause raised eyebrows, shock, and disbelief. Keeping the emotion at a manageable level is a challenge, as the employees are obviously passionate about their jobs. You manage to keep everyone calm and positive.

That's How We've Always Done It

In an effort to get to the root of the discussion, and in an indirect and non-confrontational manner, you simply ask, "So why do we do it that way?" Everyone stops for a moment, pondering the question that they have never been asked before. After a few moments, they look around at each other, then, with absolute seriousness, respond with an answer that makes you feel like someone has just driven a car into your chest. "Well, that's the way we've always done it." Here is the challenge: you must consciously remember to breathe and to conceal your absolute shock and dismay. One question immediately fills your mind: "Why? Why have we always done it that way?"

These words transport you back 30 years, to those evenings sitting around the table with your grandparents, hearing those infamous words, "Well, that's how we did it when we were growing up." Like you, I am blessed to live in the current century instead of my Great Great Grandpappy's, where they had to milk the cows and feed the hogs at 4 a.m., walk to school uphill both ways in 6 feet of snow without shoes, travel 3 miles for water, and use an outhouse filled with spiders and snakes. Like your grandparents, right or wrong, people often perceive their way of accomplishing a task as the only way to do it.

So, let's step back to understand how your team got to this point. Ten years ago, before you were there, your organization built a new service line (this scenario could apply to any industry: manufacturing, healthcare, consumer service, etc.). The line was designed and built based upon engineering and marketing insight, and then, one day, the switch was flipped on. People started working in the new process, and, as expected in any startup, issues and opportunities immediately began to surface. Engineering, facilities, quality, safety, and production teams had numerous meetings to discuss the issues. Many high-level ideas were considered, and, based on the consensus, some were immediately implemented.

Over the next couple of months, other issues kept surfacing, but were considered less critical, resulting in only minor disruptions or delays. Front line employees (the value-adding team) would bring up ideas in their start-of-the-shift huddles. They would raise their hands with ideas, to which a supervisor or manager would respond, "Great idea and observation; I will get with Engineering or Quality to discuss." Two weeks later, and still struggling with the same problem, the front-line employees raise their hands again, and subsequently receive the same response from the supervisor or manager. A month later, same thing – hands go up, supervisor gives a hollow response, yada yada yada, bla bla bla.

Engineering and Quality are never contacted or don't see the issues as a priority, and, as a result, never come out to discuss the opportunity with the employee.

Another morning huddle, but this time the front-line employees don't raise their hands, and they haven't for 10 years now. Everyone else on the team also observes this lack of engagement and the perceived lack of value in their ideas, and therefore sees no reason to raise their hands either – ever.

Wait, it gets worse. The idea that this front-line employee had would have actually solved a problem, 10 years ago. So, what has been happening for the last 10 years? Well, the problem was never addressed, and no process was ever formally defined through documented Standard Work, so little changes and adjustments have taken place here and there depending on the personal preferences of the individual employees working on line at any given time. The issues and opportunities that were not addressed 10 years ago have given birth to multiple work-arounds and Band-Aids.

> ## "The work-arounds, Band-Aids, and shortcuts eventually became the process."

The Permanent Band-Aids

To be perfectly clear, the work-arounds, quick fixes, and shortcuts became the process. Also, over the last 10 years, roughly 90 new employees have begun working in that area – each a fresh mind ready to add value, only to be trained on a broken process comprised of work-arounds, shortcuts, and temporary countermeasures. To your dismay, you realize that the waste, chaos, and pain being experienced in this process daily are a result of leadership's own failure to take advantage of the knowledge, experience, and ideas possessed by the team. You were not the victims of an unforeseen design flaw. Previous leadership created an environment that promoted and probably rewarded people for being the caped superhero or firefighter, armed with Band-Aids and temporary solutions that change with each new shift's unique superhero team.

I have seen this scenario play out repeatedly. I have seen production lines fill internal use containers to 50% capacity instead of 100%, essentially doubling the container cost, storage space, and transportation resources. When asked why they only filled them halfway, the employees responded, "Yeah, we had been wondering about that as well." The supervisors, managers, and general manager walked by the half-filled containers all day long, never giving them a second thought. When I approached the manager and dug deeper, we realized that the part size had changed the previous year, but nobody had ever readjusted the QPC (quantity per container) to an optimal amount, so everyone just worked the same way they always had.

I have witnessed employees essentially put on blinders when it came to liquid product fill lines. Instead of taking ownership of their process and working to understand

109

why bottles were arriving with their pitch oriented incorrectly, at the very first sign of an issue, they simply stopped the line, hit a call light, and waited for maintenance to fix the problem. The issue happened so often and for so long that the employee became numb to the impact the line downtime had on the organization. The maintenance team started to become insensitive to the relentless call lights and lost track of the impact the downtime had. Both production and maintenance had slipped into a coma of complacency, brought on by the failure of leadership to expect a permanent solution, not a Band-Aid.

CLASSICAL CONDITIONING

I would guess that you are familiar with Pavlov's theory of Classical Conditioning. Pavlov would ring the bell and then feed his dogs. Over time, he realized that simply by ringing the bell, his dogs would start salivating even without the presence of food. The dogs became conditioned to react to the bell. The same thing happens with employees who are conditioned to accept breakdowns, interruptions, and problems as just a part of normal daily operations. Instead of salivating, though, they become accustomed to sitting down, giving up, hitting the call light, and accepting failure. You need to create an environment where exceptional performance is the normal standard and any type of interruption or delay is seen as unacceptable and a threat to success.

Just a random thought – have you ever heard a call over the radio or intercom system by a production supervisor for more duct tape or zip strips? Chances are you are hearing a Band-Aid being applied in real time.

Super Heroes Are for Comic Books

Now, don't get me wrong. The out-of-the-box thinking and ingenuity that a superhero brings to the table can be a valuable tool. You hire people who are talented and ingenuitive for a reason, but sometimes instead of using that creativity and brain power to develop sustainable and standardized processes that add increased value, you throw them into the fire where they must learn to survive by any means necessary. The fight or flight concept is just as real in the industrial world as in is on the lion-filled plains of Africa.

When you recognize and reward this "just get it done" behavior, it leads to the development of a superhero-reliant culture, instead of a culture that promotes the development of effective teams, where the ideas and creativity of the entire group can be utilized. Think about the last superhero movie you watched. How many people on the sidelines

jumped over the barricades, rushing in to risk their lives to help the superhero? I would bet that most of the time people just stood there, patiently waiting for the superhero to save the day. This is not what a great company looks like.

So, your challenge is clear. Your predecessors have built an organization comprised of employees who have been told to just "get it done," and therefore have developed processes that mask the real problem. The problem is so big and runs so deeply through the organization that you feel completely overwhelmed. How do you fix this culture? That is the whole point of this book – *you don't.*

> **"You must teach your teams how to 'see' what has become invisible, 'smell' what has no odor, 'hear' what hides silently inside the background noise, and dig for the twisted and winding roots of waste hiding underground."**

Yes, you have a part in it, but your role will be to change how the entire organization sees the issues and waste. You must teach your teams how to "see" what has become invisible, "smell" what has no odor, "hear" what hides silently inside the background noise, and dig for the waste hiding underground in the form of twisted and winding roots. You need to set expectations that, as a company, you will no longer accept Band-Aids or duct tape as a solution for any problem. You will solve problems at their root causes, not simply implement a temporary solution by only addressing the symptom. You will "Stop to Fix." You have to be willing to miss a delivery deadline, interrupt a process that is struggling, pay for overtime, repair equipment, and refuse to make or accept any more excuses. The following acronym has proven useful throughout my career.

L   **Listen (Listen before you speak or assume; actually hear them.)**

E   **Engage (Involve the experts, develop the team, and value them.)**

A   **Acknowledge (Recognize their accomplishments and opportunities.)**

D   **Direct (Steer the ship, set the course, and drive expectations.)**

Make no mistake – it will not be easy, and you will probably receive negative responses from your leadership as well as your own team. People will wonder why you are rocking the boat. I mean, things weren't great before, but they were running decently enough to meet most customer demands and hit some of the budget, service, and quality targets. You will see who on your team is committed to the change and who is simply there because they are comfortable. It will quickly become obvious who is committed to excellence and who is satisfied with good. The latter will eventually leave and find any one of an endless number of opportunities out there to remain mediocre. Their loss provides you with the opportunity to fill those positions with winners, bucket fillers, and stars – leaders capable of building and developing an outstanding team.

One of the most difficult obstacles in any transformation is breaking down the walls and "silos" that dot the landscape of your organizational kingdom. This is the job of the leadership. People build walls for protection, just like in the ancient days. In your organization, those walls only serve to separate the people who need to work together in order to be successful. As leaders, many times you watch as people in your organization build these walls right before your eyes. They get higher and higher, followed by meeting after meeting where boulders of blame are hurled back and forth from fortress to fortress, leaving a culture of destruction. Your responsibility as a leader is to tear down the walls. Set expectations for collaboration and communication. Truly effective teamwork results in a culture of problem solving and sustainable performance.

You Can't Fake True Leadership, for Long

Remember, anyone can fake leadership ability when times are good. Elevated profits often mask the multitude of process sins, but a true leader rises to the surface when the proverbial bombs are going off all around, the rifle fire is whizzing overhead, and the radio is jammed with multiple cries for "process medics." A true leader makes the decisions that look past short-term comfort and are based on a long-term perspective, even when those decisions are not popular.

PADDLEBALL LEADERSHIP

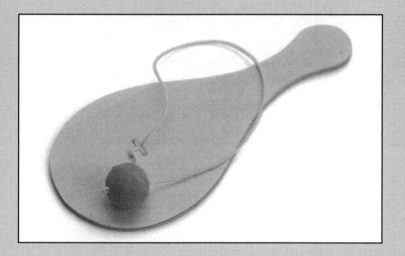

Remember paddleball? I used to get paddleball games for birthdays and holidays. They were something that parents would give kids to keep them occupied and out of trouble, which was always an option for my cousins and me. Hours were spent attempting to develop enough coordination to get even 50 uninterrupted bounces in one try. I always struggled as the ball would go this way, then that way, then up, and then down. I could not keep track of the ball's travel and could never anticipate how it would react. It was impossible, and I would eventually give up. Some leaders operate the same way, bouncing in this direction today and then in a completely different direction next week. Up and down, over and around the leadership direction goes. The staff attempt to anticipate leadership's direction based on historical behavior, but it's no use. This leadership inconsistency results in confusion and frustration within the team, who never feel like they are succeeding. How can they succeed when the leadership's direction, expectations, and definition of success are constantly changing? Eventually, many of them give up and settle into the role, defeated and unmotivated, simply surviving instead of excelling. Avoid paddleball leadership by demonstrating consistency and dedication to your direction.

As a leader, this is no time to hide in the bunker we call an office. This is the time to be walking among the troops, motivating them, encouraging them, listening to them, engaging them, challenging them, and assuring them that you are completely committed to this change in how you manage this organization.

Even in difficult and challenging times, employees can have a positive outlook when following the example of a leader who continually demonstrates confidence and courage. People follow a true leader not because they have to, but because they choose to. They follow because they trust and believe in who their leader is and that which he or she stands for, and because they desire to be a part of something special.

As a leader at any level, you may be standing face to face with what seems like a 4,000-pound rhinoceros that has no desire and no perceived reason to move. You may need to overcome years and years of complacency and apathy that created an organization that is lethargic, inflexible, and stagnated. You may find yourself in the middle of a long-standing culture that exists simply to survive, not to excel. Your directors, managers, supervisors, and employees may be uncomfortable with change or worried that they will be required to learn new ways of operating. Some may be intimidated when faced with higher performance expectations, as well as increased responsibility and a clearly defined accountability structure.

Let Go of the Bike

If you are a leader who is already committed to coaching and engaging your team, congratulations! If you are a leader who is going to have to work to develop the daily habits that demonstrate your commitment and engagement, stay the course, and don't give up just because it gets uncomfortable.

Regardless of your current leadership style or level of involvement, get into the weeds with your teams. Keep in mind that when I say, "get into the weeds," I am not suggesting that you micro-manage your teams. Quite the opposite – when you get into the weeds, it should be in order to coach and develop your team at the operational level. Remember, today's managers and staff are tomorrow's directors and executives. As you develop and coach them, you are pouring the foundation on which the future success of the company will be built.

Don't make the mistake of staying in the weeds with them forever. Get in, coach, teach, and then get out. Trust them to take what they have learned and use it to make wise and operationally sound decisions. If you stay in the weeds with them too long, they will never rise to the occasion. Instead, they will continually defer to you for decisions, preventing the development of their own leadership abilities.

This is similar to teaching a child to ride a bike. I remember this milestone for all three of my children. Their bikes were tiny, with flashy colors, training wheels, and cool stickers covering the frames. Their bikes were named things like "The Princess Chariot" and "T-Rex Rocket." As small as it seemed to me, it was a terrifying mechanical monster to my kids. Even with the training wheels that prevented them from falling over, the moment they jumped up on the seat and grabbed the handle bars, they would exclaim, "Hold me up Daddy, don't let me fall!" Once in motion and rocketing forward at a knuckle-blistering 2 miles per hour, their nervous panic would intensify exponentially: "Don't let go, Daddy!!!!!" I miss those days.

As they got older and more experienced, I would slowly reduce my stabilizing activity, even though they never knew it as I was running behind them. Eventually, they became proficient at riding, and the training wheels would come off. The process would repeat itself for a short period, but after a few scraped knees, dented fenders, and bloody elbows, they would once again be riding on their own. I haven't run beside them since that day.

As a leader, when you get in the weeds, you are, in essence, walking alongside them on their "operational bike," providing encouragement, guidance, direction, and balance. You do this to give them confidence in their own ability. Slowly you observe their riding skills improve. As this happens, you become more confident in their ability, allowing you to reduce your direct involvement. Eventually, after you have poured yourself into them, they are able to operate the "bike" on their own. You remain available, but you trust them to be successful in their role. Welcome to demonstrating servant leadership.

If you make the mistake of staying in the weeds too long, you are, in essence, still walking next to them on the bike. When my kids were small and riding tiny bikes, I could keep up with their speed, but as they moved up to mountain bikes, if I had tried to remain at their side, I would have been a hindrance, holding them back. If you never let go of your team's operational bike, at some point they will have matured to the point that your running next to them does nothing more than slow them down. This prevents them from reaching their potential and limits their ability to lead your organization in the future, negatively impacting performance, growth, and innovation.

Demonstrated Leadership

In the Marines, I had many Commanding Officers. Some were great, some were good, and some were, well, let's just say adequate. One Commanding Officer will always hold the top position, though.

I was stationed in an area that was prone to harsh winters, and this specific winter was living up to its reputation of "brutal." My fellow Marines and I were outside working on the jets one exceedingly cold, windy, and snowy night. It was miserable, to put it mildly, but we had a job to do and a mission to complete.

115

DRESSING FOR THE OCCASION

A tie makes people nervous sometimes. Whether on the production floor, in a meeting with new hires, on the call center office, or on the patient care floor, a tie screams, "Corporate employee looking for head count reduction opportunities." I know that's not true, but it's an accurate reflection of most people's perception. I learned this years ago, and, on numerous occasions throughout my career, in both operations and as a consultant, I have chosen to ditch the suit and tie in favor of the attire of the value-add team. This means jeans, a long sleeve shirt, and a hard hat for production, or a pair of scrubs for the hospital floor. Either way, what I have found is that the adjustment in my attire brings me credibility with the teams. They open up to me and give me the true picture of reality – their concerns, frustrations, and needs. By helping them and joining in to complete their duties, I am accepted rather than avoided. My objective doesn't change, but my approach does. It's one thing to go to the floor, where the value is created. It's something entirely different to dress for the occasion, sweep the floor, pick up a bed pan, deliver meals, restock the part shelves, or help with any of the other thousand tasks your teams perform every day. Set the stage for a new level of trust and engagement by dressing for the occasion every so often.

While standing on a ladder working inside of one of the electronics bays on the side of the aircraft, I asked my fellow Marine for a tool. I reached out my hand, and nothing was there. I asked again, this time with a little more attitude, since my position was less than comfortable. Again, nothing! I turned around, ready to verbally assault my partner, and saw my Commanding Officer, a Full Bird Colonel, standing there searching through the toolbox for the tool I had requested. He eventually found it, and I respectfully thanked him. For the next 15 minutes, he stood there with us, shivering and cold. In my mind, he was a Colonel and had more important things to do than hand tools to a Corporal, but he understood true leadership better than me.

> "Leadership isn't always about succeeding; sometimes it's about the example you demonstrate while courageously rising from the ashes of defeat."

I have taken this memory with me and sewn it into the fabric of my soul. It has influenced my personal life and set the standard for my professional career. This was a demonstration of true and uncompromising leadership. Did you catch that? *He demonstrated leadership!* He came to where we were, out in the cold and miserable conditions. He didn't have to come out there, but he understood that he was part of the team and his role as leader involved more than the silver eagle on his collar. He was the best Commanding Officer I ever had, and to this day I would follow him off the side of a cliff if he asked me to.

Moving from where you are today, both personally and professionally, to where you desire to be one, five and 10 years from now, may be a battle in almost every sense of the word. There will be victories and defeats. You will sometimes question your own decisions, and later, in retrospect, identify areas where you messed up. Welcome to life – those experiences are the training program for great leaders.

Take Abraham Lincoln for example. He is unquestionably one of our greatest Presidents, yet prior to his election he lost eight elections, failed at business twice, and even had a nervous breakdown. Who he was when he became the 16th President of the United States was a compilation of everything he had learned in his 56 years of life prior to the office.

If you expect your team to follow you up that operational hill filled with risks, problems, and challenges, as a leader, you had better be demonstrating true and uncompromising leadership. You need to be the first one jumping up out of that "operational fox hole" and yelling, "Follow Me!"

WHAT'S IN IT FOR ME?

An old but timeless saying holds true: *"If you aren't willing to walk at the front of the line, you're a follower, not the leader."* As you have read, this chapter, is geared toward those in leadership positions, the people who set the example and clear a path for success.

Understand that leadership isn't restricted to the executive offices; it refers to any person in a position to influence others directly or indirectly. This could be a front-line supervisor, manager, director, executive, lead mechanic, charge nurse, or a janitor with 60 years of knowledge in a facility. No leaders, no matter how driven and talented, can complete this transformation alone. The journey is for the entire team, a pilgrimage to the lofty and snow-covered mountain peak of excellence.

So, what do you take away from this chapter? Simply put, you must lead by example and work to develop this deep understanding of waste and inefficiency within your team. That sounds simple, but few leaders are willing to really do this correctly. They often simply introduce a plan with a motivational speech or memo, and then delegate the actual implementation and engagement to a subordinate. This does not work and is not true leadership. I have seen leaders try this, and, without exception, the entire initiative usually crumbled to the ground, crushing the team and smothering any hope that this was somehow different than the 20 previous "initiatives" that now fill the motivational dumpster in the back alley. This is not an initiative; this is a transformation in how you operate.

Look at every process you have, starting with the most critical. Are there standards in place to drive consistency and eliminate variation in the end product or process? What are your quality metrics telling you? Maybe that your processes are out of control or swinging wildly between the upper and lower control limits? Why? What could cause this to happen? Are you seeing differences in productivity, quality, safety, and other performance measures between different shifts, patient floors, product lines, or facilities? Why?

Process outcomes are a result of process inputs – the steps, sequence, material, tools, and other resources used in the recipe. Standard Work and work instructions are the recipes that lead to consistent and high-quality results.

As a leader, you must make the tough and unpopular decision to rock the boat and no longer allow Band-Aids or temporary solutions to be how you operate. You must set clearly defined expectations that Standard Work will be developed and utilized. Problems will be fixed, not tolerated or written off as just a normal part of doing business. You can no longer tolerate the practice of sweeping waste and problems under the rug, only to be discovered somewhere down the road by some future leader who must address the issues. When someone brings up a risk or opportunity, you must give it your attention, making it a priority and demonstrating your resolve.

Growing your organizations by developing and utilizing Standard Work will naturally surface problems, shining the once dim spotlight on the issues that have weighed your operations down. Develop your experts internally by creating small problem solving and Continuous Improvement teams that are dedicated to solving real issues. Have employees rotate on and off the team periodically so that, as they develop problem solving, waste elimination, and process improvement skills, they can then take those skills and abilities back to their own departments and continuously utilize that knowledge to reduce waste and increase value.

This constant development of your employees becomes self-propagating. Employees start asking to be part of the Continuous Improvement teams, and excitement builds, creating operational momentum that continues to pick up speed and elevate your performance. Don't make the all-too-common mistake of creating a separate department filled with an army of process improvement people. Utilize the experts from within your processes to fill the positions.

THE EXECUTIVE JANITOR

One day, while working with a new organization, I walked into the men's restroom and saw the CEO washing his hands. We exchanged the normal "good morning" greeting, and I walked over to the sink. I watched him finish and then take a paper towel from the dispenser and proceed to wipe down the counter and sink before he exited the restroom. I was taken aback, to say the least. Later that week, I pulled in behind him as we arrived at work. He had already started walking to the building, so I followed at a distance. As I watched him, I observed him bend down multiple times to pick up trash. Again, I was taken aback, as this is not the normal practice for someone in a CEO role. Sitting in his office the next week, I relayed my observations of his behavior and my honest surprise. He just looked at me and smiled. He said that he had done that for years because of coaching he received from a highly esteemed mentor from early in his career. His mentor, a wise old janitor, had provided many lessons over the years. He phrased it this way: "When I get too important to do any of the activities I require of my team, I cease to be their leader." What an example as a leader to his team, setting an example daily through his demonstrated behavior.

Develop and utilize a management system that drives the problem solving and process improvement to the value-add level, where the work is being done. Utilize the knowledge and skills of the process experts to make the processes better. Visually track the progress and performance in the departments and units where your products are produced, or where your services are provided. Make the daily status visible to the entire team, and review it daily. Organizations have called this management system by different names such as LDM (Lean Daily Management), MDI (Managing for Daily Improvement), and LVM (Lean Visual Management). Call it whatever you like, but take advantage of the what the process offers.

The tools in Chapter 21 will enable you to identify and isolate the waste and problems within your processes. As mentioned before, solving a problem is easy. Solving the real problem is the challenge. Do not make the mistake of taking a shotgun approach to problem solving. It may look impressive, making a loud noise and a bunch of holes, but it rarely finishes the job. Use a focused approach, take your time, and do it right.

CHAPTER 8:
THE ICEBERG AND THE OAK TREE

Leadership is key to change. People follow leaders and, under good leadership, will perform at levels beyond what you would ever ask of them. They do this because they believe in the person they are following. This is an awesome and humbling responsibility, one never to be taken lightly. How you as a leader see waste will ultimately set the bar for what your team is capable of accomplishing. If you are satisfied with the superficial victories that look good in reports, but provide no meaningful improvements, your team will only look for those easy and meaningless wins. If you set the example, looking deep down for systemic waste, setting expectations for true process improvements that, when woven together, produce the fabric of operational excellence, then your team will follow your lead.

Now, I know what you may be thinking when you read the title of this chapter: what do an iceberg and an oak tree have in common? Well, after years of using the iceberg to demonstrate the impact of waste and problems in processes, I have come to realize that it may, in fact, be a bad example and somewhat misleading as it relates to the identification and elimination of waste. I know, I am stepping on what you may consider sacred ground in the world of Lean and Continuous Improvement, but before you write me off as delusional, let me explain how I came to this conclusion. If, after reading this chapter, you still disagree, have constructive input, or would simply like to argue your point, I would be honored if you would share your thoughts and ideas with me through some positive forum of social media.

Whether you are a CEO, director, manager, consultant, engineer, or technician, you have probably seen this iceberg example used multiple times in your career. Here is the basic structure of the conversation that correlates waste and an iceberg.

The Old Melting Iceberg

Our problems and waste are akin to an iceberg. Icebergs are enormous frozen chunks of water, ranging from just a couple of meters across to over a mile in diameter. When we look at an iceberg, our perspective is normally from above the surface level of the water, so the visible portion is only about 13% of the total mass of the entire iceberg. When we are problem solving or looking to identify and eliminate waste, we must realize that what we see – what is plainly visible to us above the surface – is only a tiny portion of what actually exists in total.

In our operations, as we start to address the issues and solve the problems, we are basically shaving mass from the top of the iceberg. As we continue to remove ice (solving problems and eliminating waste) from the top of the iceberg, its total mass is reduced, and the iceberg becomes lighter. As this happens, more of the previously submerged iceberg continues to rise to the surface. Therefore, according to this analogy, through Continuous Improvement and the relentless pursuit of process efficiency, after a while we get to the point where we have eliminated the entire iceberg.

Sound familiar? You may have even taught this to your team or organization. You might have written a paper on this or prepared a lengthy PowerPoint presentation to demonstrate the iceberg's similarity to the reality of your processes. I understand because I have done all of the above. So, why, after 20 years, am I back-pedaling on what has been such a trustworthy and popular example? From a Lean religion perspective, this is almost Continuous Improvement blasphemy.

At this point, you may agree with me, understand my point, and see some validity, or pass my reasoning off as some sort of mental breakdown. Either way, let me try to explain my thought process.

An iceberg is made up of frozen water, rocks, and other debris that have accumulated in a glacier over many years. It has literally taken thousands of years to form. When a large chunk of ice breaks off a glacier and falls into the ocean, it becomes classified as an iceberg. How an iceberg sits in the water – both its orientation and surface exposure – depends on its shape and mass density. There is no need for me to include the actual physics calculation for mass density. If by chance you are reading this book while floating in the middle of the northern Atlantic Ocean next to an actual iceberg and feel the immediate need to calculate its volume and mass density, please feel free to Google the calculation, but make sure you put a cold water survival suit on before you jump in and start measuring anything.

If you were to start removing large chunks of ice from the exposed surface area of an iceberg, you would be decreasing the mass, making it lighter. As a result of becoming lighter, the iceberg's ability to displace water would be diminished, forcing the iceberg to rise higher in the water, leaving less total mass beneath the water line.

If you did this for long enough, you would eventually get to the "bottom" of the iceberg when it surfaced. All of this is based on physics, a science of which I am not an expert and have no desire to be. Thankfully there are people far smarter than me who have proven the science.

Here is where I believe the use of an iceberg is somewhat flawed. When we come to work every day, and observe our processes, we see the 13%. We don't just see it; we live it and breathe it. Countless production schedules, marketing programs, business plans, and operational strategies lie thousands of feet down, resting at the bottom of the "manufacturing or service oceans." Collisions happen not because of the 13% we see and avoid with work-arounds or quick fixes, but as a result of the 87% sitting below the surface that we never saw until it was too late. Similar to the tragedy of the Titanic's fate, we sink because of the 87% we failed to recognize or just chose to ignore.

If we follow the science behind the iceberg example, as we start solving problems and eliminating waste, the remaining problems and waste should automatically become evident, rising to the surface on their own for immediate resolution. We fix a problem and, just like a delivery from the Easter Bunny or Tooth Fairy, the next day we should walk in and see a brand new problem sitting there above the surface all shiny and sparkling, just waiting for us to fix it. The problem is that waste and problems don't work that way. Wouldn't every company out there have already solved all their problems if they were all so self-revealing and obvious?

The Mighty Oak Tree

On the other hand, if we were to use the mighty oak tree as an example (Figure 8:1), we would see things from a different perspective. For clarification, I use the oak tree because of its massive root structure. A single mature oak tree's root structure can total many miles in overall length.

FIGURE 8:1

When we look at an oak tree, what do we see? If it is summer time, we see big, broad, green leaves filling out massive branches that can reach up to over 80 feet high and spread to nearly 90 feet wide. We see an enormous bark-covered trunk protruding out of the dark soil, holding up the mass of green vegetation. You can't miss it. I climbed many oak trees as a child and still find myself in awe of some of these magnificent creations.

I can still remember the aftermath of a tornado that devastated an entire town in my youth. Cars were mangled, buildings were flattened, and many trees were broken, splintered, uprooted, and tossed about. To my amazement, toward the middle section of town near the courthouse, one large oak tree remained. It stood defiantly in the middle of the devastation, as if to say, "I'm not going anywhere." Most of its leaves were missing, and a lot of its branches were broken, but there it was. It was the enormous root structure that enabled it to remain stationary, firmly committed to the same plot of earth where it had stood for over a hundred years.

On our property in Indiana, we have had to remove several trees. The tree itself is fairly easy to remove, but the root structure is a different story. In fact, several years after removing the trees, we experienced what happens when the root structure decays – the yard sinks and develops holes and low spots. Sometimes the roots will eventually work their way back to the surface and do their best to destroy our riding mower blades.

To use the oak tree as an example of waste and problems in our processes, we must think about cutting down the visible portion – the trunk and the branches – the obvious opportunities. By cutting the tree down, we have, in fact, solved only a small percentage of the problems. An enormous percentage of the tree still exists; it's just not visible.

Unfortunately, just like roots, the remaining problems in our processes don't just automatically "pop up." In fact, as mentioned in the previous paragraph, if not removed, they can lead to the slow decay and rotting of our processes at foundational levels, resulting in unforeseen failure in the future that requires even greater effort to address. To get to the thousands of sub-surface roots and issues, we must dig. It took a hundred years for those thousands of roots to grow and develop, and the "roots" that exist within our processes have been growing underneath our organizational feet for as long as the company has existed.

Wait a minute! The iceberg example made problem solving sound much easier, so can't we stick with it since that is the one we are used to? The answer is yes, but only if you want to live with the majority of the problems and waste lying beneath your feet, invisible for the remainder of your career.

The oak tree analogy leaves no doubt in anyone's mind about the serious nature of our situation. Fixing the visible and obvious problems that we trip over every day is easy compared to the effort required to locate and address the ones that exist 5, 20, or 50 feet below the surface. We used to call it "cherry picking" at other companies. Anyone can pick the low-hanging fruit, the easy problems, but it takes determination and commitment to pick up a shovel and start digging deeper and deeper to locate and address the root cause problems within our processes. It requires a humble attitude and a willingness to admit that we don't know our processes quite as well as we think we do.

It takes teamwork and engagement to grab an ax and start cutting out the waste and problems one by one, both small and large, one shovel at a time, day after day. It takes leadership, commitment, and daily involvement, as well as the willingness of top management to grab a shovel, get dirty, and develop some blisters. Does this sound fun? No, probably not, but this is part of what separates the average leaders from the great leaders, good companies from the great companies, and engaged team members from people who are simply there to collect a paycheck.

Have You Lost Your Marbles?

Another and maybe easier way to demonstrate how waste within our processes exists and hides is a pretty entertaining exercise (See Figure 8:2). You can use this in training your teams and demonstrating in real life how organizations tend to focus only on the visible, unaware of and sometimes even ignoring the true magnitude of the situation. Find a glass vase or large jar. Buy a large bag of colored marbles. Now, purchase a bag of pure white marbles that is about 10% of the size of the bag of colored marbles. Mix the colored and white marbles together, and then pour as many as you can into the clear glass jar or vase.

Have the group observe the glass jar and individually count the white marbles that are visible from outside the jar or vase. Make sure everyone agrees on how many are visible. Now, pour the glass jar of marbles into a large box or another container. As a group, count the total number of white marbles that were contained in the jar. Depending on the size of the glass jar or vase you used, the actual number of white marbles contained in the jar should be anywhere from four to five times the number of white marbles that were visible from the outside of the jar. The significance of this exercise is the realization that the large majority of the "white marbles" (problems, waste, and inefficiencies) that exist within a process are hidden behind other processes (colored marbles), invisible from our normal vantage point, and that only a small percentage of the opportunities are obvious, easily identified, and, therefore, addressed.

So, turn around and look in the corner of your office. Is there a chainsaw in the corner? Are there a shovel, pick axe, and wheelbarrow covered in dirt (waste)?

FIGURE 8:2

What every organization needs is more people digging, swinging axes, and uncovering opportunities buried deep within its operations. You need teams of people with callus-covered hands, who have experience in the trenches and are not afraid of sliding on a pair of leather gloves and getting dirty. Your teams need to see "operational stains" on your clothes and dirt caked on your knees as you set the example by rolling up your sleeves and diving into the "process filth."

If you've ever transitioned from one company to another in the same industry, chances are the new company was facing a lot of the same problems, challenges, and opportunities as the previous one. The perceived greener pasture turned out to be nothing more than a difference in professional lighting, resulting from a strong desire to advance your career or improve your work-life balance.

Here is your chance to differentiate yourself from the rest of the pack. Being different from every other company out there that provides a similar product of service requires determination to think differently, to act differently, and to respond to opportunities and challenges differently. Being different from every other director, VP, manager, team leader, or supervisor also requires a willingness to think differently, to take ownership, to act differently, and to respond to opportunities and challenges differently. Look into the "operational mirror" – do you look any different than your peers?

WHAT'S IN IT FOR ME?

Don't fool yourself – most of your waste and opportunities are not apparent, popping up like one of the critters in the whack-a-mole game at the county fair. Problems and waste don't want to be found and prefer hiding just out of sight where they can wreak their havoc in your processes. Fixing the easy problems, or low hanging fruit, is easy, and some people are content with stopping here. I don't believe that you are one of those people. I believe that, if you are still reading this book, you have a total disdain for the "cherry picking" ideology. You understand that the real problems and waste, the ones that occupy the chasm between ordinary and exceptional, are going to take some work to identify and address.

Start by walking through the halls, offices, patient wings, and manufacturing floors of your organization. Just stop and watch. Look past the obvious. Look through the chaos, beyond the extra steps an employee takes, the mountain of inventory in the drawers or bins, and the defects and rework piled up in the corner. Take advantage of people from other departments or units and ask them to lend their fresh eyes to look for what you are missing. Question the process, asking "why" for everything. Why are we doing it that way? Why is that located there? Why is that activity necessary, and what value does it add? Who is involved, and why? Ask why, why, why! If everybody gives you a different answer, then what does that tell you?

Review the last problem solving or waste elimination activity event that your department or organization sponsored. What was the outcome? Were there changes made to the process that resulted in improvements? Were those improvements sustained after three months? If so, great, but how about after six months, or maybe after a year?

Did the process improve to the point where it became the model for Continuous Improvement, or, as time went on, did other problems begin to disrupt or degrade the process effectiveness? Chances are, as time passed, even with the noted improvements, new problems started to impact your team. These were the roots of the oak tree that were slowly decaying underneath your feet. If you had continued to dig when you cut down the tree, also removing the hidden roots, you may have prevented some of the issues that continued to plague you as time progressed.

Use the Process Mapping tool shown in Figure 8:3. Start by documenting a process' flow from beginning to end, capturing every single step in the process. If there are multiple options (if-then scenarios), separate the paths using a triangle and continue documenting the unique steps for each path. Be warned – this activity will reveal how complicated your "simple" process really is. You can fill up entire walls documenting what some falsely perceive as an insignificant and easy process. This is an eye-opening experience for everyone, providing a true understanding of how your operations *really* work, which is usually quite different and more complicated than how you *think* they work. Next, work with the teams to understand and document the barriers, waste, and problems that interrupt the flow of each process step and interfere with their success. Find the white marbles by dumping the entire jar into a Process Map.

FIGURE 8:3

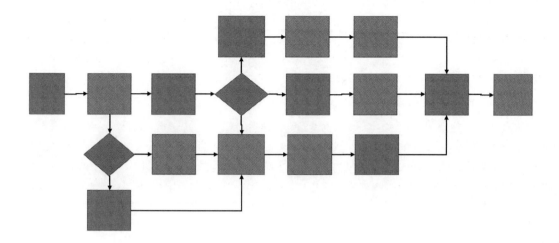

Any ordinary organization can solve the problems that they see, the ones they trip over every day, but exceptional organizations solve the problems that nobody even knew existed. These exceptional organizations not only chop down the tree, but they also dig up the roots. They fill in the "operational hole" with the dark, fertile soil of Continuous Improvement, leveling and then seeding it with Standard Work to continually produce sustainable, consistent, and high-quality results. They also continually water what they have planted and monitor its growth, while removing any weeds and thistle that do not add value.

Grab a shovel; it's time to get digging.

CHAPTER 9:
NEGATIVE VALUE

Waste, inefficiency, and problems all go hand in hand. Like the Three Stooges, Three Amigos, and Three Musketeers, they are always present together, working as a team. Unfortunately, waste, inefficiency, and problems rarely provide comic relief and are anything but humorous. As outlined in Chapter 8, finding them is critical, the first step to doing something about them. Developing a new understanding of their true impact on your organization will only intensify your desire to address them.

Patients and Patience

The patient was admitted yesterday and underwent a routine procedure. Looking at his care plan, and based on his test results, you determine he will most likely be discharged tomorrow or the following day. The patient is in good spirits, but very hungry, as he had not been able to eat for many hours prior to the procedure. The nurse helps him place the order with the Food Services group. The nurse says the meal should take about 40 minutes to arrive, and the patient is anxiously anticipating the meal. An hour goes by, and he calls the nurse to check on why the meal has not arrived yet. The nurse assures him that there is probably just a delay, and the meal is probably on its way up right now.

The meal finally arrives 90 minutes after it was ordered, and the patient is obviously irritated by the delay. The food services attendant sets the meal on the patient's bed stand and removes the lid to review the items contained on the tray since the meal order stated that he was on a diet restriction. Diet restriction? This is not the food the patient ordered. The tray contains apple juice, crackers, and chicken broth. He ordered tilapia, green beans, mashed potatoes, cherry Jell-O, toast, and coffee with cream and sugar. Now the patient is more than irritated and has transitioned into flat-out angry territory. He is viciously hungry and wants something that will pacify the ferocious bear that seems to be growling deep within his abdomen. The patient's family is also not happy at this point and, for obvious reasons, doesn't enjoy witnessing the events that have made their father angry, uncomfortable, and hungry.

The food services technician immediately calls the nurse in, and after some investigation, realizes that the dietary restriction in the system was never canceled after the completion of the procedure, so the food services group did not deliver the appropriate meal, based on the current system information and order. The patient has now made a 180-degree emotional turn and changed from a content and pleasant person to one who is totally dissatisfied, and rightly so.

FIGURE 9:1

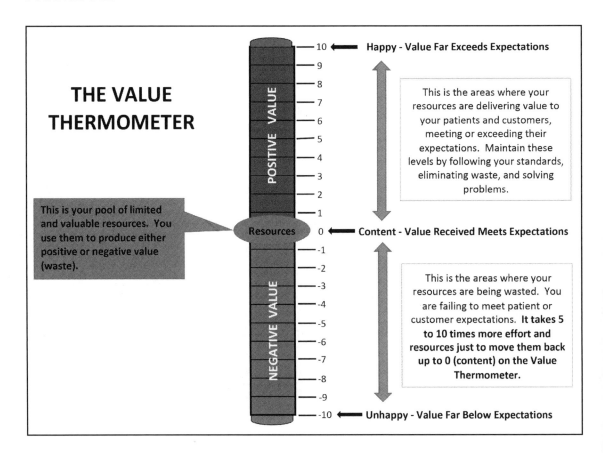

The Value Thermometer

So, let's see where the hospital is right now on the Value Thermometer. When I use the term "thermometer," I am referring to the patient or customer's individual perception of the value they are receiving, vs. the value they are expecting (See Figure 9:1). A patient who is content, believing the value he is receiving is in line with his modest expectations, would be classified as a "zero." A zero simply means that the patient is satisfied – not hot, not cold, just room temperature. A patient who receives value that far exceeds his expectations, through exceptional service, outstanding treatment, and flawless execution of his care plan, would be a 10 on the Value Thermometer. This person will tell everyone on social media how wonderful his stay was and will return to you the next time he requires care.

So, where does the patient from the above example rank? Honestly, he is probably around a negative five. The order took twice as long as it should have to arrive, and, when it did arrive, it was not the right food. To make matters worse, he then had to witness firsthand what he now perceives as incompetence by the hospital staff. Valid or not, the hungry patient's view of the entire organization is skewed by what he believes is an inability to effectively communicate between departments and follow standard procedures. Do you think that this might also have some impact on his confidence in the quality of care he is receiving? After all, if a hospital can't even get a simple food order correct, how can it effectively coordinate and perform heart surgery, respond to a Level-1 Trauma, facilitate a stroke recovery, or complete a basic outpatient procedure?

At this point, everyone involved must start jumping through hoops, bypassing Standard Work, bending over backwards, and going above and beyond just to get this patient the correct meal. All this extra effort to simply rectify a situation that resulted from a single deviation from standard procedure. Here is the point: when we analyze a patient or customer who is at a baseline of zero on the value scale, meaning that he is satisfied and content with the value he is receiving, and introduce a defect, delay, or other waste that diminishes the value he receives, we move him into the negative value zone.

> **"Your decision to produce either positive or negative value is just that – a decision."**

Once a patient is in the negative value zone, we must work five to ten times as hard just to get him back to the baseline of zero. We must go above and beyond, jump through hoops, and get all hands-on deck, including a hospital executive or director, to perform what is referred to as a "patient recovery." The amount of energy and resources you must exhaust trying to make the patient/customer content again is enormous. These resources would have been better utilized by adding value through quality care, not in recovering from a negative value condition.

A Strategic Failure

Let's look at a couple more situations where "negative" value has had a dramatic, yet overlooked impact on an organization. One company I worked with, as part of an organizational initiative, rolled out a detailed strategic plan (Hoshin) that was to be driven down through all levels of the company. The senior leadership had spent months leading up to January 1 to develop this high-level plan that detailed their financial, quality, growth, safety, and employee engagement objectives that reached out one, three, and five years. The company had seven stand-alone facilities where the general manager, directors, department managers, unit managers, and supervisors would translate this strategy into tactical action plans. The corporate level executives would support the meetings on a weekly basis.

NO JOY OR RECEPTION

As I have mentioned, we live in the country, and our internet is slow. Recently we upgraded to a "better" system, at least according to the wireless company. Everything was set up and good to go, according to the sales person at the store – it was just a matter of plugging the equipment in and entering the new password on the computers. That's not quite how it went. None of the computers would connect, so I called customer service. No exaggeration, I was transferred four times and disconnected twice. Within a 2-hour period, I had gone from an excited customer who was happy to finally be free of dial-up speed internet, to a person who was using my phone to Google other carriers in the area who I could switch all my business to. My demeanor had transformed from that of a soft and cuddly bunny rabbit to an irritable 75-pound wolverine just looking for a reason to attack someone or something.

If you were to have heard a recording of my voice, it would have been like switching your radio from a soft and smooth jazz station to one that played heavy metal – head banging, guitar thrashing hard rock. The carrier spent an enormous amount of time and resources pushing me down into the realm of negative value. By the time someone did actually help me, it took them considerable time and effort just to calm me down. They apologized profusely and ended up discounting my service and sending me vouchers for free phone gear. All this extra work and cost, just to get me back to neutral, when all they had to do was deliver what they promised in the first place.

Countless meetings took place in November, December, January, and February to train the facility leaders on effectively utilizing this process. In an effort to create a sense of urgency and transparency, each facility dedicated a moderate sized room to act as the centralized "strategy room." You, too, may have such a room in your current company – you may call it a "war room" or "Hoshin central." Every leader was assigned a section of the wall in the room where he or she would post and track his or her progress on predetermined metrics or "KPI's." Everyone was anxious yet cautiously excited about the new strategy process, as it provided a sense of positive direction that would hopefully propel the facility past some of the issues and opportunities that had seemed to weigh down the organization and trap the teams in a stagnated mire of complacency.

Over the following months, the metrics matured, and the strategy room took on a new look. Colorful graphs, charts, Fishbone Diagrams, and Process Maps (Chapter 21) filled the room. It looked like someone took a 50-pound bag of Skittles and threw them against the walls. It was one of the most aesthetically pleasing rooms I had ever seen – motivating, engaging, informative, and meaningful. If you laid on your back on the floor in the middle of the room, it felt like you were at the center of a 360-degree rainbow.

The first couple of months saw a lot of engagement in the weekly update meetings, which all leadership were expected to attend. Some leaders even brought their staff down to the room to show them how the room was making a difference. As time progressed, though, other priorities popped up. The attendance and engagement of the corporate executive leadership was less consistent, becoming increasingly sporadic. The general manager took note of this and followed the example set by the corporate executives who had previously committed to be at each weekly meeting. In fact, the general manager started to obtain confirmation of attendance by the corporate executives prior to the meeting, and started attending only on those specific days, instead of daily. This provided a false perception to the executives that the general manager were still fully engaged.

The domino effect hit quickly and hard, as the directors then started to mimic the general manager's attendance behavior and schedule. The managers and supervisors quickly got wise to the constantly changing leadership attendance pattern, and soon the meeting, which was originally scheduled to take place daily, was happening once per week, at best. Since there was never a clear idea of when the corporate executives would attend, the general manager provided a directive that the boards were only required to be updated weekly, regardless of any anticipated attendance. People updated their information on different days, so the value of the room – understanding current status at a single point in time – was lost.

So, as the year progressed, the room remained in a constant state of updating. Every week, the leadership spent countless hours updating the information, reprinting the colorful charts, and traveling to the strategy room to update the walls. Weekly attendance of the meeting was rarely above two to three people and became an excuse to hide from

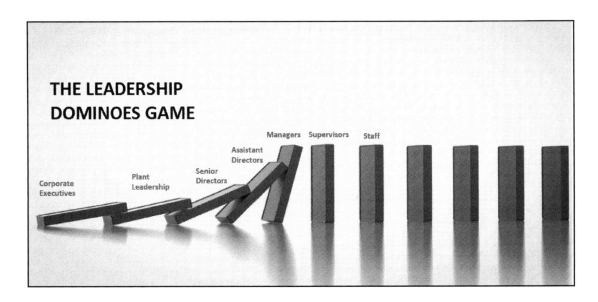

THE LEADERSHIP DOMINOES GAME

Corporate Executives · Plant Leadership · Senior Directors · Assistant Directors · Managers · Supervisors · Staff

operations for a few minutes or an opportunity to just sit and complain. "Why do we have to waste time updating this room?" Six months into the new initiative, the stunning charts and graphs were yellowed, disorganized, and meaningless, providing nothing more than a strong indication that our performance had remained unchanged.

Think about all the work that had gone into setting up and maintaining this room – the hours spent collecting data, figuring out where the reports to obtain the data were contained, creating the charts and graphs, updating the charts and graphs, and reporting out. The organization had done a great job of displaying data, but didn't connect the dots, recognizing that simply displaying the data did nothing to move the metrics performance. The real value of the strategy room and what it was intended to drive was clearly undermined for the entire organization, with the example set by the corporate executives, general manager, and directors when they made the decision not to support and attend meetings, like they had previously committed. The room became an object of jokes and ridicule, seen by employees as just another meaningless "flavor of the month" program that those "disconnected" corporate desk jockeys promoted to justify their jobs. Sound familiar?

Here is where this example, one that rings true far too often, hits home as it relates to value. If you were to summarize the different resources that went into rolling this strategic initiative out, including the training and maintenance of the room, it would probably surprise you. Every color page printed that was never reported on, or used to identify and address an opportunity, was waste and consumed financial resources that could have been used to add value in another area. The time the executives, general manager, directors, managers, supervisors, and teams spent in preparing for and attending the meetings that produced no sustainable results is astronomical. These thousands of work hours added no value and consumed value that could have been realized by utilizing that time to manage customers, vendors, people, and processes. The room itself was wasted for that period of time, when it could have been used for productive meetings and planning sessions.

Credibility Through Behavior

The most devastating negative value in this situation is the fact that you have lost credibility with your team. Your behavior produced value, but it was negative value. The team followed you in driving this process because you convinced them that it was critically important. They climbed up onto the wagon with you only to watch you jump off a short distance later, forcing them to fend for themselves and forge their own trail. They trusted in your leadership and direction and got burned. Now, in the future, when you want to drive any type of improvement or transformation, how much harder will you have to work just to get them to believe, trust, and follow you? Remember the old saying, "Fool me once, shame on you. Fool me twice, shame on me." The team that follows you is constantly watching to see if the behavior you demonstrate matches the words you say.

If you make the conscious decision to dedicate resources to activities that do not add value, you are subjecting yourselves, your organization, and your teams to the counter-productive concept of negative value. Consumed resources will result in value output, but the value may be negative, or waste. Don't kid yourself, though. In the majority of cases, you are the reason it happens – the promoter, not the victim. Make conscious decisions to understand what type of value you are producing with every process. Work to understand before you make decisions. Reflect on those past decisions that produced negative value, and learn from them. Use those experiences as a learning tool for your organization.

Mowing Air

A few years ago, my neighbor John traded in his old push mower for a new sleek John Deere riding mower. I must admit that I was a little jealous, sitting there on my 10-year-old mower, but not jealous enough to fork out the money to buy a new one. I was curious about how his mower would cut and how much tighter the turning radius was, so I just waved at him and watched as his mowing commenced. Pulling it out of the shed, he did a quick walk-around and then sat back down in the ergonomically designed seat. The mower started up, and off he went. His yard was about the same size as mine, so the speed he was traveling seemed impressive.

Around the porch, circling trees, and parallel to the sidewalk he went. I must admit that I was fascinated by the mower and wasn't paying too much attention to the cut. As he finished his first lap, he stopped the mower and got off to look at what he had accomplished. Uh-oh. I could tell something was wrong by the way he stood there scratching his head. I went over and discovered that he had failed to cut any grass in that first lap. With a little further investigation, we discovered that, in his excitement to start mowing, he had failed to lower the deck and pull the PTO (Power-Take-Off) knob to engage the mower blades.

Later, riding around my yard on my old mower, I realized that John's situation is a perfect example of negative value, or waste. He consumed the following resources: time, gas, oil, and mower life span. All of these resources produced negative value; they were wasted, never to be retrieved or utilized to produce positive value.

Understanding value at both the positive and negative level is crucial as you attempt to make decisions that promote growth, improved performance, and employee engagement. When your decisions are put under the value microscope, you see their granular impact and are in a much better position to make choices that will indeed move your organizations in the desired direction.

WHAT'S IN IT FOR ME?

Every decision you make and every action you take produce value.

Producing value requires the utilization of your limited and valuable resources. Producing positive value consumes resources to provide your customers, patients, clients, and stakeholders with what they desire and expect. Producing negative value also consumes resources, but provides the opposite of what your customers, patients, clients, and stakeholders desire and expect. Your decision to produce either positive or negative value is just that – a decision.

Moving a dissatisfied customer up from a negative six on the Value Thermometer requires the utilization of additional resources. The resources consumed that led him to that position are gone forever, wasted. In fact, you may do everything in your power to take the customer from angry to content, consuming time, energy, emotions, materials, and so on, and still never get him back to a content state of zero before he leaves. It may simply be too little, too late. That customer may never change his opinion of your organization as long as he lives, no matter what you are able to accomplish. Your opportunity to create a life-long customer is gone. Your only hope for regaining his confidence is to treat every customer as if he or she is that dissatisfied customer's best friend or family member. The only people who will sway his opinion of your organization are those whom he trusts. What they say is true.

From a process perspective, such as shipping the wrong product to a customer, any resources you initially consumed are gone, wasted. In fact, you may have to pay for shipment of the wrong product back to your facility. Your customer is in the negative value category. To fix the issue, you may have to expedite the correct part, offer the customer a discounted price, or consume additional resources to provide him with a CAP (Corrective

A PROCESS CAVITY

Several years ago, I had a root canal performed on a tooth. The root canal resulted in the application of a crown, an expensive ordeal to say the least. Recently, the tooth started bothering me again, and, since we had moved more than 700 miles away from my previous dentist, I went to a new dentist. The new dentist informed me that the previous root canal had not addressed all of the decay and that I now had an infection in the base of the roots. Swell!

To remedy the issue, the dentist would need to perform an extraction of the roots, which would require the removal of the crown and the installation of an implant and new crown. So, several thousand dollars for the previous crown was now going down the drain, and I was looking at an additional $4,000 for the oral surgeon and dentist to install the implant and new crown. Ok, it is what it is, I thought, so let's just get it fixed.

All went well with the oral surgeon, and the insert into the bone of my jaw went perfectly. It healed quickly, and we were now ready for the crown to be produced and installed. Here is where it all fell apart from a process standpoint. I was supposed to go to my dentist for one visit to have a mold taken and for a second visit to have the crown installed.

Without going into too much detail, the first visit tuned into four visits, due to multiple missteps, mistakes, and process errors. Keep in mind that I live 45 minutes from the dentist, so a single visit consumes roughly 2 hours and 90 miles' worth of fuel. After four visits, I was up to 8 hours and 360 miles, and, needless to say, my patience was fading fast. At my fourth visit, I walked the dentist's office through a specific line of questioning that would ensure the fifth visit would be my last. If it was not my final visit, all of my family's business would be taken somewhere else, a justifiable decision from anyone's perspective.

For the dentist's office, these missteps consumed four times as much time for their own staff. How many procedures could have been performed and patients seen in those hours used to service my needs?

This example was perfectly timed while writing this book. Would you have continued to use this dentist? Why would your customers continue to do business with you if you put them through the same pain and suffering? Where are your customers on the Value Thermometer?

Action Plan). You may lose the customer or damage your reputation, both of which can be catastrophic.

Negative or positive, value is produced, and it consumes your resources. Start looking at your processes and asking what specific value is being produced. Is it positive value that can be tied directly to meeting your goals and satisfying customer expectations? If not, why are you doing it, and what is wrong with your process design? Why stand at the river's edge and toss dollar bills in to simply watch them peacefully float downstream, ultimately pouring into the vast sea of waste and inefficiency?

> **"You get one, and only one, chance to make a great first impression."**

Utilize the Value/Non-Value Analysis tool in Chapter 21. Break down your processes to a granular level, and then classify each individual step according to what it is producing. Utilize the Fishbone Diagram and the Pareto tool to identify where your process is producing negative value. Use Value Steam Mapping to identify problems that are consuming vast amounts of resources, but producing no positive value, no benefit.

Make a conscious decision to design in and produce positive value in every process.

CHAPTER 10:
WASTE – THE CAPACITY PARASITE

Hope

My favorite movie of all time is the 1985 western *Pale Rider* with Clint Eastwood. It's about a group of poor prospectors and their families who have legal claim to a plot of land in the California foothills and that land's mineral rights (gold). They spend their days scratching out their meager existence panning for gold in a place called Carbon Canyon. At one point in the movie, the prospectors are near defeat, beaten down, and ready to give up when a mysterious preacher (Clint Eastwood) rides into their lives on a pale horse.

Later, Coy LaHood, the greedy landowner trying to steal their claims, returns from a meeting in Sacramento. Stepping down off the train, he asks his son if the "tin pans" (prospectors) have been driven off yet. His son informs him that they are still there and then tells him about the mysterious preacher who recently rode into town. Coy LaHood replies, "When I left, those tin pans had all but given up. Their spirit was nearly broken. A man without spirit is whipped. But a preacher, he could give them faith. One ounce of faith and they'll be dug in deeper than a tick on a hound." Coy LaHood was a parasite who fed off the hopes and dreams of this small community of miners.

I am not a preacher, and I am most certainly not Clint Eastwood, but in the same manner as Coy LaHood's statement, this chapter is about faith and hope, and should get people excited. It is about developing a resolve and commitment that is like a tick dug into the back of a hound dog lazily slumbering on the front porch of some backwoods shanty, because that's what it will take to accomplish what needs to be done.

Waste Consumes Capacity

It's a common discussion in almost every industry and in numerous companies: "How can we increase our capacity?" In reality, this is a great problem to have because it means that higher demand is probably leading to growth and the need to support increased orders, or possibly an expanding customer base. What company would not like to be having this discussion? Where this discussion goes next is where you should take notice.

Understanding your capacity is critical to satisfying customer demand and remaining profitable. If you commit to a firm order schedule from your largest customer, but have failed to go through a rigorous capacity-planning activity to understand your current demand and constraints, you may just find yourself in the same position as many companies that have failed to do so – flat on your face. Unless you are a self-contained, cradle-to-grave operation, your capacity is dependent on the capacity of your suppliers, and their suppliers, and their suppliers, and so on. Capacity may sound like a somewhat simplistic concept, but it isn't.

Capacity itself is simply a measure of the amount of value that you can produce, based on your available resources and the processes that are in place to convert those resources into the unique value that you provide to customers. Capacity isn't a concept that applies only to manufacturing. Far from it – capacity applies to any and every organization, government entity, person, resource, and process. Let's look at some examples.

Say you manage in a hospital that has a 5:1 nurse to patient ratio. You have five nurses in the unit, so, according to your capacity (ratio standard), you can effectively house and care for 25 patients. Simple math, right? Well, what if all 25 of those patients are exceptionally high acuity or extremely time consuming due to mobility issues resulting from a lack of wheelchairs?

On the manufacturing side, maybe you have a machining center that is capable of running 40 parts per hour, so it should be able to run 816 parts per 24-hour period. More simple math, right? Well, what if there is a quality issue with the raw slugs, the pallet quantity was short by 10, or the changeover tooling was not staged?

Looking at this from a service industry perspective, suppose your customer service center employees should be able to handle 12 calls per hour. You have 20 customer service representatives, so from a capacity standpoint they should service 240 customer calls per hour. What about the billing error on recent customers' statements that has caused a 300% increase in call volume, or the fact that the telephone system went down 5 minutes ago? What about the system issue that is preventing electronic notes from being added to the account during the phone call? The notes now must be added later, transferred from handwritten notes. The list goes on and on of examples of delays, constraints, obstacles, and problems that could potentially directly impact your capacity – your ability to provide value.

> **"If you *design* value into a process, you reap efficiency, quality, and consistency. If you *design* waste and inefficiency into a process, you harvest a crop of problems, confusion, variation, and defects."**

Capacity calculations themselves often consider daily events like downtime, changeovers, system maintenance, scheduled meetings, data entry, and efficiency. This is all part of understanding our true capacity, but too often we take each of these as a given, accepting that the amount of time required for each is a fixed and unchangeable number. We assume that a 30-minute changeover is the standard and cement that number into capacity calculations, never questioning the legitimacy or considering the potential for improvement.

An "Aha" Moment

A great example of accepting the status quo comes from a hospital that I worked with. The hospital's imaging equipment required periodic PM (Preventative Maintenance), so the department leadership would work with the vendor and schedule the service. For this specific hospital, the busiest time of day for the imaging department was between 11 a.m. and 9 p.m. I walked into one of the imaging control rooms at 2 p.m. one day to verify some Time Study information and was informed that the equipment was down for 3 hours for the scheduled PM. From previous experience with the imaging team, I knew that capacity always seemed to be an issue, so I found it very strange that we would schedule the PM in the middle of the busiest part of our day.

I inquired with the department director, and he informed me that this was the most convenient time for the vendor, and this time of day was when they had always scheduled it. Yes, I know you are probably shaking your head. This 3-hour downtime window was in the middle of our peak volume and was causing a backup for the Emergency Room, in-patient floors, and out-patient appointments. I asked the director one simple question, "What is the optimal time for us (the vendor's customer) to complete the PM and minimize the impact to our operations and patients?" This question realigned us with our "main thing," serving the patient.

As hard as it is to believe, this was an "aha" moment for the director. This director, and the entire imaging team, had grown accustomed to and accepted that the PM activity would be an interruption that they would have to work around. Nobody had ever questioned it, so they just walked along "carrying the gorilla." Only after realizing the true impact to the imaging equipment capacity the mid-day PM had, did they finally question it. As it turned out, the vendor had always scheduled that mid-afternoon maintenance time because nobody at the hospital had ever questioned it. After some discussion between the director and the vendor, the future PM activity was scheduled for early mornings, minimizing the impact and increasing the hospital's capacity to perform imaging procedures. The capacity was already there; we just had to reach into the "waste basket" and pull it out.

You Need Capacity Now, Not Tomorrow

Companies make the all-too-common mistake of thinking that, to increase capacity, they must build a new wing, purchase new machines, hire more people, outsource some work, increase storage space, or purchase more complicated MRP (Material Resource Planning) or ERP (Enterprise Resource Planning) systems.

The honest truth is that you have capacity available right now, but it is buried under layers, piles, and mountains of waste and inefficient processes. It exists right at your fingertips but goes unnoticed and unrecognized every day as you re-apply new Band-Aids, reinforce the layers of duct tape, and replace the weakening zip strips that hold your processes together.

Waste is a parasite that feeds off the resources you intend to use to produce value for customers, clients, patients, and staff. The formal dictionary definition of a parasite is, "an organism that lives in or on another organism, its host, and benefits by deriving nutrients at the host's expense." Now let's reword that a little and see how it sounds when applied to waste. *"Waste is a process that exists in or on an organization, its host, and benefits by consuming resources at the organization's expense."* I would consider that a perfect match.

Here is where the "hope" lies. The quickest way to immediately increase capacity is

JUST ALONG FOR THE RIDE

We adopted a beagle from the shelter a while back. He is certainly not hunting stock, as he is afraid of the dark and almost anything that moves, creeps, or crawls. His behavior and demeanor led us to name him "Goober," a name he certainly lives up to. Recently, while sitting on the couch one evening and giving him a leg spasm-inducing back and ear scratching, I felt something out of place. I pulled his ear up and found a big bump. The bump turned out to be a large, swollen, and engorged tick. Yuck! I showed my wife and son just to gross them out. A quick search on YouTube provided the proper procedure for removing and disposing of the tick, and applying antibiotic ointment. From its size, it was obvious that the tick had been there for quite some time, undetected and undisturbed. For who knows how long, it had been living off Goober, and he never knew it. Once identified, we addressed it immediately. Your processes are full of ticks, feeding off your resources and operations, swollen and engorged. It's time to remove them.

to identify and eliminate waste. Yes, it sounds almost too simple, but it is true. The best solutions are quite often those that are the least complicated. If you identify and eliminate the waste that permeates your current processes, you immediately reintroduce that capacity back into your processes. Let's look at some examples that will drive this reality home.

I worked with an organization that was attempting to improve performance and capacity. The call center was staffed with roughly 30 customer service agents. When we ran the performance reports, we saw that some CSR's (Customer Service Representatives) averaged 12 customer calls per hour, and others only averaged six per hour. We looked back 6 months and confirmed that the information was historically consistent. At that moment, the team averaged the following: six CSR's averaged 12 calls per hour, 18 averaged nine calls per hour, and six averaged six calls per hour. The team's capacity was roughly 270 calls per hour, or 2,160 per 8-hour shift. How could there be such a wide spread in the number of calls among CSR's?

To gain a better understanding, we decided to spend a couple of days shadowing multiple people who were performing at different levels. On day one, I shadowed a top performer, a CSR who was servicing the most customers on a consistent basis. I made note of her conversations, the questions she asked, how and when she entered information, her skill at navigating the software, and her overall knowledge of the product line she serviced. The next day, I sat with one of the lower performers, a CSR who was servicing the fewest customers on a consistent basis. I observed the same areas, the conversations, the questions he asked, how and when he entered information, his skill at navigating the software, and his overall knowledge of the product he serviced.

What I found was enlightening. The high performer was sincere and courteous, but refrained from lengthy sidebar conversations that had no relevance to the original purpose for the customer's call. The lower performer tended to get bogged down with these sidebar and irrelevant conversations with customers. The high performer asked questions in a specific manner that promoted precise and succinct answers, whereas the low performer asked questions in a general manner that led to long, drawn out answers that ended up requiring additional clarification. I noticed that the high performer was entering information into the system as the call was progressing and was also using a very clear and standardized script to make it easier for any future CSR to read when the customer called back. The low performer would enter his notes in the system once the call ended. His notes were not clear and tended to be very wordy and somewhat ambiguous. I observed that the high performer was very proficient in navigating the system and used two monitors to pull information between the sub-systems. The low performer only used one of the monitors and had some difficulty navigating the system.

Over the next month, as a group, the leaders and the team members identified a pre-defined and standardized script of appropriate greetings and conversation topics. We identified standard, specific questions to ask that promoted clear and succinct answers from customers. The group formulated specific, succinct, closed-ended answers to customers' questions. We developed standards for imputing notes into the system during the call instead of afterward. The team identified process standards for utilizing both monitors simultaneously to quickly access information from multiple systems more easily, and we developed ongoing training to improve overall CSR proficiency in navigating the systems.

The group also implemented and posted a visual metric that showed the performance of the entire team and how each person was performing individually. Displaying individual performance was not a punitive action; it was intended to raise the bar for the group and also surface individual deficiencies that could be addressed. In some ways, making this performance visual created a self-governing environment where everyone understood how his or her individual performance impacted the entire team and department.

So, what were the results of the actions we took? Keep in mind that there were some people who would always exceed expectations, and it was unlikely that everyone would start averaging 12 customers per hour. After a couple of weeks, we started to see results. The 18 people who had previously averaged nine calls were able to handle 10 calls per hour. The six people who previously averaged six calls per hour began averaging eight calls per hour. The six top performers were still averaging 12 per hour.

Based on this information, we were averaging 300 calls serviced per hour, or 2,400 calls serviced per day. That additional 30 calls per hour or 240 calls per day equated to an 11% increase in capacity, or, get this, an additional 3.3 employees! *We had added 3.3 employees' worth of capacity without hiring a single individual.* The call capacity was there all along, but process variation and a lack of standards resulted in waste and inefficiency that were manifested in the wide difference between the high and low performing CSR's.

> **"Waste is a parasite that lives in your operational intestines. It feeds off the resources you intend to use to produce value for customers, clients, patients, and staff."**

Maximizing Value

Let's jump into a different industry and go back to the hospital. In a hospital, the CT imaging machines are a very important revenue generating source. Maximizing CT capacity is critical to ensuring effective patient flow, providing timely care and diagnosis, meeting demand requirements, keeping providers and patients happy, and meeting fiscal targets. As always, reducing staffing cost is a top priority, so quite often a CT machine is run by a single tech. In this example, let's look at one patient in the Emergency Department who had a CT with contrast ordered by the provider. The CT tech saw the patient order pop up in his queue on the computer. The tech then pulled the order up and prepared the contrast dispenser. Once finished, the tech went to the ER and retrieved the patient and transported her back to the CT. Upon arrival, the tech brought the patient into the CT room and verified her identity.

Once the patient's identity was verified, the patient was positioned on the CT machine, and the contrast was hooked up. The tech then went into the CT control room, where he loaded the ordered test program into the system. Once the test was loaded, the CT scan was started. After the CT scan was completed, the tech went into the system to verify the quality of the images. After confirming the quality of the images, the tech removed the patient from the CT machine and transported her back to the Emergency Department. The tech then returned to the control room, where he went into the system, prepared the images, sent them to the radiologist, and closed the order in the system. The tech then cleaned and prepped the equipment for the next patient.

Now this sounds like a somewhat straightforward process. But, remember what we are talking about in this chapter? Capacity! On average, this whole process took 25 minutes. So, in a 12-hour shift (720 minutes), the team could, on average, perform 29 CT procedures. Using an average CT scan revenue of $1,200, on a normal day the hospital had the potential to realize $34,800 in billable procedures from the CT Department.

Here is where we had to step back and look at the process from a different vantage point. The overall capacity of the CT machine was pretty much locked in, based on the current process and equipment capability, providing very few options to increase overall capacity other than adding new or updated equipment. Right? Absolutely not! The key words are "based on the current process." We measure capacity based on how much time it takes for the CT equipment itself to scan a patient or add value. When the CT is not scanning, it is not adding value, and thus not maximizing capacity.

Given this information, the leadership and team sat down and took a deep dive into this process. We completed some detailed time studies to understand value vs. non-value activities. Understanding that the only person who could perform a CT procedure was a licensed CT tech, we started to separate the activities that would not require a licensed CT tech. This only made sense, given that the CT techs were hired to perform CT scans, and this was where they added the most value. Looking at the process, we realized that there were multiple time-consuming activities embedded in the process that could be performed by someone called a transporter. For example, the trained transporter could transport the patients back and forth to the ED or in-patient rooms, verify patient ID, move the patients onto the CT, remove patients from the CT, and clean and prep the machine for the next patient.

THE DREAM CAR

It was not a Mustang, Camaro, or Charger; it was a 1997 burgundy 4-door Buick Century. This was not the car that every high school boy dreams of, but it was in perfect condition, had four doors and wheels, airbags, and great tires. The perfect example of the "little old lady" car, in 20 years it had only seen 74,000 miles of road. We bought it about 6 months before Jordan started driving so that I could make sure it was in top operational condition prior to handing him the keys. During the first month of ownership, I noticed that the gas mileage (capacity) was not what I expected.

Because the car was 20 years old, I knew there were some maintenance actions I needed to take, just to give me confidence. I replaced the air filter, fuel filter, spark plugs and wires, oil and filter, battery, and PCV valve. Suddenly, the car's mileage was outstanding. These old and unaddressed items were negatively impacting the mileage (capacity) by restricting air and fuel delivery, preventing effective ignition, and causing excessive engine heat and friction. By eliminating these restrictions and problems, I saw an instantaneous increase in mileage (capacity). Your organization is no different; there are multiple opportunities to eliminate operational restrictions and friction, which will result in improved flow and process capacity.

Basically, what we did was remove the necessary but non-value-add activities from the CT tech's plate, allowing him to focus on completing CT procedures. We took numerous activities and sequenced them so that they were completed concurrently instead of consecutively. If you have ever utilized the Line Balancing technique or the SMED (Single Minute Exchange of Dies) methodology, you understand that activates are classified as either Internal or External to the actual value producing process. Internal steps are ones that can only be completed while the process is not running, while External steps can be completed while the process is running. For example, changing your radio station is External to driving your car, meaning that you do it while the car is in motion. Changing your tires, on the other hand, is Internal, meaning that the car cannot be driven while you are completing this step.

At this point, I know you may be thinking that adding a person could be considered an unnecessary cost and potential waste. That is why being able to utilize a cost-benefit analysis is so important.

This example is real, so the numbers below are from an actual hospital. The transporter role was added and tasked with the activities that did not require the actual CT tech. This allowed the tech to focus on running CT scans, preparing images, sending the reports to the radiologists, and loading the next patient orders. The amount of time between CT scans dropped from 25 minutes to 17 minutes. This means that by adding a transporter, the team was able to increase CT procedure capacity in a 12-hour day from 29 to 42.

This was a 44% increase in capacity, accomplished by simply breaking down the process into Internal and External elements and understanding it at the sub-process value vs. non-value level. On average, a transporter's salary is $36,000, which equates to roughly $138 per day, based on 2,080 hours per year. The increased CT capacity of the additional 13 scans held the potential to improve daily billable revenue for the hospital by $15,600. Not a bad return on a $138-per-day investment in a transporter.

Is this a cut and dry example? No. Are there many factors that must be considered? Yes. Did the hospital realize 100% of the additional capacity immediately? No, they had to constantly work to fill that capacity with demand, but what a nice situation to be in vs. tuning away business because you have no perceived available capacity.

Protecting Your Processes

Anyone reading this book could probably add 20 more pages to this chapter just from their experience of squeezing capacity out of a struggling process. Ultimately, every one of the 8 Wastes is a mortal enemy of your capacity. If we looked at capacity in the same way we look at our car's gas tank, it makes perfect sense. Our cars are designed to transport us and our families to school, work, church, and any number of other locations. However, we must maintain our vehicles, and, most importantly, we must fill them up with fuel. A perfectly maintained car is useless without fuel, so what we put into the gas tank ultimately determines how well our car runs, or, in other words, how much value it provides.

Have you ever purchased bad gasoline, maybe with water in it? How does that affect the value your car provides? Water can make your car run rough or completely knock it out of commission, so, like me, you probably restrict yourself to using the big names in gas stations. I admit it – I am selective when it comes to what I put in my cars, because I know that it impacts performance and the overall value delivery my car provides.

What would happen if we were just as selective when we developed processes in our organizations? How would our operations perform if we only put the highest quality gas in the tank, looking at each individual step at a granular level to understand what value each specific sub-process was delivering? In essence, asking, "Why am I doing this?" for every step. It sounds time consuming, and indeed it is, but, just like a fighter jet, the dedication to flawless design is realized in uncompromising performance. I am convinced that, regardless of industry, if we were completely committed to developing value-driven processes, we would proactively minimize the process waste upfront in the initial design.

It falls back to the adage, "Junk In = Junk Out." We can't blame others for broken processes; we own them.

WHAT'S IN IT FOR ME?

Remember what they say about starting a business or selling a house: "It's all about location, location, location." The same goes for operating an efficient and waste-free process – it's all about design, design, design! If you design value into the process, you reap efficiency, quality, and consistency. If you design a process with waste and inefficiency, you harvest a crop of problems, confusion, variation, and quality issues.

Look at the engineering and design costs for introducing a new product. The R&D alone can be mind boggling. The reason so much time and money are dedicated to these areas is so that when the product is finally launched, the market introduction is flawless, yielding huge demand and positive reviews. The attention to detail in the design phase is an investment in your organization's future.

What would happen if you dedicated as much time and effort in designing the processes within your individual departments? Design and engineering applies to every operation in every department, regardless of the industry. Clocking in is a process, and how it is designed will reveal whether it promotes efficiency or confusion. Administering medicine to a patient is a process, and how it is designed impacts patient safety as well as employee productivity. Completing employee evaluations is a process, and you probably know all too well that how it is designed can either provide for a smooth review activity or create total organizational chaos for a 3-month period while everyone scrambles to get them completed.

As you prepare to start a new process, take time to design it correctly. Even before implementation, draw it out in a Value Stream or Process Level Map (Chapter 21). If the change requires, rearrange desks, equipment, supplies, and machinery. Lay it out using a CADD (Computer Aided Design and Drafting) system first to look for flow, movement, or interference issues. You can also utilize a "Cardboard City" to accomplish the same thing. A Cardboard City is just what it sounds like, a life-size duplication of your proposed layout using cardboard boxes that you shape and size to the appropriate dimensions. The Cardboard City simulates the new process layout, and, like the CADD method, allows you to proactively identify flow, movement, or interference issues. I would need more hands to count the number of times problems were avoided and chaos was averted by completing a CADD or Cardboard City activity prior to a process launch.

For the processes you have in flight right now, step back and take some time to redesign them. What does your design look like compared to your current state? In the Lean world, what I am talking about is referred to as a "Future State Map." A Future State Map is your ideal state, a process that flows with minimal interruptions, waste, and problems. If you had a magic wand and could instantly transform your current process (Current State Map), your Future State Map is what it would look like.

Use a Process Map. Create your optimal process, your future state. Identify the differences between your current and future states, and then systematically modify your current state processes to reflect the improved future state. This will take time and require some trial and error.

I keep a saying posted in my office that sums up this chapter fairly accurately: "When you fail to effectively plan, you effectively plan to fail." This applies to the design of your processes and is manifested through the end result of every employee's activity and efforts.

CHAPTER 11:
THE 8 WASTES EXPLOSION

Instructions? Who needs instructions? These have been my famous last words multiple times over the years. Most notably are those from late at night on Christmas Eve. We have all been there – hurriedly wrapping gifts, looking for Scotch tape and the scissors nobody ever seems to put back in the drawer. So many memories of running out of Christmas wrapping paper, forced to use the comics from last weekend's paper and then fabricating believable stories for the kids explaining why Santa wrapped their gifts in comics. I have assembled bikes not fit for riding, Playskool workbenches not structurally sound, swing sets considered a safety hazard, and trampolines more dangerous than sky diving without a parachute. I fixed all of them prior to Christmas morning, but the many hours spent correcting them were completely unnecessary. If I had just trusted the proven design, as outlined in the instruction process, each would have operated correctly the first time, and I would have avoided the numerous wastes that resulted.

An Exponential Impact

So, what happens when you fail to define and document "process instructions"? What are the results when you don't take the time and effort to intentionally design a process that produces the maximum value possible? What happens when a seemingly simple and insignificant process results in waste or problems? Does it really make sense to spend time and effort worrying about the "Little w" wastes, or should we focus only on what we categorize as "Big W" wastes? In reality, there is no such thing as Little w wastes; there is only waste.

I know in Chapter 1 I said that there were 8 Wastes, but an explosion or multiplier effect results for every single waste event. When you dive deep into each waste event, you will see that there may be five, 20, 50, or even more additional process wastes generated by the "obvious" surface level, Little w waste that everyone sees. This is where the opportunity exists, where you will discover the operational gold mine, The Lean Treasure Chest.

The impact of waste is not limited to one single process or activity, but is propagated and spread through an infinite number of other processes. Understanding this allows you to truly grasp the negative impact to your organization, as well as the positive results of addressing and eliminating it.

Let's take advantage of a dramatic visual correlation. When a waste event occurs, it results in an explosion of process carnage and damage.

Years ago, we lived in a small town called Bennet Switch. The town was named after landowner Baldwin Bennet and was located where the Lake Erie and Western Railroads crossed paths. Our yard had several old and magnificent oak and maple trees. As often happens in the summer, one evening the clouds boiled up, the sky grew dark, and the wind picked up as a strong storm rolled through. While sitting in the living room with my family watching the Discovery Channel show *Dirty Jobs*, we nearly jumped out of our skin when we saw a blinding flash of light accompanied by an ear-shattering crack.

Somewhere on our property, we had taken a direct lightning strike. I thought the bolt had hit the house itself, but when I went out into the backyard, I noticed tree bark scattered all over the yard. In fact, the bark was also in my neighbors' yards, in other trees, and on top of the house. I later found some on the opposite side of the house in the front yard. My tree had been struck by lightning, and, from the visible damage, appeared to have, in essence, exploded. The strike resulted in a broken window, a bent gutter, hours spent picking up bark, dented aluminum siding, a young daughter who would forever be terrified of storms, and, ultimately, the tree dying. The dead tree required resources to cut down and remove, and it changed our yard. Its huge branches had supported a tire swing that held hundreds of wonderful memories. The single lightning strike (waste event) resulted in an explosion that damaged far more than just wood and bark – it impacted us, our neighbors, and everyone who would ever own that home.

As demonstrated by the picture in Figure 11:1, an explosion is not confined to a contained area, but expands, impacting an enormous area surrounding it in the form of a blast wave, debris, fragmentation, shock wave, and heat. A waste event works in much the same way. A process fails, resulting in a Waste Explosion that sends a shock wave across your departments, suppliers, vendors, and customers, impacting countless people and processes.

This collateral damage requires these groups to utilize already limited resources to correct the problem, impacting their other processes. Sometimes the effects are so dramatic and far reaching that you don't truly understand their ultimate impact until weeks, months, or years later, when you find yourself being pelted on the head as the residual "process debris" finally rains down from the sky.

FIGURE 11:1

FIGURE 11:2 – THE WASTE CORRELATION EXPLOSION

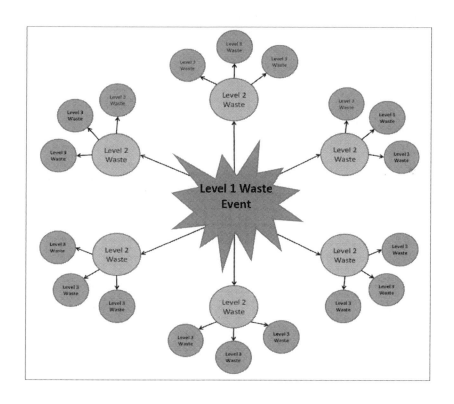

The Waste Correlation Explosion

Understanding waste and inefficiency is about seeing the big picture, and the easiest way to really start doing that is to use what I call a "Correlation Explosion." In Figure 11:2, you see an example. Every waste starts in the center; I call this the "Level 1 Waste." Each subordinated waste directly generated by the Level 1 Waste is connected, contained in a circle of its own. These are referred to as Level 2 Wastes. Each subordinated waste generated by the Level 2 Waste is also contained in its own circle, appropriately called the Level 3 Wastes.

This domino effect can go on for an infinite number of levels. I laid the tool out this way for two reasons: to clearly demonstrate the magnitude of the impact resulting from a single waste event, and to document the actual correlation of the Level 1 Waste to every subsequent level of waste generated. Even after managing for years in different industries, I did not anticipate the extent of the impact that a single waste event could have until I started drilling down. I admit that after completing several of these, I was humbled by how little I really knew about the depth to which the overall impact of waste reaches. If you find yourself in the same situation, take comfort in the fact that probably 99.99% of people are in the same boat.

A Single Defect, A Nation Impacted

I remember where I was, what I was doing, and the details of the day as if it was yesterday. I was walking between classes my senior year in high school. The date was January 28, 1986. As I passed by one of the science classrooms, I noticed the class was watching the launch of the Challenger Space Shuttle. I shouldn't have delayed, but I was captivated by the explosive power of the launch and amazed by the reality that the crew would soon be observing the earth from a vantage point that was beyond my comprehension.

Silence and horror are the only words that adequately describe the next 30 seconds. This wasn't real and couldn't be what it looked like, could it? Nobody moved or spoke; we only sat there. We looked to the teacher for reassurance that this was not as it seemed, but there was none given. The remainder of the day is a dark and dreadful memory. We had lost our heroes in a spiraling cloud of debris and smoke, and we would never be the same as individuals or as a nation.

As you read this, based on your age, you may or may not remember this event. The Challenger investigation went on for years, and the finger pointing was epic. What was finally reported as the cause for the explosion of the solid rockets boosters and external fuel tank was an O-ring seal. Yes, a simple O-ring. The below freezing temperature at launch time had interfered with the ability of the O-ring to do its job, and, as a result, through a chain of events, the mission ended in disaster thousands of feet in the sky.

I only use the Challenger disaster as an example because it is by far the most apparent example I know of how devastating a single and seemingly insignificant process defect can be. If you look at the Challenger disaster from the perspective of the Waste Correlation, it would probably expand to well over 100 levels, but let's look at just a few to show how the process itself works.

Level 1 Waste: Defective O-ring seal (based on external temperature)

> **Level 2 Wastes:** Human Impact – The loss of seven gifted and amazing people whose true value can never be measured or estimated

> **Level 2 Waste:** Loss of a multi-billion-dollar space shuttle

>> **Level 3 Waste:** The manpower utilized to design, build, and launch the shuttle

>>> **Level 4 Waste:** The opportunity cost of the value that was poured into the shuttle that could have been utilized in other projects

>>> **Level 4 Waste:** The cost of the employees who supported those designers and builders

>>> **Level 4 Waste:** The cost of the equipment, time, and effort to move the Challenger from the hanger to the launch site

>> **Level 3 Waste:** The loss of billions of taxpayer dollars that fell into the sea and added no value to the NASA space program

>>> **Level 4 Waste:** The opportunity cost of the billions of dollars that could have been used to fund other programs like education, law enforcement, military, or infrastructure needs

>> **Level 3 Waste:** The cost of the facility that was used to build the Challenger Space Shuttle

>>> **Level 4 Waste:** The cost of the facility maintenance and upkeep

>>>> **Level 5 Waste:** The cost of the manpower to provide the maintenance and upkeep

>>> **Level 4 Waste:** The opportunity cost of using the facility for a different program (hanger space at NASA is valuable)

Level 3 Waste: The cost of the equipment to design, engineer, and build the Challenger

    Level 4 Waste: The labor cost of the engineering, design, and testing of the equipment

    Level 4 Waste: The material cost of building the equipment used to design and build the Challenger

Level 2 Waste: The environmental impact of the explosion (debris and chemicals in the ocean and air)

Level 2 Waste: The resources consumed to understand why the Challenger failure occurred

    Level 3 Waste: U.S. Navy, Coast Guard, and private groups used in the location and recovery of the wreckage

    Level 3 Waste: The resources required by multiple government agencies to investigate, understand, and identify the root cause of the accident

    Level 3 Waste: The negative impact on NASA itself – a black eye to an amazing organization dedicated to excellence

Level 2 Waste: The emotional impact to everyone involved in the design, build, and launch of the Challenger. Those brilliant and dedicated engineers and scientists who now live with the scars of that terrible day and who may never be able to completely accept that it was of no fault of their own. The potential impact to their confidence and ultimately their careers may never be truly understood.

    Level 3 Waste: The impact to these people's families, friends, and communities

Level 2 Waste: The negative impact on our entire nation. We still mourn.

I have only scratched the surface, but you can see the negative impact a single defective O-ring seal can have and the resulting waste and devastation it caused. The same thing happens on a different scale within your organizations. It applies to the defective product you produce and then scrap, the blood sample that was contaminated and must be redrawn, the bolt on the brake assembly that wasn't tightened to spec, the repeat call to the customer who already paid his delinquent bill, and the fast food restaurant that forgot to include the large French fries in the bag before you drove away.

Waste propagates waste, and the cycle continues until you identify and address the source. Every single example of waste you can think of results in countless other wastes. Understanding this concept will enable you to see your processes and activities from an entirely new perspective. Remember, there is no such thing as a "little waste," as demonstrated by a simple rubber O-ring seal.

DEEP BLUE WATER

I love to fish – one of the things that sold us on our home is its two ponds. The ponds are connected by a small bridge that we often fish from. The water is beautiful, but, in the summer, we have to be mindful of algae. Nothing ruins our fun like a pond full of floating, slimy, stinky algae. In addition to the use of an aeration system to promote oxygen levels, I also use a blue pond dye. Every 2 weeks, I walk out on the dock and pour in some super-concentrated blue pond dye.

It is harmless to the fish and makes the water look beautiful, but the real benefit is its ability to prevent sunlight from penetrating past a certain depth, thus preventing algae growth. The interesting thing about this dye is that it comes in a 1-quart bottle. My ponds' total surface area is about 2 acres, with a depth ranging from 4 to 10 feet. My ponds hold roughly 3.8 million gallons of water, but all 3.8 million of them are tainted by this single quart of dye. A single waste event, like the dye, can permeate every single gallon of your "operational water." Waste is a contaminant, so, by eliminating the waste and problems, you purify your processes and deliver a clean and filtered product or service to customers.

There is no rocket science to effectively using this tool, but it does require an extremely deep understanding of your processes. In order to drive to the root cause of a problem, you must first understand the process so well that you are able to quickly move past the obvious symptoms and avoid getting dragged down a rabbit hole, stuck in the mire of the subordinated problems contained in Waste Levels 2, 3, 4, and so on.

The following eight chapters are intended to explain the 8 Wastes, but at a much deeper level than you may have explored before. As you dive into the details of each individual type of waste, you should also start to identify the accompanying Waste Explosion and the other departments, processes, and people who are impacted. As you read the chapters that detail each of the 8 Wastes, you must actively work to correlate them with your own individual systems or processes, seeing what may not have been obvious to you and your teams up to this point. Understand that when I refer to "you," I am not talking about just you, the person reading this book. I am talking about your entire team, department, and organization.

So, now that you've reached the halfway point of this book, and while I still have your attention, let's dig down deep into each one of the 8 Wastes. Like you did with the worm or frog in your high school biology class, let's dissect each one individually to understand them at a whole new level. We will identify where they originate, what causes them, how they impact the organization's operation, what they really cost, and then how to avoid, prevent, and eliminate them.

Grab your "operational scalpel," slip on some gloves, put on your mask and goggles, and let's get busy.

WHAT'S IN IT FOR ME?

This is a simple question to answer. What's in it for you is the newfound understanding of waste and its real impact. We have dissected waste in multiple ways up to this point, and, in this chapter, we have demonstrated with painful clarity that waste has an infinitely greater effect on your organization than you probably realized.

Use the Waste Explosion. If you have been to one of my seminars, you should already have a template to use – if not, draw one out. Go to your processes, and find a wasteful activity. Draw that Level 1 Waste event in the middle circle, and then start driving outward to identify every other waste generated. Look at the people and departments that now have to utilize their time and efforts to address and correct those problems. Identify the equipment used and the capacity consumed to remedy the condition. Understand the additional supplies and materials needed to make the situation right. Document the impact, too, to space, resources, employees, energy, repairs, rework, and cost. Identify the actions required to repair a damaged reputation as viewed through your customers' eyes.

Don't stop at these Level 2 Wastes. For each or these, ask the same questions to arrive at the Level 3 Wastes. If necessary, keep driving to the Level 4 and Level 5 Wastes. Since we live in a world where monetary measures provide universal clarity, put these different process wastes and impacts into financial terms, even if you have to guess. Ultimately, you will see the true power and devastation that a single waste event can have in an organization, at both a process and a financial level. By translating the Waste Explosion into both process and financial measures, you can effectively demonstrate to the entire organization the true nature of the opportunity and the justified urgency to eliminate waste.

CHAPTER 12:
WASTE #1 – DEFECTS

Defects are the simple-to-understand waste. They are simply an outcome that did not meet an expectation as defined by a standard. From the customers' perspective, Defects are something that they are not willing to accept or pay for and that must now be either reworked, scrapped, or produced again. A defect could refer to a discrete manufactured part, a wrong meal served to a customer, a package delivered to the wrong address, a wrong oil filter installed by the mechanic, or any of a thousand other examples.

A Defect Can Be Anything

As you read this section on Defects, whether you are a CEO, director of radiology, manager of assembly, VP of supply chain, or an assembly line worker, you probably pictured Defects that are specific to your organization and the services or products you provide. In addition, you also may have already started thinking about the additional wastes that are a direct result of your unique Defects. Very often, Defects are the first of the 8 Wastes that comes to people's minds, and understandably so. You experience them daily, sometimes literally tripping over them without even acknowledging their existence.

> **"You claim to have a defect, when, in reality, the processes within your organizations are so random in their design and execution that variation is the only logical outcome."**

FIGURE 12:1

Do any of these examples occur in your daily routine?

- You order fast food, but, as you drive away, you realize you only received six of the seven items you ordered.

- You get a flat tire from a nail in your driveway left by the roofers.

- You spill coffee on your pants on the way to work.

- Your car runs out of gas.

- Your pillow in the hotel room has a stain on it.

- The "7th floor" button on the elevator does not light up.

- The wiper blades are leaving streaks on your windshield.

- You receive the mail meant for your neighbor who lives three houses down.

- You forget to log a debit card transaction in your checkbook and overdraw your account.

- The toilet is running.

- The umbrella you just bought is leaking.

- Your little girl made you toast for breakfast, but she used mayonnaise instead of butter.

- Your computer spirals into a "blue screen of death" as you try to book your flight to Tahiti.

- Your company ships product without MSDS or spec sheets.

- A blood sample taken in the doctor's office is mislabeled with the wrong patient information.

- You get the shopping cart at the store that vibrates and shakes so badly that people think you are having a seizure.

- You receive an invoice from a supplier that is missing the purchase order number.

- Your server goes down, paralyzing your customer service department.

- The X-ray image is fuzzy, and the procedure must be repeated.

- You make a reservation for six people, but the restaurant tries to seat you at a table for four.

- The overhead vent on the plane is stuck open, leading to frostbite on your 5-hour flight from Los Angeles to Indianapolis.

A defect is like a floor tile in your home's entryway that wasn't laid perfectly level and continually catches the toe of your shoe – it's a nuisance at first, but after a while you subconsciously step a little higher, passing right over without even realizing it.

Defects don't necessarily have a physical presence. A defect can be a wrong answer in response to a question, an off-key note in a vocal performance, calling someone by the wrong name, or even a calendar event scheduled on the wrong day.

As demonstrated in Figure 12:1, the list is endless, and you could probably fill an entire book with nothing more than examples of Defects. I welcome additional lists that you come up with, based upon your individual perspectives, experiences, and observations. The point is this: you don't give most of these Defects a second thought. You work through or around them and their resulting inconvenience, then simply move on. In a business, though, these work-arounds, delays, interruptions, and reworks have numerous financial, process efficiency, and cultural impacts. Every one of these business examples either directly or indirectly negatively impacts the value you expect from the correlating process, and, as a result, the value you are able to provide to customers, employees, and stakeholders.

An important concept to keep in mind is COPQ (Cost of Poor Quality). COPQ looks at the actual total cost of producing a product or service vs. what the cost would have been if the process that produced the product or service had been designed and performed in a near perfect manner. In short, COPQ looks at the total resources (time, money, man hours, materials, etc.) consumed vs. the total that should have been consumed if the process' efficiency and effectiveness was optimized. Those resources consumed unnecessarily have been wasted, and the value that they could have provided went unrealized.

Wasted Joy

I was at my favorite donut shop recently, standing at the glass wall and watching the hot, fresh, sugar-drenched circles of fried heaven slowly travel down the stainless steel conveyor. I was waiting in a long line of customers, so, not surprisingly, I spent my free time focusing my attention on the process of donut making. To my surprise, what I saw was disturbing from a process and financial impact standpoint. At the end of the conveyor, an employee was picking up one in roughly 20 donuts and throwing it away. That one of 20 is equal to 5% of the donuts produced being discarded. In the manufacturing world, this is a precursor to the doors closing and an "Out of Business" sign being hung in the front window.

As I watched the process unfold up the line, I noticed that the 5% were also being coated with the glazed sugar prior to being thrown away. So, I continued to follow the process upstream, hoping to find the source of the defect. What I observed was that after the raw donut dough was dropped from the vertical conveyor rack into the hot oil, a few feet down line a second process was flipping the half-fried donut so that the hot oil would cook both sides to a golden-brown perfection. The problem was that 5% of the donuts were not being flipped and remained in their original orientation, cooking on one side only.

Down the assembly line they went, white and raw on the top. A mesh grate conveyor pulled them from the oil and carried them to a glazed sugar waterfall where they were coated in what I describe as nothing short of liquid ecstasy. After they slowly traveled another 10 feet, they were cool enough to be picked up with a straw and placed in boxes for sale to the long line of anxiously waiting consumers. The 5% of defective donuts were not boxed, but thrown into a trash bag-lined box under the conveyor.

You may be far ahead of me already, but let's take a minute and look past the obvious Defects Waste – the donuts being thrown away – and see the real impact. How many different wastes were produced by this single defect?

1. The defective donuts were scrapped.

2. The cooking oil that was absorbed by the defective donuts was also thrown away.

3. The sugar glaze that coated the defective donuts was thrown away.

4. The space on the conveyor that was designed to produce value was wasted (capacity and utilization).

5. The time of the person removing each defective donut and throwing it away was wasted.

6. The straws that were used to remove the defective donuts were wasted.

7. The box and plastic bag that held the defective donuts was wasted.

8. The cost of the time and wages of the employee who mixed the dough for the donuts that were thrown away was wasted.

9. The electricity consumed to mix the dough, heat the oil, power the conveyor, and light the store for the defective donuts was wasted.

10. The cost of the space consumed in the dumpster that now has to be picked up more often is wasted.

11. The time it took for someone to take the defective donuts to the dumpster is wasted.

12. The fact that, to potentially compensate for the 5% defect rate, management was forced to require mandatory overtime.

13. The fact that, to potentially compensate for the 5% defect rate and meet customer demand, the production rate was increased, thereby decreasing the lifespan of all of the equipment used to produce the donuts.

14. Or, on the other hand, the fact that, as a result of the 5% defect rate, the customer demand is potentially not met and there are not enough donuts for the customers when they arrive, causing them to go to a competitor (lost future sales).

15. The impact to the perspective of the customers who have a front row seat to the defect producing process, affecting their confidence in the store's business operations and potential investments in company stock.

Now, don't be fooled into thinking that this process observation interfered with my choice to wait in line to purchase two dozen hot and fresh donuts. I simply buried my disappointment beneath layers of hot, fresh, sugar-coated perfection. In fact, my family and I stop at this donut chain in every city we visit.

This was, though, a very good example of how the waste correlation explosion works. In fact, you have probably identified several wastes that I did not list. Good! That is what this book is about. Some of the wastes may seem obscure, but, in reality, each has an impact that goes deeper than just the financial statement.

> **"Defects are not random events that just happen by chance; they are produced."**

This is what I was talking about when I mentioned finding the waste at the source. Even if the source was mechanical and a repairman was a week out, the opportunity to eliminate the 5% defect was at the beginning of the process, at the donut flipper, not at the end of the line where there was no choice but to scrap the final product. From a cost perspective, what would the financial impact have been if a person was staged at the flipper to correct the un-flipped donuts instead of at the end of the line?

Well, the equipment was producing four donuts every 6 seconds. In 1 hour, the production line would have produced 2,400 donuts. At a 5% defect rate, roughly 120 donuts were being thrown away per hour. The store charges $9 per dozen, so every hour the store was losing $90 in potential revenue. Over time, assuming production occurred for 12 hours per day, 7 days per week, 356 days per year, that 5% defect rate turns into lost revenue of $7,560 per week, or – get this – $393,120 per year.

Unfortunately, instead of generating revenue, the store was basically paying for the privilege of throwing away 5% of its capacity. I know that this was just a temporary issue that was probably resolved within a couple of days, but looking at these everyday occurrences' long-term potential impact adds a unique perspective. Could you imagine that two donuts per minute wasted could add up to almost $400,000? The math may be simple, but the example is real, and you can probably see the same type of waste where you work.

Devastating Consequences

Let's look at another example that most people here can relate to at some level. Let's say you take your 1-year-old midnight black Porsche Boxter to Sparky's Garage. (I'm using a Porsche Boxter as an example for emphasis, not because there is one sitting in my garage.) The cost of the detailing service is $300. The service includes cleaning the interior, washing and waxing the exterior, applying leather conditioner, and detailing the wheels and tires. The process should take Sparky's roughly 2 hours, so you drop off the car in the morning and plan to pick it up tonight. Unfortunately, for some reason the detailer got distracted during the process and forgot to remove the wax. Your midnight black Porsche has been setting in the hot July sun, with the wax baking, for roughly 5 hours. Is this a problem? Are you going to pay for Sparky's detailing service?

This is certainly a problem, and when you arrive at the end of the day there will be some unpleasant and uncomfortable conversations taking place as the owner of Sparky's tries to explain what happened. In the end, Sparky's Garage will have to remedy the defect that they created. What will this "remedy" look like, and how much will it cost Sparky's?

1. Lost revenue of $300 for service you are not paying for.

2. Lost revenue from the detailing attendant's 4 hours of work while trying to remove the wax instead of completing other vehicles (4 hours at $150 per hour = $600).

3. The labor cost of the attendant who started to detail your car but couldn't finish (8 hours at $15 per hour = $120).

4. The materials and supplies that were used to begin the detailing of your car and to attempt to remove the wax.

5. Cost of a new paint job for your Porsche ($8,000).

6. Cost of transporting your car to and from the nearest Porsche dealership, which happens to be 300 miles away ($700).

7. Potential future revenue, as you tell 30 of your Porsche Car Club friends about the horrific event that took place, all of whom then make conscious decision to never use Sparky's services ($9,000).

8. Reputation – cannot quantify, but it could be enormous.

So, totaling it out, and including only the actual costs that Sparky's will incur to make you happy again: $300 lost revenue, $600 lost capacity, $120 labor cost of employee, $8,000 new paint job, and $700 transportation. Sparky's will end up paying $9,720 to correct a defect.

This is where the reality sets in, though. If Sparky's cost structure is such that for every $300 detailing job, he realizes a $100 profit, then, based on the $9,800 cost of rectifying the defect, Sparky will not see a profit from detailing for 98 vehicles. The next 98 people who drive in to have their cars detailed are only a means for Sparky's to get back into the fiscal black, to recover from the defect.

In terms of time, if Sparky's Garage details an average of four cars per day, as shown below in Figure 12:2, it will take almost 5 weeks to become profitable again on the detailing side of the business. That is a long time!

FIGURE 12:2

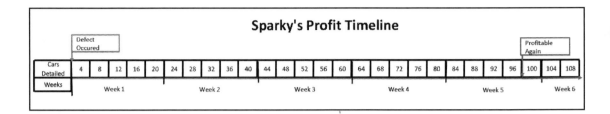

How does this example differ from the Defects that other companies experience every day? It doesn't. Every time you produce a part that does not meet spec and must be reworked or scrapped, you have consumed the profit margin for the next five, 10, 20, or more parts. Every time you must redraw and re-administer a blood culture test in the hospital lab because the nurse drawing the sample didn't wait for the prep wipe to dry and, thus, contaminated the sample, you consume resources that were needed for other tests and other patients. Every time you send out an invite that has the wrong date or wrong tele-conference information listed, you consume additional time to resend, as well as everyone else's time to recalibrate their calendars.

Getting Real

In some cases, a defect can be serious, even life-threatening. For example, say you take your wife to the local Emergency Room. She is experiencing some serious abdominal pain and discomfort. After the initial observation, the physician orders some routine lab tests. The nurse comes in the room holding a handful of vials and proceeds to fill three of them with your wife's blood. After completing the blood draw, the nurse walks into the next observation room. A few minutes later, the nurse emerges with some additional vials filled with samples from another patient.

With the handful of filled vials, the nurse proceeds to the nursing station, where she applies the patient labels and sends the vials to the lab. The lab runs the samples and sends the results back for the physician to review. After reviewing the results, the physician places an order for specific medication. A few minutes after receiving the medication, your wife starts to vomit and loses consciousness. The physician and nurse review the chart and realize that the blood samples were mixed up, and the labels were switched.

This is a potentially deadly defect, and it happens more times than you realize.

I Googled the number of flights scheduled every day around the world, and the average was roughly 102,000. Even a defect rate of .0002% means that two flights per day will crash. A defective wire, broken fuel gauge, leaking hydraulic valve, loose screw, faulty altimeter, or any of another thousand items can bring a plane crashing down, but the loss is defined by the human impact, not the destruction of metal and rubber.

Defects Don't Just "Happen"

Defects are too often seen as a simple and quickly correctable event. Nothing could be further from the truth. Defects are an indication that a process is broken or that established standards are not being followed, either by choice or because of a lack of education. Out of sight and out of mind is the easiest way for you to avoid understanding the true impact of Defects. How many times have you taken a cycle count or full audit, only to find defective parts stored all over the place with little orange tags that say, "Do Not Use" or "Hold for Disposition"? Instead of addressing the problem, you hide broken parts away – out of sight and out of mind. Even worse, how many times have you found defective parts or material just thrown away in a trash can, which explains why your cycle counts are always drastically off? Ignoring the Defects is a mistake, and it sends a very clear and confidence-destroying message to your teams about leadership's commitment to quality.

Defects are an opportunity, a "process gift." They are a shiny reminder that you can get better. Every time you experience a defect, you have been given the opportunity to dig in and understand the problem and processes at a whole new level. You have to stop using the standard "We are too busy" excuse and commit to developing a "Stop to Fix" culture. Otherwise, you will never truly solve the problem, and you will continually place your customers at risk for receiving that one defective shipment that somehow got through.

As you read this, you may be nodding your head because you know that your own processes are out of control. It is just a matter of time before the inevitable happens, and you find yourself scrambling to explain why your quality control system failed, allowing your department to ship a defective product. You may have to fabricate excuses as to why a procedure or process failed to deliver the desired results, or why a service you provided didn't meet identified customer standards. Looking at this from a 30,000-foot strategic level, these occurrences also tarnish your reputation and professional integrity, ultimately jeopardizing the future of your organization.

> **"Defects are an opportunity. They are a shiny reminder that you can get better."**

I have mentioned already that what you classify as problems are not normally the real problems. If you have not identified and documented a standard that has been tested and proven to produce a defined and consistent output, you cannot claim to have a problem. You claim to have a defect, when in reality the processes within your organization are so random in their design and execution that variation is the only logical outcome.

For example, years ago my cousin Mary Ellen gave me a recipe for chocolate chip cookies. My personal opinion is that it is the best recipe in the world. I have followed this recipe for years, and the results have been realized through the consumption of hundreds, if not thousands of these delicious chocolate chip cookies. I follow the well-defined and documented recipe, or standard, and my outcome is consistent, producing awesome chocolate chip cookies.

Once, and only once, did I make the mistake of baking these cookies from memory, not the recipe. As I combined and stirred the ingredients from memory, I created and utilized my own personal recipe, or standard. The results were catastrophic, rippling through the very fabric of space and time. One cookie out of the entire batch was eaten, by our dog. In all honesty, the dog stopped after only eating half the cookie.

What happened? My memory had failed me, and my own personal standard was, in fact, not a standard at all since it did not correlate to the desired and expected outcome – hot, gooey, and delicious chocolate chip cookies. You make the same mistake daily when you allow people in your organizations to perform tasks according to their individual and inconsistent "best" methods, either because a standard does not exist or because they simply make the decision not to follow it. A standard is, in essence, a recipe for success in any organization and in any process.

As has been said many times before, "Do it right, or do it *again*."

WHAT'S IN IT FOR ME?

Albert Einstein once said, "*Finding the problem is more important than the solution itself.*" He was absolutely correct.

It has been years since I have seen the infamous vehicle called a Yugo on the road. The Yugo was marketed in the United States from 1985-1992 and was touted as a fuel efficient and reliable alternative to other sub-compact cars. Years later, it is widely seen as the worst car every manufactured, for multiple reasons. It was a four-wheeled defect, failing to meet customer expectations, so people stopped buying them. The result? Well, when was the last time you saw one on the road?

Organizations are in business to provide a quality service or product that is in demand. When organizations are not capable of accomplishing this, they simply cease to exist. Defects are not random events that just happen; they are produced. They are produced using valuable resources, and then they are either fixed using additional valuable resources or dispositioned, which also consumes additional valuable resources. They are produced when your processes fail.

A ROOM KEY AND A CAN

I had a friend tell me a story recently about a unique day in his travels. It started when his hotel reservation was lost, and there were no rooms available, anywhere. Options were few: sleep in the car, find a comfortable spot under a pine tree, or stay in the motel with only part of its sign lit up and flashing. Unfortunately, he chose option 3. As he was checking in, he was taken aback by the carpet. It wasn't clear whether is was a floral design or just 40 years of unaddressed, intertwined stains. As he signed the log, the hotel attendant handed him a room key, and a, wait for it...can of roach spray. Yes! In all my years of Lean training, I finally found the perfect analogy for the problem Band-Aid. Instead of addressing the problem, the roach infestation, the motel had implemented a permanent Band-Aid solution. Needless to say, he handed the key and can back to the attendant and slept in his car that night. Are you, in essence, handing out cans of roach spray every day to your employees by accepting or condoning the continual use of not-so-temporary solutions in your operations?

Fixing Defects is not the answer. Preventing Defects is the answer. You prevent Defects by designing end engineering processes that deliver consistent results. You do this by developing Standard Work that defines how a process is to be completed. This includes every aspect of the process, from cradle to grave. If you can't be sure of the quality of a process' input or ingredient, then how can you be confident in the resulting output?

When you encounter a defect, walk upstream until you reach the root cause. Don't stop at the point where the defect became obvious; keep wading upstream to the process or processes where the variation originated. This is where Value Stream Mapping and Process Mapping exercises are valuable. They force you to document, in detail, the steps required to produce a product or provide a service. As you travel upstream, you begin to understand not only where the defect originated, but also the sub-processes that could contribute to the defect.

You may find that the root cause is still not completely obvious, so you may have to continue to monitor and document what you observe. Using a Run Chart and Pareto Chart are effective ways of understanding your status and trends as well as identifying the potential factors contributing to the non-standard condition. Don't start throwing solutions at the problem like you throw salt on your ice-covered sidewalk. Be methodical and cautious, implementing solutions in a controlled manner and looking for results that are in line with your expectations, while also being mindful of potential unanticipated results. If the solution does not provide resolution to the problem, don't take it personally and become defensive. Use that as a learning opportunity for everyone, and then continue to dig. You will find the root cause if you don't quit.

Applicable Tools (Chapter 21):

Kaizen/Kaizen Event

Value/Non-Value Analysis

5-Why Problem Solving

Fishbone Diagram

Pareto (Reality) Charting

Visual Management System

Value Stream Mapping

CHAPTER 13:
WASTE #2 – OVERPRODUCTION

Simply stated, Overproduction is bad – very, very bad. It occurs when you produce more than your customer or downstream process currently needs or can consume. Basically, you are producing product quantities in excess of customer demand or far in advance of the requested ship date.

Some may argue that this is not really a waste, as most often the product will eventually be consumed. In some cases that is correct, but it does not account for the resources consumed that may have provided more value if utilized to produce other products or services currently in demand.

Let's look at some simple examples of Overproduction:

1. You watch your local fast food restaurant throw out French fries that have been sitting under the hot light for too long.

2. You roast a 20-pound holiday turkey for three people.

3. A local bakery throws out 200 donuts every day because they were not purchased by consumers.

4. A shampoo company has an order for 30,000 units, but decides to run and bottle the leftover product in the hold tank since the batch was mistakenly oversized.

5. A stamping plant has orders for 900 inner door panels, but the stacks of blanks totals out to 1,200, so they decide to keep the job in and run the extra 300 panels.

6. A customer of a printing company ordered 2,400 flyers, but the paper is loaded in stacks of 500, so the company decides to run the extra 100 sheets and tries to get the customer to buy them.

7. A highway crew lays out barrels on the interstate for 6 miles when they are only capable of paving 1 mile per day.

8. An automobile manufacturer produces a large quantity of a certain model of vehicle without the marketing to support the decision.

Do any of these examples sound familiar? You have probably seen some of the above listed examples firsthand. Just like every other type of waste, Overproduction is guilty of producing multiple other wastes that are just overlooked.

Chicken Not-So-Little

To demonstrate this in a practical example that applies to everyone reading this book, let's plan a party for the Super Bowl, World Series, or World Cup. You pick. Ok, it is going to be great having all your friends over for the big game. Emotions are high, and that means lots of hungry people. In preparation for the event, you buy a bag of 100 chicken wings, which you plan to grill and smother with multiple sauces. The day of the event, several people cancel, leaving the anticipated attendance at roughly eight people. An hour before people are scheduled to arrive, you fire up the gas grill and start cooking the wings. You estimate that 50 wings will do, but since the grill is already hot, you decide to go ahead and grill up all 100 wings and put the other 50 in the refrigerator to eat next week. A couple of dinners and lunches, and those extra 50 wings will be history.

You are set; all 100 are cooked up and lathered in teriyaki, barbecue, and Cajun sauces. You put 50 wings out on the table and the remaining 50 into individual Ziploc bags, sorted by sauce, and then find a space in the refrigerator, which I suspect is a monumental task in itself.

The party is a success! Your team wins, the food is outstanding, everyone has a great time, and all attendees are either sober or have a designated driver. You put everything up, including any leftover food, stuffing it all in the refrigerator.

Life gets busy the next week, and the extra wings you cooked become a thing of the past, never even crossing your mind. Another week goes by, then another, and another until, 2 months down the road, you are searching for the dill pickles and way in the back of the refrigerator you come across three Ziploc bags filled with chicken wings. You reach for them, but one of the bags growls at you, another one tries to bite you, and the third one cowers in the corner. "Oh yeah, I forgot about these," you say to yourself as you suddenly remember bagging up and storing the 50 chicken wings last month.

Obviously, they are all bad, so you grab the three bags and start to throw them in the kitchen trash. You are stopped dead in your tracks when your spouse makes a high pitched noise indicating that, under no circumstance, are those chicken wings to be placed in the kitchen trash to stink up the house. So, you locate your closest child and tell him to take them to the trash can located in the garage. He hesitantly takes the three bags, makes a disgusted facial expression, followed by a gagging sound, then runs out of the kitchen toward the garage.

Not a pretty picture, but the impact of the Overproduction of chicken wings is bigger than you probably suspect. Obviously, you wasted the 50 chicken wings, but, as I mentioned at the introduction of this chapter, the chicken wings waste is just scratching the surface. Let's understand the big picture and break down the overall waste impact. You wasted three Ziploc bags (money), the space in the refrigerator for 8 weeks (space), the electricity consumed to cool the chicken wings that were never eaten (money), the gas used when you grilled them (money), the time you spent grilling up the extra 50 chicken wings (time), the sauce that you put on all the wings (money), and the money you spent on the chicken wings (money).

Here is the kicker – the impact that you may have missed. The next time you find yourself in the mood to gorge yourself on chicken wings, you must now stop what you are doing, get in your car, go to the store, wait in line, and fork out more money to purchase something you already had, but wasted. There is zero value in this activity; it is simply a result of the mistake of overproducing the chicken wings 2 months ago (money and time).

To understand the big picture as you see the overall impact, ask yourself these questions:

1. Where could the gas I wasted have taken me and my family?

2. How much of my car's lifespan did I consume?

3. How much of my grill's lifespan did I consume?

4. What could I have purchased, or where could I have invested the money that was wasted?

5. Where could I have spent the wasted time in a productive manner (family, hobby, sports, etc.)?

This example may seem basic, but it applies, in the same manner, to any industry. Let's look at a manufacturing example.

Pulling, Not Pushing

A useful tool for reducing Overproduction is the concept of "Pull." Historically, most organizations operate using a "Push" system, in which a process produces output at a rate that may or may not correlate with the rate of consumption with the next process down-stream. This means that you are, in essence, pushing inventory down the line. Unfortunately, if the next process down line can't consume your output as quickly as you produce it, you can end up with a glut of inventory. Your production numbers look great, but the inventory management group and the next process are struggling.

SWIMMING PIGS

On my Uncle Larry's pig farm, the animals always had access to fresh water delivered to them via an automated system that maintained a standard water level. This system added water continually as the pigs drank the water. This was a Pull system, matching the production or delivery of water to exactly what the animals consumed. One day, my cousin and I went out to feed the hogs. We found one of the watering systems was malfunctioning.

Instead of filling to the standard level and stopping, it was overflowing. The valve got stuck open and was flooding the pen, providing far more water to the pig than it could consume. This flooding is exactly what happens in your organization when your processes are not connected by a valve (Pull system) that opens and closes based on actual demand triggers. Start with a simple process, but connect the inventory level to the demand using a simple Kanban System (Chapter 21). Work it further and further back into your operations, and then to the supplier. Observe as your inventory turns increase and your inventory costs decrease.

An alternate and more effective method is to "Pull" what you need, when you need it, in the quantity you need. Your consumption acts as a trigger, with the valve opening and closing based on actual demand. A Pull system ties customer demand directly to the production of the product or service, optimizing inventory levels.

Let's look at an example of a machining operator who had an order from the next process downstream for 50 pieces of threaded couplings. He started machining the raw slugs, and the process ran well. He got to the end of the production order and realized that the pallet contained 10 extra raw slugs. The machine operator thought that, since the machine was running well, he would be proactive and run the additional 10 couplings so that when the next order came, they would be ahead of the game. So, he did just that. He ran the extra 10 pieces and then started the next order for a different item. It sounded like a great idea, and the thought process was not necessarily bad, but the decision was made without understanding the big picture and the potential consequences of the action. How could this simple act possibly impact the company? Here are the actual consequences:

1. The operator didn't know that those extra 10 slugs were needed for a different part order being completed tomorrow on another machine. That other customer order was now short 10 pieces, making the customer unhappy. The supply chain team was required to find an alternate source, paying an extraordinary amount for the expedited slugs. The small margin built into the production of the part came nowhere close to covering the extra cost of the alternate parts and expedited shipping. With the added costs now rolled in, the company, in essence, payed its customer to take the parts.

2. The operator took an extra 40 minutes to produce the extra 10 pieces that were not needed yet. The next order in line on the production schedule was expected to be on time from another downstream process in the plant. Since they started 40 minutes late, that process was delayed 40 minutes, leaving both people and equipment waiting. The actual completed order to the customer was supposed to ship that evening, but was too late and didn't ship until the following morning. Plus, the freight company truck that showed up that evening to pick up the parts had to be turned away, and the freight company charged your company a fee for not being ready and wasting their time.

3. The 10 extra pieces had no place to go since there were currently no orders that required them. The fork truck drivers had to take the time to find an empty pallet as well as open space on the floor or shelf back in the warehouse. Someone had to also prepare an inventory tag for the pallet and enter the 10 extra pieces in the system.

4. The original order of 50 pieces was actually the last order that was to be placed by the customer under that specific revision level. The 10 extra pieces produced were not needed, and never would be, because they were an old revision level and

177

now classified as obsolete. The 10 extra parts still sit in the back of the warehouse, consuming a pallet and valuable storage space. They will consume time every year when the supply chain team does their annual full-scale inventory, as well as someone's time at some point to write up the obsolescence form to remove them from inventory. They will also require fork truck driver time to move them to the dock.

5. The 10 extra pieces produced were not considered a priority at the moment, as the fork truck drivers had four other people calling for them on the radio. Instead of actually finding an open spot in the warehouse, they simply looked for the first open floor space they could find and moved on, with every intention of coming back and taking care of them later. Over the next 2 weeks, the pallet of 10 parts was picked up, moved out of the way, and pushed over and around nearly 50 times, only to finally be lost somewhere. When asked, everyone remembers seeing the parts, but nobody can find them. They have become the latest victim of the great inventory abyss.

6. We produced 60 pieces instead of 50. We were confident in the quality of the product produced and performed dimensional checks at the required intervals. Unfortunately, when the products got downstream to the next process, they found a defect in the threads, which made them unusable. The quality team isolated the original 50, but had difficulty locating the additional 10 that were floating around the factory warehouse somewhere. The additional 10 were not actually in the inventory system yet, so they were missed. Three weeks later, and now accounted for in inventory under the wrong revision number, the parts were pulled for production only to immediately get caught by the downstream process and shut the work-center down again while a full part inventory inspection event was initiated. The customer order was delayed, and the events in scenario #2 above played out again like a rerun of a bad movie.

7. The machine was on a very rigid PM (Preventive Maintenance) schedule. Because the extra 10 parts were run, the PM schedule is due sooner than anticipated, taking the equipment offline and delaying every customer order that was in line to run on that machine. The tooling and consumable cutting bits used to produce the extra 10 pieces were worn faster, requiring the purchasing and materials group to purchase tooling sooner than expected, impacting the forecasted budget and bottom line.

8. Since these 10 parts were obsolete, every dollar associated with the production, handling, processing, and disposition was a 100% loss.

All of this resulted from a single waste event – Overproduction! Overproduction has the same effect as the illustration in Figure 13:1. Producing more inventory than your process is designed to effectively utilize simply makes a mess, requiring valuable resources to clean up.

FIGURE 13:1

Overproduction is a hard one for a lot of people to wrap their heads around, as it seems intuitive to produce more in a single run and reduce changeovers. It goes back to producing JIT (Just-In-Time), or at least as close to it as you can get. Every one of the scenarios above is legitimate and may play out over and over again in your daily operations. By looking at the multiple potential impacts of Overproduction, we can see a more realistic and all-encompassing picture of where it leads us. Can you see any of these impacts in your operations now that we have dug a little deeper?

A Paradigm Shift

In all honesty, though, it is sometimes a very difficult decision to only produce what is currently needed. Changeovers are not a value-add activity, so delaying them to run just a few more remaining pieces only seems to make sense. Unfortunately, this thinking leads to a facility and warehouse filled with pallets of partial order quantities that do not correspond to firm demand. Looking to avoid the changeover as long as possible is the opposite of an efficient and Lean operation.

Customers send us orders for discrete quantities, so why produce more than what they want or need? Instead of avoiding or delaying the changeovers, why not improve the changeover process itself in order to minimize its impact. A Lean tool developed by the Japanese engineer Shigeo Shingo called SMED (Single Minute Exchange of Dies) works to optimize the changeover itself. Since the changeover activity itself produces no value and consumes valuable capacity, reducing the time required to complete it improves the value to non-value ratio of the process. Part of the SMED process is to make as many of the required changeover steps as possible External to the process, meaning that they can be accomplished while the process or equipment is still running.

In a stamping facility, the stamping dies are positioned on what is called a bolster. The dies are secured to the bolsters and then rolled into the stamping press. Years ago, a stamping press had one set of bolsters, meaning that when a job was finished, the bolsters would be rolled out, the tooling removed, the dies removed, new dies placed on the bolsters, the new tooling installed, and the bolsters rolled back into the die. This took a lot of time and consumed an enormous amount of capacity.

> **"Overproduction is used to hide production defect rates, compensate for a lack of confidence in future production schedules, hide ineffective inventory management methods, and, in some cases, mask inefficient raw material purchasing practices."**

Nowadays, a stamping press has two sets of bolsters. While the press that's running uses one set of bolsters, the second set of bolsters is staged with the dies for the next job. The tooling is installed, the blanks are staged, and the program is loaded into the computer. Once the current job finishes, the bolsters in the press roll out, the bolsters with the new dies roll in, a few adjustments are made, and the press starts running. All of the preparation of the next job is External, meaning it can be accomplished while the press is running. This saves time and enables companies to utilize the capacity that had previously been lost.

As the name implies, SMED was originally designed and utilized in a manufacturing stamping facility as described above, but the theory applies to any process, including hospital operating room turnover, oil changes, welding jig changes, and product line transitions. The theory is simple, but true. If you reduce the changeover time drastically enough, it becomes so insignificant that running JIT quantities becomes more feasible and appealing. Talk with anyone who has effectively designed and implemented SMED in their processes, and they will validate the enormous value.

Overproduction is one of the most common, devastating, and easiest wastes to generate. It is used to hide production defect rates, compensate for a lack of confidence in future production schedules, hide ineffective inventory management methods, and, in some cases, mask inefficient raw material purchasing practices. It results in inventory management nightmares, enormous write-offs, confusion with engineering change levels, space shortages, container/pallet shortages, and so on. It is not an easy waste to hide, as quite often you literally trip over it in your operations.

WHAT'S IN IT FOR ME?

Eliminating the Overproduction Waste in your processes is not easy. This waste may have become part of how your organization operates, baking in an extra 5 to 10% in every run just to compensate for process inefficiency and deficiencies. Your Overproduction may have become an operational insurance policy to protect you from your own internal processes. The last time I checked, insurance wasn't cheap, and neither is the cost associated with this waste. Isn't this similar to always running the dishwasher twice simply because you aren't confident that the dishes will get clean the first time? Gaining confidence in your processes will eliminate the fear that drives your Overproduction.

Now, it would be foolish of me to tell you to start running JIT quantities tomorrow, as you would most certainly jeopardize your entire operation. Getting to the point where you effectively run a "Pull" system takes time. You have to fix problems, address foundational issues and old habits, stabilize the value stream, and become ready to understand your current status at all times. You must be listening to the heartbeat of your operation in real time, ready to react and address issues immediately. It's like a heart monitor on a Telemetry unit in the hospital where a live person monitors the vital signs of multiple people, 24 hours a day.

To tackle this waste, you will have to slowly drain out the water of Overproduction from your processes. Instead of running at extra 10%, only run 6%. When you do this, you will either realize that your previous practice of overproducing was not justified, or you will see problems surface that can now be addressed. As you identify and address these problems, you can continue to slowly drain the water of Overproduction. Eventually you will reach the point where the quantity of product you are producing matches your firm orders or that which is being consumed by your downstream processes.

Once your quantities are in line with your actual demand, you can begin to draw your production dates closer to the required ship dates. When this happens, you are storing less finished goods. You are purchasing raw material closer to actual production dates. Your transportation coordination becomes easier to manage. Overtime and emergency runs are decreased. You also become more flexible, able to quickly accommodate customer requests and needs. Flexibility in your schedule is attractive to customers, as this flexibility allows them to become more flexible with their customers' demand needs. Achieving JIT production, or as close as you can get to it, is a win-win for you, your suppliers, and your customers.

As stated at least 20 times already in this book so far, reducing waste starts with understanding your processes, identifying your problems and inefficiencies, and then correcting them. Using SMED, Process Mapping, Time Studies, and Value/Non-Value Analysis will enable you to get to the point where you produce what your customer wants, in the quaintly they want, and in the timing that they require. The process improvements you drive by eliminating Overproduction Waste will send a tsunami of savings and efficiency through your organization that will impact every department and employee.

Applicable Tools (Chapter 21):

SMED

Visual Management System

Kanban System/JIT

Value Stream Mapping

5S

CHAPTER 14:
WASTE #3 – TOO MUCH INVENTORY

Too Much Inventory is only one of the unfortunate wastes that result from Overproduction. Too Much Inventory may also be a result of excess purchasing or poor demand planning. Many people struggle with this waste because it sounds so much like the previous waste of Overproduction. They are not the same but can certainly be related.

So, what's the big deal with Too Much Inventory? It's not like you won't use or sell it, right? The answer to that question is a resounding "No."

> **"If you don't manage your inventory, your inventory *will* manage you!"**

Over the last 20 years, we have heard a lot about the use of JIT, Kanban, Heijunka, and other types of inventory systems intended to minimize the need for enormous amounts of inventory and safety stock. There is good reason for this, as holding excessive inventory levels creates multiple burdens on a company, many of which are not commonly recognized. It may actually seem like common sense to only hold enough inventory to support your current needs, but there are many reasons why this common sense approach becomes difficult to make a reality in operations. Some of these reasons may include fear of the unknown, a lack of confidence in operational effectiveness, inconsistency of customer firm orders, minimal confidence in supplier order accuracy, overall supply chain reliability, and maybe the occasional opportunity to take advantage of a material cost savings.

The Deal of the Century

So, if we applied the same inventory principle above in our personal lives, what would it look like? For example, one day you are doing your normal weekly shopping at the local grocery store. You make your way through the produce section, pick up some lunch meat and hot dogs for the picnic with the family this weekend, grab some mayonnaise, mustard, and ketchup, and end up in the bread aisle. Hot dog buns are always a moment for pause since you can't ever remember if you got the good hot dogs or the inexpensive ones that only fill up half of the bun. You figure it out and move down the aisle to bread. Oh, my gosh! Your favorite bread is on sale for an unbelievable price of $.79 per loaf. This is an 80% savings. The dollar signs are flashing in your eyes as you start calculating the financial impact of this savings opportunity. Caught up in an emotionally charged "whole wheat-induced" shopping utopia, you fill two carts with 40 loaves of bread. At this price, you will figure out where to put them when you get home.

You get home and immediately tell your family and text your best friend about the extraordinary events of the day. As the adrenaline rush slowly subsides, the reality of purchasing 40 loaves of bread sets in, and you start trying to figure out where you are going to put all of them. You stick some in the freezer side of the refrigerator, some in the chest freezer in the garage, a couple in the cabinet above the stove, a few in the pantry, and several in your neighbor's freezer. That went well, and now you only have 20 more loaves to find a home for.

As it turns out, you really have no good location for the remaining 20 loaves, and, since you must get the kids to their soccer games, you leave them on the shelf in the garage and head out with the minivan filled with a small army of soccer players. The games run late into the night, and, by the time you get home, you have forgotten about the bread on the shelf in the garage. The next day, one of the kids needs something from the shelf in the garage where you temporarily placed the bread, so it inadvertently gets pushed back out of sight – out of sight and out of mind. The next week, you remember the bread in the garage, but, when you go to get it, you find that part of it has fallen prey to mice, and that every loaf now has colorful turquoise mold growing on the tops.

Ok, well that didn't go as planned, but you still saved a lot of money with the other 20 loaves. Several weeks later, you make your way to your neighbor's house to get the bread they graciously agreed to store in their garage freezer. Unfortunately, last Saturday, their son had all 30 members of his wrestling team over, resulting in a regional shortage of peanut butter, jelly, and lunch meat. An unanticipated victim of this sports-induced feeding frenzy were your five loaves of bread, as the guys did not realize that they were yours and technically not part of their food chain.

An additional several weeks down the line, you go to your chest freezer in the garage to retrieve some bread. Unfortunately, someone between the age of 10 and 20 who lives in your home has been rooting through the freezer searching for late night snacks and accidentally moved the frozen turkey on top of the bread, resulting in a transformation from loaves of bread to layers of pizza crust.

When it is all said and done, you calculate it out and realize that you were only able to consume 10 loaves of the bread. You do the math: 40 loaves x $.79 = $31.60 paid for the bread. You only consumed 10 loaves, though, so you actually wasted 30, or $23.70. Wait though, because at the regular price of $3 per loaf, if you had purchased 10 to match what you actually consumed, you would have spent $30, so technically you only lost $1.60 ($31.60 - $30). Ok, so not such a big deal, right?

This is where we fail to understand the other wastes that we produced as a result of Too Much Inventory. Let's list some that come to mind.

1. We wasted the time trying to find storage places for all the bread.

2. We wasted the space in our chest freezer and our neighbor's freezer.

3. We wasted the extra electricity consumed while keeping the bread refrigerated, as well as our neighbor's electricity.

4. We wasted the time it took us to go to our neighbor's home two different times to take and retrieve the bread.

5. We created wasted time and motion for everyone who had to work around the mountain of bread everywhere.

6. We wasted the required space in the trash container and landfill to house the bread that we were forced to throw away.

7. We wasted the time in the checkout line to scan and bag the bread we never consumed.

8. We wasted the time it took to stow the seats in the minivan so we had enough space to load the bread.

9. We wasted our time making six trips to unload the minivan when we arrived home.

10. We wasted the $1.60 that, as we identified in the previous paragraph, we would have saved if we had just bought bread at the regular price.

11. In reality, we did actually waste the $.79 per loaf for the 30 loaves we did not consume. If we had simply purchased only 10 loafs at $.79, for a total of $7.90, we would still have $23.70 in our pocket to spend on other necessities.

12. With the expanded food source in the first week, the mouse population exploded, and we now have to hire an exterminator to come out monthly and address the rodent issue. (It could happen!)

This example may seem far reaching, but it does not differ from daily occurrences that take place at hundreds of manufacturers every day.

A Steel Steal

John works at a fabrication company, in the purchasing department. He receives an urgent call from an approved steel mill, stating that they suddenly have a large amount of material available at 50% of the normal price, due to an order cancellation from another customer.

John's company uses the steel to make metal brackets for a customer.

- The bracket is 20" long and 42" wide and fits on a 4' x 4' pallet.

- The bracket weighs roughly 160 pounds.

- The raw material cost would be $2 per pound at the reduced price vs. $4 per pound at normal price.

- John's company sells approximately 30 pieces to the customer per month.

- Just as a side note, warehouse floor space is valued at $6 per square foot.

What should John do? This is a great opportunity to get a good deal on raw material and increase the contribution margin on the bracket. John decides to buy 100,000 pounds of the material. The concept is valid, but, is it a good business decision? Let's evaluate the logic and eventual outcomes.

1. John purchases 100,000 pounds of the discounted material for $200,000.

2. John cuts 625 pieces of the bracket and puts them in storage.

So, what's the problem? Keep in mind that we are not talking about the waste of Over-production, but only about the waste of Too Much Inventory. Let's review what takes place over the next several months.

1. The cell that produces this part is tied up for 3 straight days on this part, so every job behind it will be pushed out 3 days as well.

2. Over the same 3-day period, the company pays 6 machinists, 3 fork truck drivers, 3 quality techs, and 3 production supervisors overtime totaling $3,200 to produce the extra brackets.

3. The company is utilizing 5000 square feet of storage space to store the extra material (5,000 sq. ft. x $6.00 per sq. ft. = $30,000 of wasted space). Yes, this is an exaggerated amount, but what could the company potentially be using that space for that would actually produce value?

4. The warehouse needs 500 more pallets/stacking boards ($8 each = $4,500) to store the extra parts.

5. The company desperately needs to upgrade a couple pieces of equipment in the machine center, but the $50,000 needed is being used to purchase the extra material to make the brackets. It is hard for some people to grasp this concept, but just because you have "Inc." or "Corp." after your company name does not mean that you have a bottomless bank account.

6. Without these equipment upgrades, the machine center will experience more equipment failures and downtime, and will potentially produce more defective parts.

7. The fork truck drivers now have to work around these 500 extra pallets of parts in order to get to the parts and materials for current orders.

8. This summer has been extraordinarily humid, and rust is forming on some of the parts, requiring the team to purchase and apply additional costly long-term rust preventative chemicals.

9. There is now 21 months of inventory on hand. (625 pieces ÷ 30 sold per month) Six months after producing the parts, the customer sends over notice of an engineering change. It isn't a running change, so this leaves the company with 15 months of obsolete material ($142,000 of wasted material inventory).

As you read the example, I don't doubt that you've identified many other wastes that were produced as a result of this single waste event, and, as far fetched as it may seem, there is more reality than fiction involved in this story. Organizations are often comprised of a multitude of individual silos we call departments. If each department does not fully understand how its individual actions impact the organization as a whole, we see these types of errors in decision making.

> **"Inventory is a tool. You can use it to either build an exceptional operation or to smash your organizational thumb."**

We also see situations like this resulting from the fact that different departments may have competing metrics. Purchasing wants to reduce raw material and inventory costs, while production wants to be able to pull ahead and run any order up to 3 weeks out. To add to the confusion, the supply chain group has already committed to the customer to hold a large buffer of finished goods that we can ship on demand. It boils down to bringing the entire organization into alignment, enabling everyone to understand the broader picture and acknowledging the perspective of the other departments.

In the same manner that Godzilla repeatedly decimates Tokyo, Too Much Inventory can literally become a monster, consuming valuable resources and wreaking havoc on your organization. It can interfere with your process' flexibility and your ability respond quickly to customer demand changes. It can trample all over what started out as a fiscally sound month. It can create confusion, leading to errors in inventory control and potential shipping mistakes. Over the last couple of decades, effectively managing both raw material and finished inventory has become a priority for many companies that have appropriately realized that there are enormous benefits in becoming good at this. As someone said years ago, "If you don't manage your inventory, your inventory will manage you." This statement is true in so many ways, as many companies have failed to realize until it was too late.

If you doubt the validity of my statements, just look at someone's face when you mention the words "annual inventory." These simple words cause most people to drop their heads, roll their eyes, sigh in despair, and immediately attempt to schedule a vacation in anticipation of the event. Why? Because for most companies, this activity is painful, time consuming, frustrating, an interruption to the weekend plans of their employees, and overall a perceived total waste of time. Once completed, everyone anxiously waits in anticipation for the bomb to drop and to hear how big the write-off was this year. Great companies still perform periodic inventories, but their process is less painful because they actively manage their inventory instead of letting their inventory mange them.

THE INVENTORY VENDING MACHINE

I have a weakness for Snickers – I admit it. Whenever we are at a hotel, wrestling tournament for my son, on the road traveling, or really anytime, I often find myself holding a Snickers. Within a year's time, I probably consume 30 of them. Fortunately for me, I don't have to buy and transport all 30 around for the entire year; I simply take advantage of the nearest vending machine. The vending machine allows me to match my current need (demand) with the optimal inventory level (1 Snickers). I am also conserving capital for other purposes, as I am only buying what I currently need. If you were to manage your inventory levels the same way, what would your warehouse look like, and how would that impact the overall cost structure of your operations? Would labor, obsolescence, space utilization, material movement costs, and quality all see a positive impact? I believe they would.

As mentioned in Chapter 13, a useful tool for optimizing inventory levels is the concept of Pull. Historically, most organization operate using a Push system, in which a process produces output at a rate that may or may not correlate with the rate of consumption of the next process downstream. This means that you are, in essence, pushing inventory down the line. Unfortunately, if the next process down the line can't consume your output as quickly as you produce it, you can end up with a glut of inventory. Your production numbers look great, but the inventory management group and the next process are struggling. An alternate and more effective method is to Pull what you need, when you need it, in the quantity you need. Your consumption acts as a trigger, with the valve opening and closing based on actual demand. A Pull system ties customer demand directly to the production of the product or service, optimizing inventory levels. You can use a Pull system Internally, or you can use it as part of an inventory management system with your suppliers and vendors.

Next time you go out for fast food and grab a burger, taco, or sub sandwich, consider the humble straw as you drink your beverage. The straw is a perfect example of a Pull system. As you draw liquid through the straw, additional liquid is pulled into the straw from the cup. When you have consumed enough liquid and remove the straw from your mouth, the liquid in the straw doesn't continue flowing out, splashing you with diet soda; it retreats back into the cup until you demand more. On the other hand, try the same thing with your garden hose. If you put the end of the garden hose in your mouth and turn the faucet on, your demand has nothing to do with how much is delivered. Even after the water starts pouring out of your nose and you stand there choking, the water still runs out of the hose. The garden hose is a perfect example of a Push system, delivering product at a rate that does not coincide with the rate of demand.

Inventory Is a Tool

In a hospital operating room, space is extremely valuable. An operating room needs to have the appropriate standard supplies to support different scheduled procedures. In one hospital, I helped a team complete a formal 5S activity to optimize the flow, layout, and inventory levels for six different rooms. Five of the operating rooms were general procedure rooms and were supposed to be identical in setup, inventory, and equipment layout. This was not the case, and the word "standardized" was not the first thing that came to mind when I reviewed each of them.

One specific situation stood out above all the others. Cabinets in the OR were supposedly restocked on a daily basis. As we started our inventory of current items, we came across an entire shelf filled with anesthesia masks – literally 64 of them. The amount of space they took up was enormous, and, in fact, the shelf was so full that the masks would fall out onto the floor when you opened the cabinet door. I asked a logical question: "How many of these do we use per day on average?" The answer was four to six. This means that the number of anesthesia masks contained in that OR could support upwards of 16 days of procedures. I asked another simple question: "Are there any items kept outside of the OR that we would like to be able to store in the room?" The answer was a resounding and excited "Yes!"

You get where I am going here don't you? Each of the five rooms was stocked with the same abundance of anesthesia masks. This meant that the staff were forced to exit the OR during procedures to obtain other items stored outside the room (surgeons don't like this), instead of using the available space effectively, thus avoiding the wasted travel, waiting, risk to patients, and unhappy surgeons. In addition to the wasted space resulting from this example of Too Much Inventory, the OR had spent a large amount of money on inventory that would not be used for months. The OR had, in essence, purchased "40 loaves of bread!"

As we continued completing the inventory, we found example after example of items that had expired or were no longer used. It was not a pleasant discussion to have with leadership after we finalized the dollar amount of expired and obsolete materials, but it was expected. The reality of the situation provided justification for establishing inventory practices that promoted minimal inventories that supported current needs.

Supply chain management has become a huge priority for most companies. A lot of companies have also pushed the management of inventory to their suppliers, requiring them to hold the inventory at their facility, or to coordinate through third party warehouses. Suppliers are provided with firm and soft production schedules that can stretch for months or even years. Many inventory management systems exist – whether you subscribe to the use of JIT, Kanban, Heijunka, or third-party contractors, the key is that you are effectively managing your inventory.

Chances are your company exists to provide customers with a service or product, not to hold inventory. So why hold more of it than necessary? Like a piece of equipment or any other resource, inventory is a tool. You can choose to use it effectively and design an exceptionally efficient operation, or you can feed it until it becomes bloated and unmanageable, weighing you down, building up and clogging your processes like plaque in your arteries, and eventually leading to an "operational heart attack."

WHAT'S IN IT FOR ME?

Too Much Inventory affects almost every part of your operations. What is your inventory turns target? Are you meeting your goal?

If the answer is yes, then good for you. I could stop there, but since I am on the subject, I will ask anyway. If you are meeting your inventory turns target, when was the last time you evaluated it? When was the last time you set a new target? Is the current target what we in operations call "easy"? If so, how much money, space, time, effort, and capacity is "easy" costing you? Should you increase your inventory turns target? That's up to you, but, by increasing your inventory turns, you will quickly understand your risks and weaknesses, requiring you to eliminate waste and fix problems.

If you are up for a challenge, increase your inventory turns target. Sharpen the edge of your "operational sword" by slowly decreasing the inventory water level.

If you are not meeting the inventory turns target, then why not? Is it because you don't have confidence in your production process? What do you need to fix in your production operations that will give you this confidence? Use a Value Stream Map (Chapter 21) to identify where the opportunities are, and then fix them.

Are you not meeting your inventory turns target because you have no confidence in your customer's firm schedule, so you overcompensate? If so, when was the last time you sat down with the customer and provided honest feedback regarding their demand volatility. Complete a detailed Material and Information Flow to demonstrate the impact on your operations. Many times, customers don't understand the impact their demand volatility and knee-jerk decisions have on suppliers, or at least the extent of the impact. Collaborate with them, building a relationship where everyone benefits. Help them complete a Value Stream Map for their process if that's what it takes.

Do you consistently miss inventory turn targets because you batch your orders instead of running JIT? Does this happen because you believe that avoiding changeovers is a benefit? If reducing your inventory levels opened up a large enough footprint to install an additional production cell, what additional value could you produce? Use the SMED method to identify Internal and External steps, and then reduce the changeover to the optimal time. Reduce the impact changeovers have on your operation by reducing the time to changeover. Don't reduce your changeovers by increasing your inventory. This would be like towing a 500-gallon external gas tank behind your car. Sure, you need to stop less often to fill up, but what did it cost you in speed and fuel economy?

Applicable Tools (Chapter 21):

Kaizen/Kaizen Event

Kanban System

Visual Management System

SMED/Quick Changeover Analysis

Value Stream Mapping

5S

CHAPTER 15:
WASTE #4 – EXCESS MOTION

If you are anything like me, your typing skills would be considered by most to be less than proficient. I spend 10% of my time watching my screen and 90% of my time watching each individual finger find the next key in the sequence as my brain spits them out. Now, because my spelling skills are as poorly developed as my typing skills, writing this book was a monumental task. I usually have multiple edits to make in each paragraph, so what you are reading here is the perfect example of Excess Motion. As I finished this paragraph, I looked up and found three errors that I needed to correct – one punctuation and two spelling. This may not seem like a big deal, but considering that this book is roughly 360 pages long and contains roughly 120,000 words, the Excess Motion of scrolling back through each paragraph multiple times added up very quickly.

It's Everywhere

Excess Motion is like every other waste in that it can stand on its own, or, in a lot of cases, be a direct result of other wastes. Either way, it is prevalent in both your personal and professional environments. Identifying Excess Motion Waste requires you to understand a process, inch by inch and foot by foot. I mean this in the literal sense. If you want to know where the Excess Motion is for an employee within a process, you will have to measure and map out the entire process. One very useful tool is the Spaghetti Map. It is called a Spaghetti Map because it is normally completed in red ink and, once completed, usually resembles a giant plate of spaghetti with lines going back and forth, crossing over each other repeatedly, and winding around and around. See Chapter 21 for details on how to create and utilize a Spaghetti Map effectively.

A Not-So-Sharp Process

There are several acres on our property that my son, Jordan, and I mow. We use a Zero-Turn Grasshopper riding mower, which allows us to complete the job in a time-ly manner. Having several acres to mow means that sharpening the three blades on the 60-inch mower deck is almost a bi-monthly requirement. The job itself isn't a lot of fun – raising the deck, laying on the ground, and then reaching up inside the mower while trying to contort yourself in a manner that allows both arms to reach under the deck. The blades seem to over-tighten themselves between sharpenings, so getting enough leverage to allow the socket wrench to be effective is sometimes a challenge. Regardless, the task must be completed, or the grass gets hacked instead of cut, resulting in the mower getting bogged down in thicker or higher areas of the yard.

Recently, my son and I were in the barn preparing for the weekly mowing and noted that it had been several weeks since the blades had been sharpened. So, I started up the Grasshopper, raised the deck, and positioned the ramps in front of the wheels. I drove it up on the ramps, set the parking brake, and jumped off. I got down on the ground to look underneath the deck and scrape off any grass that had accumulated. Once that step was complete, I got up and went to the corner of the barn where I keep the toolbox.

To my surprise, it was not where it was supposed to be. I asked my son if he had seen it, but he had not. We looked everywhere in the barn and in the back of our Polaris Rang-er. No luck. It then crossed my mind that I had just changed the spark plugs in one of our cars. This meant that I had probably left the toolbox in the garage up at the house. So, we started walking down the lane toward the house and, to nobody's surprise, it was located on the far shelf in the garage, right where I had left it. Understanding the value of build-ing my son's physical endurance prior to wrestling season, I made him carry it back to the barn. Once back at the barn, we removed and sharpened the blades and went about our business mowing the yard.

Now, this may not seem like a great example, but remember when I said that waste is just as prevalent in our personal lives as in our professional lives? This is a perfect ex-ample. It may seem insignificant, but this waste event cost my son and me approximately 30 minutes. That 30 minutes added zero value and interfered with our ability to do other things later that day.

Motion Takes Time

I work in hospitals where this Excess Motion seems to be embedded into almost every process, invisible to the people who perform the clinical tasks all day. For example, when patients walk into a hospital Emergency Department, they go through the registration and triage process, many times ending up in an observation room where the provider will order specific tests. The RN will take blood samples for the lab to run any array of tests, depending on the nature of the patient's condition. The samples are sent from the ED to the lab through a tube system that runs throughout the entire hospital. It is similar to what you probably use at your local bank, but it is much more intricate and complicated.

In one hospital's ED, the tube system was located at the furthest point in the ED from where the samples were taken. This meant that the RN's had to walk a long distance every time they needed to send any sample to the lab. Again, this may not sound like a big deal, and you may see it as part of the routine process. This is where the problem lies – nobody in the ED saw it as a problem either. This was how it was always done, and nobody ever questioned it or gave it a second thought. Here is where the reality of the situation sets in. Look at the information below, and you will see that this Excess Motion, which is invisible to us, is another example of consuming resources for no value.

FIGURE 15:1

120	Avg. Distance to Tube System (feet)
240	Round Trip Distance (feet)
90	Trips per Day Average
21600	Total Distance Traveled Per Day (feet)
4.09	Distance per Day in Miles
3.1 mph	Avg. Human Walking Speed
1.32	Hours Per Day Spent Walking to Tube System
481.67	Hours per Year Walking to Tube System
60.21	Shifts Per Year Walking to Tube System

Let's review the numbers contained in Figure 15:1. The average distance an RN or tech walked to the tube system was 120 feet one way, so a round trip was 240 feet. Based on patient volumes, the average number of trips the ED team took per day was 90. The total combined distance the team walked per day on average was 90 x 240 feet, or 21,600 feet. That 21,600 feet equated to 4.09 miles walked daily to the tube system. On average, humans walk at a speed of 3.1 miles per hour, so 4.09 miles walked per day divided by 3.1 mph equals 1.32 hours a day dedicated to walking to the tube system. A hospital doesn't shut down for holidays and weekends, so with 365 days in a year, the total hours consumed to walk to the tube system was 481 per year, or an astounding 60 shifts.

195

"Motion takes time, and time *is* capacity."

Some readers may be quick to point out that, from a cost-of-employment standpoint, 60 shifts would be a fairly insignificant dollar amount for a hospital. This train of thought is why I'm writing this book. This kind of thinking misses the point – we used 60 shifts to walk, instead of adding value. What do you hire a nurse and tech to do? We consumed 60 shifts (time is a resource) walking around. Instead of treating patients, administering tests, communicating with providers, updating charts, and discharging or admitting patients, which is how a hospital provides value, we walked back and forth to the tube system. If there was value in walking, then someone would have already filled up the hospital with treadmills.

From a financial standpoint, how did these 60 shifts add value? Assuming an ED nurse makes an average salary of $60,000, we can break that down into an hourly rate of $28.84 ($60,000 ÷ 2,080 hours per year). So, at $28.84 per hour, 60 8-hour shifts gives us $28.84 x 480 hours, or $13,843.20. This doesn't sound like an enormous amount in the big picture, but you would be wrong to think that. The $13,843.20 isn't the real cost; it is only the tip of the iceberg. The true cost is realized in the patient lives the hospital didn't impact, the damage to the hospital's reputation when frustrated patients got up and walked out of the ED, the overtime paid to compensate for the wasteful process, the revenue that was not realized during the 60 shifts, and the many other opportunity costs that can never effectively be calculated.

FIGURE 15:2

Travel Distance in Feet	Travel Time			Hour Savings Per Year	Shift Savings Per Year
	Seconds	Minutes	Hours		
100	32.258	0.538	0.009	1.971	0.246
500	161.290	2.688	0.045	9.857	1.232
1000	322.581	5.376	0.090	19.713	2.464
2000	645.161	10.753	0.179	39.427	4.928
3000	967.742	16.129	0.269	59.140	7.392
4000	1290.323	21.505	0.358	78.853	9.857
5000	1612.903	26.882	0.448	98.566	12.321
10000	3225.806	53.763	0.896	197.133	24.642

Stop thinking about these numbers as time. Start thinking about them as CAPACITY! Every foot of wasted motion you eliminate is realized through additional time and capacity!

Look at Figure 15:2. This chart shows what happens when you reduce Excess Motion. It is broken down into distances in the far left column. For example, if you reduce daily Excess Motion for a single employee by 1,000 feet, you gain 5.37 minutes or .090 hours of capacity per day. That equates to 19.7 hours or 2.46 shifts per year. If you could magically stop time, what could you and your team accomplish with the free gift of an extra 19.7 hours? Assuming you have 100 employees, that 1,000 feet per day equates to 1,971 hours or 246 shifts per year. If you have 1,000, 10,000, or 100,000 employees, think about the potential!

Here is where many leaders miss the mark. Motion takes time, and time is capacity. Time is what we use to create value. We can have all the equipment, inventory, and resources in the world at our disposal, but, without time to manipulate those resources and transform them into a useful product or service, they are meaningless. When we use our time effectively, we increase our capacity and ability to add value.

Value-Based Decisions

I worked with a company in an office environment, and one situation still gives me a mild twitch when I think about it. As technology has improved, copiers have evolved from prehistoric plastic beasts that took up an entire wall to a more compact and powerful piece of equipment. In this particular manufacturing office, the old school bus-sized copier had arrived at the point where it was struggling to stay operational and was not capable of providing the services that the office of roughly 30 people needed. The old and obsolete model did still work, though, so the office leadership decided to keep it for large jobs so that the new "race car model" copier would not get tied up, causing delays in everyone's daily tasks.

The copiers were positioned in the back corner of the office, instead of centralized in the middle of the office team. Here is where my twitch starts to return. Instead of moving the old copier to the open space along the back wall of the copier room, the leadership decided to place the new copier there. After all, it would have been a big job to relocate the old copier. The new copier was located roughly 16 feet past the old copier, meaning that everyone had to walk past the old copier to get to the new copier. My gosh, we are just talking about 16 feet, right? Wrong! That 16 feet is one way, so that means that every time employees needed to make a copy, send a scanned document, fax something, or retrieve a document they printed, they walked an extra 32 feet (16 feet each way).

An average person walks at a speed of 3.1 feet per second, so these 32 feet added 10 seconds to every trip that each employee made to the new copier. Observing this for several days while working in the office, and after some discussion and investigation, I concluded that, on average, every employee went to that copier 12 times per day. It was a very busy copier. Twelve trips per day for 30 employees equaled 360 trips per day total for the team. Those 360 trips per day total, at 10 seconds per trip, turned into 3,600 seconds, or 1 hour.

Considering the average year contains 220 working days, this office team was consuming 220 hours of capacity and productivity per year (220 x 1 hour) to walk an extra 16 feet. This 220 hours equaled 27.5 shifts per year (220 ÷ 8 hours). The team was using 27.5 shifts of their capacity simply walking to the new copier, based on a decision to put it along the back wall, instead of just moving the old copier and putting the new copier at the entrance of the area. I cannot recall ever hiring someone and specifically reviewing their qualifications for walking to a copier as one of their value-add duties. In this example, the company made a wasteful and short-sighted decision, decreasing the valued output percentage of every person in that office.

If the average person in the office was paid $48,000 per year, if a shift is defined as 8 hours, and if the average person works 2,080 hours per year, this 27.5 shifts equates to $5,076.92 in negative financial impact per year, or $25,384.61 over the 5-year depreciated life of the copier. But remember, it's only an extra 16 feet, right? Truthfully though, the real cost of this Excess Motion may have never been understood and was hidden in the impact it had on the ability of the teams to complete their daily tasks in an already packed day. This directly impacted the customers who didn't get a call back in a timely manner, the vendors who were not called back quickly enough to avoid a part shortage, and the many hours of overtime worked to cover these 27.5 shifts of lost productivity. Reducing Excess Motion applies just as much in an office as it does in a manufacturing site.

Making Motion Productive

Look at Figure 15:3. Motion does not have to be measured in steps; it can also simply be measured in distance, such as the distance an employee has to reach for something. This is an example from a manufacturing environment where I was engaged to optimize both space and motion. A work cell is a station where a person performs a specific task. In this situation, the employee used parts A-H to build an assembly. The parts were assembled sequentially in the order A-H.

In example #1, the employee was reaching back and forth from parts bin to parts bin roughly nine times using both hands. From a motion standpoint, there was a lot of opportunity to promote effective flow. Completing a Kaizen and utilizing the Lean 5S tool, it was pretty easy to improve the process and place the parts into a logical sequence that reduced the overall reaching motion.

In example #2, we had improved the cell layout and flow, sequencing the parts to provide for less reaching. The employee could grab two parts with each reach, reducing the overall reaches to five, four fewer than before. This reduction in motion was realized

FIGURE 15:3

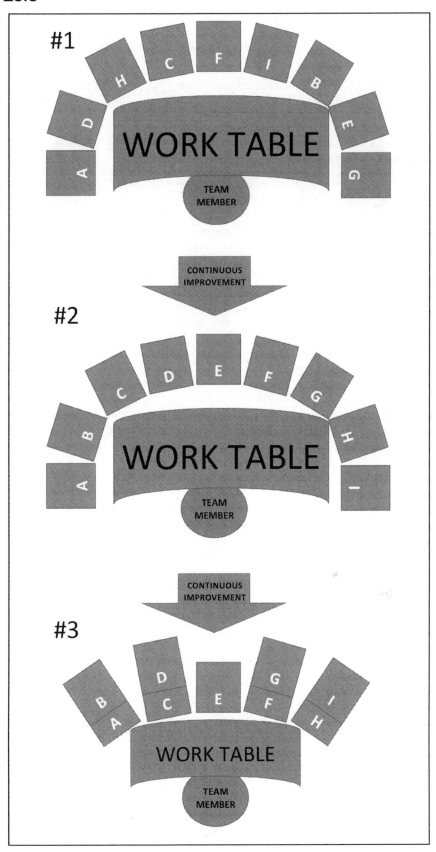

through a reduction in time to assemble the parts. The reduction in cycle time to produce the parts was then translated into an increase in both capacity and productivity.

Remaining true to the Lean and Continuous Improvement mentality, why stop there? In example #3, we made additional improvements. We reduced the reaching distance even more by stacking the parts on top of each other in the appropriate sequence. By stacking the parts and consolidating the bins to a smaller area, we were able to reduce the size of the work table and the overall footprint of the assembly cell. By reducing the size of the cell itself, we reduced the required motion, resulting in decreases in both the assembly time and the physical wear on the team members. Also, as a result of the space reduction of the cell footprint, along with the same change to other cells, we were able to add more assembly cells, allowing for additional capacity.

Excess Motion isn't always measured in distance. You can also measure it by the physical impact it has on your employees. People can literally walk miles per day and not realize it, simply because the miles are comprised of hundreds of small trips here and there. A couple trips to the copier, a trip to the wash room, several trips to the mail room, and a few trips across the building to speak with another department.

Excess Motion is everywhere and remains invisible to most of us. It is there, down at your feet, growing with every step. Through the use of some basic Lean techniques, a lot of this Excess Motion can be eliminated, or at least minimized. Some great tools are 5S, Spaghetti Mapping, and Cardboard Cities. In Chapter 21, I go into more detail on how to effectively use these tools, none of which requires an advanced mathematics degree. They are simple tools that take a common sense approach to maximizing every aspect of performing a task or process.

Just like the old 90's show *X-Files* used to say, "The truth is out there." The same applies to Excess Motion. It's out there. Finding and eliminating it will have a dramatic impact on your processes, employees, capacity, and operations.

WHAT'S IN IT FOR ME?

Honestly, more than you can imagine!

Excess Motion is one of those wastes that we don't readily see. Walking is free, and somewhat effortless. Grabbing something 12 inches away can be done without even thinking about it. It's kind of like breathing. How often do you think about taking a breath? In the same way, how often do you think about walking to the copier, stepping over to the next office, reaching for the stapler, opening the drawer to retrieve a file, or any of the other thousand things you do each day in an almost mechanical way?

Excess Motion is not an accident; it is directly related to how a process was designed.

It is a result of how an office was laid out, how an assembly cell was engineered, or how a patient floor was organized. Most companies are good at understanding equipment and employee capability during a process design stage, but very few take the time to look at motion or seek to minimize it. When this happens, you end up with what we have now, thousands of examples of Excess Motion permeating almost every company in existence.

This text you are reading was formatted to be read from left to right, with minimal space in between the lines. The computer that was used to write this book has a keyboard with letters placed in close proximity to each other. The mouse I used is right next to the keyboard, not 3 feet away. My coaster with my bottle of water is within arm's reach at the left of my monitor. I set up my office to reduce motion, and, chances are, you did too, possibly without directly thinking about it.

While Excess Motion may seem minor, almost insignificant, the resources required to complete the motion are not. As stated early in the chapter, and worth mentioning again, "Motion takes time, and time IS capacity." The less motion any activity requires, the less time it requires to complete. The less time it requires to complete, the more time you have to complete other value-add tasks. The more time you have to complete other tasks, the more capacity you have access to. The more capacity you have access to for providing value to customers, the more satisfied your customer will be. The more satisfied your customers are, the more they will return and share their experience, leading to additional customers. These result in a financially secure organization that stakeholders will continue to invest in.

Use the tools to understand your processes and the motion that is required to complete them. Identify opportunities to reduce motion, and then make it happen. Utilize the ideas that your teams already probably have floating around in their minds.

Applicable Tools (Chapter 21):

Kaizen Event

5S

Kanban System

SMED/Quick Changeover Analysis

Value Stream Mapping

CHAPTER 16:
WASTE #5 – WAITING

Similar to Excess Motion Waste, Waiting Waste translates into lost capacity, minute for minute. A minute of Waiting Waste eliminated is a minute of capacity recovered. Think about the thousands of processes that exist within your organization. How much capacity would you have immediate access to if you were to eliminate even 5 minutes of Waiting Waste from each of them? Every minute within your process that delays or interrupts your progress in producing and delivering a product or service is capacity consumed. Waiting Waste is possibly the biggest offender of all the 8 Wastes, depending on your processes. It hides in plain sight, simply passed over by everyone as a necessary delay while preparing for the next stage of an activity. We blame the location of equipment, lengthy process times, the need for quality checks, unreliable upstream production, and countless other excuses for allowing waste to rest contently within our systems. I had a friend explain Waiting Waste quite accurately: "Waiting is giving value a time-out in the corner."

> ## "One minute of Waiting Waste *eliminated* is one minute of capacity *recovered*."

Waiting is the one waste that everyone seems to clearly understand. It is almost instinctive to despise Waiting. It permeates every part of our life and is one of the wastes that can turn a normally calm and collected person into a raging bull, resulting in lost tempers, rude behavior, and regretted comments. It can cause us to exhibit less than desirable behavior in the presence of our children, coworkers, and employees. Waiting quite often brings out the worst in us.

The perceived value that customers or patients derive from the services or products you offer has a direct, but opposite correlation to the Waiting Waste that exists within your processes. For example, the chart in Figure 16:1 shows the total minutes you have available to deliver value in a typical two-shift operation (16-hour day) – 960 minutes. Every one of those 960 minutes that your customers and patients have to wait is a minute lost in your ability to provide them with value, the ultimate reason they are doing business with you.

FIGURE 16:1

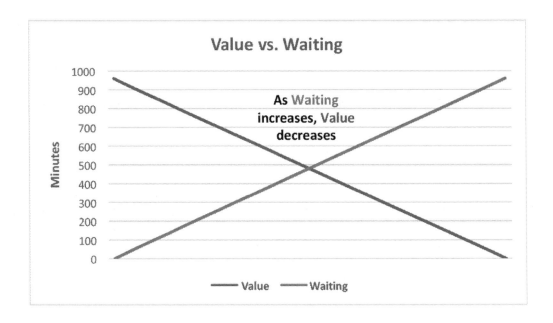

If you don't believe that this inverse relationship exists, ask any hospital if the LWOBS metric (the number of patients who Left Without Being Seen) is a critically important indicator of the Emergency Department's performance. Ask any restaurant if the customer walkout rate is important. Inquire if customer service organizations measure customer hang-ups and average wait times. Survey the local grocery store to see how often frustrated shoppers get tired of waiting in long lines and simply leave their full carts at the service desk and walk out.

When I say Waiting permeates our lives, I would be bold enough to challenge any reader to identify an area of your life where it has not been a factor. Let's run through a few scenarios and see if my claim is supported.

Fast Is a Relative Term

Suppose you and the family are out one weekend heading to a soccer game for one of the kids. You plan to stop by a local fast food restaurant to grab some burgers and fries to eat while relaxing on the sidelines in your folding chairs. You pull up and place your order at the outside drive through menu. You pull around the corner to the cashier window and find yourself behind three other cars. No big deal – it's a fast food restaurant and you are fairly confident in the "fast" part. The first two cars get through quickly, but then you watch as the car directly in front of you pays for their order, receives their bags of food, and then proceeds to return the bags of food a few moments later. Uh oh, something must be wrong with their order. This is not good.

You impatiently wait a few more minutes. The game starts at 11:30 a.m., it's already 11:25 a.m., and you are still at least 3 minutes from the soccer field. Your blood pressure begins to rise, and you start mumbling things under your breath. You subconsciously start referring to the people in front of you in less than complimentary terms. Now your family is getting upset and asking you why it is taking so long, as if you possess some supernatural power to read the minds of the cashier and driver in front of you. Three minutes later it becomes real – you are now officially late for the game. Your child, who normally starts at mid-field defender, will not be there on time for the beginning of the game, and the other team will have an advantage.

Finally, the car in front moves, and you pull up to the window to pay. You provide the exact change to the cashier, hoping for a smooth and quick transfer of cash for food. To your dismay, the cashier asks you to pull forward, as the fries are not up yet, and it will be a couple minutes before they bring them out to you. You pull forward, but then make the executive decision a minute later to drive away without the fries, just to get to the game. Waiting has cost you in several ways, so let's detail them:

1. Gas while your car waited in line.

2. Frustration and irritation for the whole family.

3. The $6 for the French fries you drove away without.

4. A disadvantage in the soccer game – the other team potentially scores before you arrive because your team was one player short.

5. Regret for the things you said while waiting in line that were the opposite of the example you like to set for your kids.

6. The embarrassment of showing up late to the game.

7. The $180 for the speeding ticket you received on the way to the field. (We will simply refer to this unfortunate cost as an expediting fee.)

My suspicion is that you have been in this situation, or at least some semblance. The point is this: we all hate to wait for anything. We hate to wait for the light to turn green. We hate to wait for the commercial to end so the game can come back on. We hate to wait in line at the ball park. We hate to wait at the airport to board the plan. We hate to wait when our flight gets delayed. We hate to wait for the attendant at the convenience store to turn on the pump. We hate to wait for the UPS driver to show up with our package. We hate to wait for the pizza to finish cooking. My point? We simply hate to wait!

> **"When we communicate effectively with customers and patients so that they understand *why* they are waiting longer than expected, they feel important, engaged, valued, and are far more accommodating and forgiving."**

It makes perfect sense that we hate to wait, as there is zero value in Waiting. We would rather be driving to our destination than waiting in traffic. It would be more fun to eat dinner than to wait on the server to take our order. It would be more enjoyable to ride the roller coaster than to wait in line to get on. Speaking of roller coasters, have you ever paid extra for the front-of-line pass at the amusement park? That purchase validates your disdain for Waiting!

A Prescription for Waiting

Unfortunately, you need to look no further than your local healthcare organizations if you want to experience Waiting. You know that when you go to the dentist, dermatologist, podiatrist, the local urgent care clinic, or the local hospital Emergency Department, you will wait. For example, how much value do you derive from sitting in the local Emergency Room waiting room for 45 minutes while holding your head back trying to stop a bloody nose? How much value do you find in sitting between two people who are coughing, sneezing, and making nasal sounds that cause you to want to revisit your last meal? Nobody in the waiting room finds value in their current situation, and the hospital itself is suffering from the long ED waiting room times.

So, how does Waiting, which results from lack of effective flow in an ER waiting room, impact the hospital? It can result in patient LWOBS (Left Without Being Seen) and LWOT (Left Without Treatment). The financial impact to the organization can be devastating, but the often overlooked impact can be just as detrimental. If a patient comes to a hospital ER and registers, only to wait for 60 minutes and then get up and leave to go down the street to another hospital or urgent care facility, the impact can result in ripples that migrate out for months and years in the form of negative perception and patient satisfaction. These happen over the course of time when this potential patient proceeds to tell everyone he meets at the county fair, bowling alley, and Friday night high school basketball game about his experience. The impact of a negative experience shared on social media can be even more devastating and far reaching.

Why would a wait be so long in the ER? Well, there are lots of potential reasons. Contrary to popular belief, most hospitals operate very differently, based on their facility layout and staffing structure. For example, when you (the patient) are registered, you may wait until a triage nurse calls you back, checks your vitals, and finds out what you came in for. Once this is done, there might not be an intake or evaluation room available, so you go back to the waiting room. Once you eventually make it back to the intake or evaluation room, you are informed that the provider will be with you in a few minutes, so again you wait. At some point, the provider, a physician assistant, a nurse practitioner, or a doctor comes in and goes over your vitals and evaluates your condition.

The provider decides to order some additional tests, which he notes in the chart. The provider leaves and takes the chart to his desk, where he enters the orders.

The RN or tech then goes and collects the necessary supplies for your tests. An electronic signal is sent to Radiology if applicable. So, you sit and wait, again. The RN comes back in and administers the ordered blood tests. Once the tests are completed, you are instructed to remain in the room and wait for the test results to come back. So, you wait, and wait, again. Meanwhile, the patients in the ER waiting room continue to wait for an evaluation room to come open, while you sit in one, waiting for tests to come back.

THE PLANE AND THE PEN

It was a late flight from Phoenix to Indianapolis. I could tell that I was not the only one anxious to get home that Friday night. We boarded the plane on time, and everything was going great. Then it happened. The pilot came over the intercom and informed us that the plane, which had been in Phoenix all day after some maintenance the previous evening, was delayed from takeoff and awaiting a maintenance sign-off that should have been completed and submitted earlier that morning. The sounds of groans, sighs, and other less appropriate comments were unmistakable.

There we sat – pilots, flight attendants, passengers, ground crew, and gate attendants, all waiting for a maintenance person to arrive and simply transfer ink from his pen to a piece of paper. In addition, the passengers in the terminal booked on the next flight out of that gate were waiting, as were the passengers on the plane that was waiting to taxi up to the gate we still occupied. The passengers scheduled to board our plane once we arrived in Indianapolis ended up waiting, as well as the family, friends, and colleagues anticipating the arrival of those on my plane. A Waste Explosion for this would have grown to well over 10 levels, impacting thousands of people. How many times have you experienced the same level of impact while a full team of medical staff wait in an OR room for a patient to arrive from Pre-Op, or a stalled assembly line full of people stand around waiting for a truck to deliver parts? How far did the explosion debris travel?

What would happen if, instead of taking up the evaluation room while you waited for your tests, you were sent to an "Awaiting Results" area, allowing that next patient in the ER waiting area to come back and start the process? What would happen if, instead of going to the desk to enter the orders, the PA, NP, or physician entered them in real time, in the room on a tablet while they were talking with you? The real question here is: how can we eliminate as much of the waiting as possible for everyone involved? How can we avoid the provider-to-RN chart hand-off? Could both be in the evaluation room at the same time, with the RN entering the orders into the system while the provider is examining you? Could the lab tests be completed on site in the ED using POC (Point of Care) testing instead of sending samples to the lab on the other side of the hospital or a mile down the street? Nobody in this entire process finds value in the numerous stages dominated by Waiting. The providers, nurses, administration, lab and Radiology teams, and most certainly the patients, are all impacted in a negative manner.

Patients Dressing for Success

Here is a scenario at one hospital I worked with. This opportunity sounds simple, but yielded enormous benefits once we identified it. Here is what we found. As patients were taken back to the ED evaluation rooms, they would wait while the RN or provider finished with other patients. Once the RN or provider did make it to the room, the evaluation was completed, and, if appropriate, an X-ray was ordered. The patient waited in the evaluation room while the order was put into the system. Five to 10 minutes later, the X-ray tech would come and retrieve the patient, taking them to the X-ray room. Once in the X-ray room, the tech would have the patient remove his or her clothes, jewelry, and all piercings from the waste up, and put on a gown. This activity of putting on the gown took roughly 3 to 4 minutes, based on the patient's condition. Elderly patients or those who had difficulty moving sometimes took even longer. The X-ray itself averaged 4 to 5 minutes. Upon completion, the patients would be instructed to remove the gown and put their clothes back on, which again took 3 to 4 minutes. This may not sound like a big deal, but let's break this down to understand how having a patient change clothes in the X-ray room reduced the value that the hospital was able to provide to patients.

- Average time to change into a gown: 3 minutes

- Average time to change from gown back into clothes: 3 minutes

- Average X-ray procedure time: 5 minutes

- X-ray hours of operation: 6 a.m. to 10 p.m.: 16 Hours (960 minutes)

- X-ray procedure capacity: 87 procedures (960 minutes ÷ 11 minutes)

Now let's look at the change we made. When a patient was brought back to the evaluation room, he or she was instructed to put on a gown immediately, even before we knew what tests were required. This proactive process benefited the provider during the examination, the RN and lab tech during blood draws or IV administration, and then most certainly the Radiology group. Now, when Radiology came and brought the patient back to have an X-ray, the only activity taking place was the actual X-ray procedure, not the changing of clothes. Here is the impact: all of the cycle times and operational times remained the same, so what was the impact to the X-ray Department's capacity?

- Average X-ray procedure time: 5 minutes

- X-ray hours of operation: 6 a.m. to 10 p.m.: 16 Hours (960 minutes)

- X-ray procedure capacity (procedure only – 5 minutes): 192 procedures (960 minutes ÷ 5 minutes)

We increased our X-ray procedure capacity by 153%! The key was understanding where the Waiting time existed within the process and then determining where it had the greatest negative impact on the value delivery within the process. We accomplished several things by instructing patients to immediately change into a gown when brought back to the evaluation room:

1. We saved time during the provider's examination of the patient, as the provider now has better access to the patient's chest, back, and extremities.

2. The RN and lab tech now have better access to the patient's arms for blood draws, IV's, blood pressure, and other potential tests.

3. The Imaging X-ray Department does not double as a changing room and can now focus on completing X-ray procedures.

4. By having the patients immediately change into gowns when brought back to the evaluation room, the hospital creates the perception of improved care and reduced waiting times.

Keep in mind that the X-ray capacity increase from 87 to 192 needed to be supported by the demand to fully realize the benefit, but that was a much better situation to be in vs. being short of capacity to support demand. As you evaluate your processes and recover the capacity, have a game plan in place to quickly fill it. It makes very little sense to buy an 8-foot-deep pool but only fill it 4 feet deep. Your "capacity pool" will get deeper, so have the demand hose ready.

Value Under Pressure

FIGURE 16:1

In the same way that we find no value in Waiting in our personal lives, Waiting also results in negative perceptions, attitudes, and reactions in a professional and business environment.

Value is like the orange in Figure 16:1. When we apply the pressure of Waiting Waste to a process, we squeeze out the value that we could be utilizing to meet customer or patient needs. As the value is pressed out by the increasing pressure of the Waiting Waste, customers and patients are left with little more than what they perceive as a handful of messy rind and seeds. They are expecting an orange, but we deliver something that fails to meet their expectations.

When was the last time you were invited to a meeting with a large group of maybe 20 people? For a lot of us, this is an everyday occurrence. How often does the meeting start on time? Sadly, starting on time is a rarity in some organizations. Not a big deal though – if the meeting starts 5 minutes late, it only costs 5 minutes. Oh really? There are 18 people in the room at the meeting start time, waiting for the remaining two participants. That means that the 5-minute delay, which yields zero value, actually costs the organization 90 minutes (18 people x 5 minutes). Two people arriving 5 minutes late costs the company 1.5 hours of value-added productivity. Here is the part that hits home with me: how many meetings do you go to every week, and how many of them start on time? The data would be very revealing and, in all honesty, quite embarrassing to most organizations.

Stamping Out Waiting Waste

In a manufacturing environment, Waiting can sometimes be easily quantified since a lot of manufacturing processes are discrete in nature, and value is based upon output over a period of time. For example, in a metal fabrication plant I worked at, a stamping press could produce 30 automobile door panels per minute. Over an 8-hour shift, the stamping press should have been be able to produce 14,400 pieces. But according to the previous month's data, for some reason the equipment had only been averaging 12,000 pieces per 8-hour shift.

After some research into the equipment maintenance logs, we determined that the reduced output was not a result of equipment failure. So, we moved on to review the supervisor's operational log, and we found that there was a consistent pattern of downtime during each shift.

Pulling the machine operators, parts loaders, and supervisor team together to investigate, we found that the pieces of metal loaded into the machine (called blanks) used to come to the machine banded together in stacks of 200. For some unknown reason, the Coil Group, who cut the rolls of steel into blanks, had begun sending them to the area banded in stacks of 100. This resulted in extra work for the parts loaders, in essence doubling their work. Loading twice the number of stacks also doubled the time required to un-band, position, and load the stacks of blanks. With the machine's operating cycle time of 30 parts per minute, the parts loader was unable to keep up at times. Ultimately, the machine had been shutting itself down automatically when no blanks were detected under the feeder cups.

The machine shut itself down because it was waiting for blanks. This was only the tip of the iceberg, though, as this one issue resulted in a number of other wastes that, for the most part, remained invisible. Let's look at some we discovered as the team dug deeper.

1. After some problem solving and discussion with the coil group, we realized that the parts blank cutting program was somehow changed to stacks of 100 instead of 200.

2. The person in the Coil Group who banded the blanks was having to band twice as many stacks, consuming substantial amounts of time and banding material.

3. Since the coil group was only allowed to place two stacks of blanks on each pallet, the number of pallets required to hold the previous lot size of blanks had doubled.

4. The floor space required to store additional pallets that held the normal lot size had also doubled.

5. The number of trips and time required for the coil group fork truck driver to move the normal lot size had doubled.

6. The number of trips and time required for the production group fork truck driver to bring the normal lot size had doubled.

7. The time and effort required for the part loader team member to un-band and load the parts had doubled.

8. The equipment downtime while waiting meant that the machine operator and parts unloader were waiting, adding no value.

9. We had produced below our target production level and were forced to schedule overtime and weekend work, which added a whole additional bucket of potential waste.

The impressive part of this story, in my mind, is how the team reacted when the problem was discovered through our investigation. Keep in mind that when I say "problem," I am actually referencing the symptom, the blanks stack size being changed from 200 to 100. The real root cause was discovered as we dug in deeper. The root cause was a system upgrade that had randomly changed blank stack quantities.

Instead of stopping after fixing the stack size for this one part, the leadership and team suggested an audit of all blanks to confirm that no other parts that had changed and caused the same kind of chaos. As it turned out, we found three other part numbers that were changed.

> **"Unless your processes involve aging wine, fermenting cabbage, or letting dough rise, Waiting is a waste that disrupts your flow, impedes your progress, and threatens your success."**

We changed them to the correct amounts. Not stopping there, the team decided to complete an audit of all parts to ensure the blanking group was stacking them in the highest quantity possible, while also eliminating some Motion and Transportation Waste.

Here is the point. When we look at our processes at the granular level and understand through Value Stream Mapping or Value/Non-Value Analysis (Chapter 21), we start to see where the Waiting Waste exists. Eliminating the Waiting Waste will drive value back into the process and positively impact the other wastes that exists within the process.

Everybody Wins

At one hospital I worked with, there was a critical need to improve operating room turnover times. The hospital was working to attract additional surgical specialists and, in order to keep surgeons happy, needed to reduce the OR turnover times between procedures. The longer a surgeon had to wait between surgeries, the fewer surgeries he or she could perform. Decreased OR turnover times also meant the OR staff would be more likely to avoid operations later in the day that could interfere with their personal plans.

When we started out, the average room turnover time was 38 minutes. Most of the leadership and staff could not imagine why it would take that long. We mapped out the process and completed a Value/Non-Value Analysis (Chapter 21). We completed detailed time studies for all groups involved in the room turnover, including EVS (cleaned the room), the existing nursing staff (removed unused items from the previous procedure and finished charting), and the incoming nursing staff (prepped the room for the next procedure).

What we found was that everyone was working sequentially, waiting for the other groups to complete their tasks. This situation was perfectly suited for a SMED activity. We mapped out all of the different groups' processes and identified which ones were External to another – which tasks the groups could be completing in the room at the same time. Some of the tasks were Internal and could only be completed consecutively in a specific sequence. One Internal process was bringing new supplies, material, and equipment into the room *after* EVS had completed cleaning the room. Many other tasks were able to be completed concurrently.

As a team comprised of EVS, nurses, techs, leadership, anesthesiologists, and surgeons, we were able to design and engineer for success a standardized, documented, and proven process that reduced the operating room average turnaround times to 21 minutes. Was this easy? No. Did it take some trial and effort? Yes. Did it require involvement by all impacted groups? Absolutely. Would it have been successful without the engagement of all involved groups? Absolutely not! Was it worth it?

With six operating rooms, in a 10-hour day, the hospital had 60 hours of capacity to utilize to produce value. With an average procedure requiring 75 minutes, plus the previous turnover time of 38 minutes, the hospital could accommodate roughly 32 surgeries (3,600 minutes ÷ 113 minutes). After completing the SMED and improving flow, the hospital still had 60 hours of capacity, but was able to support roughly 38 procedures (3600 minutes ÷ 96 minutes).

"This was a 19% increase in surgery capacity."

From a financial standpoint, this was a great opportunity for both the hospital and the surgeons. From a patient's perspective, this was also beneficial, since this additional capacity allowed for surgeries to be scheduled sooner.

This improvement also created flexibility in the procedure schedule and room management. If a surgeon was performing very quick surgeries, since we had decreased the turnover time so much, we were able to start setting up rooms faster. If necessary, we could set up a second room so fast that, as surgeons completed a procedure in one room, they could immediately move to the second room for the next procedure. When necessary, we could run the OR all day like this. Decreasing the changeover time provided the opportunity to increase the number of procedures the hospital could support, the number of surgeries each surgeon could perform, and the number of patients who could be treated. All of this was made possible by reducing the amount of Waiting Waste and injecting capacity back into the organization.

One definition of Waiting is "to remain inactive or in a state of repose, until something expected happens." The word "inactive" is quite accurate in expressing how Waiting clogs our processes, like a locomotive on its way from Denver to Seattle that has stopped in the middle of the tracks. It is inactive, but the impact is truly demonstrated by the 120 freight cars lined up behind it that are now motionless as well. The longer the locomotive waits, the longer every subsequent freight car waits.

Unless your processes involve aging wine, fermenting cabbage, or letting dough rise, Waiting is a waste that disrupts your flow and impedes your progress. It directly interferes with your success at every level and negatively impacts your organization, your suppliers, your employees, and your customers. Find it, understand it, and then eliminate it.

WHAT'S IN IT FOR ME?

For me, identifying and eliminating Waiting Waste has always been one of my favorite problems to address. It may be my own personal hatred of waiting, or it may just be that, in a lot of cases, Waiting Waste is one of the quickest to identify and the most impactful to an organization.

To identify Waiting Waste, you need to place yourself in the shoes of the customer. Now, if you are restricting my use of the term "customer" to one person, you are only seeing half of the picture. A customer can be a person, but can also refer to an organization or a downstream process. So, when I say "place yourself in the shoes of the customer," you will have to step outside of your current role and take on a new perspective.

What does the perfect Emergency Room experience look like to a customer? Draw it out step by step and minute by minute. Once you do, compare what you've drawn to your current state Process Map for the Emergency Department. What are the differences? What steps in the process are surrounded by Waiting Waste? How could you organize or rearrange the process and the resources used in that process to eliminate or reduce that Waiting? Remember, leave your perspective in the drawer of your desk, and see the process from the perspective of the person who just exited her car and is walking through your sliding double doors. What are her expectations? When we communicate effectively, so that patients understand why they are waiting longer than expected, they feel important, engaged, and valued, and they are more forgiving.

In a manufacturing environment, as difficult as it may seem, take on the perspective of the next process downstream. To be completely successful, what does that team member need? What does that supervisor need? What does that piece of equipment need? Does satisfying your downstream customer only involve providing quality parts? Or, could it also include providing those quality parts at the moment the customers need them, in the quantity they need them, in the location where they need them? Is proactively communicating status to them of value as they plan their day? Many times, Waiting Waste can be avoided simply though effective communication.

Waiting happens when there is a difference between when something is expected to happen and when it actually happens. The key to eliminating Waiting Waste is to understand why this difference exists, and then design or modify processes that prevent and avoid these obstacles.

Applicable Tools (Chapter 21):

Kaizen/Kaizen Event

Value/Non-Value Analysis

Spaghetti Mapping & Time Studies

SMED/Quick Changeover Analysis

Value Stream Mapping

5-Why Problem Solving

Transporta[tion] [...] ed with Motion Waste.
Transportatio[n] [...] material without adding
value. Motio[n] [...] otion that takes place within a process t[hat] [...]

In Chapte[r] [...] he machine blanks resulted
in Transport [...] ng their trips to move blanks
around. Tra[nsportation] [...] to be quite honest, may
never be co[mpletely] [...] ple, on a large mining truck
production [...] emblies, and such are so large
that it wou[ld] [...] nt of space on the production
line to stag[e] [...] d this wasted space. The key
is to develo[p] [...] the amount of transportation
(number of [...] mal minimum.

> "Io[...] [...]n Waste within your
> pro[...] [...]single question: What
> valu[...] [...]oduct generate for our
> [...]ation?"

It would be great if the food at you[r] [...] stablishment was always ready at the counter when you ordered it. Self-serve burgers and fries would certainly reduce transportation time and effort. Unfortunately, having a hot grill and a vat filled with boiling grease right there within little Timmy's reach is probably not the best decision for anyone. On the other hand, positioning the grill and the fry vat at the back of the kitchen is not an efficient layout either. If you look at the layout of your local fast-food restaurant, you will see that everything from the ordering line to the location of the burger drop, the French fry vat, and the shake machine has been laid out to promote flow and reduce Transportation Waste. It is also important to realize that Transportation Waste is not just measured in time or distance. It can be measured in the resources required and consumed to transport something.

Unanticipated Consequences

In a manufacturing company I worked with, there was an effort to improve the quality of a manufactured part that seemed to be getting damaged during movement from the stamping center to the dock. The team had modified the packaging to create a better fit with less potential for part-to-part contact. Doing this improved the overall quality scores, but, by making this change to the packaging, the container now only held 20 parts vs. the previous quantity of 24.

This may not seem like a huge adjustment, but when we looked at the overall burden this change had placed on the transportation process, it was staggering. Let's break it down to understand what we found.

This part had a daily demand of 4,320 pieces. As a firm believer in the Lean manufacturing process, the customer only kept 2 days of inventory on hand. An additional day was always in transit, and we kept a 1-day buffer in inventory, plus what we were producing that day for the following day's orders. At a demand of 4,320 pieces, the previous QPC (Quantity per Container) of 24 required 900 containers. With the new QPC of 20, the container requirement jumped to 1,080. At $380 per container, the company had to spend $68,400 on the 180 additional containers.

Each container had a standard footprint of 3' by 3' by 18" high. Due to the weight of the parts, we were only permitted to stack the containers two high. Previously, the 360 containers staged with both today's and tomorrow's shipments required 1,620 square feet of storage space in the warehouse. The new QPC configuration consumed 1,944 square feet, or 20% more space.

Part handling became a challenge, as the containers had to be switched out on the carousel for every 20 pieces instead of every 24. The equipment had a part producing cycle time of 8 seconds. The fork truck driver previously had 3 minutes and 12 seconds between container changeovers. This was just enough time to take a couple of the full containers to the storage area. However, at 20 parts per container, the fork truck driver only had 2 minutes and 40 seconds between container changeovers.

This was 32 seconds less, and, as time progressed and line stoppages increased while waiting for container change-outs, it became painfully obvious that 2:40 was not enough time for the fork truck driver to both store parts and keep up with the container demand on the line. So, the decision was made to allocate another fork truck driver to service the line's container needs and to dedicate the original fork truck driver to part storage.

At the dock, the transport trucks arrived to pick up the containers for the customer. The new containers required the fork truck driver to make 36 additional dock-to-trailer trips to load the parts. Also, there was some confusion because the containers ready for shipment no longer fit onto the usual five transport trucks. What happened? Well, it had previously required only five trucks to pick up and deliver the 4,320 parts. Now, with only 20 parts per container, the number of containers shipped daily had increased from 360 to 432.

Considering that the dimensions of the trailer were not going to change, it would now require six trailers daily to ship these 4,320 parts to the customer. Someone was going to have to pay for an extra delivery truck daily. Considering that we shipped 5 days per week, at a low estimate of $275 per shipment, either our company or the customer was going to see annual transportation cost increase of $71,500 (260 days x $275 per shipment) for just this part alone.

I use this example because it's not an uncommon situation for some companies to find themselves in – forced to react to a change that was made by an individual department working in an "operational silo." The department neglects to communicate the change to all groups to understand its impact across the entire organization.

The foundational reason for making the container change was appropriate, as part quality is certainly a critical priority. Unfortunately, following this event, there were numerous meetings to evaluate the financial impact this had on the organization. Many wastes were generated by this decision, but let's just look at the additional transportation that resulted from this situation:

- 180 new containers – $68,400

- $18,000 for the used fork truck needed for part handling on the production line

- $32,000 (annual salary and benefits) for the cost of the additional fork truck driver dedicated to part handling at the production line

- $71,500 for the additional 260 transport trucks required each year

Considering that the margin for the parts was originally calculated and quoted based on the production and transportation of 24 parts per container, how and where will these additional transportation costs be absorbed? Will the sales team need to humbly approach the customer to negotiate a new piece price? How will the customer react, and will they require you to go back to the old containers? Keep in mind that all of the additional transportation time, resources, and costs associated with moving the parts internally at your facility will be mirrored at the customer's site. So that begs the question: was this change approved by and communicated with the customer as well?

MOVING, MOVING, MOVING

I was performing a cycle Time Study during a Process Mapping session at a manufacturer. I soon realized the area I was working in was dangerous as a result of the forklift traffic. I had my orange vest on and used eye contact and hand signals to communicate with drivers. I was working on one area, but the interactions taking place in a cell across the aisle is what really caught my attention. I watched a forklift driver bring over a pallet of parts from the dock and set it down in the area. Roughly 3 minutes later, a second forklift driver picked the pallet up and set it down in a space 20 feet away. A third forklift driver then picked up the pallet of parts and moved them over about 5 feet. An assembler then came over a few minutes later with a pallet jack and pulled the parts over into their cell. In a 15-minute span of time, the parts were moved four times, requiring four people, three forklifts and a pallet jack. I later measured it out, and the distance these parts were transported during this circus of activity was 120 feet total.

How much time and energy were wasted picking up, putting down, moving over, picking up, putting down, picking up, moving over, and putting the pallet down again? Everyone was blind to the waste, working within the confines of their process walls, unaware of the absurdity taking place around them. I later took a video of the process and showed it to the department leaders and team. Needless to say, we created a standard inventory process utilizing a Kanban System (Chapter 21) that eliminated all but one leg of the transportation.

Free Home Delivery

You may already have a very good understanding of Transportation Waste. How can I just assume that? Well, I would bet that you or someone in your family has an Amazon Prime account. I do, and I use it constantly. How is this a demonstration of reduced Transportation Waste? I am glad you asked. In my business, I use a clicker that allows me to scroll through PowerPoint presentations with ease. If, during one of my meetings, I accidentally drop and break the device, I have two options.

My first option is to get in my car and drive to every office supply store within a 100-mile radius to find the exact model I want. I could call my wife and let her know I won't be home for dinner tonight. It may take me 4 hours, five gallons of gas, a little wear and tear on my car, and unimaginable aggravation with the traffic situation. All this for a $60 clicker!

My second option is to take 5 minutes and open the Amazon app on my phone. I search for clickers and then scroll through the 30 different options before finding the exact replacement for mine. I enter the appropriate information and complete the order. Actually, it only took me 3 minutes and 42 seconds. Instead of spending 4 hours of my time, paying for and consuming five gallons of gas, and getting aggravated with traffic, 2 days later the clicker is delivered to my front door.

Delivery companies make their living out of our desire to reduce Transportation Waste, whether personal or business related. They deliver products to us at home or work so that we don't have to go get them ourselves. Your value lies in the product or service you are providing to your customers, not in going to the store to purchase the resources. Delivery companies plan their routes based on distance, turns, traffic, and any other interruptions. If you measure the distance, fuel, and time it takes for just one truck to deliver the 60 to 70 packages it is transporting on average, and then compare that to the distance, fuel, and time it would require for each individual customer to go to the store and purchase those same 60 to 70 items, the difference is enormous.

Moving Without Value

I was working with a hospital to identify opportunities to improve patient satisfaction scores. This is an absolute priority for hospitals, as the HCAHPS (Hospital Consumer Assessment of Healthcare Providers and Systems) is the standard national measurement tool that potentially impacts how Medicare, Medicaid, and insurers compensate them.

I was with a staff nurse on a patient floor one afternoon and observed another nurse transporting a patient out of his room and to the elevator. I waved to the patient, as we had previously had a conversation, and I knew he was scheduled for an inpatient CT scan later in the day. The nurse and I went about our business of mapping out a patient flow process. Thirty minutes later, I observed the other nurse pushing the patient's bed off the elevator and towards his room. I greeted him and asked how the CT scan went. He responded as politely as he could, but I noticed some frustration. The look on the nurse's face mirrored the patient's frustration.

I followed the patient to his room and asked him patient what had happened. Apparently, when they arrived at the CT, there was some confusion. The CT scan had been ordered by the physician earlier in the day, but, because of some scheduling and coordination missteps, the actual scan procedure time had been pushed to the following day. Unfortunately, that information had not been correctly entered into the system or communicated. After all the effort that went into unhooking his bed, maneuvering the bed out of the room and into the elevator, then out of the elevator and over to the Imaging Department, nothing was accomplished. 100% of this transportation was wasted because of a defect in communication and coordination.

This doesn't take into consideration the negative value created for the patient, who had his lunch interrupted, missed the second half of his favorite show, and was paraded through the halls past 20 different people in his stylish gown. The patient and his family are now probably questioning the quality of the care they are receiving since they have doubts regarding the hospital's ability to simply communicate effectively between departments. This negative value will be reflected in the hospital's HCAHPS scores and will also take a toll on the employee and physician satisfaction scores.

You may think it odd that I use a hospital patient in the Transportation Waste example, but it is valid. When critically wounded patients are brought in by ambulance or helicopter, they are normally taken immediately to an Emergency Department Trauma Room. The Trauma Room is equipped to save patients by addressing any one of a thousand threats to their lives, and to stabilize them for transportation to surgery if necessary. The team in the room resembles a small army, each member with a specific set of skills that aligns and complements each other. Sometimes, the Trauma Room outcomes are heartbreaking, and sometimes they are thrilling and inspiring, but every time is impressive.

Any information that can be obtained without moving the patient from the Trauma Room is critically important. If there are questions about the extent of injuries, for instance broken bones or bleeding, transporting the patient to the X-ray room, even 70 feet away, would be difficult and dangerous. Every second counts.

In response to this, hospitals use portable X-ray machines. When a trauma patient is brought in, an X-ray tech stands outside of the Trauma Room waiting for the call. If an X-ray is requested, the tech maneuvers the portable X-ray machine into the room, positions the patient and equipment, takes the image, and then instantly displays the results on location for the trauma team to evaluate. No transportation needed.

This is a perfect example of adding value by eliminating transportation. Granted, the patient will, at some point, need to be moved to either surgery or an inpatient floor, but, instead of transporting the trauma patient between the different departments required to save his or her life, (ED, lab, imaging, respiratory, surgery, anesthesia, patient access, etc.), the value is delivered to them in one place. Completing more of the process steps without the need for transportation allows for a higher percentage of resources to be dedicated to adding value.

A ONE STOP SHOP

The next time you need to take your car in for maintenance, consider the effort that would be required if, instead of taking your car to the dealer that can complete everything under one roof, you had to take it to a specialty shop for every unique need. You need the oil changed, so you take it to Jiffy Lube. You need the brakes replaced, so you take it to Meineke. You need the muffler replaced, so you take it to Midas. The tires are worn, so you drive it to Firestone. The transmission is slipping, so you have it towed to AAMCO. The list goes on and on, and the time and resources required to actually complete this task would be ridiculous. Fortunately, most car dealerships are capable of completing all of these repairs while your vehicle sits in one spot, resting safely on a car lift where a certified mechanic brings the value to your car. Less transportation, less time, less effort, less gas, and more value.

Transportation Waste, for the most part, can never be completely eliminated, so the key is to see it for the waste that it is and reduce it to the point where it is having the least possible impact. Understanding flow is a critical part of reducing Transportation Waste. Distance and time studies are valuable when you are looking at laying out process and inventory locations. Spaghetti Mapping isn't just a tool used for the elimination of Motion Waste; it is also a great way to provide a visual indication of how you are moving product and how to optimize your routes.

Identifying the impact of Transportation Waste within your processes can be understood by asking yourself a single question: "What value does transporting this product generate for our customer and our organization?" The answer is probably little if any at all. So, the obvious question is how to eliminate or reduce it. The accompanying answer is never easy, but once you start to see the lack of value generated through transportation, you will find yourself not only fixing current Transportation Waste opportunities, but also starting to use this knowledge to minimize waste when setting up and designing new processes.

WHAT'S IN IT FOR ME?

Eliminating Transportation Waste results in a direct injection of value into your processes. How is value being created or added by picking up a part and moving it from here to there? How is value being created or added by transporting a patient from this room to that room? How is value being created or added by transporting a loan application file among 10 different offices to finally receive final approval? The answer is obvious – it isn't.

The value creation doesn't take place during transportation; it starts once the transportation is completed and the person or material can re-enter the process. In the Introduction, I talked about the 20% value delivery. You may have thought that I was exaggerating, so let's put it to the test.

Pick a process in your operation. Engage your team to identify the value that this process was designed to generate. Now, follow the process from cradle to grave, documenting the time dedicated to each individual step, from actual value creation to transportation, waiting, error correction, clarification, and so on. Don't be fooled by thinking that if your process is electronic, it must be faster. If, for example, the process you are documenting is an electronic loan application, any time the application spends between approval steps is Waiting Waste. Any time dedicated to sending it to the next process step is Transportation Waste. Electronic applications do not guarantee process speed.

What you have basically completed is a detailed Process Map, Time Study, and Value/Non-Value Analysis. What did you find? Were you surprised at how little of the overall time was spent in the value creation?

Consider this example. People spend roughly $800 million for fireworks on July 4 in the United States. The fireworks manufacturing process only takes several minutes and four to five parts. On the other hand, the overseas transportation from the manufacturer in China to a consumer in Michigan takes months. What value did that 4 months of Transportation add to the light show that lasted a mere 6 seconds? None; it only delayed the value realization. If reducing Transportation time is not important to you, then why do you sometimes pay extra for expedited delivery?

Look at your processes and identify every single touch point. Is there a reason the part needs to be moved? Can it be stored in a location closer to the next value-add process? Can more parts be stored together, or can the packaging be modified to reduce the frequency of Transportation? Are there opportunities to utilize space more effectively to reduce or eliminate Transportation between value-add processes? Can you move value-add processes closer together to reduce or even eliminate any required Transportation and improve flow?

What can you do to reduce the amount of overall process time between cradle to grave that is consumed by Transportation? Once you do this, then how will you utilize that time to increase your capacity, productivity, and value delivery?

Applicable Tools (Chapter 21):

Kaizen/Kaizen Event

Value Stream Mapping

Spaghetti Map

5S

Value/Non-Value Analysis

Time Study

CHAPTER 18:
WASTE #7 – OVER-PROCESSING

Over-Processing Waste is one that can be kind of confusing, so we will look at some specific examples. Basically, Over-Processing is a waste that results when you utilize limited resources (time, material, equipment, hours, movement, etc.) unnecessarily to provide products or services that exceed your customer's requirement. The effort you put into the Over-Processing activity can consume resources that were not built into the original quote or pricing structure. In some cases, the activity may have no value whatsoever from the customer's perspective. The customer didn't ask for it, they don't find value in it, and they are certainly not going to pay for it. Over-Processing Waste results from your decisions as a provider of products or services and is not driven by a customer need or request.

Above and Beyond?

Let's pretend one evening you are driving to the local convenience store to get gas for your car. You pull up to the pump, remove the gas cap, fill up the car, and walk into the store to pay. The young man behind the register is very friendly and obviously motivated to ensure that every customer receives the best convenience store experience of his or her life. You purchase $16 worth of fuel and hand the attendant a 20-dollar bill. He puts the cash into the register drawer and takes out four 1-dollar bills.

Instead of handing them to you, the attendant then turns around to an ironing board that is set up behind him. You thought that was odd when you saw it earlier, but figured someone was ironing clothes between customers. Over the next 2 minutes, the attendant meticulously irons out each of the 1-dollar bills, removing all wrinkles, straightening out the edges, and steaming them to like-new condition. He even tapes up a couple of small tears. He finally turns around and, with a huge smile that screams "outstanding service," hands you four crisp 1-dollar bills. They are so nice and crisp and will fit into your wallet perfectly. Unfortunately, you don't have your wallet. So, you wad them up and stuff them in your pocket as you walk out.

The attendant certainly went above and beyond, but how much value did you, the customer, receive from the freshly ironed bills? From an operational perspective, how much wasted time, energy, motion, and resources did the attendant consume while adding zero value? How many customers were waiting in line or at the pumps during this activity? I highly doubt that any of them found value in it either. Did this Over-Processing Waste impact the convenience store in the long-term, with multiple customers making future decisions to go somewhere else?

Slow Boiling Water

Over-Processing is not normally one of the top impactful wastes and is usually not something you originally design into processes. It happens gradually, taking place over time as you look for ways to improve a process or add value, sometimes without adequately considering the impact it has on the organization. The reason behind it may be valid, but the slowly increasing impact is often not felt until it's too late, like a frog that unknowingly perishes in a pan of water slowly brought to a boil. Very often there is also a failure to completely understand the resources consumed and the cost incurred when compared to the end value delivered.

Let's take a look at an example using Bob the contractor. My wife and I decide to replace the five windows in the front of our house. Bob provides me with a quote to come out and replace all five windows in a single day. The $2,500 estimate is acceptable, so I give Bob permission to go ahead with the work. Here is the sequence of Bob's activities:

1. I hire Contractor Bob to replace five windows on the front our home.

2. My wife and I pick out the windows we like for $1,800 total.

3. When Bob the contractor picks up the windows, he decides to get a higher UV rated glass, but does not charge me the difference ($400 upgrade).

4. After he installs the windows, Bob notices my gutter has a leak and replaces it, for free.

5. While fixing the gutter, Bob notices that my roof is old and a couple shingles are missing, so he repairs the worn spots, for free.

6. While roofing my house, Bob notices my chimney is dirty, so he buys the necessary equipment and cleans it, for free.

7. While cleaning my chimney, Bob notices my furnace vent is rusty, so he replaces it, for free.

Admittedly, Bob is a jewel and would probably be voted the nicest contractor in the world! But, how long do you think Bob will stay in business?

Let's look at it from a project perspective:

I paid Bob $2,500 to replace the five windows in 1 day, but here are Bob's project costs:

- The windows cost $2,200.

- The new gutter cost $350.

- The roof repair cost $675.

- The chimney cleaning material cost $160.

- The furnace vent replacement cost $12.

If we look at Bob's total costs incurred vs. the $2,500 that I paid him, you will see that Bob actually spent $3,397 on the windows and other projects, and, in addition, he consumed 3 days of his time instead of 1. Bob has suffered a financial loss of $897, not to mention the opportunity cost of the 2 extra days he could have utilized to service other customers and generate revenue.

This may seem far-fetched, but Over-Processing is a real risk and, for the most part, goes unseen as you make tiny and almost unnoticeable changes within your processes. Years down the road, you find yourself reevaluating the cost structure for a product or service and, while validating the current process against the documented standard, find any number of deviations and variations. These process variations are often quickly explained away and justified as necessary to provide added value to the customer through reduced Defects or improved quality. Unfortunately, they were made in a vacuum, a departmental silo where the overall organizational impact was hidden from view, buried deep within the multiple process layers.

> **"Continuous Improvement isn't always an improvement if you don't understand the sum total impact of the change across the entire organization."**

Delivering Expected Value

Let's look at a real scenario from a manufacturing organization. The company had just signed up a new customer who produced and sold farm equipment and implements. Here were the details regarding the customer's requirements:

- The part we made was attached to an implement assembly that our customer then sold to retail customers.

- We sold 1,000 of these parts to our customer monthly.

- Our customer was billed $220 for each part.

- Our profit margin for each part was $26 (11.8%).

- The customer simply wanted a good, reliable, welded part with a marginal quality coat of paint (as outlined in the specs).

Our company wanted to start out on the right foot to promote a long-term relationship. As a result of this admirable desire, we went above and beyond by also taking the following actions:

1. We fabricated the part, but added several extra welds to reinforce the structure, even though the prints did not call for it.

2. We spent 20 minutes grinding, smoothing, and removing weld bb's, even though the customer did not require it as outlined in the original part specs.

3. We decided to run the part through the paint booth twice just to make sure that it had a good thick coat of paint, even though the specs called for only a single coat.

4. When we started shipping the parts to the customer, they were surprised by and impressed with the parts we were providing. Nobody else provided this level of finish, and these were the best looking parts on the implement.

Again, a happy and satisfied customer is always critically important, but staying in business is also a priority. So, let's take a look, from a financial perspective, at how this product line was operating.

Assuming an hourly rate of $22.40 for the manufacturing employees, what impact was this well intended Over-Processing having?

1. Extra welds: 10 minutes x $22.40/hr. = $3.73 per part

2. Extra Cost of Grinding and smoothing: 20 minutes x $22.40/hr. = $7.46 per part (also grinding and smoothing the additional welds from item "a")

3. Extra cost of applying second coat of paint: Time to apply is 5 minutes x $22.40/hr. = $1.87. Cost of paint is 1oz. of paint x $1.20 per oz. = $1.20 (This extra coat of paint also required an extra trip through the paint oven.)

The standard process that the customer requested provided a per-part margin of $26, but as a result of the extra work and deviations introduced, the realized per-part margin was only $11.47 at best – a $14.26 difference. The well-intended but negative impact to the organization's operating plan would have been a reduction in margin of $14,260 per month and $171,120 per year. Keep in mind that budgets set at the beginning of the year were based on planned volumes and their respective margins. This negative $14,260 monthly hit would be felt by everyone at some level. The increased cycle times would also impact every other subsequent job or product produced in those cells and processed through the paint booth.

To make this scenario even more meaningful, assume that we had continued this Over-Processing for several years. Halfway into the 5-year contract with the customer, a couple savvy and motivated managers dig into the process and discover these Over-Processing activities. Everyone is shocked that we have been doing all of this extra work and, after a careful review of the quote and specs, the decision is made to produce the parts strictly as required in the original contract.

A month down the road, the Quality Department gets a frantic call from this customer demanding to know what has failed in the process, as the part quality seems to have taken a turn in the wrong direction. We spend the next 3 months in countless meetings and phone calls digging ourselves out of a hole. We tirelessly negotiate with the customer, attempting to convince them that the parts they are now receiving are being produced according to the original specs. In essence, by Over-Processing the parts, we have conditioned the customer to expect the "luxury car version" of the parts, not the "economy version" that they were originally quoted and are paying for.

Taxing My Patience

Recently I experienced an Over-Processing example that still makes me laugh. If you own land or a home, you must pay your appropriate property tax every year, at least in most states. Last month, I received three property tax bills. They all originated from the same county government office and were all postmarked on the same day. I was a little confused, as I never get a bill for my home property because it is paid through escrow. I knew that I needed to pay taxes for a piece of land I owned, but what could the other two tax bills be for? As I opened them up and identified the specific parcel numbers, I realized that they were all for the exact same piece of property. Each one had a different assessment value, and, as a result, each one had a different "Taxes Due" amount. One even had an amount due of $0. For obvious reasons, this is the one I was hoping was correct.

Being the responsible tax-paying citizen that I am, I called the County Tax Assessor's office, and they explained that it was a processing error. Well duh! Where is Captain Obvious when you need him? This situation spans both Over-Processing and Defect Wastes, resulting in multiple other wastes as well.

If we looked at this through the "waste microscope," we would see the following:

1. The county used three stamps to send the bill instead of one.

2. The county used three envelopes instead of one.

3. The county office printed three pages and used three pages' worth of ink instead of what was required for one tax bill.

4. A county employee spent the time to generate three tax bills instead of one.

5. The mail carrier delivered three envelopes instead of one.

6. I spent 30 minutes scratching my head and another 30 minutes on the phone with the Assessor's office.

7. A person in the Assessor's office had to stop what he was doing for 30 minutes and figure out the mistake.

8. Potentially 10 other local citizens didn't get their tax bills that day because the county employee was generating two extra ones for me.

9. Now an audit will have to be performed to ensure that this same type of mistake was not made for the other 300 tax bills generated that day.

Over-Processing isn't one of the wastes that jumps up in your face like Defects. Without understanding the standard process design, it is very difficult to identify this waste. Here is where very effective companies take advantage of this opportunity by utilizing visual management and posting very detailed work instructions, product specs, and Standard Work. There is truth in the old adage that "a picture is worth thousand words." Regardless of whether you are involved in a manufacturing, service, medical, or other field, having clearly defined work instructions and Standard Work at the point of operation is, in essence, a mirror that quickly surfaces process variation or deviation that doesn't "look right."

In a hospital, there are numerous examples of Over-Processing Waste. Walk into any hospital and count how many times you are asked the exact same question: "What problem are you having?" The registration person will ask you, the triage nurse will ask you, the X-ray technician will ask you, and the nurse practitioner or physician will ask you. Every time you must re-explain your problem results in a delay of treatment.

A Rainbow with No Gold

Another example that stands out in hospitals is what many refer to as a "Rainbow" (See Figure 18:1). A Rainbow refers to a set of five or six different colored tubes used to hold blood samples. When a patient is admitted into the ED, and after the initial evaluation, in many cases it is standard practice to draw blood to aid in diagnosis. There are many different tests that can be run on blood samples, so each of the different tests uses a different tube. Depending on the hospital policy, either the nurse in the ED or a lab tech will draw the samples. A patient may only need one or two specific tests, but in a lot of cases the standard is to fill the entire Rainbow and send them to the lab.

FIGURE 18:1

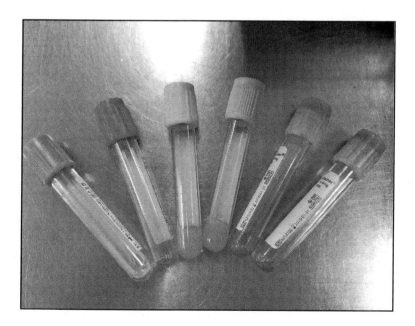

So, to step back, in this situation we have filled six different colored tubes, of which only two will be used for testing. Each of the six blood sample tubes requires separate labeling, which the nurse or lab tech must print off and apply. All six blood sample tubes are sent through the hospital delivery tube delivery system and received by the lab. The lab tech must enter them into the system and then deliver them to the appropriate testing equipment and operator. If a specific test exists in the system for the sample, the testing equipment operator runs the test. If no test exists, then the blood sample is placed in a holding tray just in case an order is entered later. If a test is never ordered, the blood sample must be disposed of through an expensive and labor-intensive biohazardous material management process.

Advocates of this process argue that the benefit of taking the samples in advance outweighs the process waste and inefficiency that results. In some cases, this may be valid, but, according to an article published in the January 2017 edition of the *Journal of the American Medicine Association* by the American Medical Association, only 7% of the extra blood sample tubes were ever used for future add-on tests. This means that, on average, 93% of them served no purpose and added no value.

This 93% isn't invisible; it is an Over-Processing Waste that impacts the entire hospital. This example demonstrates how powerful the waste explosion can be and how far the impact can reach. Only 7% of the sample tubes were used to add value through diagnosis, so the hospital purchased 93% of them for no reason. This money was used for nothing more than filling up a biohazard trash can. The time used by the nurse or lab tech to draw the blood for the 93% of tubes never used for diagnosis could have been dedicated to other patients. The portion of the printer's limited lifespan that was used to print the labels for the 93% was wasted.

The time and motion that the lab tech used to process the 93% of the blood samples that were not used for diagnosis were all wasted. 93% of the blood that was drawn from the patient, blood that the patient needed and was fond of, was taken but never used for diagnosis. The cost incurred to dispose of the 93% of blood samples never used for diagnosis was wasted. The time and effort that everyone spent handling and processing the 93% of the blood samples that were never used directly impacted those patients who were waiting for their blood samples to be processed.

Drawing six vials of blood before they are needed is certainly in line with Overproduction, but Overproduction normally occurs when you are confident that all of what you are producing will eventually be required and consumed. In this example, the majority of the time the nurses know that not all of the samples will be used by the lab, therefore resources and capacity are being consumed "just in case" the samples are needed. This is a good example of how a single event or act can cross over multiple waste types.

Don't get me wrong – customer satisfaction is critically important, and providing outstanding products and services directly impacts this. On the other hand, you must be careful that you don't get so caught up in going above and beyond that you make the mistake of peppering your processes with so many small enhancements and improvements that you lose sight of the overall cost and impact to the organization as a whole. A minor improvement or modification may be well intended, but without understanding the

Resources, Capacity and Value wasted, never to be captured......

financial ramifications and process effects for all groups, decisions can be made in a silo that result in negative consequences that may remain hidden for years.

WHAT'S IN IT FOR ME?

The key to eliminating Over-Processing is understanding. Understand what your customers want, and then provide it to them. Always couple the desire to improve with a deep and detailed understanding of process change impact. Continuous Improvement isn't always an improvement if you don't understand the sum total impact to the entire organization.

Understand your process cost, and then measure any improvements, modifications, or adjustments to understand the financial impact they have on your operations. Constantly look for ways to improve the value you provide, but with fewer steps, less material, reduced motion and transportation, and better quality. It is possible – that is why they call it "Continuous Improvement."

Over-Processing isn't a waste that you set out to sabotage your processes with. It normally starts with good intentions – a desire to provide more value to your customers or downstream processes. The changes and improvements seem minor, almost insignificant. A few seconds of process time added here, a few steps over there, another label applied here, or a small addition of material here, but nothing that will ever really impact your organization. This is the thinking that leads to Over-Processing, done for the right reasons but without a true understanding of the ripples this tiny pebble dropped into the "process pond" will cause.

The key to avoiding Over-Processing Waste is to ensure everyone who adds value within a department, unit, cell, or assembly line understands the basic concept of cost structure as it applies to their processes. I am not referring to the granular level of detail that was required to bid on and win the product or process award; I am referring to their understanding of profit margin. Educate the teams on how their specific roles, as insignificant as they may seem, are instrumental in remaining profitable as a company. Help them understand the fragile nature of what is probably a very small margin that is realized from the product or process they provide.

Don't make the mistake that many companies make in assuming that only managers and above care about cost and that the front-line teams and supervisors don't have the time or desire to understand the cost structure of their roles. When everyone in an organization sees their roles from both a process and financial perspective, Continuous Improvement, waste, and value take on a whole new meaning. Teams see a 10-second savings, a 5-foot travel reduction, a material utilization enhancement, and other improvements for what they really are. They understand that even a tiny positive change can equal an exponential increase in value delivery, and that even the most seemingly minuscule negative change can result in devastating consequences.

This understanding is taken for granted many times. You assume that because a person has the title of vice president or director, he or she understands the complicated and far reaching effects of Over-Processing. When individual teams can visualize and document how a small process change in their "silo" ripples out through the entire organization, you create an environment where everyone is aware of their dependencies and connectivity.

Applicable Tools (Chapter 21):

Value/Non-Value Analysis

Value Stream Mapping

Time Study

Kaizen/Kaizen Event

CHAPTER 19:
WASTE #8 – UNDERUTILIZATION OF PEOPLE

Out of all the wastes described previously in this book, this is by far the most critically important. Understanding, recognizing, and minimizing this waste has the ability to literally transform an organization. Unlike the other wastes, this is a culture-driven waste. When I say "a culture driven waste," I mean that it is a result of an organization's philosophy and practices, and thus manifests itself through the behaviors, attitudes, engagement, and commitment of employees. As a leader, you may feel like this subject steps on your toes, but to candy coat this issue would be a disservice to every reader of this book. Underutilization of People Waste is not an accident you fall victim to; it is a decision made by leadership.

> **"An organization is like a garden. The more effort you pour into it as its servant, the more productive it will be, yielding a bountiful harvest of personal and professional success."**

Whether you are an existing leader or a leader-in-the making, take this chapter to heart and recognize the unimaginable potential that you have access to.

The Market Downturn Opportunity

Let's take a look at a common misstep that many companies make. If you listen to the rhetoric conveyed through employee brochures, HR initiatives, and other company-sponsored communications, it seems that every organization touts the employees as their most important resource. This is quite true, as employees are in fact the faces, voices, ears, hearts, minds, arms, and legs of every organization, regardless of the industry. We cease to exist without employees, and they are without question absolutely invaluable.

In reality though, few companies live this belief in their operational practices. The "Employees are our most valuable asset" hype becomes nothing more than propaganda. Yes, a hard statement, but if you look back over your career, when things got tight for the company, what was the first thing that started happening? Very often, it was that management and leadership started identifying a strategy to reduce headcount. Why? Because it has an immediate impact to the bottom line and can be used as a method to calm the concerns of the company board or "Wall Street" analysts and, as a result, allow the company to maintain stock prices, dividend forecasts, bonus structures, and shareholder satisfaction.

At this point, as a leader who has had to make these tough decisions, you may be writing me off or even calling me names under your breath. I have seen this situation play out numerous times, so call me what you will. Now, don't get me wrong – I understand that productivity is absolutely an essential measure of performance, and there comes a time when headcount and employee resource allocation must be evaluated. And yes, I believe in some situations a headcount reduction is unavoidable and necessary. My issue is with the point at which this decision is being made. Provide me with some professional grace, and follow my thoughts over the next several paragraphs.

Let's say you see a downward trend taking place in your market or industry. Most often, this takes place in a gradual manner, and, unless you have your heads buried in the sand, gives you at least a little time to both understand and proactively react. It doesn't require an advanced degree to recognize that a company must maintain profitability to survive. Ask anyone what happens to a company that doesn't make a profit, and you will most often hear something along these lines: "They will go out of business." Bingo!

So, knowing that a market downturn is imminent, instead of looking to purge the ranks, why don't you involve the teams in the process of keeping your head above water by identifying and reducing waste? Instead of slicing and dicing the rank and file and ultimately pushing your intrinsic knowledge base (employees) to your competition, why not instead utilize their vast experience and untapped expertise to find ways to become more efficient, reducing waste and operational costs the right way. Think about this long and hard. When you start pushing your "greatest assets" out the front door as the first line of financial defense, the following things happen:

1. You literally increase your rival's competitive advantage while at the same time reducing your own. Letting your talent go sounds like a simple decision. You can put that labor cost savings into a nice neat report, but the indirect cost and impact to your organization will never be truly understood. Don't think this is important? Take a look at what happened the last time you experienced a RIF (Reduction in Force). The rumor that a potential RIF is coming always gets out to the masses,

and so the real talent doesn't wait around for the axe to fall. These people are already in high demand and probably need only to reach out to any one of five recruiters or competitors that have been calling them for the last 6 months to see if they were open to an opportunity. In a lot of cases, when your top performers leave, you are left with an overall talent base that is lower on average than before the RIF took place.

2. The process of watching your colleagues and friends walk out the door with their belongings box in hand is demotivating. I know this for a fact personally. It creates an environment of fear and nervousness. People start looking around corners to see who is next. Instead of looking to excel, people just start looking for ways to survive. This fear does not promote constructive competition; instead, it creates a culture where people are aggressively looking for ways to cover their rear ends, and, in some cases, subvert others' achievements in order to appear more knowledgeable and valuable to the organization. Instead of a team, we create an army of individuals dedicated to self-preservation.

3. When you start to recover from the downturn, getting the talent to return is nearly impossible. You have, in essence, burned a very valuable bridge. You are asking people to come back when they may have endured a very painful and traumatic financial period because they were released. Now you expect all to be forgiven, for them to trust you and come back, like nothing ever happened? Except for some union jobs, in most cases this will not happen. Even if it does, do you honestly think that people won't always have an immediately executable backup plan on hand if there is even a hint of another market slowdown?

4. Probably the most important and devastating impact of a RIF is that people no longer trust leadership. Another strong statement, but if you stated prior to the downturn that "Our employees are our most valuable asset," then why didn't the company sell off equipment, land, buildings, or other underutilized assets before turning to a RIF? This may sound like an ignorant question, but don't you think that the employees are asking themselves these things? These may not be viable options, but doesn't it make sense to take the time to explain why not to your "most valuable assets"?

I have personally seen examples where leadership bonuses are voluntarily suspended and temporary salary reductions are agreed upon in order to avoid letting employees go. These acts made a statement to, demonstrating that leadership did, in fact, care about employees, truly valued the team, and were willing to sacrifice and take a seat next to them in the same boat on those uncertain and rough seas ahead. It said that, as a team, we win together, we lose together, we suffer together, and we persevere together. This demonstrated example of committed leadership is tangible, going beyond words, catch phrases, or mottos.

I say all of this is to drive one simple idea home. Instead of reducing employee head-count first, why not use their heads and minds to generate ideas to improve operations and the related costs? Why not ask them what they think? Every leader knows that the further you get away from the front-line activity, the more you forget about the day-to-day activities that create value. Understanding this should spur you on to run, not walk, to the people on the front line to solicit their ideas and suggestions. Use the ideas that make sense and are truly impactful, and disregard those that are not.

In the long run, you may still have to adjust employee numbers, but if the process savings are enough to avoid the elimination of even 10% of the forecasted reduction, isn't it worth it? Think about what that level of engagement says to the employees, those remaining as well as the ones who are ultimately let go. It says to your teams, "The leadership tried everything," and cultivates a level of trust and loyalty that few organizations have experienced.

WE'RE SINKING

It was a long voyage, and the ship was far out at sea somewhere in the middle of the Atlantic. It was loaded down with supplies for the lengthy trip and rode deep in the water. Late one night, and almost out of nowhere, a vicious squall rose up, churning the waves and wind until it was almost impossible for the crew to maneuver around the deck. The waves towered above the ship, breaking over the bow and washing the men up against the railing. Desperation set in, as many feared that these were their last moments on Earth. The decision was made to throw the heaviest cargo over the side.

Everyone's first thought was the gold and gunpowder, but these were far too valuable. Then came the idea of the cannon balls and cannons, but these also were far too important. Finally, a decision was made. The crew worked hurriedly to hoist out the large barrels from the belly of the ship, roll them over to the railing, lift them up and dump them into the ocean. At last, the ship was riding higher, and the crew were saved. They joyfully celebrated as every last barrel of their fresh water sank to the bottom of the sea. In their panic and haste to survive, this crew lost perspective, made poor choices, and ultimately perished. As a leader on your ship, what would you be throwing overboard?

The best part of this whole process is that when the downturn is over, all of those improvement ideas that have been implemented are still in place. From an operational standpoint, you will come back stronger, leaner, and more agile than you were before the market downturn. What does it say to your competition and to their employees when you take a different path during a downturn? When you utilize the team's knowledge and experience to eliminate waste, improve flow, promote efficiency and utilization, reduce inventory, free up space, and create Standard Work, those improvements become a sustainable competitive advantage as you ramp back up. In accomplishing these things, your employees also increase their knowledge base and skill level, transforming themselves through a self-directed Continuous Improvement journey, driven by a desire to remain employed and keep the company profitable.

The "We Know More" Opportunity

Let's face it – as we get promoted and move into different roles, we do tend to think that we know more than the average employee. After all, isn't that why we were promoted? This is accurate in some ways, but the more we get involved in productivity reports, HR issues, volume forecasting, project management, and annual budgeting, the less we understand about the ever-changing day to day processes where value is added. As we spend most of our time managing, we spend less and less time directly connected with what we produce.

Keep in mind that I wholeheartedly believe this, as I can personally attest to its legitimacy in my own career. If you think that the direction in which I am headed in this section is off base with reality, then humor me. If you are in a production leadership role, go to the floor. Find an assembly line station or pitch. Tell the team leader that you would like to fill in for the assembly team member for 10 minutes. If the team leader is sharp and confident, you will receive a resounding, "I appreciate the offer, but no." Why would you be turned away? Well, let's think about this. You probably don't know the part sequence of the assembly. You probably don't know what sub-assembly parts to use. You may be unfamiliar with the tools for assembly. You have most likely not been trained on defect identification and recent quality alerts. I doubt you are wearing the proper PPE (personal protective equipment), and you are way too slow and will most likely cause the entire line to stop.

Take another example, such as the director of the ED in a hospital. A director is probably well-educated, knowledgeable in the clinical and financial aspects of running the department, with numerous certifications listed after his name in his email signature. This director has risen to this position over the last 10 years, after gaining experience at the clinical level within several units at the hospital. On a Monday morning, let this director take the seat of the Emergency Department HUC (Health Unit Coordinator) for a day.

This ED HUC is quite literally the traffic light, telephone, bull horn, fax machine, and vending machine for the ED. Her job is non-stop and constantly changing. How long would it take for the director to ask his first question, maybe something like, "How do I page on this new phone system?" Within an hour, I would suspect that the ED charge nurse will have ordered the director to vacate the role. This is not a negative reflection of the director's skill level; he simply doesn't have the knowledge of the day-to-day requirements to competently fill that role. He is not face to face daily with the changes in staff and providers, the new standards and protocols put in place last week, the migration of information between the old and new computer system, or the upgraded phones.

None of this is intended to negate the importance of any leadership role in an organization. Without leadership, just as without employees, a company cannot exist. Leadership must develop strategies, direct resources, cultivate a culture, observe the market, provide direction, and align priorities to ensure the survival of the business. Without these activities, a business is nothing more than a doomed fish floundering helplessly up on the muddy bank of a river.

As mentioned in Chapter 7, there is a limitless amount of knowledge available to you as a leader. It resides within the minds of your employees. But, just like a treasure chest that is never unlocked or a book that is never opened, the priceless resource inside will never be realized unless you purposefully access it. Employees want to be seen as more than just the assemblers, nurses, secretaries, service representatives, clerks, deliverers, welders, and technicians. They want to be part of your success as an organization. They want to be part of your growth, innovation, service, and quality. They want to create an environment where the grass is greener here than anywhere else. The solutions to many of the opportunities you struggle with on a daily basis are already out there; you just have to look in the right place. Open your office door, and step out into the hall. Go for a walk in the assembly area, hospital hallways, or office floors. The solutions you seek are walking all around you.

WHAT'S IN IT FOR ME?

What's in it for you is only what you are willing to sacrifice for others.

Years ago, in the Marine Corps, I was taught that the team was everything. This didn't just apply in the lower ranks; it was demonstrated by my leadership. It was lived. Common professional philosophy says that the higher you go on the corporate ladder, the more important you become. This idea demonstrates a "me" mentality, where, as a leader, you are focused on one objective, promoting and advancing one person – you. This is not leadership; this is pride and ego fueled by arrogance and self-obsession. If your toes are feeling some slight pressure, use these truths as an opportunity to grow as a leader.

MORE THAN WORDS

Our general manager was scheduled to go out of town on vacation on the coming Saturday. He was excited, and we were excited for him. It was Friday before the weekend, and the day was going well, until we got the call. A customer informed us that there was an urgent need for additional parts from multiple product lines. Evidently their demand management and material management groups had gotten their planning wires crossed and were in an operational pickle. We were not expecting this and didn't have the materials in house to support the demand, so at 11 a.m., we started jumping through hoops. We would have to expedite material, modify the production schedule, require employees to work both Saturday and Sunday, and coordinate outbound shipments. It was going to be a circus.

Saturday morning arrived, and, as we walked in, who did we see out on the floor helping move parts? It was our general manager. He informed us that he had sent his family on ahead and that he would catch up with them on Tuesday. As disappointed as we were that he was not on vacation, we were relieved that he was there to provide direction. His presence gave us confidence in our ability to succeed. His sacrifice for his team required no verbal explanation. His actions spoke volumes.

Leadership isn't simply a word or a title; it is a way of life. As I stated in the previous paragraph, my Marine Corps superiors "lived it." Your ability to advance professionally is a result of the commitment, dedication, and faith that others offer up to you. True leadership is not about you; it is about the team you are leading. It is about doing everything in your power, including sacrificing, to ensure they have what they need to succeed.

One of the most meaningful and profound quotes I have ever heard comes from Jack Welch, the former CEO of General Electric: *"Before you are a leader, success is all about growing yourself. When you become a leader, success is all about growing others."*

Barbara and I plant a garden every year. We grow green beans, potatoes, okra, squash, Brussels sprouts, peppers, radishes, and many other delicious vegetables. We freeze, can, and pickle everything, benefiting from this garden year-round even though the growing and harvesting season is only 6 months long. The only reason we benefit from the garden is because we are its servants. We dedicate hours and hours of time to till the dirt, plant the seeds, fertilize the soil, pull the weeds, and water the plants. We protect the garden from rabbits, deer, and occasionally the neighbor's dog. It grows based on the effort we

pour into it – the more effort, the better it grows.

Regardless of your current position as a president, VP, director, manager, or supervisor, your organization is like our garden. The more effort you as a leader put into planting the seeds (setting clear expectations), fertilizing the soil (educating and developing the teams), pulling the weeds (removing barriers and solving problems), tilling the dirt (challenging the team), and watering it (providing the tools for success), the better your "garden" will grow.

Your garden will produce bushels and bushels of process value that your customers, employees, and organization will benefit from. By becoming a genuine servant to your teams, you harvest a crop of personal and professional success. Instead of climbing to the top by stepping on top of people, you are elevated by the branches and vines of the team members you have put so much effort into growing and developing.

> **"A full glass can be a very empty life, but an empty glass poured out over and over again for others is a life overflowing with the true meaning of success."**

If you are climbing the ladder for *you*, you will never realize the potential contained within your team, or yourself. If, on the other hand, you are holding the ladder, stabilizing it for the team as they file past you to climb toward something greater, you will experience success in a way that few can comprehend. Ask yourself: are you climbing the ladder or holding it?

Applicable Tools:

A Mirror (Take a good, long, honest look.)

CHAPTER 20:
THE CORPORATE CRUTCH

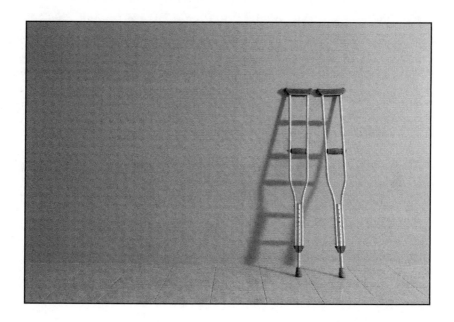

The previous eight chapters detailed each individual type of waste. I would expect that you now have a deeper understanding of each and can probably see some examples in your own operations that may not have been visible prior to reading these chapters. In an effort to preemptively address a potential knee-jerk reaction, I have added this chapter. The last thing I want, now that your eyes are open to this enormous opportunity, is for you to make a hasty decision.

This is a fairly short chapter, but, as an operations consultant myself, I am including it as a precaution so that those reading it don't get caught in the trap that could, in essence, debilitate your organization. I have seen from personal experience the long-term cultural and operational impact and problems resulting from the inappropriate and misguided utilization of consulting resources. Please read the entire chapter before you pass judgment on the idea that I am attempting to convey. I am and always will be a strong advocate of the knowledge, experience, innovation, insight, and leadership guidance that the consulting industry offers.

It is not a coincidence that every company I have worked for over the last 25 years has, at some level, fallen into the same trap. Let's say you know that waste, problems, and opportunities saturate every corner of your organization. You are desperate to stop the fiscal bleeding and the resulting operational carnage, so in an attempt to turn it around, you hire a large outside management or Lean consulting group to come in and remind you of something you already know: "Yes, you have waste and endless opportunities for improvement in your processes."

You sit through extravagant PowerPoint presentations that demonstrate through colorful pictures, eye-popping graphs, emotionally charged videos, and high impact charts the unimaginable magnitude of the potential improvements that exist. You see the calculations unfold before your eyes, revealing the millions of dollars that are being left on the table, on the production floor, in the OR department, in the billing department, and so on because of your current conditions. You may have experienced similar situations personally and be vigorously nodding your head in agreement. You may even be a consultant thinking that I have a vendetta against the consulting industry, but I don't.

The Value of Consultants

I am a consultant myself, and I have a lot of well-respected and close personal friends who work in this industry and who are providing value and a positive impact for their clients. I am absolutely an advocate for the use of consultants, but only for the right reasons, in the correct context, and with the appropriate expectations. True-to-the-trade consultants, if acting according to their purpose and with their client's best interest in mind, should be, by nature, working to make their services unnecessary.

> **"The solution to waste resides within the people who live and breathe your purpose every day, who are, in essence, the voice and face of your companies to your customers."**

Hold on one second. What am I saying? It makes no sense and even seems counterintuitive. As a consultant, shouldn't I be writing about how I can turn your company around and help you create processes that will leapfrog you to the forefront of your industry? Shouldn't I be demonstrating through endless reports and data that it is in your best interest to hire me to come in and show you how to run your operations? Well, remember my last sentence in the previous paragraph, about how consultants should be working to make their services unnecessary? I truly believe it.

I believe to my core that, as leaders, executives, managers, supervisors, and front-line team members, you have to start taking a different approach to fixing the problem of process waste. The solutions to the waste problem already exist inside your companies. I am not talking about new software or new equipment. I am talking about you, the person sitting next to you, and the people you pass a hundred times a day in your organization. It starts with the process experts who fill your ranks and are referred to as: employees, team members, front line staff, workers, welders, nurses, technicians, waitresses, customer service representatives, cashiers, stewardesses, team leaders, managers, etc. The solution resides within the people who design, produce, and distribute your products and services. These are the people who live and breathe your purpose every day, who are, in essence, the voice and face of your companies to your customers.

UNFAMILIAR TERRITORY

I utilize a lot of rental cars. Regardless of the available vehicle options, I like driving a Toyota Camry. Every rental company uses them, and so I will walk right by the Malibu, Mustang, Camaro, Maxima, and Elantra just to snag a plain white Camry. Those other cars are excellent vehicles, but I am familiar with the Camry's layout, performance, and functions. During one unfortunate trip to Palm Springs, I arrived at the airport to find that no Camrys were available. I took another vehicle and spent far too much time fiddling around with lights and levers, pushing buttons, and fumbling through the radio and A/C options. One switch turned on the heated seats, which I quickly realized was not a wise selection. By the end of the week, I had finally figured out how to turn on the Bluetooth and connect my phone for hands-free phone calls, just in time to turn the car back in at the airport. My point is nobody knows more about a car than the person who drives it every day. Your employees understand your processes better than you do, so any improvement activity should have the team members positioned in the center of the process.

The challenge comes in effectively harnessing and leveraging the enormous amount of knowledge, talent, and experiences these internal experts already poses. Think I am off base? Just look back at the last time you hired a new employee who already had some great experience in your industry. I would bet that it still took him, at minimum, several months to understand your organization and become truly proficient in his new role. But why? Well, as his new employer, your company is managed, operated, equipped, supplied, staffed, and organized differently than his previous company. He had to get to know new faces and names, remember new passwords, learn the new layout, and become familiar with the shortcuts unique to your IT systems.

There is a learning curve anytime someone joins your ranks, regardless of his or her level of responsibility. So, how do you justify the belief that bringing in an outside group of self-proclaimed "industry experts" for 6 months to solve your problems will produce sustainable results? Did you catch the key word in the previous sentence? *Sustainable.* Quick fixes quite often lead to quick results, followed by a quick regression to the previous condition or even worse. Think about it. To arrive at your current state, and for your problems to have gotten to the point where they are now, it has potentially taken numerous years and multiple generations of management. How can you think it realistic that a group of people who don't even know where the nearest restroom is will be able to, in a short period of time, develop a deep understanding of your operations, organization, and culture, let alone solve your underlying foundational issues?

Transferring the Torch, Not the Crutch

The main objective of using these outside groups should always be to create and develop a team of internal experts who are capable of carrying the torch and driving operational excellence once the consultant's contract has ended. If this is not the main objective, you create an environment where you tell employees, "You are not smart enough, talented enough, or knowledgeable enough to drive this company to succeed." You, in essence, rob the company and teams of the priceless knowledge and experience that is gained from deeply understanding your processes, investigating the problems, and implementing solutions. When you use consultants as the problem solvers for these situations, the value of that knowledge and experience walks right out the door with them once the contract is over.

You can also create a very expensive management behavior pattern in which every time a problem arises that seems overwhelming or is so messy and politically charged that nobody wants to become associated with it, you simply call a consultant group. This provides an immediate out as everyone can now just blame the consultant if the project fails. The use of consultants, if not managed, can become a crutch.

Several years ago, my daughter, Brittany, decided to play football with her friend in the middle of winter in a foot of snow. She had no concerns, as the snow would absorb any impact with the ground, right? Well, as it turns out, you can, in fact, still break your ankle in a foot of snow. As a result, she remained on crutches for roughly 6 weeks. The crutches were vital, as they provided a way for her to stay mobile and continue her junior year of college. There came a time when she had to reduce her reliance on them, put weight on her foot, work through the pain of regaining flexibility and strength, and ultimately stop using the crutches. If she had not stopped using them, she never would have completely healed, and, as a result, would have been handicapped by her own conscious decision to continue to rely on the crutches.

In the same way, a company can become so reliant on consultant groups that they, in essence, make the conscious decision to remain on crutches, operationally dependent on what was initially intended to be a short-term solution. The company fails to regain its "operational strength, flexibility, and endurance."

In some ways, the use of consulting groups has become what I call a "corporate drug." On an individual level, the only way to truly solve a drug addiction is to first admit and take responsibility for the addiction, and to then correct the situation through counseling and treatment programs. Unfortunately, when faced with the impending withdrawal symptoms, many times people simply ignore the short-term and long-term consequences of the addiction and instead choose another quick fix to get rid of the pain.

The trouble with this action is obvious – the quick fix is only a temporary solution or Band-Aid. In a very short period of time, the shakes, sweating, and pain return, leading to another quick fix and an endless cycle of misery and addiction. In the same way, when a company becomes overly reliant on outside groups to fix its problems, the easiest way to eliminate the "operational shakes, sweating, and pain" is to call a consultant.

Just like the drug addiction, though, once the consultant leaves, and without the internal competencies necessary to address and solve your own problems, the operational shakes, sweating, and pain will return, quickly leading to another "consultant fix." Just take a look back on the money your company has invested over the last 10 years in outside consultants. If the money you spent cannot be validated by documented, measurable, and sustained performance improvement results that continue to this day, then where was the value in the consulting investment? What value could that same money have potentially provided if it had been invested somewhere else in the organization?

Consultants as Partners

Don't get me wrong by thinking that consultants and outside groups do not play an important role in creating a platform for success. They absolutely do, but as a partnership, not as a group of Armani-wearing superheroes who your employees automatically line up behind. These outside groups do have a critically important role in that they can provide the knowledge, experience, guidance, training, mentoring, skills, and tools that enable you to develop internal expertise and establish continuous and sustainable improvement systems. They are often comprised of talented and experienced people who have held positions that range from team leader to president. They bring to the table fresh eyes,

251

unique perspectives, out-of-the-box ideas, and insight that can be vital to your company's continued growth and development.

By elaborating on this subject, I simply want you to understand that, to maximize the problem solving and process improvement potential of both the in-house experts (employees) and the outside consulting groups, we must first understand the unique tools, knowledge, and expertise that each brings to the table. When combined into one focused and undivided front, together they can accomplish infinitely more than either could on its own.

The Parable of the Onion

To use an illustrative example that will hopefully hit home with every reader, let's take a trip to your kitchen. If you are like my family, the kitchen refrigerator is a place of awe and wonder, with its multiple levels of different foods, sauces, drinks, dips, vegetables, and meats. Some items found in the furthest reaches where light barely penetrates probably date back to the early 20th century.

We organize our refrigerator like most families, I suspect. Our top shelf is for drinks and large containers. We have the milk, wine, juice, a gallon jar of dill pickles, half empty sport drinks, and, along with many other things, a large jar of pickled garlic that we just can't seem to get enough of.

The second and third shelves are for other miscellaneous smaller items like mayonnaise, butter, margarine, sweet pickles, and other seldom-used items that are relegated to the very back. The door is for the salad dressings, ketchup, mustard, water bottles, and an array of hot sauces that have origins from all over the world. Some contain titles that are not appropriate to verbalize in our home.

The first drawer is dedicated to meats and multiple packets of different cheeses. Finally, the bottom drawer is for fruits and vegetables, containing apples, cucumbers, lettuce, cabbage, kiwi, carrots, lemons, and, finally, onions. The unsuspecting onion is the whole point of this paragraph.

Several years ago, I helped my wife prepare a dinner. She asked me to cut up an onion for the main course. I complied and did what I considered a fine job, demonstrating culinary skills rarely seen east of the Mississippi River. Here is where it got interesting. Since I only used about half of the onion, I put the rest in a resalable bag and placed it not in the bottom drawer, but on the third shelf. To add to my error, I failed to seal the bag correctly, meaning that it wasn't actually sealed at all. It was a very nice meal, and the onions were absolutely the star of the dinner. The next morning, we left for a 1-week vacation.

You already know where I am going with this, don't you? Upon our return home a

week later, my youngest son made the mistake of opening the refrigerator. Oh, my goodness! You guessed it, the smell was overwhelming. We located and disposed of the onion immediately, but, over the next several days, we began to notice a trend. Everything in the refrigerator either smelled like or tasted like onion. Needless to say, I am now restricted to chopping up only carrots and celery.

The point is everything in the refrigerator was tainted by its exposure to the onion. The ketchup smelled like onion, the apple tasted like onion, the cheese was transformed into an onion derivative, and even the ice had a mild hint of onion. This made for some interesting drink flavors – onion orange and onion cranberry juice are something everyone should try at least once.

When a company brings a consulting group into its organization (the refrigerator), the results should be the same as what took place with the onion. Every department, unit, area, production line, group, and level of the organization should, in some way, smell like the onion. It may not be a direct impact (onion flavor), but there should at least be an indirect impact (onion smell).

If the only reason you use consultants is to receive recommendations regarding your productivity, consistently leading to layoffs and RIF's, why would your teams ever see them as a resource? Why would they ever welcome them and provide them with honest and accurate information? Why would they ever want to partner with them, learn from them, or work together to develop long-term strategies for success?

Now, if you took my advice and read the entire chapter, you now understand that I am not campaigning against the consulting industry. Quite the opposite, in fact – I am an advocate of using consultants, but only so long as they are utilized in a responsible manner that adds sustainable value to your organization, leaving it stronger and more capable than when they arrived.

CHAPTER 21:
THE TAKING ACTION TOOLBOX

Over the last 20 chapters, we have taken a deep dive into the concept of waste. We have jumped into a submersible and journeyed 36,070 feet down to the bottom of the deepest part of the ocean, the Mariana Trench. Hopefully, through this journey you have discovered things about your operations, processes, people, and maybe even yourself that you were not aware of before. Here is where the rubber meets the road.

All of this newfound knowledge is of little value without the ability and determination to take action and address the opportunities. Talking about process waste and inefficiency is easy, since we all know it exists within every part of our lives. The challenge comes in doing something about that waste – actually identifying and eliminating it. I believe that you would be hard-pressed to find anyone who would argue that there isn't waste in any one of the processes they work in on a daily basis. Even in the most successful companies such as Toyota, Apple, Amazon, and Google, waste is present. What should convict and motivate you is that these industry leaders are the first ones to acknowledge the existence of waste and the urgent need to eliminate or minimize it.

This book is about action, not theory. It's about enabling you to understand, identify, and eliminate waste. This chapter is intended to point you in the right direction and then give your bike a big push down the hill we call action. There are many well-written books available to help you search for and destroy waste, and many other problem-solving tools and methodologies that can be of great benefit. In this chapter, I will briefly detail the purpose and use of several of my go-to tools that I utilize to achieve meaningful and sustainable results.

TRAINING FOR THE IRONMAN

I am in awe of those who compete in and complete Ironman competitions. These races consist of a 2.5-mile swim, a 112-mile bike ride, and a 26.2-mile marathon. I'm in pretty good shape, but this sounds like a recipe for catastrophic heart, lung, and leg failure. Sharks live in the water, big ones, and a 2.5-mile-long group of swimmers sounds like an aquatic buffet line – a Golden Corral for sharks. Training for an Ironman is a serious and long-term commitment. Let's pretend I make the decision to complete an Ironman. I buy a $2,000 bike, several pairs of the best custom fitted running shoes, and a couple of sleek Speedos. I am ready for action. I go out to the garage occasionally and oil the wheels and air up the tires on the bike, but I never actually ride it. I slide on and lace up my new shoes, but never actually run any farther than the mailbox. I even model my Speedos and sometimes wear them in the hot tub (to my kids' shame and embarrassment), but I never use them in a pool. I have all the tools I need to complete an Ironman, except one – effort. Buying the tools was easy; using the tools to accomplish something amazing requires strength, discipline, endurance, commitment, and effort.

I like these tools because they can be applied in almost every situation, by almost anyone, without the need for an advanced degree in mechanical engineering or quantum physics. As I mentioned early in the book, I am not a borderline genius waiting at the mailbox for my Mensa membership card to arrive. I prefer simplicity and ease of use over complicated systems that lead teams down rabbit holes or become so encumbering that they lead to analysis paralysis. The value in simplicity and ease of use is recognized when we begin to see the experts (team members) using these tools every day as part of their normal routines. Instead of being viewed as external tools, they become part of the operation, embedded into the fabric of the process itself.

Don't tiptoe around these tools like a 1964 Lamborghini 350 GT, afraid to open the hood or even touch the door handle. Jump in, buckle your seatbelt, and start it up. Take the tools for a drive, burn some rubber, redline the RPM gauge, and test the suspension on some sharp curves. Learning to use them effectively comes from driving them, and the more you drive them, the better driver you become. The tools in this chapter are only effective when you "drive them." Start it up!

Kaizen/Kaizen Event

Purpose: To drive a sustainable organizational transformation and to engage every employee in Continuous Improvement.

Kaizen is a Japanese term that means to continuously improve. Kaizen is a way of life, a way of thinking. It is not something you accomplish in one week, but is a continuous, never-ending journey. Of all the tools found in this and other books, I believe Kaizen is the greatest and most impactful, possessing the potential to deliver results and rewards beyond what most think possible. Kaizen is not just a tool; it is a method for cultural transformation.

There is no magic formula behind Kaizen; it is simply a mindset that permeates every aspect of an organization – its people, its processes, and its strategy. Kaizen saturates a culture like a wet sponge. Kaizen is the arch enemy of contentment and complacency, refusing to surrender to average or acceptable, always striving to improve. When I say "improve," I am not referring only to quality or productivity. I mean every aspect of a company – the engineering, production, customer service, quality, delivery, research, innovation, human resources, finance, accounting, purchasing, and so on. Every single

aspect!

A lot of people and organizations misuse the term Kaizen to refer to a group event or team activity, such as: "We organized a Kaizen to fix the productivity problem." This is not Kaizen; this is a Kaizen Event or activity. A Kaizen Event is centered around improving a discrete process or fixing a defined and measurable problem.

Continuous Improvement (Kaizen) is just that, continuous. It is not completed in a week, month, or even a year. It is ongoing, driving further and further toward operational perfection. Operational perfection is not a final destination and is located beyond the reach of any organization, but through Kaizen you can move closer to it on a daily basis. The gears of Continuous Improvement are not perpetual, turning forever as if driven by some mystical power. They require force and energy to maintain momentum.

Newton's First Law of Motion (inertia) states that "an object at rest will remain at rest, and an object in motion will remain in motion unless the object is acted upon by an outside (unbalanced) force." This means that it takes work to set your teams in motion, building momentum by utilizing tools to eliminate waste and fix problems. Once they are in motion and have picked up speed, the success they experience, coupled with leadership's daily engagement, will sustain the momentum and provide the energy for Continuous Improvement.

A Kaizen Event is a team activity that is focused on improving a specific opportunity. The event and team must operate in an effective manner, or the activity will serve no value. For instance, the team size is not standard and can be made up of 2-100 people, but the larger the team, the more complicated managing the activity can become. The team should be comprised of a broad range of employees working in multiple of departments because every process touches multiple groups and departments. Any improvement activity actions must be cross-functionally measured against every affected group to understand the overall organizational impact.

In addition to the process experts, a Kaizen Event should also contain people who are not directly associated with the process. This provides a "fresh eyes" perspective. These are the people who exist outside the normal operational forest and have a unique perspective that isn't tainted or influenced by the daily routines, problems, and habits. They are the ones who won't be tempted to say, "Well that's how we've always done it."

The Kaizen Team should contain every level of leadership – executive leaders, directors, managers, supervisors, staff, and support groups. You can also involve suppliers, vendors, and sometimes consultants to help facilitate the event or provide industry insight. A hard pill for some leaders to swallow is that there is no rank or position on a Kaizen team. Every member of the team has the same voice and is valued as equal. If this was not the case, the assemblers would be very reluctant to voice an idea, knowing that they could be quickly shot down by a VP or director. As a leader, this will require you to

FIGURE 21:1

Kaizen Event Scope and Tracking Form

Basic Data		Event Team	
Kaizen Event Title / Scope		Executive Sponsor	
		Process Owner	
Event Dates		Team Leaders	
Event Times		Kaizen Event Team Members	
Event Facilitator/Trainer		Team Member Role	Team Member Name
Process Improvement Tools			
Team Meeting Room			
Report Out Time/Dates to Leadership			
Report Out Location			
Event Final Report-Out Date & Time			
Event Final Report-Out Location			
Scope Boundaries			

Event Objectives

How is the need for this event based on current goals, metrics or KPI's?

GOAL STATEMENT

Metrics of Success

Key Performance Metric	Before Kaizen Performance Baseline	End of Project Target Performance	Performance End of Month 1	Performance End of Month 2	Performance End of Month 3	Performance End of Month 4	Performance End of Month 5	Performance End of Month 6	Sustained Performance %

PROJECT ACTION PLAN

Start Date	Improvement Activity	Owner/s	Action Status (Month 1)	Action Status (Month 2)	Action Status (Month 3)	Action Status (Month 4)	Action Status (Month 5)	Action Status (Month 6)	Action Status (Month 7)

Support/Special Services/Materials Needed?

take a humble approach, especially when you are providing ideas or challenging the ideas of others. It is very easy for the comments or ideas of a leader on a Kaizen Event team to be taken by the others as direction, not suggestions. Just be aware.

A Kaizen Event's length can vary from a single 4-hour activity to months or even years of scheduled activities on an ongoing basis. The length of a Kaizen Event depends on the magnitude of the problem, the complexity of the process, and the overall breadth of the scope. For instance, addressing a material storage issue on an assembly line would require far less time than tackling a quality issue that spans four suppliers located in three different countries.

A Kaizen Event is a formal activity that should be documented through the use of a Charter. Figure 21:1 is an example of a basic Kaizen Event Charter. A Kaizen Event Charter can be as complicated or simple as your needs require, but keep in mind you are dedicating a lot of time and resources to this event, so understanding the value that it delivers is critically important.

Regardless of your format, a formal Kaizen Event Charter should always include these items at a minimum:

1. Kaizen Event title

2. Event scope (Define boundaries.)

3. Event dates/time/location

4. Executive sponsor (executive leader who is accountable)

5. Process owner (leader of process being improved)

6. Team leaders (those facilitating and leading the event)

7. Team members and titles

8. Event objective (What are you working to accomplish?)

9. Goal statement (Define success in a single sentence.)

10. Performance metrics (leading and lagging/current and target)

11. Project plan (time driven/owners/activity/updated status)

12. Special needs and support requirements

A Kaizen Event Charter can have an infinite amount of information and be painfully complicated, but putting too much information on the Charter tends to negate its usefulness. I would recommend using supporting documents that provide specific details, and referencing those documents on the Charter. Do not make the mistake of focusing too much attention on the format of the Charter. The Kaizen Event is not about creating a great Charter; it is about solving a problem or improving a process, so don't lose sight of the real objective.

The Kaizen Event is an opportunity to develop a Kaizen mentality and culture in your organization. It is an opportunity to open your team's eyes to see the world in a new way and to be aware of the potential that exists within arm's reach. There are multiple tools that can be utilized during the event that will allow the team to break down and understand the process, identify the barriers and obstacles, and then develop meaningful action plans. Many of these tools are detailed in this chapter.

None of these tools are more valuable than "Gemba," or the place where value is being created. To truly understand a process or problem, the team must leave the meeting room and spend an adequate amount of time on the floor observing the actual process. Process Maps, Time Studies, and Spaghetti Maps are meaningless if they have not been verified and validated with your operational reality. Without going to the Gemba, you are just speculating, and 99.9% of the time, you are missing something because of your limited perspective. I wish I had a quarter for every Process Map or Value Stream Map that a team has corrected after they compared the perceived process flow against reality. Go to the Gemba!

There is no such thing as a perfect Kaizen Event. Your first one may be clunky and awkward, and you may find yourself digging your way out of a rabbit hole you inadvertently jumped into, but that is to be expected. Don't let it discourage you. Identify an opportunity, assign an executive owner who will be accountable and an advocate, identify a couple of motivated leaders or process owners, and give them the Kaizen Event reigns. Put together a cross-functional team, and start using the tools in this chapter. If needed, contact me or another experienced facilitator who can set your team in motion.

Be prepared though. Once you and your team see how effective a Kaizen Event is, the flood gates will open, and everyone will be requesting an Event for their process' opportunities. Be careful not to let your Kaizen Event become nothing more than a paper trophy. A Kaizen Event without meaningful actions and results is what we would call in this book a complete *waste*.

The 5S Way of Life

(Sort, Set, Shine, Standardize, and Sustain)

Purpose: To create an organized and sustainable environment that promotes the flow of service/product to maximize efficiency, productivity, safety, quality, and performance.

5S is not an activity; it is a way of life. It is manifested in the fabric of an organization's culture. It is one of the most useful Lean tools and is one of my favorite to use because the results are realized in real time as you make the changes. Unfortunately, many times people have a misguided understanding of what 5S really is. I have heard managers tell a group of employees to "5S" their area, so everyone grabs a broom and starts sweeping. 5S is so much more – it's about the effective utilization of limited space, minimization of waste, process flow, efficient equipment layout, visual controls, and a safe and clean work environment. 5S is intended to maximize the value that you and your team can produce by improving every aspect of your process' layout and flow.

I have mentioned "flow" several times. Flow is the progress of your process. I used to live in a town in Central Indiana called Kokomo. No, not the town the Beach Boys were referring to in their 1988 hit. To get from one end of the town to the other you would take State Highway 31. This short 7-mile drive could take up to 30 minutes, all because of the number of stoplights. If I jump in my car and drive 7 miles on the highway, it takes about 7 minutes, so my flow on the highway is 1 mile per minute. My flow on Highway 31 through Kokomo is less than perfect, at 1 mile every 4.3 minutes.

It isn't just my time that is being impacted by the traffic light interruptions to my flow and progress. I am also consuming more fuel, placing more wear and tear on my car, getting stressed out, and potentially falling behind schedule for an upcoming meeting. Flow is about time and the resources required to complete a process as designed. Quite often, we live in processes that don't flow well, simply because flow was not considered a priority when the cell was laid out, the program was designed, or the process was engineered.

Here's a quick example of 5S that I mentioned earlier in the book. It is worth repeating. Open your silverware drawer and observe the location of the forks, spoons, and knives. I will almost guarantee that the spoons and forks are next to each other, and the knives are on the outside. How often do you use a knife? In my home, we seldom use knives. On the other hand, we almost always use a spoon and fork. By having the spoons and forks together, you eliminate that tiny extra motion of reaching over the knives every time you collect the silverware to set the table.

Figure 21:2 shows two rivers – poorly drawn rivers. In all rivers, the objective of the water is to flow to a final destination. Water may start as snow at the top of a mountain in Colorado, or it may begin its journey as a rain drop in the Mississippi Delta. Regardless

FIGURE 21:2

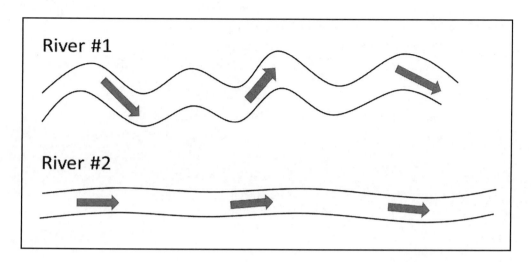

FIGURE 21:3

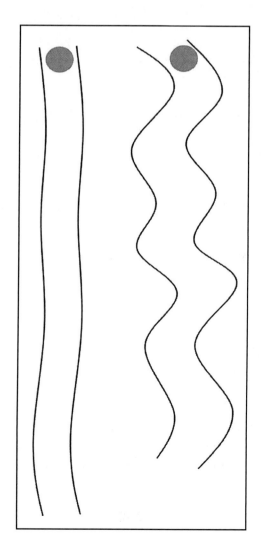

of where the journey begins, water wants to flow to the sea, and the quicker the better. Which of the rivers in the figure do you think flows faster? What would cause the water flow in the two examples to be different? The flow of water in River #1 will be slower than the flow or the water in River #2 because there are curves and bends in the river path that disrupt the flow. The curves and bends also increase the actual distance the water must flow.

Remember what they say: "The shortest distance between two points is a straight line." The same applies to your processes. The shortest time between the process' beginning and end is a straight line. A straight line contains no curves or bends – no obstacles that interrupt the progress or disrupt the flow. By eliminating those obstacles and interruptions, you allow your process to progress quickly and efficiently from step to step. Effective flow benefits you, your teams, downstream processes, organization suppliers, and certainly your customers. Even if you turn Figure 21:2 on its end and remove the water from the flow analogy, gravity itself validates the concept of flow.

See Figure 21:3. Drop a ball in the top of both examples and see which one finishes first. When you design processes to flow, the results are the same. The 5S tool utilizes five unique steps or stages: Sort, Set, Shine, Standardize, and Sustain. Each of the five steps is defined below.

5S STEP #1 – SORT

Purpose: Identify and inventory everything contained in a specific area of operation, keeping what is needed for current operations and removing what is not.

1. Sort through all items, inventory, supplies, tools, and equipment in the area.

2. Document the location and quantities of all items, inventory, supplies, tools, and equipment.

3. Keep what you need for current operations.

4. Remove items not needed for current operations.

5. Keep only the appropriate quantities to support current operations.

6. Acquire the items that you do not have to support current operations.

7. Red Tag items removed from the area. A Red Tag Process (Figure 21:4) involves identifying an area where all items removed from a process during a 5S activity will be stored until evaluated and transferred to other departments, placed back in inventory, disposed of, sold, or held for later use. Red Tagging is literal in the

sense that you are placing a red tag on items you remove from the area. A Red Tag should contain the area the item was removed from, the date, and the 5S Event name.

FIGURE 21:4

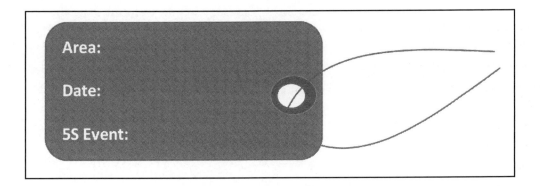

The identified Red Tag storage area is controlled and not open to the general population to pick through like a local flea market. The Red Tag area has one to two people who control it and can authorize the transfer of items.

The Sort activity is to reset the area. Normally, during the Sort stage, you will find obsolete materials, old tooling, 5-year-old cans of Vienna Sausage, old reports and forms, 600 pens and pencils, dead mice, and that blue binder everyone was looking for 3 years ago. During Sort, you also tend to realize that you have 10 times the amount of materials and supplies that you would need to support operations for a month. Sorting is taking a step back and asking, "What is absolutely necessary to be successful and support current operations?"

5S STEP #2 – SET

Purpose: Identify a place for everything, and put everything in its place.

1. Identify the optimal location for all items based on their use (frequency, sequence, dependencies, etc.).

2. Locate items that are used together in the same area.

3. Focus on safety and ergonomics by eliminating repetition and Excess Motion.

4. Utilize location indicators and min/max quantity levels.

5. Use visual management (color coding, work instructions, pictures, shadow boards, floor tape, etc.).

6. Make the process flow.

The purpose of the Set step in 5S is to create an environment that promotes success. By first Sorting and removing all excess or unnecessary items, you eliminate the clutter and chaos, allowing you to design the process layout in a manner that flows. Think about the last time you moved. Remember the boxes all over the living room, dining room, kitchen, and bathrooms? All of these boxes made it difficult to move around, prepare dinner, and even take a shower. Once you had removed the boxes and organized each room, life became much easier.

Think about your remote control sitting on the arm of the couch or the coffee table. It is a perfect example of 5S, especially the Set stage. You pick it up, turn on the television, turn on the cable or satellite, select "Guide," scroll through the channels, and select a program – probably without ever actually looking at the remote. You can do this because the engineers who designed the remote understood how your hands work. They realized that you would be using your thumb for 99% of the remote control's functions, so they organized the buttons to accommodate this. In some homes, the remote control is almost an extension of your body, like an extra appendage. The remote control buttons are designed to promote your entertainment process flow.

A few Lean tools that can help in the Set stage are Spaghetti Maps, Value/Non-Value Analysis, SMED, and Cardboard Cities. These tools can help you to first understand your processes, and then develop and experiment with different layout options in order to implement the optimal process flow. Even after you implement the optimal layout, you and your team will naturally find additional opportunities to continuously improve.

5S STEP #3 – SHINE

Purpose: Clean everything inside and out.

"Clean everything" means just that – everything. This includes shelves, work benches, closets, cabinets, equipment, floors tools, walls, bins, desks, computers, and so on. It can also include painting, patching holes, filling cracks, straightening fixtures, removing tape and adhesive from the wall, and many other things. Shine doesn't necessarily mean making an area look beautiful, but it does mean making an area your employees would be happy to work in. It also means making an area that you would be proud to show your customers or clients on a tour.

The fact that the area is now clean and shiny is not the only benefit. A clean environment speaks to you. What do I mean by that? Well, take my garage for example. I keep my garage clean, including the floor. Imagine I pull out of my garage one morning and notice a big black spot on the floor. I get out and walk over to find that it is a small puddle of oil that has dripped from my car. Based on that knowledge, I take my car to the dealer to identify and correct the problem.

If, on the other hand, I did not keep my garage clean and just let the dirt, leaves, rocks, and other debris that blows in accumulate for months, this scenario could end very differently. I pull out of my garage one morning and use the remote to close the door. The garage floor is filthy, so I am unaware of the oil spot. Twenty miles down the road, my oil light comes on in the car. Being 50 miles from the nearest dealer, I risk it and keep driving. Twenty miles later, my engine makes a spine-chilling noise and then freezes up. I coast to the side of the road and call for assistance. After being towed to the dealer, I am informed that my car had a catastrophic failure and now needs a new engine.

A clean environment makes problems stand out. This is called "Inspection Through Cleaning" and is extremely effective. An environment that "Shines" will also result in improved quality and productivity. When the hospital room floor is maintained in an immaculate manner, even the smallest scrap of paper, syringe cap, tissue, or used glove stands out, promoting the maintenance of the standard.

> **"Inspection Through Cleaning requires documented and posted visual standards for sustainment."**

Shine goes beyond just cleaning up the current dirt and debris; it means putting processes in place that prevent the dirt and debris from returning. For example, in a machining center where metal chips are flying out of a lathe and onto the floor, a guard could be installed to keep the chips inside the equipment area.

In a city park where the trash can is always overflowing and allowing paper, trash, bottles, and wrappers to blow all over the children's playground, possible solutions could be to install additional trash cans, utilize trash cans with hinged lids, or increase the pick-up frequency of the trash.

Kitchen stoves are a great example. Years ago, we had a stove with heating coils that sat inside silver trays on the top of the range. If something being heated up would boil over, the mess went everywhere and took a lot of time and effort to clean up. Now, we have a smooth ceramic cook-top. If something boils over, it's no big deal, as the mess is minimal and easy to clean up.

Shine is a critically important step that some make the mistake of skipping, thinking that it's just about a broom and a spray bottle of all-purpose cleaner. It's not; it's about creating an environment that promotes pride, establishes clear expectations for sustainment, and visually speaks to you. Clear expectations and accountability should be reinforced through visual standards (Standard Work) that show what the area should look like and what "clean" means. Using a daily or shift audit to drive accountability is an effective tool. When people leave an area clean for the next shift, they come to expect the same when they return. This audit process drives a level of self-accountability across the teams, opening avenues of communication between shifts or groups that typically ascribe to an "us vs. them" attitude.

5S STEP #4 – STANDARDIZE

Purpose: To develop processes and procedures to sustain the previous three steps.

1. Engage employees, and utilize their knowledge.

2. Develop robust Standard Work.

3. Document roles and responsibilities for the team.

4. Training, training, and more training.

5. Establish location and min/max quantities for items.

6. Create and post cleaning schedules and procedures.

7. Share information through visual controls.

8. Use color coding, status boards, and floor layout.

Standardizing as it applies to 5S is proactively answering two questions: "Where does this belong?" and "What am I supposed to do?"

If a co-worker borrows a tool from you and brings it back, but you are not in the area, an effective 5S program will show them where to place the tool. The tool has a home, and making that home visual prevents misplacement and the resulting search and rescue operation that takes place later. As shown in Figure 21:5, every wrench, ratchet and drill in this work space has a unique home. If, at the end of your shift, you need to take an inventory the tools, this Shadow Board allows you to do it quickly vs. rifling through a toolbox and counting everything. The Shadow Board gets its name from the shadows or outlines it contains, showing each item's storage location. Shadow Boards can be used to visually identify the home for tools, cleaning equipment, fixtures, supplies, and many other items. Different sized wrenches will have different sized shadows, broom shadows look like brooms, and so on. This is the visual management side of an effective 5S program.

FIGURE 21:5

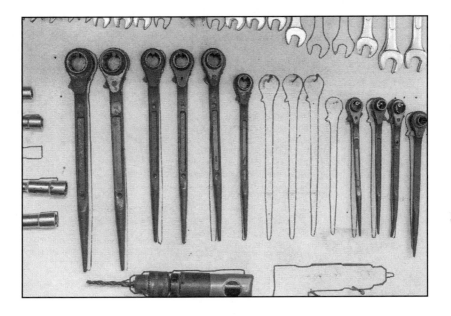

The term "board" in Shadow Board does not mean that you must actually use a board. Shadow Boards can be utilized on walls, tables, on the sides of equipment, inside cabinets, and on shelves. Also, the term "shadow" does not imply that you must use a simple outline. For instance, in a toolbox, you can insert a piece of foam material in the drawer and then cut out openings in the foam in the distinct shape of each tool, creating a unique home for each one.

How do you maintain this level of organization and sustain the accompanying improvements in performance? Simply stated, by establishing clear expectations and driving accountability – an expectation is nothing more than words if there is no method for verifying compliance. I can tell my children to clean their rooms, but if I never check to see if the rooms are cleaned, they will eventually figure out I am not serious. You can tell your employees to clock in and out on time for lunches, but if you never run a report that measures their compliance, eventually they will figure out that your expectations are hollow words.

FIGURE 21:6

Production Area - 5S Daily Audit

Area: _____ Date: _____ By: _____

Item	Item Description	Yes	No
1	Does the area contain only tools needed for current production?	▓	
2	Are the fixtures in the area ones required for current production?	▓	
3	Does the area contain only parts that area needed for current production?	▓	
4	Are the parts/tooling/fixtures in area correctly identified?	▓	
5	Is production area clean and free of dirt/chips/oil on floor?	▓	
6	Is the area free of any trip hazards?	▓	
7	Is there a 5S cleaning board in the area and is it equipped?	▓	
8	Are all parts/equipment/tooling in the designated areas?	▓	
9	Are white boards updated with production plan and current status?	▓	
10	Are recent quality and production issues displayed in cell?	▓	
11	Are tooling and inventory storage areas adequately marked?	▓	
12	Are previous week's audit cards located in cell?	▓	

Green Boxes = Score | |

Comments:

The 5S SCORE GOAL IS 12 "Yes"
Score: 10 - 11 = Good
Score: 8 - 9 = Need to improve
Score: 5 - 7 = Unacceptable
Score: 0 - 4 = Need Immediate Action

OR Area 5S Audit

Room: _____ Date: _____ Time: _____ By: _____

Item	Item Description	Yes	No
1	Are the fire extinguisher and electrical box unobstructed?	▓	
2	Is the Nursing Station organized to standard?	▓	
3	Is all of the standard equipment in the room?	▓	
4	Is the room equipment organized to the standard?	▓	
5	Are cabinets 1 & 2 organized according to the standard?	▓	
6	Are cabinets 3 & 4 organized according to the standard?	▓	
7	Are cabinets 5 & 6 organized according to the standard?	▓	
8	Are cabinets 7 & 8 organized according to the standard?	▓	
9	Is the count board cleaned?	▓	
10	Are all supplies from previous case put away?	▓	
11	Are trash and linen containers emptied?	▓	
12	Is the room clean?	▓	
13	Is the anesthesia equipment organized to standard?	▓	

"Yes" Boxes = Score | |

Comments:

The 5S SCORE GOAL IS 13
Score: 10 - 12 = Good
Score: 7 - 9 = Need to Improve
Score: 4 - 6 = Unacceptable
Score: 0 - 3 = Need Immediate Action

A tool for validating compliance with your expectations for maintaining the 5S standards is a simple audit. I am not referring to a process that takes 10 minutes; I am talking about a simple 2-3-minute defined process that measures adherence to the standard and provides enough information to correct any deviation trends.

Figure 21:6 shows a couple of simple audit cards that I used with a hospital and a manufacturing organization. These cards are formatted in Excel – three audits fit on a letter sized sheet of paper or card stock. There is nothing complicated about them, and each took roughly 2 minutes to complete. After each audit is completed, the cards are placed in a designated slot, and then the performance score is entered into a tracking tool that is posted in the department for everyone to see. The key to success in sustaining 5S is immediately resolving any deviations from the expected standard as outlined on the audit. For example, if the score for the OR totaled 9 instead of 13, the auditor should address the deficiencies with the team in real time, instead of waiting until the next day.

5S STEP #5 - SUSTAIN

Purpose: To develop habits and behaviors that result in a positive cultural transformation.

Sustain is all about leadership. What is important to the leaders becomes important to the team. A priority expressed by a leader is translated into action by an employee. The proverbial "flavor of the month" epidemic that most organizations suffer from is a direct result of the ever-shifting wind of expectations from leadership. Sustained success or failure rests on the shoulders of leaders

An effective 5S program is sustained when you:

1. Define and communicate expectations clearly, consistently, continually, and visually.

2. Ensure the team is trained in the 5S process.

3. Continue to look for opportunities to improve.

4. Use visual management tools wherever possible.

5. Develop Standard Work to drive consistency and eliminate variation.

6. Develop systems to measure and communicate 5S performance to the team.

7. Immediately address and resolve any deviations and deficiencies as defined by the standard.

There is no way around it; 5S Step #5 is the hardest. It's hard because 4 weeks after implementing 5S, when the excitement and celebration start to fade, it becomes work. It becomes work to sweep under that shelf, clean behind the grinder, pick up that paper behind the printer, and wipe off that equipment. It becomes work for the supervisor or manager to complete the 2-minute audit when there are so many other pressing issues. It becomes work for leadership to monitor performance and address issues.

Yes, it is work, but the real benefit isn't realized in the first or even third month. Its realized 6 months down the road, when a clean and efficient process becomes just a normal part of doing business – when 5S isn't something we do; it's how we live. The benefit is realized two years down the road when an employee who has lived 5S is transferred to another department and immediately starts driving a transformation in the new area to deliver the same organized, efficient, and effective flow.

A 5S EXERCISE

A fun 5S exercise for the team that I have seen used many times over the years at various companies is something I call the Numbers Exercise. This concept was originally developed by RWD Technologies, but has since been modified and manipulated thousands of times to suit different needs. I have created my own version that adds some additional twists.

The premise behind the Numbers Exercise is simple: circle the numbers 1 through 50 in sequential order. First find the number 1 and circle it, then find the number 2 and circle it – all the way to 50. Success is reaching 50. The exercise has four stages, with the page format changing in every stage.

There are four pages in the exercise, and they are to be completed in order. Only give the team one page at a time.

PAGE 1:

Start by handing out the first page of the exercise as shown in Figure 21:7. Hand it out face down and direct the team not to turn it over until you say so. Use a stopwatch or timer, and allow them 3 minutes to complete the exercise. Instruct them to find and circle the numbers 1 through 50 in sequential order. Clarify that they are not allowed to circle a number unless they have located and circled the previous number. Also clarify that they are not allowed to circle the entire page at once or to circle only parts of numbers (circle the 2 in number 28 and claim to have found the actual number 2). There is to be no talking or sharing of information. Tell them to turn over the page and begin.

FIGURE 21:7

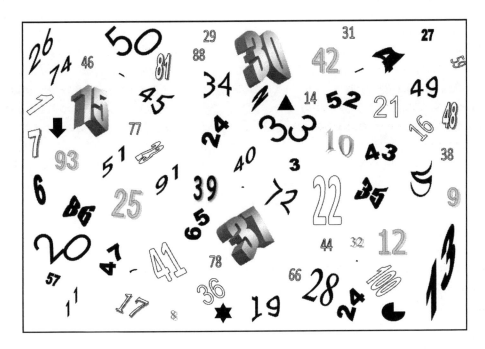

After the 3 minutes have passed, tell them to stop, and then review their performance together. Ask the team how many of them got to 10, 20, 30, 40, and 50. On the board, draw out a matrix as shown in Figure 21:8, and fill in the boxes with the number of team members who reached each level.

FIGURE 21:8

	Page 1	Page 2	Page 3	Page 4
Score of:	3 Minutes	2 Minutes	1 Minute	30 Seconds
10				
20				
30				
40				
50				

Most people will probably get to around 15 or 16. A few people may get into the 20's, and some will probably get frustrated and not get past 10. Ask the team why they struggled to get to 50 when everyone in the room can easily count to 50.

Their struggle to reach 50 is a result of several factors, but start by pointing out and addressing only one – the instructions involved the numbers 1-50, but the page contained numbers higher than 50, as well as shapes and letters. These additional items were nothing more than distractions. Mathematically, the team spent roughly 36% of their time looking at numbers, letters, and shapes that had nothing to do with their success and served only to interrupt their progress. From a 5S perspective, these numbers, letters, and shapes were the clutter in their work areas – equipment rarely or never used, obsolete parts and material, duplicate tools or fixtures, old monitors and printers, excessively large tables, and unneeded shelves or cabinets. Just like the numbers, letters, and shapes in the exercise, all of these items interfere with their progress and disrupt their process flow.

PAGE 2:

Prepare the team for Page 2 (Figure 21:9). Inform them that, as a dedicated leader who listens to employee feedback, you are going to eliminate everything from the page that could interfere with their success. All the letters, shapes, and numbers over 50 will be removed. Instruct them that, with the improvements made, they should be able to find more numbers, and therefore they now have only 2 minutes to complete the exercise. Hand them the second page face down, and then instruct them to all start at the same time.

FIGURE 21:9

After 2 minutes, instruct them to stop. Ask the team how many reached 10, 20, 30, 40, and 50. Fill the matrix out with their performance information, and then discuss why they once again didn't succeed. Many times, people will actually do worse on this second page than on the first. Discuss the page's lack of organization or flow. Acknowledge that numbers are sequential and should be laid out in a manner that flows. Right now, the page is just one big jumbled blob. Maybe if it were broken up and organized, it would be easier to navigate. Inform the team that you will make some improvements personally to help them.

PAGE 3:

Prepare the team for Page 3 (figure 21:10). Inform them once again that, as an engaged leader, you have taken their concerns to heart and have made some changes that you are certain will enable them to succeed. Also, in light of the improvements and your resulting confidence in the process, you are now allowing them only 1 minute to complete the exercise. Hand them the third page face-down, and have the team start at the same time.

FIGURE 21:10

Be prepared. As they turn over the page, you will hear groans and moans. They were hoping for something better. They were hoping for something organized that flowed well.

After 1 agonizing minute, instruct them to stop. Ask the team how many reached 10, 20, 30, 40, and 50. Fill the matrix out with their performance information, and then discuss why they once again didn't succeed. What you will hear from the team at this point is that the numbers are different shapes and sizes, and they are not all vertical. The biggest obstacle the team will surface is the fact that the numbers are *still* not in sequence, and this does not provide for effective flow.

Inform them that they are mistaken. There is actually a very distinct flow, as shown in Figure 21:11. This pattern from block to block continues all the way from 1-50. When the team sees the pattern, they will have an "aha" moment. This is the opportunity to drive home the importance of documented standards. As their leader, you created a process that flowed, but unfortunately, you didn't document it or train the team. Your personal Standard Work was just that – yours alone. Nobody else knew about the pattern, and, as a result, everyone continued to flounder around like fish on the beach.

FIGURE 21:11

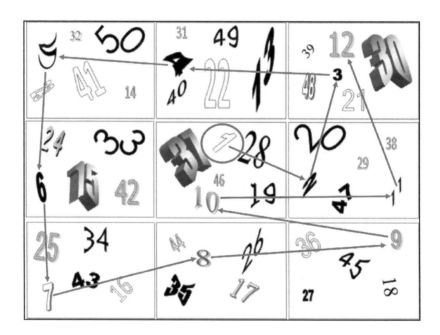

At this point, the team should very clearly understand the importance of standardizing the format, color, size, and orientation of the numbers. They should also demand that the numbers be ordered in a manner that is sequential, makes sense, and flows.

PAGE 4:

Prepare the team for Page 4 (Figure 21:12). Explain to them that all of their suggestions and ideas have been implemented, and, as a result of the process improvements, they have only 30 seconds to complete the exercise. Hand them the fourth page face down, and instruct them to start at the same time.

FIGURE 21:12

1	2	3	4	5	6	7	8	9	10
11	12	13	14	15	16	17	18	19	20
21	22	23	24	25	26	27	28	29	30
31	32	33	34	35	36	37	38	39	40
41	42	43	44	45	46	47	48	49	50

After 30 seconds, stop everyone. At this point, everyone in the room should have circled 1 through 50 easily. Take a count, though, and put the information on the matrix. Assuming you have 20 people in the room, and they are not all astrophysicists from MIT, your matrix totals should look similar to the numbers in Figure 21:13.

FIGURE 21:13

Score of at Least:	Page 1 3 Minutes	Page 2 2 Minutes	Page 3 1 Minute	Page 4 30 Seconds
10	6	7	5	0
20	14	12	9	0
30	0	1	3	0
40	0	0	1	0
50	0	0	2	50

Put this into perspective for the team. Originally having 3 minutes at their disposal, but working in a chaotic, unorganized, non-standardized process, nobody probably got past even 20. On the other end of the exercise, with only 30 seconds at their disposal, but working in a clean, organized, effective, and standardized process, everyone got all the way to 50. In the last exercise, everyone succeeded in meeting their goal!

5S EXERCISE SUMMARY:

Circling the numbers 1 through 50 was a simple process, but it was still a process. The characteristics of this exercise are no different than any process, regardless of the industry. If your processes are filled with obstacles, barriers, excess material, obsolete equipment, or anything else that produces waste, your team experiences the same confusion, frustration, stress, discontentment, and failure as they did during the first three exercises.

If, on the other hand, you are able to make your process organized, standardized, visual, and clean, providing for effective flow, you will utilize less time and resources to accomplish far more, as demonstrated in the fourth exercise. Your team will be more engaged, disciplined, committed, and focused. This is an enormous step in a successful cultural transformation and becomes the foundation for an organization filled with empowered and accountable people who refuse to settle for second best.

Value/Non-Value Analysis

Purpose: To improve the value that a process produces by identifying and then minimizing or eliminating steps that consume resources and capacity, but produce no value.

So, how do we identify and eliminate waste? Let's first start by identifying it – by understanding the processes at an entirely new level. Every process, without exception, is comprised of individual steps or actions that, when combined with others, lead to an end product or service. Identifying and categorizing them as either Value, Waste, or Necessary-Waste is the first step in understanding. Necessary-Waste is still waste – a less than optimal situation that cannot be avoided due to the current process layout or design. The goal would be to eliminate it at some point, but for now it is accepted as required.

Let's use an example that everyone should hopefully be familiar with – brushing our teeth in the morning. I will run through what I believe to be a generic process that most probably follow, and then we will break it down. This same activity can be applied to any process in any organization.

Ok, I wake up in the morning. I crawl out of bed, walk to the bathroom, open the door,

278

and walk over to the farthest of the two sinks. I reach down and open the top drawer. I grab my toothbrush and the toothpaste tube. I close the drawer. I unscrew the toothpaste lid and squeeze about 1 inch of toothpaste onto my toothbrush. I screw the cap back on the toothpaste, open the drawer, put the toothpaste back in the drawer, and close the drawer again. I reach over and turn the water on and run my toothbrush under it. I reach back over and turn the water off. I stand there for some time brushing my teeth – I think about 2 minutes or so but am not sure as I have been known to fall asleep standing up.

Once finished scrubbing my teeth, I bend down and spit in the sink, then turn the water on to rinse out the sink, and then turn the water off. I turn around and wipe my mouth off with a towel. I then turn the water back on to rinse my toothbrush off, turn the water off, and then turn to dry my toothbrush off with the towel. I then turn back around and turn the water off. I open the drawer and put my toothbrush back in the drawer for the next use.

FIGURE 21:14

Step #	Activity	Cycle Time	Value	Non Value	Process Improvement Ideas
	BRUSHING MY TEETH - PROCESS VALUE				
1	Wake Up	5	X		
2	Crawl out of bed	6	X		
3	Walk to bathroom	5	X		
4	Open the bathroom door	2		X	Leave the bathroom door open
5	Walk to far sink	3	X	X	Switch to the closest sink
6	Open the drawer	2	X	X	Store my toothbrush/paste on the counter
7	Grab my toothbrush	1	X		
8	Grab my toothpaste	1	X		
9	Close the drawer	2		X	
10	Unscrew the toothpaste cap	3	X	X	Use toothpaste with pop-cap
11	Squeeze 1" of toothpaste on toothbrush	2	X	X	Do you need 1", or would 1/2" work
12	Screw cap back onto toothpaste	3	X	X	Use toothpaste with pop-cap
13	Open the drawer	2		X	Leave the drawer open from step 6
14	Put toothpaste in the drawer	1		X	Do this when you put the toothbrush away
15	Close the drawer	2		X	Leave the drawer open from step 6
16	Turn water on	2	X		
17	Wet toothbrush	1	X		
18	Turn water off	2	X		
19	Brush my teeth	160	X	X	Use an electric that has a 120 second timer
20	Spit in the sink	2	X		
21	Turn on water	2	X		
22	Rinse drain	3	X		
23	Turn Water off	2	X		
24	Wipe mouth off with towel	4	X		
25	Turn water on	2		X	Rinse toothbrush at the same time you spit
26	Rinse toothbrush off	4	X		Rinse toothbrush at the same time you spit
27	Rinse drain	3		X	Rinse drain only once from step 22
28	Turn water off	2		X	Rinse drain only once from step 22
29	Wipe toothbrush with towel	4	X	X	Do this when you wipe your mouth
30	Open the drawer	2		X	Leave the drawer open from step 6
31	Put toothbrush away	1	X		
32	Close the drawer	2		X	Store my toothbrush/paste on the counter
	Total Process Time	238			

We could look at breaking this process down in several ways, but ultimately, what we are trying to achieve is the elimination of waste. Don't fall into the trap of thinking this is a simple attempt to save time. This process, when done correctly, identifies the non-value activities responsible for the consumption of **any** resource. (See Figure 21:14)

I know this is a very simplistic process, but it makes sense to use an example that I am hoping all readers can relate to. On the surface, everything described above is of value, as it is just part of the process I follow daily to effectively brush my teeth. Upon a deeper look though, we can find multiple wastes buried inside the process. Let's look at each step, asking the questions that seem a little more obvious now that we have them documented:

1. Why do I close my door to the bathroom at night while sleeping? Unless I am afraid of something crawling out of the drain in the middle of the night, what value does closing the door provide when I will just have to open it in the morning?

2. Why do I use the farthest sink? What would prevent me from using the nearest sink and eliminating a couple of steps.

3. Why not store my toothbrush and toothpaste on the counter in a cup, eliminating the need to open and close a drawer?

4. Instead of taking time to unscrew and screw on the toothpaste cap, why not buy toothpaste that has a pop-open cap to reduce the time spent opening and closing the toothpaste?

5. Is it necessary to use 1 inch of toothpaste on my toothbrush, or is 1/2 inch enough to effectively brush my teeth? If 1/2 inch is sufficient, I can double a single tube's lifespan and cut in half my future expenditures for toothpaste.

6. Why am I closing the drawer over and over, knowing that I will just have to open it again later in the process? Why not leave it open until the very end of the process?

7. Why take the time to put the toothpaste away individually when I will have to mimic these steps when I put my toothbrush away? Why not wait and put them both away at the same time?

8. I am normally half asleep when I brush my teeth, and, in some instances, have probably dozed off while completing the task, leading to a process time that is longer than required. Why don't I use an electric toothbrush that has a built-in timer? This will limit this step to the optimal required time.

9. Why not spit and rinse my toothbrush in sequence, requiring only one occurrence for rinsing the sink?

10. Why not wipe my mouth and toothbrush off in sequence?

Look at the opportunities we just listed for what most of us consider the simplest and most monotonous of tasks. As simple as this is, now look below to see what the process looks like with these improvement opportunities now embedded into the process.

FIGURE 21:15

Step #	Activity	Cycle Time	Value	Non-Value	Necessary Waste
	NEW: BRUSHING MY TEETH PROCESS VALUE				
1	Wake Up	5	X		
2	Crawl out of bed	6	X		
3	Walk to bathroom	5	X		X
4	Walk to **near** sink	2			X
5	Grab my toothbrush	1	X		
6	Grab my toothpaste	1	X		
7	Pop open the toothpaste cap	1			X
8	Squeeze **1/2"** of toothpaste onto toothbrush	2	X		
9	Close toothpaste cap	1			X
10	Turn water on	2	X		
11	Wet toothbrush	1	X		
12	Turn water off	2	X		
13	Brush my teeth (electric timed toothbrush)	120	X		
14	Spit in the sink	2	X		
15	Rinse toothbrush off	4	X		
16	Rinse drain	3	X		
17	Turn Water off	2	X		
18	Wipe mouth off with towel	4			X
19	Wipe toothbrush off with towel	4			X
20	Put toothbrush away	1	X		
21	Put toothpaste away	1	X		
	Total Process Time	170			

If you want to go to the next level of efficiency, you could take it even further. People tend to laugh at me when I tell them this, but how much more time could be saved if you staged your toothbrush sitting next to the sink with toothpaste already on it, so that it was ready (kitted) for the next use. I know, the toothpaste might get a little crusty sitting there, but it would still work.

So, the original process took 238 seconds, or 3 minutes and 58 seconds. After we broke down the process (see Figure 21:15), identifying value and non-value activities, we combined steps, eliminated redundancies, reduced travel and motion, and reduced the overall process to 170 seconds, or 2 minutes and 50 seconds. Not a big deal, right? It's just brushing your teeth. Actually, it is a very big deal – that's the point of this simple yet insightful exercise. That difference of 68 seconds equals a 28.5% improvement in process time, not counting the toothpaste savings, the wear and tear on the drawer, the reduced water consumption, and so on. Based on the assumption that you brush your teeth twice per day, 365 days per year, that 28.5% improvement equates to 827 minutes, or 13.8 hours per year. Calculate how much you get paid per hour at your job, multiply that amount times the 13.8 hours, and then tell me again how this is not a big deal.

In a small manufacturing organization I worked with, we completed a detailed Value/Non-Value Analysis in a small assembly cell. The process flow was actually fairly well organized already, but the cycle time of the downstream process was several seconds quicker, meaning that, since we were running a single piece flow line, the downstream process was often waiting for parts. We videoed the process and documented the Value/Non-Value Analysis. We were surprised to find that what we had previously thought was a decent flow was in fact quite congested and riddled with waste.

Many of the process steps were simply a result of how the cell was laid out. There was Excess Motion, Transportation, and Over-Processing Waste everywhere. The Spaghetti Map revealed that a day in this cell was like walking a mini-marathon, in steel-toed boots. As we broke the process down step by step, we started to ask the same question over and over again: "Why are we doing that?" The answers were fairly straightforward. We had laid out the cell and materials in a manner that necessitated waste to assemble the part.

As a team, we identified each non-value activity and worked to eliminate it. Instead of just moving the cell around, we completed a Cardboard City of the cell, equipment, tools, and materials. The team used the Cardboard City to run a mock production line for an hour. After every iteration, we re-evaluated the results and modified the Cardboard City layout again until we arrived at the best process cycle time. We moved cardboard equipment, fixtures, tools, materials, and parts.

As a result, we took a process with an original cycle time of 2 minutes and 46 seconds down to 2 minutes and 21 seconds, a 25 second reduction, or 15.1% improvement. The real benefit became evident as we realized that the cycle time for this cell was now 12 seconds faster than the cycle time for the downstream cell. You know where we went next! Yes, we completed the same activity for the downstream cell and then simply continued this process over and over again. As Eliyahu M. Goldratt explains in his Theory of Constraints, continually identifying and eliminating the limiting factor (constraint) will always drive you to the next limiting factor as you work toward your goal. This is where Continuous Improvement and the Theory of Constraints align perfectly, creating a perpetual and self-sustaining path of improvement.

Picture just one of your hundreds of processes. It might take 20, 100, 200, or even more lines to document it in the Value/Non-Value manner shown in Figure 21:15. It may take you days or weeks to get it right and validate the steps and times. Once completed, though, what do you think it will tell you? Understanding your process at the micro-process level is absolutely critical and extremely revealing. You don't know your processes as well as you think you do, and breaking them down using this Value/Non-Value activity will help you understand them at an entirely new level.

The resources you are consuming will become obvious, whether utilized through value or waste. Keep in mind that there are some processes that do not add value, but are required to complete a process. For instance, walking to the bathroom is motion and really adds no value, but, unless you want to brush your teeth at the bedside and spit into the nightstand drawer, I would suggest walking to the bathroom. In these situations where a non-value but necessary step is required, the goal is to minimize them, like walking to the nearest sink vs. the further one.

The "New Shoes" Matrix

Purpose: To build the foundation for improvement by identifying and documenting the value expectations for all participants in a value stream.

The "New Shoes" Matrix is a quick but very useful tool. It forces you and your teams to take a step outside of your box and slide over to a different and even unfamiliar box. It is the operational version of the old saying: "Don't judge a person until you have walked a mile in their shoes." The team takes the perspective and wears the shoes of every other participant within a value stream, or process. This tool requires you to understand exactly what value you expect to derive from a process, as well as the value expectations of every other person or group. This activity also provides a sounding board for ideas for improvement so that you can understand how a single change may benefit one group, but at the same time have no effect or possibly even a negative effect on others.

I call this the "New Shoes Matrix" because it requires you to ask the question of every value stream participant: "What are your expectations, and what do you value?" Why is this so important? It's important because you are not the only person or department impacted by a process. There are many dependencies that exist, stretching out laterally and horizontally across the organization. You and your department are a single spoke on the "operational wheel," and every bump in the road impacts everyone else as well; you just may not understand how. The New Shoes Matrix is important because it connects the dots for team members who previously didn't realize that a mistake or problem in their circle of influence migrated out to multiple other circles, causing problems and chaos.

FIGURE 21:16

Cath Lab Kaizen Event – "New Shoes" Value Matrix		
PATIENTS	Timely Treatment Good Communication Friendly and Compassionate Clean Environment Safety Up-to-Date Equipment Well Trained Staff Family Accommodating Environment Professionalism of Staff	Trained and Capable Staff Good Flow & Turnover Times Up-to-Date and Innovative Equipment Special Accommodation Requests Flexibility of Scheduling Streamlined Information Entry Friendly Staff Clean Facility Safe Environment	**PHYSICIANS**
STAFF	Safe Work Environment Teamwork Physician Timeliness Good Management/Leadership Improved PAT Processing Support from Administration Effective Flow Efficient Flow Good/Reliable Equipment	Effective Flow Increased Capacity Perception as Best in Area In Compliance Effective Scheduling Safe Environment Happy Engaged Employees Attractive to New Physicians	**HOSPITAL**

Building a New Shoes Matrix is easy. You simply list the participants of a value stream and then start listing the value expectations for each group. Figure 21:16 is an example of a New Shoes Matrix that a team I was working with completed. You can see in the different quadrants what the team listed as value for each of the four groups. Did the Kaizen Event team come up with all of these on their own? Absolutely not. We went to the Gemba and asked the groups what value they expected. Even now, I know there are additional items that could be listed, but this provides a strong foundation.

By documenting these value expectations, you begin to share a common perspective. You begin to understand that you are not the only one who struggles daily with obstacles, but that everyone shares in those struggles. You also start to realize how an improvement impacts not just you, but potentially all three of the other groups.

I like to use the New Shoes Matrix tool at the beginning of a Kaizen Event or any problem-solving activity, simply to lift people out of their own process forest and take a new look as a team from above the tree tops. It's common to hear comments like: "Oh, I didn't realize that," or, "I hadn't thought of it that way before," as the "perspective explosion" goes off. As you develop a game plan for improvement, understanding each of these expectations enables you to ask the question, "Will this change provide a value increase or decrease to each value stream participant?" Understanding this will prevent you from making well intended changes that actually result in unexpected consequences.

The Value Stream and Process Mapping Tools

Purpose: To provide a detailed visual representation of the material, people, and information flow within an organizational process in order to identify constraints, understand dependencies, and formulate improvement action plans.

I am not going to go into a lot of detail regrading Value Stream Mapping, as there are some exceptionally informative books out there dedicated to teaching this skill. My personal favorite is *Learning to See* by Mike Rother and John Shook. It provides details and examples that are useful and clearly explained.

The tool's name itself, "Value Stream Mapping," is somewhat misleading because in completing one, you are documenting the entire value stream, both value and non-value steps. The purpose of the process is once again to understand value at an entirely new level. Value Stream Mapping gives the team an even higher-level view than the New Shoes Matrix – more of a 10,000-foot perspective of an organization's processes and how they interact.

This tool gives teams a big-picture idea of things like how materials move from one area to another, how orders are communicated, how much inventory is needed in between processes, how long processes take, how many people are required, what individual process times are, etc. You may have heard of an M&I Flow, which stands for Material and Information Flow. This shows the order-to-delivery flow for a product or family of related products. These are good to visualize an enterprise or organizational level flow of product and information.

A more detailed and actionable approach to the Value Stream Map is the PLM (Process Level Map). A PLM dives to the same level of detail that we identified in the Value/Non-Value activity at the beginning of the chapter. The main difference is in the way it is portrayed. A PLM is a visual indication of the steps within a process – hence the word "map." In a PLM, every detail of the process is documented, down to the who, what, when, and where. By creating a visual depiction of a process, it becomes easier to identify specific barriers or constraints that are related to each unique step in the process.

To understate the importance and value that a PLM can provide would almost be criminal. When developing a PLM, the real complexity and challenges faced every single day are made painfully obvious. The entire team learns not just the details of their own processes, but also the dependencies and interactions that exist among every unit, department, and system that are part of the process. A great exercise to validate the comment I made earlier – "you don't understand your processes as well as you think you do" – is to pull together a team of managers from different departments.

FIGURE 21:17

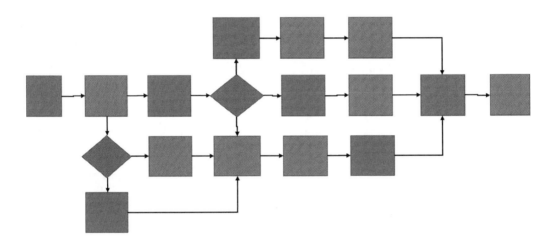

Using sticky notes and arrows connecting them, complete a PLM of a process that crosses over all the managers' areas of responsibility. Once completed, go to the floor, pull together some team members from their departments, and have them come up and evaluate the PLM the managers developed. Give them a pad of sticky notes that are a different color than those the managers used. Without exception, this is what will happen. The team members will look at the PLM and start making statements like: "You forgot this step," "We don't do this anymore," and "This doesn't happen unless..."

The point? Even the managers of a specific process are missing some degree of understanding in the flow of the process simply because they are not "working inside" the process daily at the floor level. At this point, correct the PLM with the new sticky notes based on the team members' input. Next, go to some of the ancillary and support departments. Have team members from these departments come up and look at the PLM. Give them a third color of sticky notes. The exact same thing will happen as when you brought in the first group of team members. The PLM is much closer to our actual reality, but, based on their perspective and unique roles, the new group will quickly identify gaps and omissions in the documented process. Have them fix the process with their sticky notes.

You will end up with a PLM that looks somewhat like a rainbow (Figure 21:17), but what does that tell you? Don't be discouraged by this. There is enormous value in the revelation that, as individuals or individual departments, you really don't know your process that well, and, as a result, you struggle to effectively eliminate waste and solve problems that result in organizational-level impacts.

Another win that comes from completing a Value Stream Map or PLM is that the entire team becomes painfully aware of how their actions impact every other department, unit, and organization as a whole. They realize that when they don't document something at the appropriate time, it causes a delay or possibly 12 extra steps for a person downstream in the process. They realize that not collecting and delivering replenishment parts in the correct sequence can potentially cause a 15-minute delay in part availability and ultimately a line stoppage. The registration group realizes that not putting a "Fall Risk" or "Restricted Diet" wristband on patients at the time of admission can cause multiple reworks for the nurse upstairs, not to mention the potential safety risks for the patients themselves.

Once you are comfortable with the PLM, understanding that it will never be 100% perfect, you can start identifying specific barriers and constraints at individual process level steps. I like to document these directly on the PLM, under each process step. In Figure 21:18, you can see an example. The boxes represent the individual process steps, the decision steps, and the barriers or constraints that are specific to that unique process step. It takes very little time to correlate the current level of performance in an area with the fact that it almost seems like a miracle that parts get manufactured, patients get treated, or service is provided at all, given the number of barriers and opportunities that exist.

Now, be prepared – most teams will default to two specific obstacles when they complete this PLM – the need for more staffing and more equipment. These are the go-to excuses, applicable to every situation known to the business world. Fortunately, they are just that – excuses. In the vast majority of these situations, staff and equipment are nothing more than a temporary solution for a broken process filled with waste and inefficiency. The quickest path to increasing capacity and better utilization of your limited resources is to eliminate the waste that is consuming those resources.

Don't stop here. Once you have completed (documented and validated) the Value

287

Stream Map or PLM, you can then start using the tools described in this chapter to understand and address the opportunities. The Value Stream Map or PLM will probably contain a vast list of obstacles and barriers, so you will need to prioritize the problems based on impact and risk. Don't try to "boil the ocean;" focus on a few issues at a time. Utilize the Kaizen Event team to then begin using the tools to improve the processes.

FIGURE 21:18

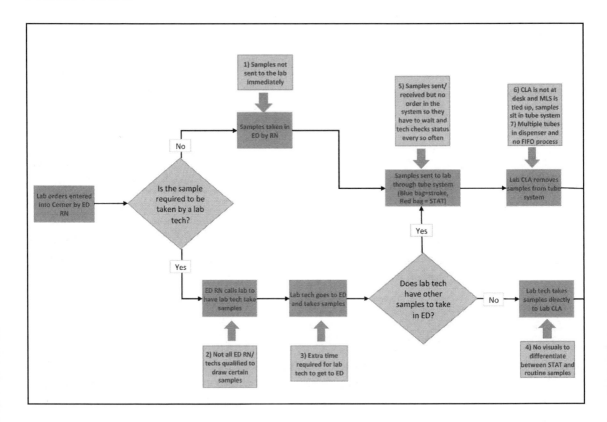

The Pareto (Reality) Chart

Purpose: To break down a problem by its individual contributing factors to understand the significance of each.

The Pareto Chart is one of my favorite tools for one simple reason – it documents your reality. The Pareto Chart is named after its developer, Vilfredo Federico Damaso Pareto, an 18th century Italian engineer who is also known for the 80/20 rule. Now, what do I mean when I refer to "your reality"? Well, if you are a leader of a department, unit, or an entire organization, try this one simple exercise, and you will most likely gain an immediate understanding of my intent.

Bring your entire team into a room – hopefully between 10 and 20 people. Give each person one individual sticky note. Instruct your team that this is an individual exercise and that there is to be no talking. Ask the team to write down on their sticky note what they as individuals believe to be the single biggest improvement opportunity for your departments. Give them a couple of minutes to sort through the plethora of available answers that are flooding their minds. After everyone has stopped writing, have them fold up and then turn in their sticky notes. From my experience, out of 20 sticky notes, you will get 12 to 15 different answers.

That being said, how can you or your team expect to actually solve problems and improve your performance if you can't even agree on what the most significant opportunities for improvement are? You can't! At best, you will pick one and maybe get lucky, but you can't effectively solve your most critical problems based on everyone's perception; you need to take actions based upon your reality. You need to be able to prioritize the opportunities and address them in the order of their impact or risk to you, your team, and the organization.

I like to use an example from a 1977 film called *Day of the Animals*. In the movie, the earth experiences some sort of sun flare that floods earth with radiation, messing with the minds of all the animals in a small northern California mountain community. Every animal goes nuts. Man's best friend turns against him, snakes and rats become aggressive, birds of all kinds become carnivores, and you can only imagine what starts going through the minds of mountain lions and grizzly bears. I am not advocating watching the movie, and I don't really remember much except that Leslie Nelson loses a one-on-one wrestling match with an enormous grizzly bear.

Ok, moving on to my excessively belated point. Let's pretend that you were one of the unfortunate hikers walking through the mountains that day. You like to be prepared, so you decided to carry a Winchester 270 rifle and a 12-inch Bowie knife with you as you trekked through the wilderness. Aside from a wayward charging elephant, this rifle should protect you from just about anything you encounter. Your day is going well, until you walk over the ridge of a hill.

As you come over the ridge, you see a line of animals standing about 20 yards out, poised and ready to attack. In the lineup, you see a mountain lion, wolf, chipmunk, grizzly bear, possum, raccoon, bull moose, wolverine, and porcupine. This is not good, so you quickly evaluate your options. Realizing you only have five rounds in the clip of the 270 rifle, you slowly shoulder your rifle, take aim, and eliminate the wolf, raccoon, bull moose, porcupine, and chipmunk. Ok, now you're feeling far more confident in your odds of survival. At this point, you can just use the Bowie knife to finish off the remaining mountain lion, possum, grizzly bear, and wolverine.

Does this sound like the best plan? No, you chose poorly, and have just signed your own death certificate. Facing this lineup of animals, your obvious decision would be to prioritize the animals by risk to life and then use your five rifle rounds to eliminate the most dangerous animals first, starting with the grizzly bear, bull moose, mountain lion, wolf, and wolverine. The four remaining animals, the possum, chipmunk, raccoon, and porcupine, are far less of a threat and thus lower on the priority list. You can easily handle these four with the Bowie knife.

Now, I know you may be formulating in your mind the reasons that I should have chosen a different order for elimination of these first five crazed animals, but the important thing is that you survived. If you must, though, email me your order of threat elimination and reasons, and we can have some fun arguing and justifying our decisions.

You may be asking yourself what this dramatic and vivid literary tangent was intended to accomplish. Well, when we look at how we problem solve in our companies, in some ways, we make the same mistake. If we take that list of 15 sticky note priorities that our team of 20 people produced and just start working to solve them without truly understanding the level of risk and the overall threat that each one presents individually, then we cannot prioritize them. If we are unable to prioritize them, we run the risk of wasting our valuable and limited resources (our five rounds/bullets) on items that were actually not a risk at all, ultimately leaving us in a position where we don't have the capability to address the most dangerous threats.

This is the beauty of a simple Pareto Chart – it removes our individual perceptions and puts our reality into a visual format that everyone can understand. Let's use an example from an ordinary hospital. In a hospital, the operating room department is very important from both a patient care and operating revenue perspective. A key metric for any OR department is FCOTS (First Case On-Time Starts). If a hospital has five operating rooms, each one has a first case, and that case should always start on time.

If the first case does not start on time, every case after that one is at risk of starting late, impacting surgeons, staff, anesthesiologists, technicians, and vendors, not to mention the patients and family members of everyone scheduled for a procedure in that room. It is the proverbial domino effect, with the potential to impact patient health, surgeon satisfaction, staff retention, organizational fiscal health, and more. Knowing how important this FCOTS metric is, most hospitals measure it daily.

So, we start to measure FCOTS using a Pareto Chart. This means that every time we have an OR first case that does not start on time, we document it on the Pareto Chart – both the date and the reason. As we progress through the month, we remain disciplined and continue to accurately and timely capture this information. We discover that there are numerous reasons that an OR first case doesn't start on time. As a matter of fact, as we progress through the month, we realize there are delays for reasons we were never even aware of: lacking equipment, waiting for the surgeon, waiting for staff, waiting for anesthesiology, system issues, patients rescheduling, and waiting on the vendor. If you look at Figure 21:19, you will see the Pareto Chart with these factors listed at the bottom.

Occurrences	Lacking Equipment	Waiting Surgeon	Waiting Staff	Waiting Aneshestesiology.	System Issues	Patient Reschedule	Waiting Vendor
27							
26							
25							
24	5/30						
23	5/28						
22	5/25						
21	5/24						
20	5/20						
19	5/18						
18	5/18						
17	5/18						
16	5/16						
15	5/14						
14	5/14						
13	5/12						
12	5/11						
11	5/9				5/28		
10	5/9				5/26		
9	5/8				5/24		
8	5/7				5/19		
7	5/5				5/14		
6	5/5	5/27			5/12		
5	5/4	5/19	5/26		5/9	5/27	
4	5/3	5/16	5/22		5/8	5/21	
3	5/2	5/8	5/16		5/6	5/16	
2	5/2	5/4	5/9	5/28	5/4	5/15	5/24
1	5/1	5/2	5/5	5/14	5/2	5/1	5/9

OR FCOTS Delays — Factors

Something specific to note on the Pareto is that every occurrence gets its own box. For example, as shown in Figure 21:19, if there are two FCOTS failures on 5/2 due to lacking equipment, then two boxes get filled out. Look at the date 5/18 – there were three separate FCOTS failures due to lacking equipment, so three boxes are filled out with that date. Over time, you are building a bar chart to show the severity of each factor.

So, at the end of the month, we pull the entire OR team together – all 20 of them. We go through the same exercise as we did above. We give them all a single sticky note and ask them to once again write down what they believe the biggest factor or obstacle is in achieving 100% FCOTS, but we add one step. In the middle of the table, visible to all of the team members, is this Pareto Chart with the data we have recorded. We ask them to write their answers on the sticky note and turn them in. The process goes much faster this time, and, instead of getting 15 different answers, how many answers do we get? We get one!

The reason is because we have eliminated random individual perceptions and documented our reality. Our reality is clear and obvious – our biggest threat to FCOTS is lacking equipment. There is no doubt what our priority must be and where we should expend our resources to address the problem. We must find out why we are lacking equipment, and here is where we start to problem solve. But wait, isn't the factor "lacking equipment" kind of generic? There could literally be a hundred pieces of equipment in an OR, so can we really problem solve at this point, or would we still be guessing, using assumptions and individual perceptions? We would be chasing our tail until we understood the problem a little better. The example in Figure 21:19 is what I call a Level 1 Pareto. From a problem-solving perspective, this is the first couple of shovels full of dirt you get when digging a fence post hole.

This information in Figure 21:19 is valuable and puts you on the path of being able to take meaningful actions that lead to the elimination or minimization of this problem in your operations. It does not, however, drive far enough into the problem for us to really understand at the level we need to in order to change our situation.

As mentioned above, the term "lacking equipment" is far too generic. What type of equipment specifically are we lacking, leading to the delay in start times for OR first cases? This is where we use what I refer to as the Level 2 Pareto. So, we confirmed in May that lacking equipment was our biggest barrier to success. In June, we will continue to track the Level 1 info, but also add a Level 2 Pareto to the chart to break down the lacking equipment issue. What we are driving toward is answering the question, "What equipment is causing the delay in start times?" Looking at Figure 21:20, you can see that as we progress through the month, every time a first case doesn't start on time due to lacking equipment (as captured in the Level 1 Pareto), we also specify which piece of equipment specifically we are lacking (as captured in the Level 2 Pareto).

By the end of June, actually very early in June, we realize that it is the Neptune machine that is causing our FCOTS delays much of the time. We have taken a not-so-uncommon situation, where we had simply surrendered to being unfortunate victims of our circumstances, poor FCOTS performance, and worked to truly understand the problem.

That is the amazing side effect of digging into our reality – we actually accomplish two very important things: first we understand our processes at a far deeper level, and second, we utilize this understanding to take meaningful actions that promote Continuous Improvement. We avoid the "shotgun effect" of shooting at everything and hitting nothing.

FIGURE 21:20

OR FCOTS Delays

Occurrences	Lacking Equipment	Waiting Surgeon	Waiting Staff	Waiting Aneshestesiology	System Issues	Patient Reschedule	Waiting Vendor			Ranger	Neptune	IV Pump	Bair Hugger	SCD Machine
27														
26	6/30													
25	6/30													
24	6/29													
23	6/28													
22	6/28													
21	6/28													
20	6/27													
19	6/26													
18	6/24													
17	6/23													
16	6/21													
15	6/18													
14	6/15													
13	6/15										6/30			
12	6/14										6/28			
11	6/12										6/28			
10	6/10										6/26			
9	6/8										6/21			
8	6/7				6/29						6/15			
7	6/7				6/27						6/14			
6	6/7	6/29			6/24	6/29					6/8	6/30		
5	6/6	6/27			6/22	6/22					6/7	6/27		
4	6/4	6/19	6/28		6/17	6/17					6/6	6/23		
3	6/3	6/14	6/26		6/14	6/9				6/18	6/4	6/15		
2	6/1	1/8	6/17	6/27	6/11	6/2	6/22			6/12	6/3	6/12	6/29	6/24
1	6/1	6/1	6/8	6/18	6/3	6/1	6/2			6/1	6/1	6/7	6/7	6/10
	Factors									Level 2 Pareto				

Now, you could continue to drive down further into a Level 3 Pareto if you wanted to. For instance, why are lacking Neptunes for the first cases? Maybe we have 10 OR rooms and only eight Neptunes total. Could some Neptunes be broken or loaned out to other hospitals? If so, does the procedure scheduling team know this? Are there surgeons who prefer a specific model of Neptune and will delay their cases until one is available? You could use the next level of Pareto to dive deeper, but you could also start using the 5-Why and Fishbone problem solving tools we'll discuss next at this point.

The 5-Why Problem-Solving Tool

Purpose: To break down an obstacle or barrier in order to understand the underlying symptoms and ultimately identify the root problem, allowing for the implementation of an effective long-term solution.

FIGURE 21:21

Why #1: _____

    Answer #1: _____

    Why #2: _____

        Answer #2: _____

        Why #3: _____

            Answer #3: _____

            Why #4: _____

                Answer #4: _____

                Why #5: _____

                    Answer #5: _____

                    Why #6: _____

                        Answer #6: _____

                      Why #7: _____

                        Answer #7: _____

The 5-Why problem-solving tool is an effective way to drive down to the root cause of a problem. It is fairly simple and does not take an advanced level degree to understand or use. It can be used by anyone who understands both its purpose and flow. Many people try to over-complicate it and end up getting lost in rabbit holes or an endless loop of tangents. The premise is simple – ask "why" until you identify the ***root cause*** of the problem. Notice I specifically called out the term "root cause"? I make this point for a reason. In many situations, you have grown accustomed to digging until you hit a root, the first thing you can fix. You have been conditioned to stop there, and this is where the mistake takes place. As mentioned in an earlier chapter, the very first thing that you identify as broken and are able to fix is most often not the true root cause; it is merely a symptom. You can tell whether you have addressed the root cause when you sit down and review your meeting notes. If you see the same problem discussions being regurgitated week after week, month after month, and year after year, it is a pretty good indication that you have only addressed symptoms, not the root cause.

The name "5-Why" is misleading – this problem-solving tool is not bound by or limited to asking "why" five times (see figure 21:21). In your journey of discovery, you may find that sometimes it takes asking "why" 12 times to arrive at the root cause, and in other cases only requires asking "why" three times.

The important thing to remember is to use the tools and to take the time to intentionally dive into the issue with open eyes and no preconceived notions of solutions. If you start with the solution in your mind, you will quickly get diverted and end up on some desert island in the middle of an ocean of meaningless information.

FIGURE 21:22

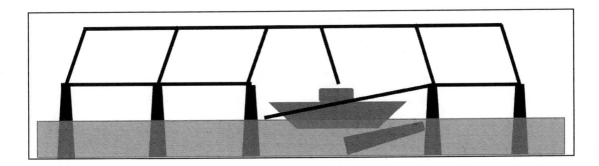

Look at Figure 21:22 above. What this poorly drawn picture shows you is a ship that has attempted to pass under a bridge. Something has happened to cause a section of the bridge to fail and fall on the ship. Let's use the 5-Why tool to understand and answer this question: Why did the bridge fail?

Question 1: Why did the bridge fail?

Answer: A section fell onto the passing ship.

Question 2: Why did the section fall onto the ship?

Answer: The ship ran into the pylon holding the section up.

Question 3: Why did the ship run into the pylon?

Answer: The steering on the ship failed.

Question 4: Why did the steering on the ship fail?

Answer: Someone spilled a cup of coffee on the control panel console.

Question 5: Why did the coffee cause the control panel to fail?

Answer: Because electricity and liquid don't behave well together, and the control panel shorted out.

Ok, at this point we know why the ship ran into the pylon – the control panel shorted out when someone spilled liquid on it. At this point, we could take meaningful action to eliminate the risk of this happening again in the future. For instance, we could design steering control consoles to be waterproof, only allow spill-proof drink containers on the ship's bridge, or develop a standard that does not permit any liquids to be located near the control console.

Wait one second. What was the original question we were wanting to answer? "Why did the bridge fail?" Did we actually answer that question, or did we get caught going down a rabbit hole and instead answered the question, "Why did the ship run into the pylon?" Unfortunately, we had a "squirrel moment" and got distracted. We took the obvious and easy path, unknowingly missing the original intent of the 5-Why activity: "Why did the bridge fail?" This happens a lot and is why working as a team is so valuable, allowing us to stay focused and on target.

So, let's try this again and avoid getting diverted.

Question 1: Why did the bridge fail?

Answer: A section of the bridge fell onto the passing ship.

Question 2: Why did the section fall onto the ship?

Answer: The bridge structure did not support the impact of the ship.

Question 3: Why did the structure not support the impact of the ship?

Answer: The tonnage of the ship and the force it produced were in excess of the impact that the bridge pylon was engineered to sustain.

Question 4: Why was the impact force in excess of what the bridge was engineered to sustain?

Answer: The bridge was designed and built in 1920, when ships were much smaller and lighter.

So, the answer to the original question, "Why did the bridge fail?" is now clear – it was not engineered and designed to absorb the impact of ships as large and heavy as the ones that are currently in use. If we would have stopped with the first 5- Why exercise, we would have only been solving the problem for that one ship, and none of the other 600 ships that pass under that bridge annually, which means we could have been in the same situation a year, month, or week from now when another ship ran into one of the bridge pylons.

FIGURE 21:23

5-Why Action Plan	Department

Opportunity Statement:
Why:
    Why:
        Why:
            Why:
                Why:
                    Why:
                        Why:

Opportunity Statement:
Why:
    Why:
        Why:
            Why:
                Why:
                    Why:
                      Why:

PROBLEM DESCRIPTION		*	Date	Action Plan	Owner	By When
Action Plan #A		A				
Action Plan #B		B				
Action Plan #C		C				
Action Plan #D		D				

* Place the Action Letter on the Pareto chart on the date you took this action

In the second 5-Why, we addressed the reason the bridge failed. Knowing what we know now, we have several options: reinforce the bridge to meet current ship size impact risks, restrict shipping on that river to ships under a certain size, or rebuild the entire bridge with new engineering standards that accommodate current and future ship size and weight impact risks.

Figure 21:23 is an example of a 5-Why tool that I like to use. It is basic but provides a simple format that allows people the ability to actually write out the 5-Why questions and answers. It also provides another critical opportunity to document what actions you are taking once you have identified the root cause problem. It provides an area to document when you take action, the action plan, the action owner, and the target completion date. The key to using the 5-Why tools is simple – just use it. Even if you find yourself 30 feet down a rabbit hole, you will realize it and have now gained a much better understanding of the problem. Doing something wrong is part of learning, just like taking a corner too sharply on your bike when you are 10 years old, digging that pedal into the pavement and skidding across the road into the ditch. The road rash you must tend to for 4 weeks is a great teacher, so you will find yourself a little more aware of your situation and conditions the next time you take that corner. The same applies to using the 5-Why. You will make mistakes and end up on a desert island tangent, and that's ok. As you start to dive in again, you will be more aware of the pitfalls, quicksand, and mirages as you encounter them. The more you use and practice the 5-Why tool, just like any sport, musical instrument, or skilled trade, the more proficient you become, and the better your results.

The Fishbone Diagram

Purpose: To create a visual representation of the multiple factors that contribute to a current condition. Each factor can be broken down to an infinite number of levels to understand and identify the process at a granular level.

I can remember going with my dad to a place in Indiana called "Haunter Bridge" to fish at night. The name was appropriate, as the local myths of someone getting buried in the cement during construction had been passed down for many years. I would sit there late at night, fishing pole in hand, as close to my dad and the dim lantern as possible, certain that there were eyes fixed on me from deep within the thick woods. We would catch carp and catfish and take them home. The carp would be used as fertilizer and buried next to our trees or in the garden.

The catfish, though, served a much more noble purpose – they were dinner. I am not a big fan of fish, but fried catfish is the exception. The thing about catfish, though, is they have a long skeleton comprised of an amazing number of bones. If you are not careful, these can jab you in the side of the mouth or end up in your throat.

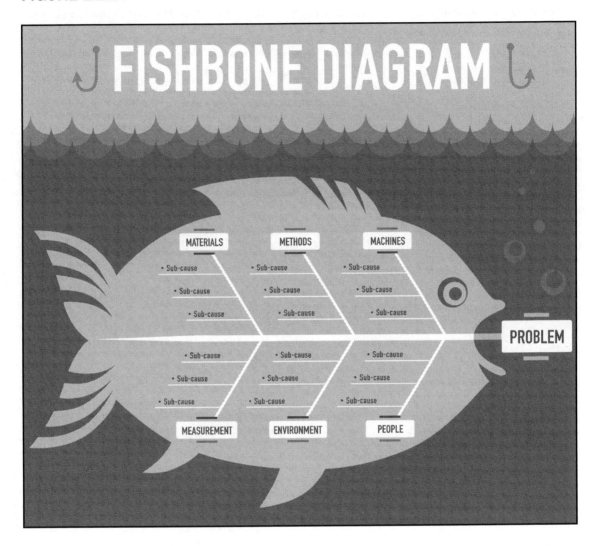

Either way, the Fishbone Diagram (Figure 21:24) – also known as the Cause and Effect Diagram or the Ishikawa (named after Dr. Kaoru Ishikawa) – is extremely useful and makes a lot of sense once you get familiar with it.

I'll offer you a word of caution, though, as it's easy to get entangled in the many "bones" created as you dive deeper and deeper into the problem and contributing factors. A Fishbone Diagram works very well to visualize the potential contributing factors of a problem. It provides a method to show in a written format the numerous possibilities leading to the current situation. Sometimes we get so caught up in the impact of a problem in our own world that we forget the impact it has on numerous others outside the walls of our span of control.

Most problems can be categorized into one of six areas of impact and cause: materials, method, machines, measurement, environment, and people. As you work to complete the diagram, you may find that there is no relevance for one of the factors, and that's fine. Don't artificially fabricate a connection to one of the six factors just to make the diagram look complete or symmetrical. Your objective is content, not cosmetics.

FIGURE 21:25

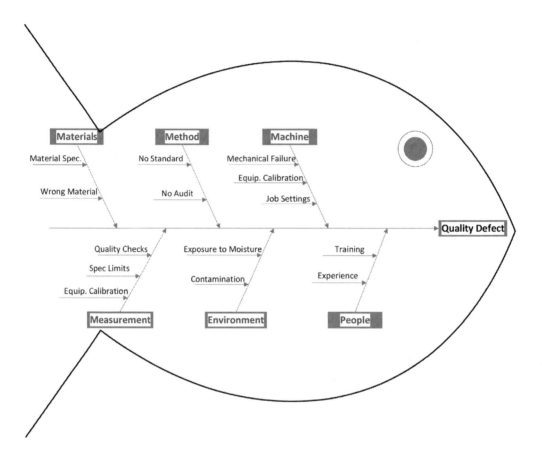

In the simple example illustrated in Figure 21:25, you can see that the problem, a quality defect, can be caused by many different factors. Understanding these factors allows you to investigate and validate whether these specific factors are or are not contributing to the resulting defect. Each of these factors can be broken down further, as illustrated in Figure 21:26.

For instance, under the Materials factor, there could be multiple sub-components that go into a part. Using this method, we would first verify that each sub-component was comprised of the correct material, as called for in the engineering design. Once we have validated the sub-component materials, we could then investigate to verify that the material itself was also within spec limits. Both activities are part of validating the correlation or lack of correlation of these factors to the defective condition. In some ways, using this process is like looking at a grain of sand under a microscope, uncovering the details that are not apparent to the naked eye.

FIGURE 21:26

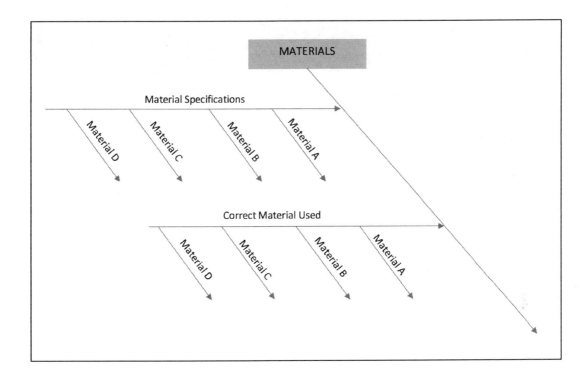

The Fishbone Diagram is, in some ways, a map that allows you to retrace your steps, as you do when you lose your keys. In a hurry, you reach for your keys, but they aren't there. Frantic to get out of the door, you check each pocket and then retrace your steps to eventually find them laying on the top of the washer, where you had set them down to grab a new light bulb out of the cabinet. In the same way, the Fishbone Diagram provides you with the ability to retrace your process to identify potential factors (materials, method, machines, measurement, environment, and people) that resulted in your current situation.

SMED (Single Minute Exchange of Dies) Tool

Purpose: To reduce the time required and resources consumed while transitioning from one process to another.

Do not be fooled into thinking that, because it refers to a stamping die, SMED is only a manufacturing tool. It applies to every industry and organization, leading to improvements in utilization, capacity, and response times.

SMED is a tool that is purposeful in its application. As we discussed in Chapter 13, it is intended to accomplish one thing – reduce the amount of time, resources, and effort required to transition from one process to another. Remember the equations below as they relate to Motion, Transportation, and Waiting Waste.

"Motion takes time, and time *is* capacity."

"Transportation takes time, and time *is* capacity."

"Waiting takes time, and time *is* capacity."

Reducing any one of or all three of these wastes in a change-over or process transition will be immediately realized through an increase in overall capacity. A minute saved in Process A is a minute that can be instantly be applied to completing Process B. Time savings equates to a 1:1 ratio.

SMED can be used by hospitals to improve (reduce) room turnover times in the OR, ED, and in-patient floors. It can be used in an oil change business to reduce the wait time between vehicles serviced. SMED is applicable to restaurants that want to reduce the time it takes to clear a table and seat the next group of customers. It most certainly applies to manufacturing, where changing over equipment between two product lines is an everyday occurrence. The Navy can use SMED to reduce the amount of time required between fighter jet launches and recoveries. Oil companies or manufacturers can use SMED to reduce the time required in periodic maintenance shut-downs. The uses of SMED are limitless.

You already benefit daily from an effective utilization of SMED that resulted from improved technology. Pick up your smart phone. How many songs are contained on that small hand-held device? I have close to 1,800 songs downloaded, which is probably low compared to most. Remember the days of the cassette player? Look at all the music you have on your phone, and then translate that into physical cassette tapes. With an average of 14 songs per cassette tape, I would have to be carrying around roughly 129 individual tapes (and a Sony Walkman) to have access to the same songs.

Currently, I can transition from an intense jam session with the group Journey to a soft and jazzy session with Adele in all of about 5 seconds. I can even add a second or two to locate a specific song. To accomplish the same task with my Sony Walkman and 129 cassettes would require at least 3 minutes, between locating the correct cassette, removing the old cassette, loading the new one, and then repeatedly rewinding or fast-forwarding to the song I wanted to hear.

Transitioning from artist to artist is a change-over in the same sense that a company changes over a process. See, you are the unknowing beneficiary of the use of SMED by Apple, Sony, Samsung, and many others.

Remember computers from years ago? At one point, I purchased an IBM PS-2 486-DX2 that was state-of-the-art. It was the fastest computer on the market…for about a week. These days, that computer wouldn't compete with even the low-end graphing calculators. Think about how many processes a current computer can complete at the same time. Years ago, logging on to the internet and waiting for a web page to load consumed the entire processing capacity of the computer. Improvements in processor speed and capability over the years have resulted in a reduction in the time required to complete individual tasks – another example of SMED in action.

FIGURE 21:27

Ink Cartridge Replacement Process Steps	Time Required (Seconds)
Wait for the printer to finish current job	80
Acknowledge and close the message pop-up	2
Walk over to the supplies cabinet	8
Open the cabinet drawer	2
Locate the black ink cartridge	5
Close the cabinet drawer	2
Walk back to the printer	8
Select "Tools" on the printer screen	2
Select "Ink Cartridge Replacement"	2
Wait for printer to position ink carriage	4
Open the ink cartridge access panel	3
Remove the old ink cartridge	5
Install the new ink cartridge	5
Close the printer ink cartridge access panel	3
Wait for printer to align ink cartridge carriage	10
Acknowledge cartridge replacement on printer screen	2
Load old ink cartridge into recycle bag	5
Walk to recycle container and place old cartridge in	12
Walk back to desk	12
Select next print job on computer screen	4
Add paper to printer paper tray 1	9
Start printing 2nd job	2
Print 2nd job	45
Total Time Required (seconds)	232

To effectively use the SMED tool, you must understand the concepts of *Internal* and *External* activities. An Internal activity is a process step that can only be completed while the equipment is *not* running, or when the value-add action has been paused. An External activity is a process step that can be completed while the equipment *is* running or while the value-add action is operational. A piece of equipment or a process is producing value when it is in operation, so, by reducing the amount of time that the equipment or process is not operational, you improve efficiency and utilization, and also increase capacity.

This concept can be somewhat confusing, so let's take a look at an example that should provide some clarification. If you are reading this book, there's a good chance you drive a car. Your car is providing value when it's in motion, transporting you, your family or friends, and other items such as groceries. Activities that are Internal (actions that can only be completed while your car is not operational) would be changing a tire, replacing an air filter, filling the tank with fuel, checking your oil level, replacing a headlight bulb, airing up a tire, and changing your wiper blades. None of these can be completed while your car is in motion. Activities that are External (actions that can be completed while your car is operational) would be changing the radio, turning on your wipers, using your turn signal, reclining your seat, activating your GPS, changing the A/C temperature, and adjusting your mirrors. These items can be completed while the car is in motion.

I have an HP LaserJet printer in my office. Let's say, while printing a document using paper tray 1, a notification pops up on my computer screen informing me that my black ink cartridge is running low and will soon need to be replaced. Let's complete the black cartridge replacement using two different methodologies.

The first methodology, identified in Figure 21:27, is sequential – all required activities are completed consecutively, one after the other. Using the sequential method, we can complete the task in 232 seconds, or 3 minutes and 52 seconds.

The second method, identified in Figure 21:28, separates the ink cartridge replacement process steps into Internal and External activities, completing steps concurrently when-ever possible. Using this method, I can identify which tasks could be completed while the printer was running, preventing me from interrupting its operation and reducing the amount of value it could produce. A printer is adding value when it is printing, not sitting idle.

SMED forces you to understand and identify dependencies within a process. For example, walking to the cabinet to retrieve a new ink cartridge is not dependent on the printer operations, and vice versa. I can walk to the cabinet whether the printer is running or not, and the printer's operation is not affected by my decision to walk to the cabinet or not. On the other hand, installing the new ink cartridge is absolutely dependent on whether the printer is running or not. The printer cannot be running while I replace the ink cartridge, and the ink cartridge cannot be replaced while the printer is running. When you understand the dependencies within an operation, you are able to separate them into

Internal and External activities and then organize them in a manner that takes advantage of concurrent vs. consecutive completion.

FIGURE 21:28

Internal Activity		External Activity	
(Can only be completed while printer is not running)	Time Required		(Can be completed while printer is running)
Printer finishing current job	80	2	Acknowledge and close the message pop-up
		8	Walk over to the supplies cabinet
		2	Open the cabinet drawer
		5	Locate the black ink cartridge
		2	Close the cabinet drawer
		8	Walk back to the printer
		2	Select "Tools" on the printer screen
		4	Select next print job on computer screen
Select "Ink Cartridge Replacement" on printer screen	2		
Wait for printer to position ink carriage	4		
Open the ink cartridge access panel	3		
Remove the old ink cartridge	5		
Install the new ink cartridge	5		
Close the printer ink cartridge access panel	3		
Wait for printer to align ink cartridge carriage	10		
Acknowledge cartridge replacement on printer screen	2		
Start printing 2nd job	2		
Print 2nd job	45	5	Load old ink cartridge into recycle bag
		12	Walk to recycle container
		12	Walk back to desk
		9	Add paper to printer paper tray 2
Total Time Required (seconds)	161	71	

So, what were the overall results? Originally, following a consecutive method, the entire process took 232 seconds. When I broke the process down into Internal and External activities, I was able to complete 71 seconds of process steps Externally (while the printer was running). These 71 seconds of External process steps were completed concurrently with the Internal activities. This means that the time from the start of the first print job to the completion of the second print job was reduced from 232 seconds to 161 seconds, an astounding 31% improvement.

What would you accomplish if you woke up tomorrow morning and had 31% more capacity in your operations? Maybe a better question would be what could you accomplish with that 31% additional capacity? Start thinking about it now, because if you are serious about utilizing the SMED tool, you will discover and recapture capacity that may have been hidden for a very long time.

If you noticed, I rearranged some steps in the process to accommodate completing some tasks concurrently. You may have noticed that, in the first example, I was utilizing paper tray 1 on the printer, but in second example, I loaded paper into tray 2. Having the ability to print out of two trays provides flexibility and allows me to fill one while the other is running. You may have also noticed that I had to walk to the cabinet to retrieve the ink cartridges. Could I reduce or even eliminate that step if I stored the cartridges at the printer? A SMED activity can utilize other Lean tools, like 5S, Process Maps, and Cardboard Cities to identify opportunities to improve flow by reducing Excess Motion, Transportation, and Waiting.

SMED is another Lean tool that forces you to understand your operations at an entirely new level. By using it, you start to see more clearly the dependencies and connections in what may have previously appeared to be a twisted and mangled ball of string you call a process. Don't get frustrated when you mess up or forget steps, as that is just part of becoming proficient. You don't have to organize a formal team or activity to complete a SMED, but the more people involved, the more likely you are to avoid omitted steps, and the broader the stroke of the paint brush used to drive cultural transformation.

After reducing the amount of time consumed between the value-add activities, you can then re-capture and utilize that time for value producing activities. A word of caution for those that tend to jump in without looking first – never implement a SMED-driven improvement without first involving every impacted group to verify the project assumptions and proposed changes. If possible, pilot the new process multiple times prior to implementation. You will be amazed at the additional wins you will discover from this proactive activity.

The Cardboard City Tool

Purpose: To design a process layout that provides the most value by promoting effective flow and the efficient utilization of limited space.

Remember playing with Legos or Lincoln Logs as a child? Both of my sons, Justin and Jordan, had extensive collections of Legos and spent thousands of hours building everything from castles to cities, cars, bridges, jet fighters, and spaceships. Actually, now that I think about it, my daughter Brittany used to jump in with her brothers and create some amazing things, too. Though not normally historically accurate or compliant with the known laws of physics, their designs were born from imagination. All three of my children are brilliant and exceptional students, and I believe that the Legos played a big part in their development.

I am not directly promoting Legos, but they are a valuable tool, just like a Lean tool explained in Chapter 10 called a Cardboard City. Don't be misled – a Cardboard City is not a literal city made of cardboard. It is only the title for a tool. Think about your house for a moment. If you had it built from the floor up, you probably met with a designer and engineered the layout. You created, in a digital or blueprint format, the actual home itself before pouring even one cubic yard of concrete. Why did you do this? Was it to waste thousands of dollars on a designer, or was it to ensure that the end product was exactly what you and your family wanted to live in for the next 5, 10, or 30 years? I believe it was the latter and that you spent that time and money to ensure that you received the maximum value possible for the large amount you invested in the home.

In the same way, designing a process correctly can yield the same value. I have worked for companies that built a facility and then fit their processes into the available footprint, spending the next 10 years arranging and re-arranging in order to identify value. Smarter organizations design their processes to yield maximum value, and then build the facility around the process. They build value into the process.

A Cardboard City does not have to involve an entire plant or 20-story building, but it can. Even the most advanced design software cannot account for every factor that comes into play in a process on a daily basis. Simulating a layout design and the multiple activities that take place can validate the software design, as well as uncover unforeseen interactions of obstacles, prior to actual implementation.

This is in line with one of the greatest project management quotes ever delivered. President Abraham Lincoln once said, "Give me 6 hours to chop down a tree, and I will spend the first 4 sharpening the axe." A Cardboard City is meant to prepare for value delivery by avoiding process waste creation.

"An ounce of prevention is worth a pound of cure."

A Cardboard City is nothing more than a process or area generically built out of cardboard. There are numerous companies out there that sell cardboard that you can use to simulate a work environment. Taking a piece of cardboard and bending it into the shape of a desk, cabinet, piece of equipment, copier, inventory rack, and so on is actually quite simple. All you need is a tape measure, a box cutter, razors, stop watches, and lots and lots of masking tape.

Start by fabricating the equipment, furniture, and fixtures in an area. If you are looking to optimize the layout and flow in an office area or assembly cell, use masking tape to outline the room or area dimensions. Note power sources, doors, and other items that are contained in or on walls of the current area. Fabricate trash cans, benches, carts, chairs, and other random items that are also part of the area, or just use the real ones. Do not forget to include these items, or you will later be scrambling to locate homes for them. Without going off the deep end, concentrate on realism, fabricating each item to the exact dimensions of the real objects contained in the area.

For items that are stationary or far too large to mock up, simply outline their location with tape on the floor. The outline should mirror the largest profile shape of the item, not just the footprint on the floor. For example, a piece of equipment may have a square footprint on the floor, but it may have a 24-inch overhang 2 feet higher than the base. Once you have outlined the confines of your available work space and then used the cardboard to fabricate the equipment, fixtures, and other items contained in the work space, run some real-life processes.

Simulate reality as if you were actually running production, servicing clients, packing materials, assembling parts, treating patients, and such. You will need to understand your process' Internal cycle times and mimic them to the second. Have people with stopwatches located throughout the process to keep the simulated times accurate and realistic. Simulate the use of tools and equipment to mirror reality. Walk around the area as if the process was the real working environment. Move the carts, material, patients, inventory, customers, supplies, and equipment around as if you were actually completing the process. Have people bring in supplies, have quality checks performed, or pretend to experience a defect or equipment breakdown. Make this process real.

I have completed Cardboard Cities with different organizations ranging from manufacturers, hospitals, office buildings, and service organizations, and one thing continually rings true. "You don't know what you don't know." The purpose of a Cardboard City is to maximize value through the effective flow and efficient utilization of space, but this can only happen if you take the time to complete it correctly. Without exception, every Cardboard City event has led to the discovery of unforeseen problems that ranged from material storage to delivery obstacles, Motion and Transportation Waste, process dependency conflicts, cycle time discrepancies, space availability conflicts, and equipment movement barriers.

As shown in Figure 21:29, we identified specifics like equipment located where no power outlet was available, entry ways that were too narrow for carts or mobile equipment, vertical interferences with part manipulation and handling, area congestion, and safety risks. Any one of these issues we discovered would have resulted in chaos and confusion if realized later after implementation, but, by identifying them in advance, we avoided the negative impact to our customers, suppliers, employees, patients, downstream departments, and higher level organizational processes.

When running a simulated work environment, don't limit it to one or two process cycles; run if for multiple cycles. Have one of the team members complete a Spaghetti Map. Identify the Excess Motion and Transportation Waste, the duplication of steps, and the backtracking. Look for inefficiency in the location of tools and materials, areas where people get in each other's way, situations that could result in safety risks, and scenarios that don't happen often but could be a show-stopper.

After every iteration of the exercise, look for opportunities to improve. Rearrange the area based on those observations, and then run the simulation again. Run, identify, adjust, and then run again until you arrive at the optimal layout and flow. The hours you spend simulating a process flow using a Cardboard City can return literally thousands of hours of value and capacity by proactively avoiding barriers, obstacles, and problems that would have otherwise resulted in interruptions to your processes. A Cardboard City allows you to fix potential problems now, before they become real problems.

FIGURE 21:29

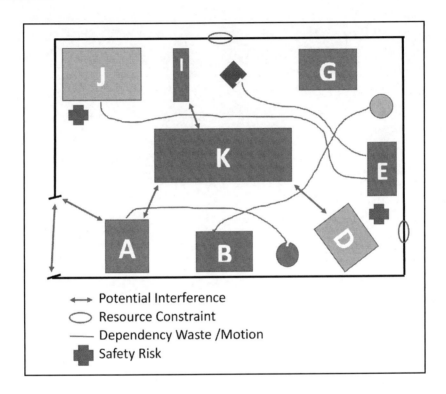

The Spaghetti Mapping Tool

Purpose: To provide an accurate depiction of the motion, travel, and time required to complete a process as currently designed.

As mentioned in Chapter 15, the Spaghetti Map is useful because it puts into a visual format what a process' motion and travel look like. Once you complete the Spaghetti Map (using red ink), you will understand how it gets its name. Few people realize how much repetition and unnecessary motion and travel actually takes place within a process until it is drawn out.

Draw the layout of the environment where the process takes place, and then measure the distances between every different point of interaction, like equipment, desks, inventory shelves, and computers. Once you have the measurements, you can map the motion and travel distance of a person within that process. Prepare for a surprise, as you will most likely be taken aback by the total distances your team members travel on a daily basis.

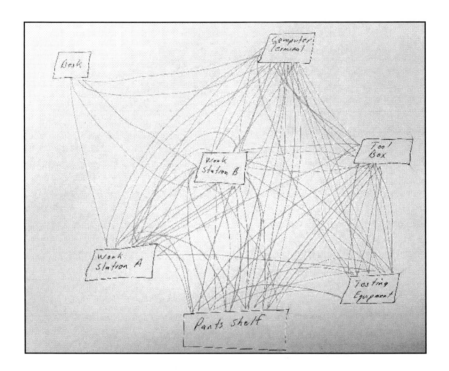

What you are looking for is wasted motion. As you look at the Spaghetti Map, look for duplication of steps or motion that adds no value. Are there pieces of equipment or materials that are used together on a consistent basis, but are located at opposite ends of the process? Are there part storage bins that are not accessible from the optimal direction?

Look for ways to reduce the amount of motion required to complete the process. This may require you to move equipment, storage bins, tools, and desks around, but finding the optimal layout is worth the effort. Prior to moving everything, you could utilize a Cardboard City to simulate the exercise, or you could use simple paper cut-outs and a piece of paper scaled to the correct dimensions for the area.

Either way, run the process through again and again, measuring the distances between interactions. Document the process steps as shown above in the Process Travel Flow Line. It is simple and shows the actual interaction flow.

DISTANCES							
	A	B	C	D	E	F	G
A							
B							
C							
D							
E							
F							
G							

Use a matrix like the one shown above to document the distances between the different points of interaction. Use these numbers to arrive at the total distance traveled while completing the process. Evaluate your findings and identify the optimal layout that reduces your overall motion waste and drives additional capacity into your processes through the recaptured time.

Be careful not to focus so much on motion reduction that you compromise safety or the ability of other groups to efficiently complete their activities that are required to support your department.

The Standard Work Tool

Purpose: To drive process consistency, promote repeatability, and eliminate variation by defining and documenting the individual steps and parameters involved in producing a safe, efficient, and quality service or product.

I am not going to write in detail regarding the value of Standard Work, as Chapter 5 goes into great detail already. I cannot emphasize enough the importance of Standard Work and the critical role it will play in enabling you to perform at levels you currently think impossible.

Do not be misled into believing that you must perfect a process before you document the Standard Work. Even a broken and imperfect process, when documented and performed consistently by trained team members, will achieve improved results, simply as a result of the consistency. Design and engineer repeatability into the process to drive consistency and reduce variation. Three shifts completing a process in three different manners is a breeding ground for variation and Defects. This variation promotes inconsistencies in performance and productivity.

> **"By definition, a process standard dictates the output, so, without a process standard that defines both input and process parameters, it is impossible to realistically expect a consistent output."**

Understand your processes, document them, train your teams on them, and then hold people accountable to follow them. Engage your teams in constantly looking for ways to improve the standard. Once you identify a potential improvement, document, train, and follow. Repeat this process for eternity. Monitor your progress, and make it visual to the entire team. Review your status – not monthly or weekly, but daily. Discuss in detail your victories and your defeats. Learn from both, and continue to grow. Define what success looks like by developing Standard Work, and then watch your teams succeed.

FLYING HIGH, AND FAR

Standard Work drives improved performance. It reduces variation and provides for consistent, repeatable, and elevated levels of performance. Here is a simple and fun exercise will prove the point.

Take a group of team members, and give them each a regular piece of copy paper. Instruct them to use the next 2 minutes to build their very best paper airplanes. Give them each an individual number to write on their airplane. Inform them that this is an individual exercise, and there is to be no talking, sharing ideas, or watching each other. While the team is building their paper airplanes, place a piece of masking tape about 2 feet out from a back wall.

After 2 minutes, instruct the team to line up along the back wall, with only one person standing behind the tape. Instruct the team to stand behind the tape and give their paper airplanes the best toss they can. They are to take turns throwing their airplanes one at a time, and only when behind the tape on the floor. One person throws, then moves out of the way for the next person in line. Tell everyone to not pick up their planes, but to leave exactly them where they land.

Remember, an airplane is meant to fly high and far, so success is defined by distance. After everyone is finished throwing their paper airplanes, ask them about the results.

They should be absolutely inconsistent. Some airplanes will have flown all the way to the other wall, while some probably will have turned immediately after launch to perform an aerial attack on their designer. Some will have gone up, some will have gone down. Some will have gone to the left, and some will have gone to the right. The results will not be standard or consistent because the design was not standard.

Now, measure the distance every plane flew from the piece of tape on the floor and document it. Once you have finished measuring and documenting the distances for every individual plane, give each of the team members another blank piece of paper. Identify the owner of the plane that performed the best in the first round, and have him or her slowly walk the entire team through the design process for building that exact same plane. If team members mess up, give them a new sheet of paper to start over. Take enough time to allow for the entire team to build paper airplanes that are standardized according to the best performing plane design, or as close to standard as possible.

Run the team through the same launching process, with each taking a turn behind the tape. Let the designer of the best performing airplane go first and demonstrate his or her angle of launch and velocity at release. Once again, instruct them to leave the airplanes where they land. After the final airplane is launched, measure the flight distance for each and then discuss the results. Without exception, you will find that the overall performance of the entire team will have improved drastically. Ask the team to explain why the average performance improved. They will answer that the standardization of the optimal design, launch angle, and velocity is what resulted in the improved performance. Below is the summary of the actual exercise from one of my engagements.

Simply by standardizing the process and training everyone to follow it, the average performance (distance traveled) for the team improved 86%, from 6.75 feet to 12.58 feet. The combined distance traveled went from 81 feet to 151 feet. These same results will

Aircraft #	Flight Distance		
	Test Flight #1		Test Flight #2
1	18		19
2	3		12
3	8		14
4	-1		10
5	4		11
6	6		12
7	11		7
8	7		18
9	8		14
10	2		14
11	1		9
12	14		11
	6.75		12.58
	Average		Average

be realized when you develop and utilize Standard Work in your own processes. It's not magic; only the commonization and utilization of optimized processes.

The Time Study Tool

Purpose: To understand at a granular level the activities that comprise the individual and total cycle time of a discrete process.

How long does it take you to drive to work? Is it always exactly the same amount of time, or does it vary based on traffic conditions?

How long does it take to cook dinner? Is it always the same, or does it change depending on what you decide to cook?

How long does it take to mow your yard? Does the time required vary based on the height of the grass or the sharpness of the blades?

Just like I have mentioned throughout this book, everything is a process. Every action you take, even every thought that goes through your head, is a process. Not taking an action is actually a process in itself.

In manufacturing, service, healthcare, government, or any other industry, understanding how long a process takes is the foundation for staying in business. If you were a service company that charged $30 for a service that took your employees 6 hours to complete, you would be out of business quickly. On the other hand, if you were a plumber who consistently scheduled your day with ten 3-hour jobs, you would never have a repeat customer. Understanding how long a process takes allows you to manage and schedule your operations in a manner that maximizes your capacity.

A Time Study does exactly what it says – studies your process time. It requires a stop watch, a piece of paper, and attention to detail. But why do you need to complete a Time Study? Look at some of your processes, and think about how long they have been in play. Over that time, how many modifications and adjustments have been made? How have those additional error checks, packaging changes, IT system modifications, equipment upgrades, inventory location changes, and tooling layout changes impacted the cycle time? In many cases, you just assume that there has been no change as a result of these, when in reality the impact has been dramatic.

Five years into a process, the upstream department is struggling to keep pace with their downstream customer for some reason. It must be a people issue, right? Nope. Chances are that the downstream process has made some improvements that decrease their overall cycle time, while the upstream process has been burdened with extra quality checks that now add time to the completion of every part. All of this invisibly takes place within the disconnected silos of each department or operation.

> **"Just like an equipment preventative maintenance schedule, a Time Study should be performed for each process on a regular basis to confirm your system parameters."**

To accomplish effective flow, especially single piece flow, processes must operate in conjunction with each other. There is no value in an upstream supplier drowning their downstream customer in inventory, and there is certainly no value in a downstream customer repeatedly waiting for their upstream supplier to send the next part or item to process. In a fast food restaurant, it would be absurd to have a single person flipping burgers while six people take orders. The burger flipper would never be able to keep up with the tidal wave of orders. On the other hand, it would make no sense to have six people flipping burgers while only one person manned the register. The burger flippers would spend the majority of their time waiting for an order.

The same logic applies to a manufacturers, hospitals, and service organizations. On an assembly line, single piece flow is optimal. It minimizes inventory and finished goods, reduces the risk of large-scale quality events, and provides for flexibility in production. An assembly line is balanced so that every person in the process can complete his or her task in roughly the same amount of time. If an improvement is identified in one specific area of the production line, then the cycle times are evaluated, and the line may be re-balanced to distribute the work across the line in a way that promotes effective and uninterrupted flow.

FIGURE 21:30

				Burn Room Tip Change Study
Activity	Start Time	Stop Time	Time Total	Activity
1	0:00:00	0:00:05	0:00:05	Brought torch to home
2	0:00:05	0:00:54	0:00:49	Walk to breaker boxes on west wall
3	0:00:54	0:00:55	0:00:01	Turn off breaker box for torch and coolant
4	0:00:55	0:01:40	0:00:45	Walk back to burn table control panel
5	0:01:40	0:02:10	0:00:30	Remove nozzle and electrode
6	0:02:10	0:02:28	0:00:18	Replace electrode
7	0:02:28	0:03:22	0:00:54	Replace nozzle
8	0:03:22	0:04:01	0:00:39	Walk to wash station to remove coolant from hands
9	0:04:01	0:04:28	0:00:27	Wash hands
10	0:04:28	0:05:15	0:00:47	Walk back to breaker box on west wall
11	0:05:15	0:05:16	0:00:01	Turn on breaker boxes for torch and coolant
12	0:05:16	0:06:03	0:00:47	Walk back to burn table control panel
13	0:06:03	0:06:16	0:00:13	Blow coolant out of nozzle
	Total Time		0:06:16	

Figure 21:30 is an example of a simple Time Study for a tip change procedure in a metal fabrication burn room where metal parts are cut out of large sheets of metal. Similar to a Value/Non-Value activity, you are observing, measuring, and documenting the granular level steps in a process. Notice how many times the word "walk" appears? Once we understood this waste, as identified in the Time Study, we were able to address it and eliminate it. Many times, this simple tool creates a realization of how impactful those tiny and insignificant steps truly are. Those numerous 2, 3 and 5-second steps become a major factor when summed up and compared to the total time.

In a hospital, reducing wait time in the Emergency Department is critically important for both patients and hospital performance. Many hospitals have implemented a system that separates patients into two flows – one flow for patients in need of more extensive evaluation, and another for patients with minor or less complicated issues. The problem that many hospitals run into is that the patients can be registered far faster than they can be seen and evaluated by the nurse and provider. This is why "Patient Wait Time" is such an important metric for hospitals.

FIGURE 21:31

Process A	
Cycle Time	30 Sec.
Operators	1
C/O Time	90 Sec.
Uptime %	95%

Process B	
Cycle Time	28 Sec.
Operators	1
C/O Time	90 Sec.
Uptime %	95%

Process C	
Cycle Time	29 Sec.
Operators	1
C/O Time	92 Sec.
Uptime %	95%

Process D	
Cycle Time	30 Sec.
Operators	1
C/O Time	90 Sec.
Uptime %	95%

Take a look at Figure 21:31 above. The operation is comprised of four unique processes. The boxes define the parameters for each process. For example, Process A has a cycle time of 30 seconds, utilizes one operator, requires 90 seconds to change over, and has a historical up-time average of 95%. If you look at all four processes, you see that each of them is close to even with the others. This provides for effective flow and minimization of both Waiting Waste and in-process inventory. You will also notice the triangles, which represent inventory between processes. This is required to account for inherent and unexpected issues that will arise even in the most robust of processes. The inventory acts as a buffer that prevents a downtime event in once cell from immediately causing a domino effect in every subsequent cell. The example is Figure 21:31 should flow effectively.

FIGURE 21:32

Process A	
Cycle Time	30 Sec.
Operators	1
C/O Time	90 Sec.
Uptime %	95%

Process B	
Cycle Time	60
Operators	1
C/O Time	90 Sec.
Uptime %	95%

Process C	
Cycle Time	29 Sec.
Operators	1
C/O Time	92 Sec.
Uptime %	95%

Process D	
Cycle Time	45
Operators	1
C/O Time	90 Sec.
Uptime %	95%

Now look at the example in Figure 21:32. Notice that there have been some changes made that have extended the cycle times of Process B and Process D to 60 seconds and 45 seconds, respectively. This means that Process A will be flooding Process B with inventory, Process C will be waiting idle for Process B to furnish inventory, and even Process D, which is now at a 45-second cycle time, will be waiting as a result of Process B. Your entire operation is only as fast as your slowest Internal process. Regardless of how fast Processes A, C, and D are, they are constrained by the cycle time of Process B.

So, what are your options? You can live with the operational pain and discomfort, or you can work to understand. Completing a Time Study will allow you to understand what changed and what makes up the 60-second cycle time of Process B. If the additional time is non-negotiable as a result of new requirements, you may be able to balance the production line and transfer some of the process activity to both Process A and Process C, as shown in Figure 21:33. All three processes now average roughly 40 seconds.

FIGURE 21:33

Process A	
Cycle Time	40
Operators	1
C/O Time	90 Sec.
Uptime %	95%

I = 10 Pieces

Process B	
Cycle Time	40
Operators	1
C/O Time	90 Sec.
Uptime %	95%

I = 10 Pieces

Process C	
Cycle Time	39
Operators	1
C/O Time	92 Sec.
Uptime %	95%

I = 10 Pieces

Process D	
Cycle Time	45
Operators	1
C/O Time	90 Sec.
Uptime %	95%

If, as a result of layout or equipment constraints, you are unable to transfer some of the new activities to Process A and Process C, you may be required to add an additional operator, as shown in Figure 21:34. Splitting up the Process B total cycle time of 60 seconds between two people decreases the process cycle time to 30 seconds. Now, with Process B's cycle time once again at 30 seconds, the entire operation flows smoothly. Or does it?

FIGURE 21:34

Process A	
Cycle Time	30 Sec.
Operators	1
C/O Time	90 Sec.
Uptime %	95%

I = 10 Pieces

Process B	
Cycle Time	30
Operators	2
C/O Time	90 Sec.
Uptime %	95%

I = 10 Pieces

Process C	
Cycle Time	29 Sec.
Operators	1
C/O Time	92 Sec.
Uptime %	95%

I = 10 Pieces

Process D	
Cycle Time	45
Operators	1
C/O Time	90 Sec.
Uptime %	95%

What about the fact that Process D is now at 45 seconds? You may have gotten so tied up in addressing the Process B constraint that you forgot about the new constraint, Process D.

Simply go through the same motions as you did with the Process B constraint. Work to reduce the times internal to Process D. If you are unable to reduce it to the target cycle time, then look to balance the line. Make the operation flow uninterrupted.

Time Studies are useful for understanding your processes and should be a part of your normal mode of operation. Accepting status quo is a mistake waiting to happen, and assuming that your process cycle times have remained unchanged over the last three years is a recipe for disaster. Just like an equipment preventative maintenance schedule, a Time Study should be performed on processes on a regular basis to confirm system parameters.

Consider what is at stake here. Your entire operation depends on the system-defined cycle times. Your staffing, inventory, purchasing, scheduling, capacity, and quoting activities all rely on system cycle time data. When this data is not accurate, it results in waste, inefficiency, frustration, finger pointing, and general chaos throughout the entire organization.

The "Kanban" Tool

Purpose: To optimize inventory levels and connect your supply and demand. It is _not_ an inventory reduction tool; it is an _optimization_ tool.

"Kanban" is a Japanese term that means "signboard" or "billboard." When used in the context of inventory management, a Kanban is physical or electronic. We spoke of JIT (Just-In-Time) in the previous chapters. The purpose of JIT is to optimize inventory to the minimal level required to support current needs.

Why would you only want enough to support current needs? How about space availability and reductions in Transportation, Defects, and almost every other waste mentioned in chapters 12-19. Purchasing, holding, moving, and tracking inventory takes a lot of effort and resources, so keeping inventory levels to a safe minimum is an advantage for everyone.

Be careful, though. Notice in the preceding paragraph I used the word "safe." Any JIT or Kanban System must take into account known inventory flow interruptions, as well as other potential factors. I have seen organizations implement a Kanban System based on bare-bones minimums, only to be caught off-guard by a quality defect inspection, broken down tractor trailer, power outage, or lost inventory issue. To effectively implement a Kanban System, you must ease into it, slowly dropping the inventory water level over time. As you slowly drop the inventory level, you discover new rocks and remove them. Continue this process until you reach your optimal inventory level.

FIGURE 21:35

Part #	QPC	Process Location	Kanban #
125-45-352D	12	Weld Cell #2 Rack 4 - Shelf 3	1 of 6
Inventory Storage Location			
Warehouse 2 Row 4 - Shelf D2		Picture of Part	
Manufacturer			
Name	**Revision Level**		
Acme Mfg.	3		

A Kanban can be a physical card, an electronic signal, or even a container itself. An example of a Kanban Card is shown in Figure 21:35. A Kanban Card should contain the part number, the QPC (Quantity Per Container), the storage location in the warehouse and at the process, the number of Kanban Cards in the system, the manufacturer information, and even a picture to improve visual identification and avoid part mis-picks. You probably use a type of Kanban System in your home. If you use a Keurig coffee maker, you may have one of those metal racks that holds any one of a thousand different flavored coffee pods. What do you do when you use the last coffee pod? Hopefully, you load the rack back up. The rack itself is a visual Kanban System, each empty slot an indication that inventory has been consumed. In the office at work, if you empty the coffee pot, what are you supposed to do? Obviously, you are supposed to make a fresh pot so that the next person isn't left without his or her caffeine fix.

Let's look at a simple Kanban System used in an office. Assume that the copier paper is kept in a cabinet. On average, you and your office team use one ream of paper per day, it takes 2 days for your supplier to deliver paper once you order it, and you normally order 10 reams at a time. You should always have, at a minimum, two reams in inventory when you place your order. What happens when you don't have at least two reams, and you haven't placed your order yet? You run out of paper. So, what tells your team it's time to order paper?

FIGURE 21:36

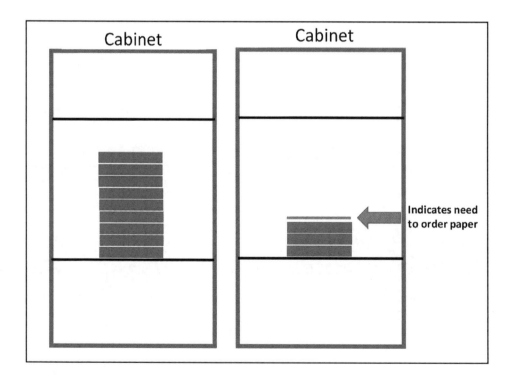

A simple Kanban System would provide this information to them. It can be done a couple of ways. First, if you look at Figure 21:36, you see a cabinet with stacks of paper in it. Behind the paper is a red line, or visual Kanban. When the paper level drops to the point where the red line becomes visible, it provides an indication that directs you to order more paper.

This same process could be accomplished with a simple piece of yellow, orange, or red letter-sized paper that says, "Order 10 reams of paper." and is placed between the bottom third and fourth reams of paper. This way, when someone takes the fourth to last ream, the sheet of paper provides a visual indication to order more.

The visual Kanban method can be used in countless situations. It can be used for tires in a dealership, bedsheets in a patient's room, parts inventory in an assembly cell, pens in the supply cabinet, coffee in the break room, or surgical gloves in an operating room. Have you ever stood at the counter of a store and been handed a receipt that is covered in red? This red ink is a visual message to the cashier that the receipt paper is almost empty, enabling the staff to prepare for the replacement and avoid impacting customers.

In a production environment, an assembler may use Kanban Cards to tell the inventory person when more parts are needed. For example, if a cell uses 10 parts per hour, and containers hold 20 parts each, the assembler will consume one container of parts every 2 hours. It takes the inventory person 1 hour to replace empty containers. In this example, the containers themselves can be used as Kanbans. Each container must be labeled with the part number and the QPC. As the assembler empties the container, he places it in a designated spot. The inventory person making his routes sees the container and picks it up. The empty container is a visual indicator to the inventory person that the supply needs to be replenished. The inventory person then brings the assembler a full container of parts, and the cycle continues. Following this system, instead of needing four containers on the line to support the 8-hour shift, the assembler only needs two.

A Kanban System can be used to drive inventory all the way back through the value stream in to Tier 1, Tier 2, and other suppliers. It can be used to control raw material and purchased parts ordered from suppliers, work-in-process parts between Internal processes, or tooling, supplies, and material inventory management. It is meant to eliminate Overproduction, which results in the creation of almost every other waste.

Calculating a Kanban System requires you to understand your takt time, cycle time, planned downtime, QPC, replenishment time, and any potential or historical risks.

I have included an example of a Kanban calculator below. The calculator I use considers the following variables:

DD = Daily Demand (number of parts)

LT = Lead Time (replenishment days, or how long it takes to get more parts)

SS = Safety Stock (days of extra inventory to account for unforeseen issues or interruptions)

KBS/QPC = Kanban Size

Let's assume that we are talking about an assembly cell that produces the Hammer XPS. As shown below in the table, the Daily Demand is 60 pieces per day, the Lead Time is 2 days, we decide on a Safety Stock of 1 day, and the Kanban Size is 30 pieces.

The chart below automatically calculates the number of Kanbans required by the system. The top four gray boxes on the right side require the manual entry of information, and the darker gray box on the bottom right is automatically calculated.

SCENARIO 1:

	Kanban Calculator	
	Input	
Manual Input	DD	60
Auto Calculated	LT	2
	SS	1
	KBS	30
# OF KANBANS		6

According to Scenario 1, to fill the system, we would need to have a total of 6 Kanbans, or containers, since the container is the Kanban in this example.

What if, a year down the road, the demand for the part increases? With more demand, we will be producing more finished goods and, therefore, consuming more parts. Let's assume that our Daily Demand jumps to 90 pieces, the Lead Time remains at 2 days, we decide to keep our Safety Stock at 1 day, and our Kanban Size remains at 30 pieces. As shown in Scenario 2 below, this increase in volume now requires 9 Kanbans to fill the system.

SCENARIO 2:

		Kanban Calculator	
		Input	
Manual Input		DD	90
Auto Calculated		LT	2
		SS	1
		KBS	30
	# OF KANBANS		9

The manual Kanban calculation is contained below.

$$\#KB = (DD*(LT+SS))/KBS$$

Keep in mind that any change to the Daily Demand, Lead Time for replenishment, Kanban Size, or your confidence level in process reliability must be reflected through adjustments in the Kanban calculation inputs. For example, if the transportation company begins to have delivery issues or your supplier starts to have frequent equipment issues, to protect your own processes, you may increase your Safety Stock levels.

To maintain the integrity of the Kanban System, periodic checks must be made to verify all Kanbans are still in circulation. Each Kanban should be labeled and numbered, for example "1 of 6," "2 of 6," "3 of 6," and so on. This way, if one is missing, you know which.

CHAPTER 22:
A LEAN MANAGEMENT SYSTEM

I am including this chapter simply because everything up to this point is based on understanding and taking meaningful action. Locating and utilizing The Lean Treasure Chest is not a simple quest; it is a complicated and far-reaching journey that will stretch you beyond the point of comfort and potentially into the realm of actual operational pain. You may experience frustration as you trip over yourself, and your teams might want to quit when the going gets tough.

Remember, Lean is not just something you do; it is part of who you are as an individual and an organization and is demonstrated daily through your habits and behaviors. It is woven through the threads of your cultural fabric. Lean, Six Sigma, High Reliability Organization, PDCA, and Operational Excellence are all meaningless without people. These systems improve nothing by themselves and provide no value without hands to manipulate them.

Any Lean Management System must focus on the people as the drivers and sustainers. Managing the hunt for The Lean Treasure Chest requires an immense amount of coordination. It requires a management system that ties the strategic objectives of the organization to every single person who plays a part in its success, or simply put, everyone. It requires a management system that breaks down the departmental and unit silos, connecting them all to a single unyielding purpose.

Like the ancient weapon of a Spartan warrior, Lean is the shaft of your strategic spear. It translates your Mission, Vision, and Values into purposeful action. Lean defines objectives, develops metrics, sets targets, establishes standards and expectations, drives daily accountability, visually communicates performance, and, most importantly, drives meaningful action. The system must be transparent, sharing information across the entire organization both vertically and horizontally. There are no hidden agendas or secrets, only honest and open communication regarding reality that provides for innovative and out-of-the-box thinking designed to break down the walls of mediocrity and average. There are, of course, certain areas of business and types of information that require confidentiality, so these areas should be handled in the appropriate manner.

> **"Every organization already has a management system in place; it just may be ineffective."**

You may be looking at this chapter and thinking, "We already have a management system." You are correct. Actually, every organization already has a management system; it just may be ineffective. It may be an unspoken one without a title or formal documentation, but it is still a management system. What value does it provide, and what purpose does it serve if it is only designed to monitor status, not to drive improvements and success? Look at the traction control system on your car. How useful would it be to you if it merely informed you that the road was slippery, and didn't automatically adjust your vehicle operation? In the same way, if your current management system is only a blinking red light alerting you of the problem, but not doing anything about it, what value is it providing?

In my experience, the more visual you make your strategic objectives, the easier it is to tie them directly to the day-to-day operations that ultimately yield the results that allow you to achieve those objectives. By translating 5-year goals into tactical activities and performance measures, you engage the floor level employees – the value creators. You connect the dots for the nurse who now understands how his explanation of medication side effects ultimately impacts the hospital's ratings and, as a result, the perceptions and survey results from patients within the community. You connect the dots for the welder who now understands that a clean weld affects the multi-billion-dollar customer who is evaluating supplier quality prior to their award of a new multi-million-dollar contract. You connect the dots for the customer service attendant who now understands how his tone of voice and courteous demeanor plays an absolutely critical role in retaining customers in a cut-throat industry.

Any Lean Management System is only as effective as the leaders are engaged. Simply put, if leadership sees a management system as an activity intended only for directors and below, it will fail, every single time. As stated before, when leaders demonstrate their commitment and belief through personal engagement and involvement, the teams will mirror that same level of commitment and belief. Leadership is the key – that's why they call it "Leader"-ship. Leadership is not a word; it is an action-based characteristic that must be demonstrated while walking at the front of the line.

I don't have enough pages to go into detail regarding the enormous amount of work and effort that is required when implementing of an effective Lean Management System. There are many versions of Lean Management Systems out there, but I have found that, without exception, the most effective contain several key components.

1. *Daily* monitoring, reporting, action, and organizational engagement

2. Leadership commitment to *daily* involvement (real engagement, not simply lip service)

3. An uncompromising focus on customer and patient satisfaction

4. An obsession with removing waste and driving operational efficiency

5. Clearly defined organizational Strategy (Hoshin)

6. Clearly defined and communicated Mission, Vision, and Values (everyone understands the "why")

7. *Daily* involvement and engagement at every level of the organization

8. Visual management of goals and metrics in all departments

9. Collaboration between leaders and staff to identify meaningful metrics

10. Clearly defined expectations and standards

11. Rigid accountability and ownership

12. Effective use of problem-solving and waste elimination tools

13. An unwavering commitment to "Stop to Fix"

14. Commitment to respecting and valuing employees

15. A focus on the long-term, not the short-term

16. Maturity and discipline to avoid "knee-jerk" reactions

17. A willingness to constantly look in the "operational mirror" and admit the weaknesses and opportunities present

18. A commitment to not just report problems, but to fix them

19. Action, action, action, and more action

A Lean Management System is not as much about the tools being used as it is about the people using the tools. Effectiveness results from a team's dedication and commitment to a common cause – a uniting banner that waves over their heads, providing a constant reminder of what they are a valuable part of. It's not about the forms, it's about the process.

I have included an example of a visual method for implementing a Lean Management System. What you call your own system is only mildly important. I have seen it called MDI (Managing for Daily Improvement), LDM (Lean Daily Management), LMS (Lean Management System), LOM (Lean Operational Management), LLS (Lean Leadership System), and many others.

What you call it is not critical; what is important is how you operate from day one. Believe me, your teams will be watching. They will be watching to see if your commitment and excitement are skin-deep or internal, temporary or long-term, superficial or genuine. They will look to see whether you start digging with a small hand tool or a full-size, heavy duty, contractor grade shovel.

Lean Applies to Everyone

So, who should get the Lean training in your organization? To make it easy, you can narrow it down to a select group referred to as "everybody." Seriously? Yes, everybody. When I refer to Lean training, I am not referring to a 3-day training session. I am talking about basic Lean training to understand the concepts of waste, flow, and efficiency. If you must exclude someone, just look for someone who adds no value to your organization. Hopefully, you don't have anyone who fits that description.

The reason for training everyone is because every single person in your organization has ideas for improvement. If, for example, you make the mistake of only training 10% of the team, whether you intend to or not, you create a culture of exclusivity, where 10% are seen as the "chosen ones" and the other 90% believe they are not important or valuable enough to train. Lean provides a method for capturing those ideas that everyone has residing in the back of their minds. Understanding Lean will enable people to see their processes differently, opening their eyes to opportunities that up until now have remained hidden behind the cloudy blur of "operational cataracts."

Training everyone in Lean is an investment, no different than an IT system upgrade or an equipment enhancement that yields a 10% increase in production. The difference is that the potential return on investment of training your teams in Lean makes a system or equipment upgrade ROI (Return On Investment) seem insignificant in comparison. Remember, your greatest asset is your team, so upgrade that asset with Lean skills.

Why Daily?

You may have noticed my preoccupation with the term "daily" in the key components for an effective Lean Management System. There is a good reason for that. Think about the last road trip you took. Chances are you spent a fair amount of that trip on major interstates or highways. Unlike a lot of the county roads in Indiana, most of these major travel routes have lines on the sides of the road as well as lines separating the lanes. As you drove, whether you realized it or not, you were constantly managing your vehicle's alignment with the lines on the road. Now, be honest, there have been times late at night or early in the morning when your eyes have been heavy, like someone has lined them with lead. When that has happened, you may have struggled to maintain alignment, resulting in the heart-stopping roar of the rumble strips that immediately bring you back to a conscious state, for a couple of minutes at least. The point is that when you take your eyes off of the road, for whatever reason, you end up drifting off course. In some situations, this leads to tragic consequences.

> **"Lean Management isn't necessarily about being in control; it's about being aware."**

Monthly, weekly, or even bi-weekly management doesn't work. It results in reactive management that is permeated with answers like, "I'll look into that," "I'm not sure, but we will find out," and "I wasn't aware of that, but we will let you know in next week's meeting." Do any of those sound familiar? An effective Lean Management System understands current status, on a moment-by-moment basis. It is proactive, not reactive. If you doubt that managing daily and minute-by-minute is important, see if these examples could wait for you to react on a weekly or monthly basis:

1. Your heart stops beating.

2. Someone steals your identify.

3. A check for $1,000,000 gets delivered to your mailbox.

4. Your flight gate has changed.

5. While driving on the interstate, your car tire blows out.

6. Your 4-year-old child runs up to you and says, "I need to go – bad!"

7. The truck just left your dock with only half of the shipment.

8. As a pilot, you lose one of two engines while cruising at 34,000 feet.

9. A patient is showing an allergic reaction to the anesthesia.

10. Your most loyal customer calls with an urgent need.

None of these are situations that you can manage on a weekly or monthly basis; they all require your immediate attention, or daily management. The same applies to understanding your operations. It isn't always a matter of being completely in control; it's more of a matter of being aware.

A Line of Destiny

To demonstrate this, complete this simple exercise. Doing so will drive home to your leadership and teams the importance of managing in real time. This can be done with either a small group or a full conference room. You will need a piece of paper and a pen or pencil for everyone. Follow the directions below:

ROUND #1

1. Draw a dot at the top of a piece of paper.

2. Draw a dot at the bottom of the paper.

3. Place the tip of your pen/pencil on the bottom dot.

4. Close your eyes.

5. Connect the two dots.

99% of the time, nobody connects the dots. Why not? The obvious answer is that you were not looking at where you were going, so you missed the dot at the top of the page and went either to the right, to the left, or simply stopped short. Some may have gone too far and written on the table.

So, what is the difference between this exercise and an organization that meets at the beginning of the month to set end-of-month goals and targets, waves their operational wand, and then doesn't meet again to review performance or status until the end of the month? There is no difference. At the end of the month, the group sits around a table, and the VP or general manager asks why the goal or goals were not met. Everyone avoids eye contact or immediately reapplies a coat of Teflon. The finger pointing may start, or you may start hearing layers upon layers of excuses.

Since you haven't been meeting on a daily basis, the honest answer is, "We don't know." Every day has its own challenges, and so, as each day passes, you lose the detailed understanding of what took place and why you struggled. Without understanding the details, you lose the ability to dig into the granular level of problem-solving that

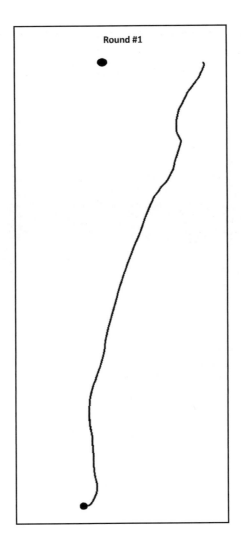

Round #1

prevents reoccurrence of the issues. This results in the same meetings every month with identical discussions, excuses, empty promises, and hollow commitments.

Now, let's try a different method.

ROUND # 2

1. Use the same sheet of paper.

2. Draw another dot at the top of the piece of paper.

3. Draw another dot at the bottom of the paper.

4. Place the tip of your pen/pencil on the bottom dot.

5. Keep your eyes open this time.

6. Connect the dots.

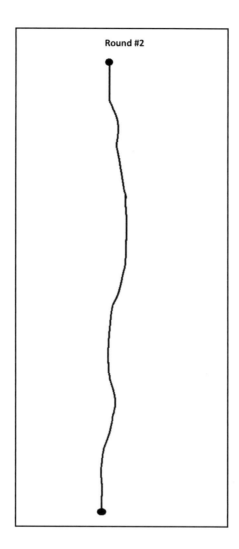

Round #2

Hopefully, 100% of those completing Round #2 actually connected the dots this time. If they didn't, chances are they took their eyes off the target.

So, what was the difference? Why were you able to connect the dots the second time? It was because you were watching your progress the entire time. You were monitoring your status over every single millimeter between the two points. You never took your eyes off of the objective.

The most significant part of this exercise is this. Look at your line in Round #2. Is it straight? The answer is no. Your line winds this way and that way, all the way up to the second dot. If you were to place your second line under a microscope, you would see literally thousands of small deviations. That is the point. Since you were constantly aware of your direction and end goal, you consciously made numerous course corrections to ultimately arrive at your desired target point.

If you manage your operations like you managed your progress in the second round, even if you didn't achieve your goal, at the end of the month you understand *why!* By understanding the problems and situations that prevented you from reaching your goals, you can then make adjustments and corrections so that you are able to achieve or at least get closer to your goals the next month. In the first round, you weren't watching, so you have no idea why you failed to hit your targets, and therefore, next month, you will end up with the same result, sitting in the same painfully awkward end-of-month meeting, providing the same excuses.

Daily management enables you to understand and react in a timely manner that promotes success. If you are actively managing your processes daily, and, on the 5th of the month, you see risks or potential problems, you have time to react and course correct, addressing the risks and shifting back to a level of performance that enables you to achieve your goal. If, on the other hand, you are managing your processes weekly or monthly, you reduce your ability to react and correct problems. Face it, by the time you get to the 20th of the month, if you are off course; you have very little chance of meeting your end-of-month targets. There is simply not enough time to react and course correct. Like the Titanic, you see the impending disaster, but changing the direction of the ship takes not just time and effort, but distance. By managing daily, you become agile and flexible, able to react and respond on a moment's notice. Surprises become rare as you monitor your operations in a manner that promotes a clear view of what is just ahead in your "operational ocean."

Implementing a Lean Management System

MISSION, VISION, AND VALUES

Where are you going? What is your purpose? What do you want to become? Without answering these questions, it becomes very difficult to reach your potential or even define success as an organization. A company opens its doors for a reason, and the reason is not simply to make money. Regardless of the industry, making money or being profitable is a direct result of providing value to someone who will pay for that value. To provide that value now and in the distant future, you must have a plan. You must have a strategy, and developing a strategy begins with understanding and defining your Mission, Vision, and Values. Your Mission, Vision, and Values enable you to develop a strategy that moves you toward your ultimate objective as an organization.

Your Mission

Your Mission is simply a statement of what you want to accomplish. It defines why you opened your doors in the first place. A hospital's Mission is normally something like, "To provide quality healthcare to our community and to improve lives." That sums up why they exist. A manufacturer may have a Mission that reads, "To provide efficient, safe, and reliable motors to our valuable customers."

I like to look at a Mission as "why we exist." Ultimately, you hire people who believe in your "why" and will give of themselves to fulfill the Mission. People will sacrifice of themselves and go beyond superficial obligation when they believe in something. When they are part of the Mission, the "why," they will reach further down and display levels of loyalty seldom seen.

Your Vision

Your vision is simply a literary description of who and what your organization is working to become. Whereas your Mission defines what you want to accomplish, your Vision defines what the organization looks like and how it can make that Mission a reality. It defines who you are serving and why they are important to you.

Values

Your values are what you believe are the essential and uncompromising characteristics of your organization. They define how you operate and the standards you and everyone in your organization will adhere to. They define not just the organizational level character, but also the individual character of those who carry your flag on a daily basis. Your values are what you believe are the ingredients for success.

I have included the Mission, Vision, and Values below for my own company, Jay Hodge & Associates, as an example.

OUR VISION

To be a trusted, respected, and valued partner to the industries and organizations with which we engage.

OUR MISSION

To harness and develop the knowledge, experience, and skill of every organization with which we engage, and to create world-class sustainable processes that provide the foundation for continued growth and success.

OUR VALUES

Continuous Improvement – To be committed to systemically refining our work to achieve measurable success.

Integrity – To demonstrate sound moral character, and to do what is right even when no one is watching.

Honesty – To speak and act truthfully without exception.

Perseverance – To improvise, adapt, and overcome in the face of challenges or obstacles.

Confidence – To trust in the knowledge and experience of the team in order to drive change.

Humility – To be modest, respectful, and continually open to new ideas and learning.

Determination – To analyze and understand a situation, and to be willing to take action.

Empathy – To understand the unique situation of everyone we work with in order to see their needs.

Sincerity – To communicate and act truthfully in order to reinforce trust and collaboration.

THE "GLASS WALL"

If you have not documented your Mission, Vision, and Values, you need to. Developing a strategy requires direction, and these provide that direction. Once you have a strategically defined direction, you need a way to measure your organizational performance. Some companies call this mechanism a Balanced Score Card or a Dashboard. Your first objective in building a Lean Management System is to lay the foundation for transparency.

Your organizational report card may not be called a Balanced Score Card, but your transparency implies that your entire team is working toward the same goal. That said, regardless of the industry, most departments know how they are performing, but lack knowledge of how other departments are doing. This is because many are so departmentalized and "silo-ed" that nobody can see over each other's walls. That's a problem, considering every department is part of the same body of business. If my left ankle is broken, my right leg had better be aware and compensate. If I have something in my eye, my hand and fingers should be part of the solution to remove the object. This is the kind of involvement and collaboration we need across a company.

In the same manner, when organizations are filled with disconnected departments and groups functioning almost autonomously, how can they work as a team? How can good ideas be shared, and how can offers of assistance and resources between departments be provided when nobody understands everyone else's needs and problems?

In a Lean Management System, this is addressed through the use of what I call the Window, sometimes called the Glass Wall. Glass is most often transparent. The Glass Wall is a meeting that takes place at the beginning of each day, either first thing or soon after the teams are lined up and the operational ball is rolling. The attendees include the executive leadership, directors, and managers. The meeting should take no more than 10 minutes and include a standard to ensure both timeliness and effectiveness. The meeting takes place in the same room every day, a room I like to call the Glass Wall Room. On the walls of the room are the organizational level metrics that are critical to the success of the company, organized by strategic pillars or category.

FIGURE 22:1

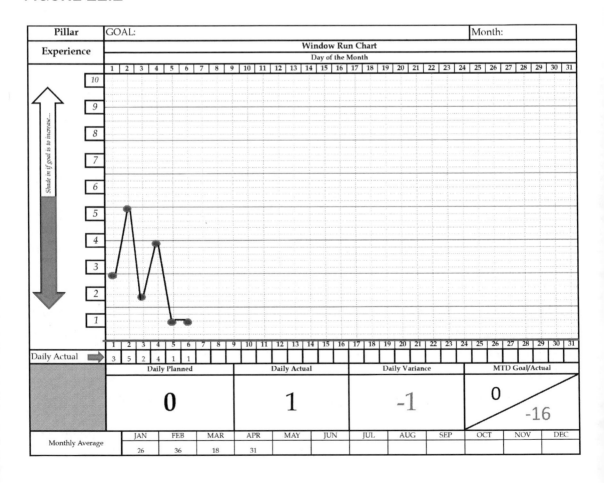

Most company strategies involve pillars such as Quality, Safety, People, Profitability, Productivity, and Growth. These priorities are used as headers on the wall, and the organizational level metrics that impacted these are displayed underneath them. For example, in almost every organization, under the Safety pillar, a common metric would be "Near Misses." Under the Productivity pillar, you may have individual departments' performance. Under the Growth pillar, you may have demand volume or orders for individual product or service lines. These metrics are displayed in the form of a Run Chart (Figure 22:1) and must be updated daily prior to the meeting with the previous day's information.

You may be thinking to yourself that the walls in the Glass Wall Room will fill up quickly. Don't fill up the walls just to fill them up. Identify the specific metrics that are absolutely critical to success and should be reviewed daily to maintain constant awareness. Also identify other metrics that are your focused priorities for improvement. Don't blanket the walls with metrics that are performing at or above targets; use the walls to show where you are struggling and need to improve. In the above Productivity pillar example, only the departments that are struggling should be listed.

FIGURE 22:2

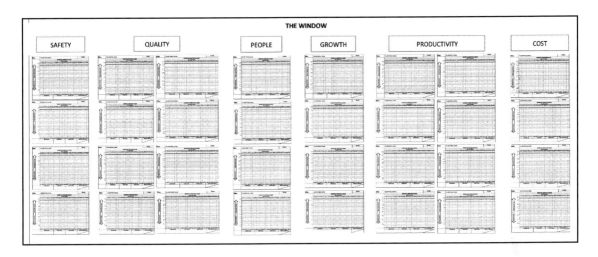

The Glass Wall Room layout looks similar to the example in Figure 22:2, depending on the number of metrics you have listed. By using colors when updating the graphs, you provide a quick visual indication of performance and status. The graph owner is responsible for reporting out their data. To keep the meeting on schedule, only metrics that failed to meet their goals are reviewed. Metrics with daily performance that is at or above target are skipped over.

By discussing the metrics as a group, you are realigning every single department on a daily basis to the organization's "True North." Since the captain of the ship (CEO or president) is always at this short meeting, this provides a daily opportunity for him or her to reinforce expectations, step in to remove any obstacles, and then coach and motivate the entire leadership team.

Below is a quick list of the standards for running an effective Glass Wall meeting. These should be posted in the room. A single leader should run the meeting daily, with that role rotating weekly or daily to provide development opportunities for the entire group.

1. Show respect to all members at all times.

2. Begin on time and end on time.

3. Five consecutive days of red requires an action plan.

4. Manage by exception: discuss only metrics that didn't meet the goal.

5. Explanations of performance should be no more than 10 seconds.

6. No side conversations, phone calls, or texting.

7. Update your run chart's metrics prior to the beginning of the meeting.

8. Share any important information with your department teams.

9. Celebrate the progress and wins for metrics that have been improved to meet target levels and then sustained.

10. Do not try to problem solve at the Glass Wall; go to the Gemba.

Take special note of number 10 on that list. The Glass Wall meeting is not where problem solving takes place. The Glass Wall points you to where the opportunities are – out on the floor, on the assembly line, and in the processes where value is created. The problems and waste are solved at the Gemba.

THE GEMBA BOARD

As described in Chapter 10, Gemba is a Japanese term that means "go to the floor" or "go to where value is created." If you think about it, the only place you can really solve problems is where they happen. The second part of a Lean Management System is about identifying and solving problems, using the knowledge, skills, and experience of the experts who know the processes best. The tool used is called the "Gemba Board," a quick visual representation of how the department is performing against key measures.

Every unit or department should have its own Gemba Board. Doubt that? Give me an example of a single department in your organization that does not, in some manner, impact your success. A Gemba Board is comprised of metrics that are specific opportunities for improvement related to that individual department. For example, falls may be a big opportunity in a department on the production floor, but not a real risk in the accounting department. The metrics contained on a Gemba Board should reflect the department's priorities and immediate needs for improvement, based on their unique characteristics and operational objectives.

Picking the Right Metric

Figure 22:3 contains an example of a tool I use with teams to identify meaningful metrics for a Gemba Board. Gemba metrics should be identified through collaboration between the department leadership and staff. The metrics should not be dictated by leadership, and, on the opposite side, the staff should not have free reign to choose any metrics. The metrics need to be tied to impacts and improvements that are reflected in customer and organizational value, as defined by a Balanced Score Card, for example. In a hospital, metrics should center around improving the care provided to patients, not reducing missed lunches for employees. In a manufacturing environment, the metrics should center around improving productivity, quality, and satisfying customer requirements. The key is to remember who your ultimate customer is and what value delivery they are expecting. Remember why you exist, and measure what reflects that.

Step back and put yourself in your customer's shoes. Ask yourself what matters most. Take a minute and write down every single item your customers value, down to the smallest detail. Chances are your competition has never done this to that level of detail. Once you have the list, work to deliver that value through every single process you perform. If an activity within the process doesn't provide for one of those items valued, work to eliminate it or transform it into one that does.

The tool in Figure 22:3 is a simple tool to help the teams identify potential metrics and then relate them to the organizational priorities. Start by writing your idea for a metric in the middle box. Now, write in the Customer box how this metric is important to the customer. After that, fill in the other four boxes explaining how the metric impacts those organizational pillars. The four pillars I have listed may not be the same as yours, so modify them to meet your needs. Sometimes, what sounded like a great metric at first turns out to be a metric that ultimately provides very little meaningful impact.

A Gemba Board can have as many metrics as you believe appropriate, but I recommend having no more than four. More than four can become overwhelming for a department whose main objective is to service customers, produce product, care for patients, or ship product. Having more than four also prevents the teams from focusing on the issues and leads to a process of just reporting data vs. actually solving problems.

Also, utilizing a VOC (Voice of the Customer) program is a way to stay grounded and avoid becoming distracted from your ultimate goal – satisfied customers. Using VOC is a way of continually stepping back into the customer's shoes and aligning your operations with their expectations and perspective. Keep in mind that the customer's perspective is their reality. Similar to the baby penguin who recognizes its parents' unique calls while surrounded by a crowd of 10,000 other penguins, become so in tune with your customer's "voice" that everything else is just background noise.

FIGURE 22:3

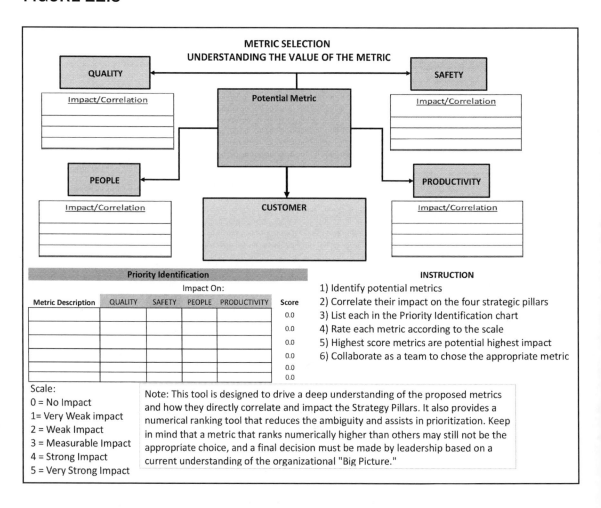

You can also post on a clipboard or on the Gemba Board itself a sheet that allows the team to document ideas for future metrics. Doing so allows you to have a running pool of meaningful and impactful ideas for Continuous Improvement. It is a proactive activity that demonstrates your team's awareness of the endless opportunities that exist. See Figure 22:4.

Keep in mind that once a metric has been selected for the Gemba Board, there needs to be a standardized method for removing or replacing it. If a metric is important enough to be on the board, you need to make sure that the results have been achieved and processes are in place to sustain the improved performance. It makes no sense to remove a metric just to find that 3 months down the road the problem has resurfaced because it was, in fact, not corrected. It is counterproductive when performance has only improved due to the well-known impact of the *Hawthorne Effect,* a change that occurs simply because a process is being watched.

FIGURE 22:4

Gemba Board Future Metric Ideas		
Metric Idea	**Date**	**Suggested By**

Below, in Figure 22:5, is a tool that I have used to standardize the removal of Glass Wall and Gemba metrics. It provides very rigid guidelines that ensure that the metric performance is not simply a result of luck. The tool I use is made up of seven basic questions and contains conditional formatting to provide a quick visual indication of the status. As you answer the questions with either "yes" or "no," the boxes change to the appropriate color.

FIGURE 22:5

Glass Wall & Gemba Metrics Removal Management Standard

Metrics contained on the Glass Wall and Gemba Boards have been identified as critically important to the success of this organization. Removing the metrics from the Glass Wall or Gemba Boards is not a decision that should be made without a clear understanding of the opportunity and careful consideration of overall impact. As a result, a standard shall be used to reduce ambiguity and provide clearly defined criteria for the management of the metrics.

The 7 requirements defined below must be evaluated before the metric can be considered for removal from the Glass Wall or Gemba Boards. Answer each as Yes or No. The cells are conditionally formatted to turn Green for Yes and Red for No.

	Glass Wall	Gemba Board
1) Are we meeting our defined goal?		Yes
2) Is our goal set at the appropriate level? (Did we set the bar too low - if yes, then reset the goal)		Yes
3) Have we maintained the desired level of performance for the defined period of time? Glass Wall: 4 Weeks Gemba: 4 Weeks		Yes
4) Can we correlate specific actions taken in the problem solving process that have led to the improved performance level?		Yes
5) Have standardized processes been documented and implemented to sustain the improved performance levels?		Yes
6) Have all impacted staff been trained in the developed standards to sustain the performance?		No
7) Is a documented process in place to continue to measure the performance "offline" once removed from the Glass Wall or Gemba Board?		Yes

Note: If any of the questions above were answered with a "No," then a process is not currently in place to support the sustained level of desired performance, and the metric must be maintained on the board until the process gap is corrected.
Metrics must remain on the board until all 7 answers are "Yes."

Understanding and using this or a similar tool to standardize your metric removal will eliminate an enormous amount of work for everyone involved. Notice the seven questions all point toward one objective – sustainable improvement. A "no" answer to any of the seven questions prohibits you from removing the metric. If you remove a metric prior to confirming all of these factors are met, you will undoubtedly find yourself struggling with the metric again at some point down the line. This rollercoaster of inconsistency is powered and driven by your own decisions to move on to another metric before actually solving the root cause of a problem. Are you on an "operational rollercoaster" right now? If so, reflect back on these seven questions, and see if any explains why.

THE GEMBA BOARD LAYOUT

Gemba Boards, as I use them, contain four documents: a Daily Status Chart, a Run Chart, a Pareto Chart, and a 5-Why Problem Solving Tool. As shown below, I also like to include Roles and Responsibilities (R&R), a Report out Schedule, a Win Capture document, and a laminated version of the Gemba Standard Work for training and reference purposes. The R&R communicates the role and expectations for everyone involved in the Gemba Board Process. The Report Out Schedule allows the department manager to schedule her team in advance for the daily report out. The Win Capture is where the team records when they have successfully met and sustained their goal and subsequently replaced it on the Gemba Board with another metric that needs to be addressed. I like to call the Win Capture the team's "Trophy Case." The Gemba Board in each department should also have a header showing what department it applies to. An example Gemba Board is shown in Figure 22:6.

LDM: Roles and Responsibilities

Executives (Attend Glass Wall and Gemba Routes)	Director & Managers (Attend Glass Wall and Gemba Routes)	Staff (Attend Gemba Routes)
• Lead by example • Set clear expectations • Encourage and coach directors and staff • Coach directors through problem solving process • Facilitate cross-departmental problem solving • Remove obstacles for directors and staff • Drive BSC and Glass Wall/Gemba metric correlation • Hold yourself and team accountable • Focus on the patients	• Lead by example • Set clear expectations • Schedule the daily Gemba report outs • Manage metric mix with staff and executives • Manage the problem solving process (Gemba Board) • Coordinate cross-departmental problem solving • Facilitate improvements • Remove obstacles for staff • Develop the standards with teams • Hold yourself and team accountable • Focus on the patients	• Update and present Gemba Board • Participate in problem solving • Generate solution ideas for experimentation • Help directors and executives to understand • Stay engaged and work as a team • Constantly look for new opportunities • Develop the standards with your directors and managers • Focus on the patients

Monthly Gemba Report Out Schedule - Department: _____ | Month:

	Sunday	Monday	Tuesday	Wednesday	Thursday	Friday	Saturday
Date							
Team Member							
Date							
Team Member							
Date							
Team Member							
Date							
Team Member							
Date							
Team Member							
Date							
Team Member							

GEMBA BOARD "WIN" CAPTURE TRACKING

DATE	METRIC	OPPORTUNITY	ACTION TAKEN	BASELINE PERFORMANCE BEFORE ACTION	PERFORMANCE AFTER ACTION	SUSTAINED PERFORMANCE AT 3 MONTHS	SUSTAINED PERFORMANCE AT 6 MONTHS

FIGURE 22:6

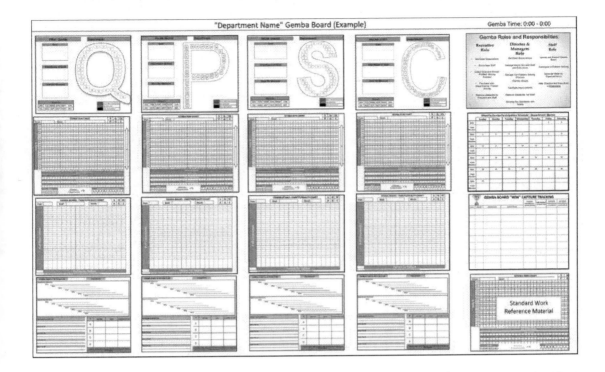

FIGURE 22:7

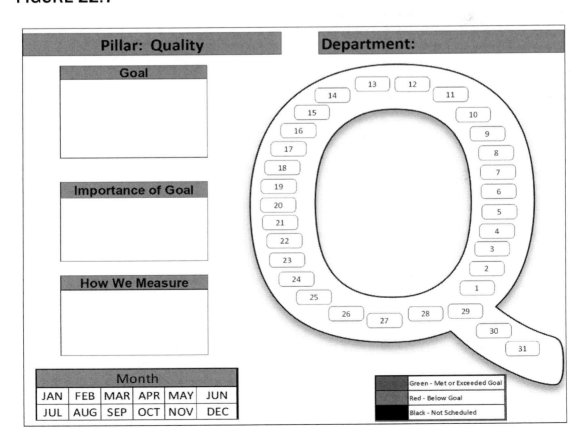

The first document is the Daily Status Chart. It serves no other purpose than to provide a visual indication of status and progress toward the goal for the current and preceding months. It allows for a quick visual understanding of status. In Figure 22:7, you see an example of a Quality metric. Notice there are 31 boxes inside the letter Q. Each of those boxes represents the day of the month. As identified by the legend, when the goal is not met on a day, that specific date box is colored in with red. If the goal is met, that day's box is colored in with green. If nothing was scheduled for that day, the box is colored in with black. The department will list the Goal, the Importance of the Goal, How We Measure it, and highlight the current month.

Instead of a "Q," for a Safety metric you would use an "S." For a Productivity metric, you would use a "P," for Growth you would use a "G," Cost a "C," and so on, based on your unique core strategic pillars.

The next document on the Gemba Board is the Run Chart. Like the Run Chart in the Glass Wall, it provides a visual indication of performance trends for the current month. A Gemba Board Run Chart is displayed in Figure 22:8.

FIGURE 22:8

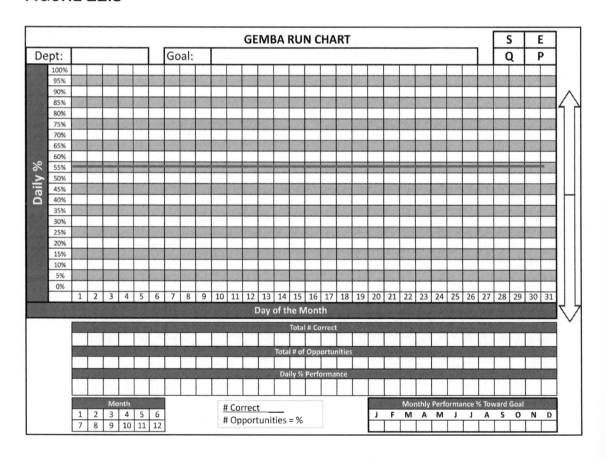

You can track performance by percentage or actual numbers. The chart has two blank arrows on the right side. Color in the one that indicates your desired performance direction. The bottom right is where you note the previous months' information to show long-term trends. Obviously, the bottom left (1-12) indicates the current month, which should be highlighted. The three lines of boxes at the bottom are for tracking actual data: Total # Correct, Total # of Opportunities, and Daily % Performance. The upper right contains boxes with the abbreviation for strategic pillars, so you simply color in the one applicable. The Department and Goal should be completed as well.

The third and fourth documents contained on the Gemba Boards are the Living Pareto Chart and the 5-Why Action Tool. Figure 22:9 shows the example charts again.

FIGURE 22:9

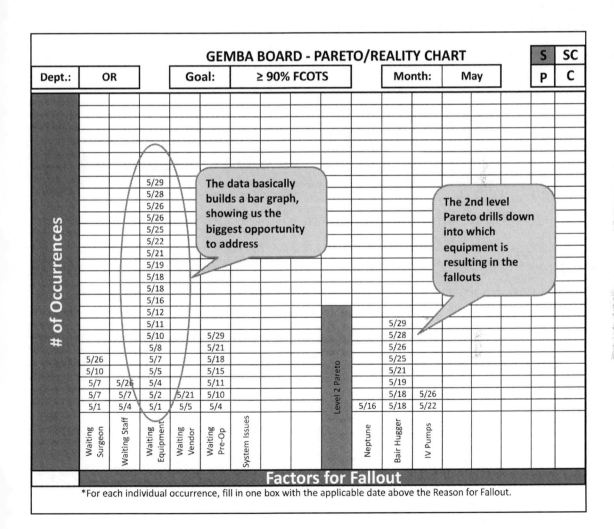

GEMBA 5 WHY & ACTION PLAN		Department	

Opportunity Statement:
 Why:
  Why:
   Why:
    Why:
     Why:
      Why:
       Why:

Opportunity Statement:
 Why:
  Why:
   Why:
    Why:
     Why:
      Why:
       Why:

PROBLEM DESCRIPTION	*	Start Date	Owner	Completion By Date
	A			
Action Plan #A				
	B			
Action Plan #B				
	C			
Action Plan #C				
	D			
Action Plan #D				

* Place the Action Letter on the Run Chart above the line on the date you took this action

Keep in mind that this is a single format. I have created and used multiple different formats, based on each organization's unique needs, but the content itself is very consistent. All four of these documents are important to the process. The first three are for identifying where to dig, and the fourth (5-Why Action Plan) is for digging for, locating, and addressing the problem.

Remember, the Gemba Board is not a tool for reporting status; it is a tool for collecting data that drives action. As stated before, data without action is meaningless and a waste.

The Gemba Board process is what differentiates this type of management system from so many others. After the daily Glass Wall meeting, the leadership team in attendance breaks up into assigned groups and heads out on a Gemba Board Route. A Gemba Board Route could contain two to five boards. Each Gemba Board is presented to the leadership by one or two people from that department team. The team reports out on status and actions being taken to solve the problems and improve performance. The leadership team engages the Gemba teams and removes barriers and provides support as needed. The process takes no more than 3 minutes per board. The leadership then moves on to the next Gemba Board.

Every leadership team I have ever worked with expresses a desire to improve engagement, trust, and communication between senior leadership and staff. This is how it is done. If you desire loyalty, commitment, engagement, trust, and motivation from your teams, then set the example by meeting with them daily in their world, where value is created.

Your organization may have the potential to operate like a $3,000,000 Formula 1 race car. You may have the horsepower to surpass every other competitor, with the industry leading engine, transmission, controls, and electronics. But all of this awesomeness and power relies on four simple rubber tires which cost only $800 each, or $2,400 combined, equaling only .0008% of the car's total value. These tires are your management system, and, though it may seem insignificant, the success of your entire organization rides on them – literally.

Don't settle for discount tires on your Formula 1 business; invest in the best tires, get some traction, and then drive to win.

SUMMARY:
A NEW HORIZON

I would pay to know what's going through your mind as you read the title to this summary. If you have taken the time to completely read this book and truly understand it, then most likely you are now seeing waste for what it truly is – *opportunity*. Waste *is* the treasure in The Lean Treasure Chest. Just like the perspective change that takes place when you watch a sunrise from your front porch, and then experience the blessing of watching one from 30,000 feet on a plane, your perspective should have changed dramatically. The horizon from a car is limited, but the horizon at 30,000 feet appears almost infinite. Such should be your new "organizational horizon."

You should now begin to see the vast number of opportunities within your processes that you may not have been consciously aware of prior to reading this book. What your organization looks like in the next 1, 3, 6, and 12 months depends on what you decide to do moving forward from this very moment. Your first option, and the one I find a personal disdain for, is to simply take this book after reading it and stick it on your shelf at home or in the office. There it will sit for the next 20 years, collecting dust, sandwiched between some other outstanding resources. It will be nothing more than a grain of sand on the beach of your professional development literature that has served no purpose and provided no value to you, your career, your team, or your organization.

If you choose that option, the time you wasted reading this book is akin to the man who walks into the doctor's office for his annual physical. The nurse checks his weight, height, and blood pressure and leads him to an observation room. There the nurse takes several blood samples to be used for routine tests. A short time later, the doctor walks into the room to perform the physical and review the test results. Upon reviewing the test results, the doctor informs the man that his weight and cholesterol are very high and that he is at serious risk of heart disease.

The doctor provides the man with a list of activities that will promote a more appropriate body weight as well as a reduced cholesterol level. He emphasizes the critical importance of exercise, a healthy diet with lots of vegetables, a good sleep regimen, reduced alcohol consumption, and not smoking. The man is more than appreciative for the doctor's honest and direct instructions. He folds the doctor's instructions, puts them in his back pocket, vigorously shakes the doctors hand, and promises that he will carry these instructions everywhere with him for the next 6 months as a reminder of what is at risk and the potential for improvement.

Six months go by, and the man returns for his follow-up. After all the tests are run, the doctor enters the room with the results, and just stands there shaking and scratching his head. He explains to the patient that he is confounded as to how the patient's cholesterol and weight have gotten so much worse since the last appointment. The doctor asks the patient how he has progressed in the diet, exercise, sleep, alcohol consumption, and smoking recommendations.

The patient confidently explains to the doctor that he didn't actually do anything different – he didn't change his behavior and still smoked two packs per day, drank a six-pack of beer each day, consistently ate five pieces of bacon for breakfast each morning, got only 6 hours of sleep on an average at night, and added 200 more channels to his cable package so he never had to leave his recliner. In an attempt to address the stunned expression on the doctor's face, the man excitedly states, "On the positive side, I did carry your recommendations with me everywhere for the last 6 months and read them on a daily basis."

This patient's health will continue to suffer, and he will remain at a very high risk for a catastrophic heart failure or stroke. Like this patient, if you ignore your condition and do nothing with this book to address it, you might as well just sit back and wait for the inevitable. It will be no surprise as you, your team, and your organization continue to experience "operational chest pains, lethargy, bloating, gas, cramping, elevated pulse, and potentially, complete heart failure." Regardless of the thousands of pharmaceutical commercials that bombard us during prime time, there is no magic pill or quick cure for this patient, and there is no magical pill for your process waste, inefficiency, and problems.

The second option you can choose is to utilize what you have gained from reading this book. The many examples and previous experiences I have shared should coincide with your current situation on multiple levels, regardless of your industry or role. Tailor what you have learned to your specific needs. Take a long, hard, and honest look in the operational mirror. Dive deep into your processes to see, hear, and smell what is happening. Challenge the norm and commonly accepted. Reach higher by digging deeper. The tools work, but only when used.

Chances are there are a lot of people in your organization – leaders, peers, and subordinates – who like things just the way they are. A common battle cry may sound something like this: "No, things are not perfect, and yes we spend a lot of time chasing our tails and running in and out of the phone booth, but it has always been this way. We are comfortable in our uncomfortable state. We have grown accustomed to the pain." Sadly, but truthfully, your own team may be the biggest initial obstacle to driving forward. Don't get disheartened, and don't give up. Nothing worth doing is ever easy. Use this book to see your reality in a whole new way. Become the Lean, responsive, proactive, agile, effective, and efficient organization that you have the potential to become. Pull the doctor's recommendations out of your back pocket, and, instead of just reading them, implement them in every part of your organization.

Use the tools, remain determined, maintain process discipline, and expect greatness. I wish you, your team, and your organization the greatest of success in this exciting journey.

Jay H.

*"Destiny is not a matter of **chance**. It is a matter of **choice**. It is not a thing to be waited for, it is a thing to be achieved."*

William Jennings Bryan, Former U.S. Secretary of State

"Success is not final. Failure isn't fatal; it's the courage to continue that counts."

Sir Winston Churchill, former British Prime Minister

"He is not fool who gives up what he cannot keep to gain that which he cannot lose."

Philip James Elliot, martyred missionary to Ecuador

"Continuous improvement is better than delayed perfection."

Mark Twain (Samuel Langhorne Clemens)

"If you want to be extraordinary, the first thing you have to do is stop being ordinary."

David Cottrell, business leader and author

WHAT NOW?

There is a lot information in this book. I have tried to include as much as possible to provide you with the knowledge, tools, and resources necessary to both understand and jump in with both feet without hitting a hidden rock. There is infinitely more to learn about eliminating process waste, recovering capacity, and Lean Management Systems, but even a dozen more books this size would only begin to scratch the surface.

If you have questions, are concerned about your next steps, or are in need of additional assistance, please contact me to discuss different options available to you as you undertake this journey in search of The Lean Treasure Chest. I am available for leadership coaching and development, "Train-the-Trainer" sessions, and large-scale seminar activities. I can provide hand-in-hand coaching for your organization and teams to drive a greater and deeper understanding of the opportunities and potential contained in The Lean Treasure Chest. If you need "in the trenches" support, I can also work at the value-add levels to implement these tools and design sustainable management systems that will promote long-term growth and success.

Please reach out to me directly at jayhodge@LeanTreasureAcademy.com.

Our website is www.LeanTreasureAcademy.com. On the home page, I have provided a short video to introduce myself and review the concepts contained in this book. The "Bridging The Gap" tab contains short videos where I offer insight regarding specific topics, some of which I have not covered in this book. They deal with leadership, communication, and a variety of other topics. There you will learn more about the book, and I will continue to post new tools and examples on the website to provide you with continuing opportunities for growth.

I also invite you to continually share with me your experiences, both victories and lessons learned. With your approval, I will post them for the benefit and development of the entire group on the "Your Stories" tab.

ACKNOWLEDGEMENTS:
AN IMPOSSIBLE TASK

Where do I start, and where should it end? I have been and continue to be blessed beyond my ability to adequately articulate in words. So many people in my life have played a part in the contents of this book.

I need to start by thanking David Cottrell, who has inspired me through his numerous books. His insight has been reflected in my leadership for many years. David is also responsible for connecting me with Stephen Williford, my editor. Stephen has provided me with honest and purposeful direction in a manner that still astounds me. I have written and re-written so many pages based on his recommendations and experience, and I have yet to find one valid reason to argue with him. His mentorship in developing a useful and purpose-driven book has been greatly appreciated.

Thank you to my content and layout editor, Brittney Anderson. I am a terrible writer, my English is atrocious, and my typing skills are criminally poor, so putting my thoughts onto paper was only half the battle. Brittney fought the other half by organizing, editing, and laying out this book in a manner that people could read and use as a tool. She is patient and professional, and I look forward to working with her on many more books.

Thank you to my mentors over the last 25 years who sacrificed of themselves and took me under their wing. They deserve immeasurable gratitude. The list is not long but so very meaningful: Staff Sergeant Howe (USMC), Thomas Durocher (Vallen Safety Supply), Ken Riefler (General Motors), Brian Bold (Toyota), Mike Morris (Caterpillar), Charles Holder (Hol-Mac Corp.), Dan Williams (KIK Custom Products), and Stan Holm (Abrazo West Hospital). You gave of yourself, and I am humbled.

Thank you to my close friend who has been a part of my professional career for almost 16 years, Traye Lisanby. Over the years, Traye has been my coach, instructor, buffer, filter, voice of reason, sounding board, shoulder, cheerleader, muzzle, friend, and ultimately brother. His constant encouragement and belief has carried me in times of doubt and fear, and I am eternally grateful for his friendship.

My parents, Jim and Kathy Hodge, taught me so much. They showed me that, though not always easy, life is what you make of it. I carry with me the examples of love, determination, perseverance, and faith they have demonstrated and continue to demonstrate.

My family has remained committed to me for 30 years, so what can I say that would do them justice? They have moved from state to state to support my career, changing homes, schools, friends, and communities. They have remained my foundation and reason for waking up in the morning. They have endured many long work hours, missed dances, forgotten matches, and Sunday afternoon flights to meet with clients. My children, Justin, Brittany, and Jordan, are how I define the words "pride" and "joy."

My wife, Barbara, is my better half. I am both happy and humbled to admit it. She has endured so many challenges in our marriage and remains my unwavering anchor. She is my best friend, my rock, my greatest supporter, my wise counsel, and how I define "perfection." She is my life. Thank you, Babe.

Finally, I need to thank my Father in Heaven. God has blessed me with an amazing family, career, and life. I deserve nothing, yet He has poured out His grace and mercy upon me. His unfailing love is my greatest blessing.

ABOUT THE AUTHOR

It is a strange thing to sit down one day and start writing a book. I have always perceived authors to be the pinnacle of knowledge and expertise in their respective fields, and, in some cases, they most certainly are. But now I realize how misguided my perception may have been. This book has been written over a three-year period of time. Its pages have been filled while sitting in airports, waiting for Uber drivers, on 737's cruising at 32,000 feet, relaxing in hotels in the evening, and in my home office.

I started my career in a small town in Indiana called Avon. My parents were extremely hard-working people and set the bar high for me. We did not have much in the way of possessions, so I learned at an early age that working hard would provide opportunities to do what I wanted. My family moved to Boulder, Colorado, when I was 16, forcing me to venture out and make new friends. My early career includes prestigious positions like mowing yards, delivering pizzas, working in fast food restaurants, and bagging groceries at the local supermarket.

I met my wife while in high school, and we married after my first year of college. I had always considered serving my country as the greatest of all honors, so shortly after our marriage, I enlisted in the United States Marine Corps. I wanted to complete my degree, but serving my country was my heart's desire at this point in my life. During my five years as a Marine, I was exposed to many levels of operations. Obviously, discipline and commitment were the standard, and I have benefited from that exposure my entire life. Barbara and I were blessed with our first two children (Justin and Brittany) during those five years in the Marines.

After the Marine Corps, Barbara and I decided that it was time to finish what I had started and complete my degree. After the family spent three years sharing a 576-square-foot apartment, living off very little, sacrificing, and yet always appreciative of our blessings, my graduation day came.

The time that has passed since that day seems like merely the blink of an eye. During the next 20 years, my family, and I moved to five different states to support my career, saw the birth of our third child (Jordan), and experienced countless other significant events. I have, in every sense of the word, been blessed. I have had the privilege of being mentored and coached by some of the greatest leaders in the industry, and have been a part of exceptionally gifted teams who showed me the true meaning of teamwork. The world-class organizations that make up my career have provided growth and development opportunities that are reflected in who I am today. Simply put, I am blessed.

Even after 25 years of managing in multiple industries for companies such as Toyota, General Motors, Caterpillar, Ford, and Tenet Healthcare, I remain a wide-eyed pupil. I spend my days soaking up knowledge and experience at every opportunity, constantly in awe of how much I truly don't know. I am a perpetual student of unforeseen circumstances, problems, discoveries, mistakes, victories, failures, and challenges, while studying under the constant and relentless tutelage of my Master Sensei I respectfully refer to as "life."

RECOMMENDED READINGS

If I was told that, for the remainder of my life, I would be stranded on a desert island and could only take 16 books with me, in addition to the Bible, these are the books I would chose. Some of these are time-tested, and others are more recent works. All of them have impacted my career and personal life in ways that would require another book to explain. I would recommend these to anyone with a desire to grow personally and achieve levels of influence and success that few are courageous enough to dream of.

The Seven Habits of Highly Effective People by Steven R. Covey

Creating a Lean Culture by David Mann

The Toyota Way by Jeffrey K. Liker

Kaizen by Masaaki Imai

The Goal by Eliyahu M. Goldratt and Jeff Cox

The Tipping Point by Malcolm Gladwell

The 21 Irrefutable Laws of Leadership by John C. Maxwell

Monday Morning Leadership by David Cottrell

How to Win Friends and Influence People by Dale Carnegie

Toyota Kata by Mike Rother

Learning to See by John Shook and Mike Rother

The Lean Turnaround by Art Byrne

As Iron Sharpens Iron by Howard and William Hendricks

Good to Great by Jim Collins

It's Our Ship by Captain D. Michael Abrashoff

Fearless by Max Lucado

Ordering Additional Copies for Your Teams

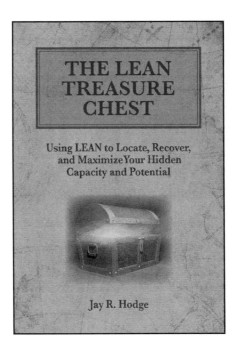

Available through Amazon. For quantity discounts, order through our website at www.LeanTreasureAcademy.com

---

THE LEAN TREASURE CHEST QUANTITY DISCOUNTS

1-4 copies $35.95   5-9 copies $33.95

10-19 copies $31.95   20-99 copies $29.95

100+ copies $26.95

Order by calling us at (812) 789-6404 or

by visiting our website at:

www.LeanTreasureAcademy.com

The Lean Treasure Chest Workbook

THE LEAN TREASURE CHEST

WORKBOOK

*Using the Lean Tools to Locate, Recover and Maximize
Your Hidden Capacity and Potential*

Jay R. Hodge

A 98-page workbook designed to help you and your teams apply the knowledge and skills you have learned in order to transform your reality.

Available through Amazon. For quantity discounts, order through our website at www.LeanTreasureAcademy.com

THE LEAN TREASURE CHEST WORKBOOK

1-4 copies $16.95   5-9 copies $15.95

10-19 copies $14.95   20-99 copies $13.95

100+ copies $10.95

Order by calling us at (812) 789-6404 or

by visiting our website at:

www.LeanTreasureAcademy.com

INDEX

5S — 71, 190, 198, 200, 262–279

5S Way of Life — 262

5-Why Problem Solving Tool — 294–298, 343, 347

Ability — 13, 36, 41, 45, 55, 60, 75, 79, 90, 112, 115, 123, 143, 156, 159, 188, 194, 197, 198, 204, 222, 237, 243, 255, 298, 301, 306, 311, 330, 333

Accomplish — 22, 26, 33, 36, 57, 69, 75, 78, 79, 91, 138, 142, 151, 197, 252, 256-257, 260, 278, 290, 293, 301-302, 305, 315, 334

Accountability — 14, 24, 29, 53, 101, 106, 114, 268, 270, 325, 327

Action — 15-18, 22-23, 28-29, 36, 56, 75, 95, 134, 138, 147, 177, 251, 255-256, 261, 271, 285, 296, 298, 303-304, 314, 325-327, 335, 338, 348

Adjust — 82, 240, 308, 326

Ambiguity — 69, 83, 85, 107

Audit — 100, 169, 213, 232, 268, 271

Authority — 75

Average — 27, 126, 148, 150, 167, 169, 190, 195-198, 205, 213-214, 221, 234, 239, 241, 257, 302, 313, 317, 320, 326, 352

Awareness — 61, 337, 341

Band-Aid — 34, 51, 64, 109–111, 118, 144, 171, 251

Barrier — 244, 261, 278, 286–288, 292, 294, 308

Battle — 117, 353

Behavior — 14, 55, 56, 69, 110, 113, 119, 135, 137, 204, 237, 250, 271, 325, 352

Believe — 18, 26-27, 59, 62, 82-83, 85, 88, 100, 114, 121, 123, 128, 137, 144, 189, 192, 205, 238, 241, 249-250, 255, 257, 278, 289, 292, 306-307, 326, 328, 334, 339

Benefits — 41, 144, 188, 192, 209, 219, 264

Big W — 153

Bridge — 295–298

Burden — 88, 183, 218, 315

Buried — 23–24, 34, 63, 127, 144, 165, 229, 280, 298

Capability — 148, 201, 290, 303

Capacity — 16–19, 26–27, 33, 77, 141–150, 160, 165–167, 179–180, 191, 196–198, 200–204, 209–210, 214, 225, 278, 287, 301–305, 309, 311, 315

Capacity Recovered — 203–204

Capital — 31, 33, 91, 189

Cardboard City — 151, 282, 306–310

Change — 14, 19, 23, 28-30, 40-42, 44, 55, 59, 69, 75, 80, 109, 111-112, 114, 116, 118, 121, 138, 151, 180, 187, 200, 205, 209-210, 218-220, 229, 235-236, 284-285, 292, 302, 314-317, 323, 335, 341-342, 351-352

Chaos — 32, 53, 69, 109, 128, 151, 213, 266, 284, 308, 318

Chaotic — 44, 99, 278

Choices — 83, 102, 138, 240

Clean — 70, 99, 148, 159, 178, 181, 262, 267-268, 270, 272, 278, 326

Cleaning — 50, 61, 71, 166, 214, 228-229, 268-269

Collaborate — 192

Collaboration — 25, 327

Collateral Damage — 154

Color coding — 77, 266, 269

Comfortable — 68, 72, 81, 90, 102, 107, 112, 116, 171, 287, 353

Commitment — 29, 39, 51, 56, 114, 126, 142, 169, 237, 243, 256, 326-328, 349

Committed — 14, 94, 112, 114, 124, 135-136, 150, 188, 239, 278, 335

Common Sense — 14, 183

Competition — 45

Competitive Advantage — 238, 241

Complacency — 22, 26, 37, 61, 95, 110, 114, 135, 257

Complexity — 260, 286

Compromise — 30, 93, 311

Confusion — 79, 83, 85, 107, 113, 143, 151, 180, 188, 219, 222, 278, 308

Consistency — 69-70, 83, 113, 118, 143, 151, 271, 311

Consistent — 69, 73-74, 77, 102, 118, 129, 135, 146, 170-171, 211, 310, 312-313, 348

Constraint — 142

Consultant — 116, 122, 247, 248, 250-251

Consume — 32, 34, 50-51, 60, 77, 91, 101, 138, 168, 173, 175-176, 178, 185, 189, 227-228, 278, 321

Content — 16, 27, 37, 81, 89, 128, 132-133, 138, 299, 348

Continuous Improvement — 19, 43, 100-101, 118, 122, 128-129, 200, 229, 235-236, 241, 257-258, 282, 293, 335, 341

COPQ — 164

Corporate Crutch — 247

Cost — 25, 164, 167, 231, 346

Cost Savings — 183, 238

Create — 19, 36, 59, 68, 71, 85, 90-91, 100-101, 110, 135, 138, 151, 188, 193, 197, 218, 236, 239-242, 248, 250, 262, 266, 298, 306, 328, 334

Cultural Transformation — 257, 271, 278, 306

Culture — 14, 30, 55-59, 80, 95, 100, 106, 110-114, 168-169, 237, 239, 242, 250, 257, 261-262, 328

Current Needs — 183, 191, 319

Customer — 14, 17, 29, 31, 55-56, 64, 67-69, 76-77, 89, 96, 98, 112, 132-134, 138, 140, 142-144, 146, 158, 161, 163, 165, 169, 171, 173-174, 177-178, 181-183, 186-189, 191-192, 201, 205, 211, 215, 217-221, 224, 227-231, 234, 243, 249, 257, 315, 326-327, 329, 339, 340

Customer Demand — 31, 76-77, 142, 165, 173, 177, 188-189

Customer Satisfaction — 14, 56, 67, 234

Cycle Time — 75

Daily Status Chart — 343, 346

Data — 17-18, 63, 96, 136, 143, 211, 248, 292, 318, 337, 340, 347-348

Defects — 17, 23, 52, 83, 102, 128, 143, 161

Definition — 32, 69, 86-87, 91, 97, 99, 113, 144, 214, 312

Delivered — 72, 161, 176, 190, 221, 223, 228, 232, 307, 329

Delivery — 35, 63, 91, 97, 112, 123, 149-150, 176, 210, 219, 224-225, 233, 236, 257, 285, 307-308, 323, 339

Demand — 26, 31, 51, 76-77, 89, 96-97, 142, 147, 150-151, 165, 171, 173, 176-177, 179, 181, 183, 188-190, 192, 210, 218-219, 239, 243, 276, 319, 322, 337

Demonstrated — 56, 105, 117, 119, 154, 159-160, 163, 214, 239, 242, 278, 325-326

Department Ownership — 75

Dependencies — 236, 265, 284-286, 304, 306

Design — 18, 51, 57, 69-70, 83, 85, 109, 140, 143, 150-153, 157-158, 162, 170-171, 191, 201, 214-215, 228, 232, 249, 264, 266, 278, 296, 300, 306-307, 313, 355

Digging — 29, 42, 61, 126-127, 129, 231, 261, 292-293, 295, 298, 328, 348, 353

Directors — 28, 95, 105, 114, 134-136, 258, 326, 336

Discipline — 5, 94, 256, 327, 353, 360

Discomfort — 33, 52, 168, 317

DMAIC — 17

Document — 57, 73-74, 128, 153, 156, 171-172, 197, 236, 276, 283, 287, 290, 298, 304, 310-313, 341, 343, 346

Documentation — 78, 326

Dominoes — 136

Downtime — 110, 143-144, 187, 211-212, 317, 321

Drive Consistency — 83, 118, 271, 311

Effective — 13, 18-19, 63-64, 69, 71, 74-75, 99, 110, 112, 147, 149, 172, 177, 189, 194, 198, 207, 215, 232, 257-258, 261-262, 267-269, 271-272, 276, 278, 294, 302, 306, 308, 315-317, 326-327, 329, 338, 353

Effective Standard — 69

Efficiency — 19, 23-24, 40-41, 43, 45, 47, 51, 69-70, 93, 95, 103, 143, 151, 163-164, 182, 241, 262, 281, 304, 327-328

Eliminate — 17, 23, 57, 72-73, 79, 82, 86, 88, 100, 118, 122, 146, 149, 160, 166, 181, 191, 203, 208, 215, 224-225, 241, 251, 256, 258, 262, 266, 271, 274, 278, 282, 287, 289, 290, 296, 306, 311, 316, 321, 339, 343

Employee Retention — 25

Employee Satisfaction — 53

Empowered — 278

Encumbered — 53

Engaged — 57, 101, 126, 135, 198, 206, 215, 275, 278, 326

Errors — 139, 187-188, 193

Evaluate — 41, 99, 186, 210, 219, 223, 286, 289

Evaluation — 207-210, 233, 316

Excellence — 19, 30, 34, 55, 101, 112, 117, 122, 158, 250

Excess Motion — 31, 193-203, 265, 282, 306, 308

Expectations — 31, 71, 75, 97, 161, 270

Experts — 52, 57, 100-101, 103, 112, 118-119, 249-250, 252, 256, 338

External Activity — 149-150, 192, 304-305

Firefighter — 97, 109

Fishbone Diagram — 140, 298-301

Flavor of the Month — 57, 136, 271

Flexibility — 181

Flow — 19, 40, 43, 51, 56, 96, 128, 147, 149, 151, 190, 198, 207, 213-215, 218, 222, 224-225, 241, 261-262, 264, 266, 272, 274-278, 282, 285, 287, 295, 306-310-319, 328

Focused — 30, 43, 119, 242, 252, 258, 278, 296, 337

Follower — 117

Forest — 44, 59, 79, 258, 285

Format — 74, 260-261, 272, 276, 290, 298-299, 306, 309, 348

Foundation — 114, 278, 283, 285, 315, 335
Frustration — 32, 45, 95, 113, 222, 278, 318, 325
Gemba — 261, 284, 338--348
Gemba Board — 338-343, 346-348
Gemba Metric Selection Tool — 340
Goal — 50, 59, 278, 282-283, 330, 333, 335, 338, 340, 343, 346
Gorilla — 9, 47, 50
Granular Level — 63, 140, 150, 213, 236, 298, 314, 316, 330
Growing — 23, 60, 92, 107, 125, 184, 200, 243-244
Growth — 14, 24, 33, 101-102, 115, 129, 134, 138, 142, 159, 242, 252, 335, 355, 360
Habits — 14, 43, 55-56, 114, 181, 258, 271, 325
Horizon — 19, 37, 105, 351
Hoshin — 106, 134, 135, 327
Iceberg — 121-125, 196, 212
Identity — 148
Immune — 64-65
Impact — 14, 25, 33-34, 44, 49, 52, 54, 56, 60, 62, 67-68, 72, 80-81, 93, 95-96, 98-99, 107, 110, 122, 128, 131, 133-134, 138, 143-144, 154, 156, 158, 160, 164-166, 169, 175, 177, 179, 182, 184, 187, 189, 192, 196, 198, 200, 207-210, 213-214, 217, 219, 224, 228-231, 234-235, 238-239, 247, 248, 250, 253, 258, 287, 288-290, 296-299, 308, 315, 339, 341
Impact of Waste — 67, 80-81, 122, 154, 156
Improve — 17, 23, 41, 43, 45, 69, 83, 115, 127-128, 146-147, 150, 179, 198, 213, 218, 222, 225, 228, 235, 240-241, 257, 267, 271, 278, 288-289, 302, 304, 306, 308, 312, 320, 325, 334, 337, 348
Improvements — 18-19, 43, 69, 106, 121, 128, 182, 200, 234-236, 241, 248, 270, 274-275, 277, 301, 315, 326, 339
Inconsistencies — 312
Inconsistent — 69, 170, 313
Industry — 14, 19, 23, 28, 34-35, 63, 80, 91, 97, 108, 127, 142-143, 147, 150-151, 176, 238, 248-250, 253, 256, 258, 278, 301, 315, 326, 333, 335, 349, 353
Inefficiency — 17-19, 23-24, 28-29, 33-34, 44, 53, 56, 63, 67, 83, 85, 100, 117, 131, 140, 143, 147, 151, 156, 181, 234, 255, 287, 308, 318, 353
Influence — 14, 117, 284, 361
Input — 69, 71, 122, 171, 287, 312
Inspect — 54
Inspect Through Cleaning — 267
Inspection — 69, 178, 319
Internal Activity — 149-150, 192, 304-305
Inventory — 17, 23, 31, 43, 64-65, 99, 128, 176-178, 180, 183-184, 187-192, 197, 217-218, 220, 224, 241, 264, 269, 285, 307-308, 310, 315, 317-322
Inventory Monster — 188
Inverse Relationship — 87-88, 205
Invested — 91, 176, 251, 307
Investment — 45, 102, 150-151, 251, 328
Journey — 13, 18, 30, 37, 47-50, 57, 73, 98, 101, 105, 117, 241, 255, 257, 262, 264, 295, 325, 353, 355
Just Get It Done — 37, 110
Just-In-Time — 179, 181, 319
Kaizen — 198, 225, 257-258, 260-261, 284-285, 288
Kaizen Event — 225, 257-258, 260-261, 284-285, 288
Kaizen Event Scope — 259
Kanban — 42, 176, 183, 191, 220, 319-323

Kanban Card — 320

Knowledge — 7, 18, 26, 31, 91, 101, 109, 117-119, 146, 224, 238, 241-242, 248-252, 255, 267-268, 334-335, 338, 355

Layers — 24, 33, 63, 144, 166, 185, 229, 330

Layout — 96, 151, 190, 198, 207, 218, 249-250, 262, 266, 269, 278, 282, 306-311, 315, 318, 337, 357

Lead — 14, 18, 36-39, 82-83, 95, 115-118, 122, 125, 250, 256, 278, 292, 329

Leader — 37, 56, 78, 106-107, 112-121, 127, 135, 237-244, 251, 258, 260, 271, 274-276, 288, 338, 354

Leaders — 19, 26, 44, 57, 69, 79, 91, 112-113, 117-118, 121, 126, 135, 146, 197, 220, 249, 256, 258, 260-261, 271, 326-327, 353, 360

Leadership — 14, 17, 19, 23-24, 27-28, 30, 55-57, 68, 79, 102-106, 109-118, 121, 126, 134-137, 143, 148, 169, 191, 197, 213-214, 237-243, 248, 258, 271-272, 326, 330, 336-339, 348-349, 355

Leader Standard Work — 78-79

Leading — 33, 43, 54, 71, 79, 83, 101, 134, 142, 163, 188, 191, 201, 243, 251, 253, 260, 280, 292, 299, 301, 349

Lean — 10, 13-14, 17-19, 23-25, 27-28, 41, 43-45, 49, 60, 63, 100, 119, 122, 152, 154, 171, 179, 198, 200, 218, 248, 262, 266, 306, 325-329, 333, 335-336, 338, 351, 353, 355

Lean Management — 18-19, 325-329, 333, 335-336, 338, 325, 355

Legacy — 36-37

Limited Resources — 13, 31, 34, 73, 91, 102, 154, 227, 287, 290

Little W — 153

LWOT — 207

Management — 18-19, 119, 172, 182, 192, 325, 326-329, 333-338, 348-349, 355

Management System — 18-19, 172, 182, 192, 325-329, 333, 335-336, 338, 348-349

Manager — 28, 37, 52, 64, 68-69, 79, 91, 101, 106-109, 117, 122, 127, 134-136, 161, 243-244, 272, 330, 343

Marbles — 126

Market downturn — 237-241

Matrix — 52, 273, 275-277, 310

Meaningful — 19, 36, 80, 95, 121, 135, 231, 243, 256, 261, 292-293, 296, 325, 327, 339, 341

Microscope — 138, 232, 300, 332

Migrate — 207

Min/Max Quantities — 268

Mission — 55, 106, 115, 157, 325, 327, 333-335

Mistakes — 59, 95, 139, 188, 298

Modify — 49, 75, 88, 152, 215, 243, 339

Monster — 115, 188

Motion — 31, 193-203, 213, 217, 224, 258, 265, 282, 302, 306, 308

Motion Is Capacity — 196

Movement — 31, 65, 77, 151, 189, 217-218, 227, 308

Negative — 34, 87, 98-99, 112, 131, 133-134, 137, 138, 140, 154, 158, 198, 207-211, 222, 231, 235-236, 242, 284, 308

Negative Effect — 284

Negative Impact — 34, 154, 158, 210, 231, 308

Negative Value — 131, 133-134, 137-140, 222

New Shoes Matrix — 284-285

Non-Value — 140, 213, 224-225, 236, 266, 278-283, 286, 316

Oak Tree — 124

Objective — 49-50, 116, 242, 250, 261-262, 299, 332-333, 335, 340, 343

Objectives — 53, 86, 134, 325-326, 339

Obsolescence — 178, 189

Obsolete — 97, 178, 187, 191, 197, 265, 274, 278

Obstacles — 19, 40, 112, 143, 215, 261, 264, 278, 285-288, 307-309, 335, 338

Operational Mirror — 35, 39, 127, 327, 353

Opportunities — 17-18, 29, 43-44, 55, 57, 62, 67, 85, 93, 99, 107-109, 112, 116, 125-127, 135, 149, 191, 201, 222-225, 242, 248, 255, 261, 267, 271, 281, 287-289, 306, 308, 327-328, 338-341, 351, 355, 360

Opportunity — 18, 33, 35-36, 45, 56, 69, 80-81, 95-96, 108, 112, 118, 136, 138, 154, 157, 160, 166, 169-172, 183-186, 196, 198, 209, 214, 229, 232, 239, 242, 247, 258, 261, 276, 289, 298, 338-339

Optimal — 31, 88, 109, 144, 152, 189, 192, 217, 265-266, 278, 280, 308-315, 319

Optimization — 319

Optimize — 179, 190, 198, 224, 307, 319

Organize — 42-43, 215, 252, 305-306

Organized — 43-44, 201, 250, 258, 262, 266, 272, 275, 278, 282, 336

Our Most Valuable Asset — 238

Outcomes — 69, 83, 96, 118, 186, 223

Output — 69, 83, 137, 165, 170-171, 176, 189, 198, 211, 312

Over-Processing — 31, 227-236, 282

Overproduction — 31, 173-183, 186, 234, 321

Overtime — 23, 51, 92, 95, 112, 165, 186, 196, 198, 212

Paddleball leadership — 113

Pain — 33, 102-103, 109, 139, 168, 251, 317, 325, 353

Parable of the Onion — 252

Parameters — 69, 311-318

Parasite — 141

Pareto Chart — 288-292, 343, 347

Performance — 17, 19, 30, 33, 35, 37, 45, 55, 67, 85, 93, 105, 110, 112, 114-115, 118-119, 136-138, 146-147, 150, 163, 205, 238, 249, 251, 262, 270-276, 287-289, 292, 312-313, 316, 325-326, 330-342, 346-348

Permanent Solutions — 34

Perspective — 19, 27, 32, 35, 44, 57, 61, 68, 80-82, 95, 113, 122-124, 138-139, 143, 157, 161-166, 188, 214-215, 227-230, 236, 240, 258, 261, 274, 278, 283-292, 340, 351

Pilot — 15, 97, 208, 306, 329

Positive impact — 107, 189, 248

Positive Value — 138, 140

Potential — 13, 18, 23-24, 27, 31, 33, 35, 44, 57, 63, 68, 72, 81, 83, 88, 95-96, 99, 101-102, 115, 143, 148-150, 158, 165-166, 172, 177, 179, 188, 197, 207, 210, 212, 218, 237-238, 244, 247-248, 252, 257, 261, 287, 290, 299, 301, 309, 312, 319, 321, 328, 333, 339, 349, 352, 353, 355

Precedent — 53

Predictable — 69

Prepare — 15-16, 23, 94, 151, 177, 252, 266, 307, 321

Prioritize — 57, 288-290

Priority — 80, 108, 118, 148, 178, 188, 191, 219, 222, 230, 262, 271, 290, 292

Problem — 17, 33, 37, 40, 51-56, 63, 68-69, 82, 92, 100, 102, 106, 108-112, 118-119, 122-123, 125, 128, 142, 154, 159, 164, 167, 169, 170-172, 186, 195, 212, 233, 249-250, 252, 256, 258, 260-261, 267, 284-285, 288, 290, 292, 294-295, 297-300, 316, 326-327, 330, 335, 338, 341, 343, 348

Problem Solving — 63, 112, 118-119, 122, 125, 128, 212, 252, 294, 327, 330, 338

Process Description — 75

Process Flow — 128, 261-262, 266, 274, 282, 309

Process Level Map — 151, 285, 286

Process, Not People Dependent — 67

Process Owner — 260

Process Variation — 74, 83, 147, 232

Process Waste — 18-19, 26, 45, 57, 62, 72, 77, 81-82, 85, 151, 234, 249, 255, 307, 353, 355

Produce — 26, 31-32, 34, 51-52, 68-69, 77, 88, 91, 95, 122, 129, 133, 138, 140, 142, 144, 147, 158, 165, 168, 170-173, 176-179, 182, 184-189, 192, 200, 211, 214, 231, 241, 244, 249-250, 262, 278, 304, 340

Productivity — 18, 23-24, 33, 36, 51, 53, 69-70, 92-93, 95, 118, 151, 198, 200, 211, 225, 238, 241, 253, 257, 258, 262, 267, 312, 339

Progressive Time — 75

Promote Repeatability — 311

Purpose — 75, 257, 262, 264, 267-268, 271, 278, 283, 285, 288, 294, 298, 301, 306, 309, 311, 314, 319

QPC — 109, 218, 320, 321-322

Quality — 14, 17, 19, 23-24, 28, 32-33, 45, 51-56, 63-64, 69-70, 72, 77, 82-83, 89, 93, 97-98, 102, 108, 112, 118, 129, 133-134, 143, 148, 150-151, 169, 171, 178, 186, 189, 203, 215, 218-219, 222, 229-231, 235, 241-242, 257, 260, 262, 267, 300, 308, 311, 315-316, 319, 326, 334, 339

Random — 110, 162, 166, 170-171, 292, 307

Reality — 13-14, 17-19, 26, 29-30, 35, 39, 41, 44, 48, 50, 59, 63-64, 73, 81, 87, 91, 93, 95, 98-99, 105, 107, 116, 122, 142, 146, 153, 156, 162, 166-167, 170, 183-187, 191, 195, 238, 241, 261, 287-293, 308, 315, 325, 334, 340, 353

Red Tag — 264-265

Reduce — 18, 45, 57, 77, 88, 115, 118, 179-180, 187, 192, 197, 200-201, 213-218, 221, 224-225, 238, 241, 250, 280, 301-302, 306, 310-311, 318, 333

Reduced — 85, 122, 186, 198-200, 209-211, 214, 220, 229, 235, 282, 305, 352

Reduce Variation — 311

Reducing — 26, 45, 51, 148, 176, 179, 181, 192, 198, 200, 214, 224-225, 238, 240, 304, 306, 316, 339

Reduction — 42-43, 47, 116, 198, 200, 231, 236, 238, 240, 282, 303, 311, 319

Repeatable — 312

Resource — 29, 31, 44, 91, 94, 142, 191, 196, 237-238, 242, 253, 280

Resources — 13, 31, 33-34, 41, 50-54, 73, 88, 90-95, 98, 101-102, 109, 118, 133-138, 140, 142, 144-145, 147, 154, 158, 160, 164, 168, 171, 173, 178, 188, 195, 197, 201, 215, 218, 220-223, 227-228, 234, 242, 248, 257, 260, 262, 278, 283, 287, 290, 292, 301, 319, 336, 352, 355

Respond — 65, 79, 107-108, 127, 133, 188, 333

Responsibility — 52-53, 67, 75, 79, 100-101, 105-106, 112, 114, 121, 250, 251, 286

Resulted — 7, 19, 23, 53, 128, 133, 139, 147, 153-154, 178, 211-212, 217, 219, 301-303, 308-309, 313

Results — 18, 19, 33, 35, 51-53, 60, 69, 73, 77, 83, 102, 106, 112-113, 118, 129, 131, 136, 147, 153-154, 159, 168-172, 180, 207, 211, 223-224, 227, 233-234, 250-251, 253, 256-257, 261-264, 282, 298, 305, 311, 312-313, 318, 321, 326-329, 331, 341, 352

Revision Date — 75

Reward — 21, 110

Rewarding — 41-42, 61

Risk — 23, 64, 67, 94, 105, 111, 118, 169, 190, 229, 267, 288-290, 296, 316, 339, 352

Roles and Responsibilities — 268, 343

Root Cause Problem — 126, 298

Run Chart — 172, 337, 343, 346

Safety — 25, 322-323, 337, 346, 357

Satisfaction — 13-14, 28, 52-53, 56, 67, 71, 207, 222, 234, 238, 290, 327

Scope — 260

Set — 14, 19, 28, 30, 32, 42, 48, 53, 57, 64, 82, 90, 95, 111-112, 117-118, 121, 127, 134-136, 174, 180, 191, 194, 201, 206, 214, 220, 223, 227, 231, 233, 235, 240, 258, 261-262, 301, 330, 349

Shadow Board — 266, 269

Shine — 262-268

Shipwreck — 64

Shock wave — 154

Silos — 112, 187, 315, 325

Six Sigma — 13-14, 17, 100, 325
SMED — 17, 149, 179-180, 213-214, 266, 301-306
Social Media — 64, 98-99, 122, 133, 207
Solution — 37, 44, 51, 110-112, 170-172, 248-251, 287, 294-295, 336
Solutions — 19, 34, 51, 59, 100, 109, 118, 146, 171-172, 242, 249-250, 268, 295
Solve — 17, 23, 111, 122, 129, 169, 250-251, 287-292, 338, 348
Sort — 85, 123, 289
Spaghetti Map — 193, 225, 282, 308-310
Staff — 53-54, 65, 68, 91, 95-99, 105, 113-114, 133-135, 139, 144, 147, 190, 208, 213, 222, 242, 249, 258, 287, 290, 321, 327, 339, 349
Stakeholder — 88, 102
Standard — 67, 70, 73-79, 82-83, 85, 109, 118, 129, 133, 171, 232, 241, 268, 271, 276, 311-314, 343
Standard Work — 67-83, 85, 109, 118, 129, 133, 171, 232, 241, 268, 271, 276, 311-314, 343
Sticky Note — 95, 289, 290-292
Stop to Fix — 23, 51, 112, 169, 327
Strategic Plan — 134
Strategy — 134-136, 238, 257, 333-335
Strategy Room — 135-136
Struggle — 8, 17, 183, 242, 274, 287
Struggles — 48, 285
Success — 18, 26, 37, 67-69, 73, 75, 79, 82, 89, 102, 110, 113-114, 117, 128, 170, 174, 213-215, 237, 242-244, 251, 253, 258, 260, 266, 271, 274, 292, 312, 325-326, 333-339, 349, 353, 355
Superhero — 14, 109-111
Supervisor — 14
Surrender — 90, 102, 257
Survive — 34, 98, 110, 114, 238-240
Sustain — 18, 258, 268, 270, 297, 341
Sustainability — 67
Symptoms — 34, 159, 251, 294-295
Takt Time — 75
Target — 16, 96, 105, 191, 212, 260, 296-298, 318, 332-333, 337-338
Teflon Salute — 105-106
Temporary Solutions — 51, 59, 109, 118, 171
That's How We've Always Done It — 107, 258
Theory of Constraints — 282
Time — 15-18, 21-23, 27, 31-36, 39-42, 45, 49-54, 56, 59-62, 65, 69-71, 75-77, 80-82, 87-88, 90-91, 96-97, 99-101, 103, 105, 107-111, 114, 116, 119, 124, 126, 128-129, 133-139, 141-145, 148, 150-153, 156-157, 160, 164-171, 175-181, 184-185, 189, 191-193, 195-196, 197, 200-201, 204-205, 207-214, 217-218, 220-229, 232-243, 249-251, 260-262, 264, 266, 268, 270-272, 274-275, 277-282, 284, 287-288, 290, 292, 295, 298, 301-309, 311-321, 326, 330, 332-333, 338, 351-353
Time Is Capacity — 196-197, 302
Time Study — 143, 220, 224-225, 236, 314-318
Tool — 28, 36-37, 42, 69, 72, 110, 116, 137, 140, 156, 159, 176, 179, 187, 189, 191, 193, 198, 222, 224, 257, 264, 268-271, 283, 285, 294-295, 298, 301, 304-306, 319, 328, 338-339, 342-343, 348
Toolbox — 18, 94, 116, 194, 255, 269
Tools — 13, 17-19, 29-30, 37, 41-42, 57, 68-69, 77, 102, 116, 118-119, 128, 200, 241, 244, 251-252, 256-258, 261-262, 264, 266-267, 269, 271, 274, 282, 287-288, 294-295, 298, 306, 308, 310, 327, 353, 355
Too Much Inventory — 31, 183, 185-186, 188, 190-191
TPS — 17
Trail — 49, 82, 137

Transformation — 36, 112, 117-118, 137, 185, 257, 271-272, 278, 306
Transportation — 23, 109, 167, 181, 217-225, 235, 323
True Leadership — 112, 116, 118, 243
Trust — 114-116, 137, 239-240, 335, 349
Understand — 13-14, 18-19, 22, 25-27, 30, 36, 39, 41, 44, 47, 52, 59, 63, 72, 80-82, 85-88, 93, 95, 98-99, 106, 108-109, 122-123, 128, 137, 142, 148-150, 154, 158-161, 169, 172, 175, 181, 185, 187-188, 191-193, 201, 204, 206, 209, 213, 215, 218-219, 228-229, 235-236, 238, 241, 249, 252-253, 256, 258, 261, 266, 276, 283-288, 290, 292-295, 298, 304, 306, 308-309, 314, 317, 321, 326, 328, 333, 335, 351, 355
Understanding — 18-19, 35, 44, 71, 83, 85, 89, 138, 142, 148, 154, 156, 159, 194, 224, 237, 240, 283, 285, 300, 315, 328, 343
Unique — 18, 32, 37, 40, 44-45, 69, 83, 99, 106, 109, 128, 142, 162, 166, 171, 223, 250, 251-252, 258, 264, 269-270, 286-287, 317, 335, 339-340, 346, 348
Unrealized — 35, 81, 164
Utilization — 13, 92, 95, 103, 138, 165, 189, 236, 241, 247, 262, 287, 301-308, 314
Utilize — 14, 19, 27, 31, 72, 91, 95-96, 101-102, 118-119, 149, 151, 154, 160, 178, 180, 193, 214, 225, 227, 238, 241, 249, 256, 268, 278, 293, 306, 310, 314, 353
Utopia — 37, 184
Valuable Resources — 33, 138, 171, 178, 188
Value — 33-34, 85-86, 88, 90, 96, 97-98, 102, 132-133, 138-140, 147, 151, 171-172, 182, 191-192, 197, 201, 210-211, 213, 216, 222, 224-225, 230, 236, 248, 261, 266, 278-286, 316
Value Analysis Tool — 140, 278-283
Value Creation — 26, 31, 44, 101, 224-225
Value Stream — 151, 171, 191, 213, 261, 285
Value Thermometer — 132-133, 138-139
Variable — 26
Variation — 65, 69-71, 74, 83, 118, 143, 147, 151, 162, 170-171, 232, 271, 311-312
Victim — 137, 178, 184, 237
Victory — 37, 102
Vision — 55, 106, 325-327, 333-335
Visual Management System — 43
Visual Standards — 267-268
VOC — 340
Voice of the Customer — 340
Volume — 36, 51, 123, 143-144, 241, 322, 337
Waiting — 19, 24, 32-54, 63, 65, 72, 81, 88, 98, 102, 111, 123, 164, 177, 190, 203, 205-215, 218, 223-224, 228, 234, 256, 271, 282, 290, 303, 315-318
Walls — 17, 29, 44, 70, 112, 128, 135, 220, 267, 269, 299, 307, 326, 335-337
War Room — 135
Waste — 13, 16-19, 23-24, 26-29, 31-34, 36, 38, 40-45, 47, 53-57, 59, 60-64, 67, 72-73, 77, 80-83, 85-88, 91, 95, 100-103, 109, 111, 117-119, 121-123, 125-128, 131, 133, 136-138, 140-141, 143-144, 146-147, 149, 151-161, 166, 173-178, 180-189, 191, 193-194, 203-204, 209, 212-217, 220, 224, 227, 232-238, 241, 247-249, 255-256, 258, 262, 278, 280, 282-283, 287, 306-307, 311, 316, 318-319, 321, 327-328, 338, 348, 351, 353, 355
Waste Eliminated — 203-204
Waste Event — 153-154, 156, 159-160, 178, 187, 194, 217
Waste Explosion — 153-154, 159-160, 208, 234
Waste Immunity — 59, 62-64
Waste Octopus — 63
Window Meeting — 335-338
Window Wall — 335-338

Why Am I Doing This? — 150
Win Capture — 343
Work-Around — 51, 53
World-Class — 35-36, 106, 334

Made in the USA
Columbia, SC
09 February 2019